Maya to Aztec: Ancient Mesoamerica Revealed

Edwin Barnhart, Ph.D.

THE
GREAT
COURSES

PUBLISHED BY:

THE GREAT COURSES
Corporate Headquarters
4840 Westfields Boulevard, Suite 500
Chantilly, Virginia 20151-2299
Phone: 1-800-832-2412
Fax: 703-378-3819
www.thegreatcourses.com

Edwin Barnhart, Ph.D.
Director
Maya Exploration Center

P rofessor Edwin Barnhart is Director of the Maya Exploration Center. He received his Ph.D. in Anthropology with a focus on Archaeology from The University of Texas at Austin in 2001; his dissertation was entitled *The Palenque Mapping Project: Settlement Patterns and Urbanism in an Ancient Maya City*. Professor Barnhart has more than 20 years of experience as an archaeologist, explorer, and instructor in North, Central, and South America and has published more than a dozen papers and given presentations at eight international conferences.

Professor Barnhart's involvement in Maya studies began in 1990 as an archaeological intern in the ruins of Copan, Honduras. In January of 1996, he was invited to return to Copan and help a team from the University of Pennsylvania excavate the early acropolis and the tomb of the city's lineage founder. From 1992 to 1995, Professor Barnhart studied New World art, iconography, and epigraphy (hieroglyphic translation) under the late Dr. Linda Schele at The University of Texas at Austin. During that time, he intensively studied the Andean culture, writing a number of papers about Moche shamanism as seen through art and iconography.

In 1994, Professor Barnhart began working as a surveyor and University of Texas field school instructor in the jungles of northwestern Belize. After finding numerous small villages, he discovered the ancient city of Maax Na ("Spider-Monkey House"), a major center of the Classic Maya period. Professor Barnhart mapped more than 600 structures at Maax Na between 1995 and 1997 before moving his research focus to Chiapas, Mexico. He received his master's degree in Latin American Studies in May of 1996 and began teaching anthropology classes at what is now Texas State University the following September. He taught archaeology and anthropology classes there until 1998, when he was invited by the Mexican government to direct the Palenque Mapping Project, a three-year effort to survey and map the unknown sections of Palenque's ruins. More than 1,100 new structures were documented, bringing the site total to almost 1,500. The resultant map has been celebrated as one of the most detailed and accurate ever made of a Maya ruin.

In 2003, Professor Barnhart became Director of the Maya Exploration Center, an institution dedicated to the study of ancient Maya civilization. He has led dozens of student groups on journeys through Mexico, Guatemala, Peru, and Bolivia.

Over the last 10 years, Professor Barnhart has appeared multiple times on the History Channel; the Discovery Channel; and NHK, a Japanese public television network. In addition, he is a Fellow of the Explorers Club and teaches University of Texas travel courses for college professors on ancient Andean and Mesoamerican astronomy, mathematics, and culture. For The Great Courses, he has also taught *Lost Worlds of South America.* ■

Table of Contents

Table of Contents

Table of Contents

Maya to Aztec: Ancient Mesoamerica Revealed

Scope:

This course is a tale of two great cultures, and many of others in between—often great in their own right—that helped make them possible. The Maya and the Aztecs occupied a land that's collectively called Mesoamerica. Mesoamerica encompasses all of Mexico from coast to coast, from the Sonoran Desert, just south of the Pueblo cultures of the American Southwest, down through Guatemala and Belize and partway into Honduras and El Salvador, bordered by the Lenca culture of eastern Honduras. The territory is delineated not so much by its varied geography—from deserts to rainforests—but by the presence of a certain set of mutually held traits that allow us to call these cultures *empires*. Those traits include shared use of plants, a commonly held calendar, a pattern of organizing themselves into city-states (even in the dominant-capital model governing the tribute empire of the Aztecs), ancestor worship, and the infamous penchant for human sacrifice.

The Maya have been around for millennia, while the Aztecs appeared late and lasted only a few centuries. Preceding both were thousands of years of transition from nomadic to sedentary life, after which the peoples of Mesoamerica went through three major periods of cultural development. Maya archaeology calls these the Preclassic, Classic, and Post-Classic periods. The lines between these periods are marked by major changes in the trajectory of Mesoamerican civilizations. The Preclassic (2000 B.C.–200 A.D.) is typified by the rise of Mesoamerica's first great civilization—the Olmec. Rising from the agriculturally rich lowlands of Tabasco around 1700 B.C., these people built massive earthen pyramids and multi-ton stone effigies of their leaders. Their ideas were transmitted along trade networks far and wide, and ideas from abroad came back to the Olmec through the same channels. The exchange between the Olmec and their neighbors set the foundations of a cultural pattern that would persist until the Spanish arrived some 3,000 years later.

One by one, the Olmec cities we call San Lorenzo, La Venta, and Tres Zapotes faded away by around 500 B.C., but Olmec ideas of urban living and divine kingship continued to flower. More and more cities were built across Mesoamerica, growing in size and number for centuries. In particular, the Maya built such cities as El Mirador and made interconnected advances in mathematics, calendar making, and astronomy, which influenced their buildings, their art, and even their creation story, the *Popul Vuh*.

The opening of the Classic period around 200 A.D. is marked by the emergence of notably larger cities that absorbed smaller ones around them into city-states. In the Peten rainforest in and around northern Guatemala, a collection of Maya cities, such as Tikal, Palenque (in the west), Copan (southeast), and Calakmul (north), established regional power through a complex system of alliances, intermarriages, and wars. Farther to the west, in Oaxaca, was the Zapotecs' hilltop city of Monte Alban. But the biggest force of the Classic period sprang from a single great capital even farther west, the northern city of Teotihuacan. Growing steadily from 250 B.C. in a valley just north of modern-day Mexico City, by 300 A.D., Teotihuacan was ready and willing to push outward. Its military-backed influence spread south and east across Mesoamerica, pushing through Oaxaca into the Maya world and, ultimately, as far as modern-day Honduras.

The extent and nature of Teotihuacan's control over Mesoamerica remains shrouded in mystery, but its influence is evidenced everywhere by a clear escalation of violence and warfare. However, as we know, those who live by the sword die by the sword: Teotihuacan's end came when the city was burned to the ground around 650 A.D. The demise of the city left a power vacuum that was felt everywhere. Some city-states struggled on longer than others, but one by one, the great cities of the Classic period were abandoned. By 850 A.D., virtually every city that had started in the Early Classic period was crumbling and growing moss.

No chain of historical events is as neat as archaeologists would like to make it appear, and those in Mesoamerica are no exception. Not every region was on the decline as the Classic cities failed. New cities emerged after the fall of Teotihuacan, especially in Central Mexico. The exchange of cultural ideas and trade goods actually increased at that time. We see Maya people adopting ideas from Central Mexico and peoples of Central Mexico adopting Maya ideas. In the middle, the long rule of the Valley of Oaxaca by the Zapotecs of Monte Alban came to an end, and the Mixtec people rose to fill the void.

The Post-Classic period, starting roughly at 900 A.D., began with exchange between newer Mesoamerica city-states, with no clearly dominant culture. The strength of cultural exchange during the Early Post-Classic, and our continued weak understanding of its mechanisms, is typified by the "twin cities" of Chichen Itza and Tula, located more than 800 miles apart at nearly opposite ends of the Mesoamerican world. Archaeologists still debate which city influenced which. One southeast in the heart of Maya Yucatan and the other the Toltec capital (later idealized by the Aztecs) northwest of the Valley of Mexico, they shared a nearly identical program of art and architecture, and they did so until the end, when both cities were abandoned in the early 1200s.

The pattern of independent city-states continued until the Aztecs from the northern deserts came to settle on the shores of Lake Texcoco in the Valley of Mexico. They began as mercenaries for hire and interlopers but slowly gained the favor and respect of local lords. They put themselves in the service of the valley's most powerful group, the Tepenacs, in exchange for the right to build their own city on manmade islands in the lake. Then in the early 1400s, the Aztecs led a rebellion against the Tepenacs, assuming power as part of a partnership called the Triple Alliance. Together with their new partners, they dominated all of Central Mexico, creating a super-state over all of the once-independent city-states. Military dominance, demand of tribute, and frequent human sacrifices were the hallmarks of this new empire. Though they were in an alliance with their neighbors, the Aztecs maneuvered their capital city, Tenochtitlan, to be the nexus for all deliveries of tribute. By controlling the wealth, they controlled the empire.

The Aztecs ruled with an obsidian fist, controlling their ever-expanding empire through fear. City-states either obeyed and paid their excessive tribute or faced the wrath of the Aztec army. By the time the Spanish arrived, the Aztecs had expanded to the border of the Maya world and an assault was in process. Rumors of strange, hairy men in oddly built boats had been circulating for years, and one fateful day in the spring of 1519, Hernan

Cortes and his conquistadors landed on the shore of modern-day Veracruz. Mounted on four-legged beasts, they marched into the Aztec capital. For a time, a friendship was beginning, but then a Spanish attack on unarmed citizens resulted in the deaths of hundreds of conquistadors. Those who survived escaped and regrouped back in Veracruz.

Over the next year, allied with tens of thousands of native peoples who hated the Aztecs, Captain Cortes and his army attacked the Aztec capital. On August 13, 1521, the Aztec empire officially surrendered, and the Spanish proceeded to build a colonial empire of their own, using the cities, labor, and resources they had conquered. The Aztecs' name for themselves (the Mexica) was revived in the 19th century with the founding of the nation of Mexico, which has retained interesting aspects of its former Mesoamerican heritage down to today.

During the decades immediately following the conquest, a combination of infectious diseases and Spanish military campaigns subdued most of Mesoamerica. The Maya of Yucatan and the northern jungles of Guatemala were a notable exception, resisting and rebelling against Spanish domination well into the 19th century.

Today, 500 years later, only fragments of once-vibrant cultural traditions remain, but archaeologists continue to find new cities, discover new treasures, and glean surprising new insights. Whether concealed by remote rain forests or modern-day cities (such as ancient Kaminaljuyu under Guatemala City or Tenochtitlan beneath present-day Mexico City), what does remain is important to our global patrimony and worthy of both preservation and celebration. ■

Monte Alban and Zapotec Rule over Oaxaca
Lecture 25

B uilt on top of a mountain, the city of Monte Alban had a commanding view of the entire Valley of Oaxaca in southern Mexico. From there, Zapotec rulers controlled a vast kingdom for more than 1,000 years. At Monte Alban's peak, there was no other city for hundreds of miles that even came close to rivaling its sophistication or scale. In this lecture, we take a step back in time to the Preclassic and Classic periods to understand the history of Monte Alban; its massive, decades-long construction; the rich art objects found in its tombs; and the powerful city's mysterious disappearance.

Monte Alban: A Massive Construction Project
- The city of Monte Alban was built on arid highlands in a location perfectly situated to control all three arms of the Valley of Oaxaca. The mountaintop it sits on was uninhabited before 500 B.C.; at that time, the largest city in the valley was San Jose Mogote, which flourished between 1300 to 500 B.C. During its existence, San Jose Mogote was very much influenced by the Olmec.

- The building of Monte Alban was a massive labor project; just leveling the mountaintop was a huge undertaking. It must have taken decades and at least hundreds, if not thousands, of builders working on it full-time. Archaeologists speculate that the construction of Monte Alban was almost certainly initiated by the people controlling San Jose Mogote.

- This speculation is supported by several important facts.
  o San Jose Mogote's population dropped as Monte Alban's rose around 500 B.C.

  o Monte Alban's earliest architecture was very similar to that of San Jose Mogote.

- The people of Valle Grande resisted Monte Alban, just as they resisted and fought San Jose Mogote.

- By 500 B.C., Monte Alban's plaza was finally leveled and its first temples were erected. Below it on the hillside were terraces with housing compounds for the elites. These elites seemed to be administrators, artisans, or people running workshops. By 300 B.C., there were 5,000 people living in Monte Alban, and San Jose Mogote was completely gone.

"Disembedded Capital" Model of Oaxaca
- By 100 B.C., archaeologists believe there were more than 17,000 people living in and around Monte Alban. Zapotec power was undeniable at that time; Monte Alban represented only a fraction of the lands the Zapotec controlled. The political and economic strategy of the Zapotec unified the entire Valley of Oaxaca and bound its inhabitants in a new Zapotec cultural identity.

- By the beginning of the 1st millennium, Monte Alban had complete control of the valley. The city did not simply control the trade, however; it created an organized division of labor.

- Each village in the valley specialized in a different product. Monte Alban was the administrative center that kept all that in order. Goods were redistributed through a centralized government structure in the city of Monte Alban. The capital itself was supplied by the valley, in a scheme some scholars have called the "disembedded capital" model of Oaxaca.

Early Excavations at Monte Alban
- At Monte Alban's peak, there was no other city for hundreds of miles that even came close to rivaling it in sophistication or scale. At the heart of the city was a huge plaza, 300 by 200 meters. All around the plaza were temples and palaces that reached their largest form about 680 A.D. Other cities, such as those in the Maya world, were accretional. But Monte Alban was master planned from the very beginning.

- Alfonso Caso was the first excavator of Monte Alban; he worked at the site from 1932 to 1953. He was also the founder of the Instituto Nacional de Antropologia e Historia (INAH) in 1939. Caso was most famous for discovering Monte Alban Tomb 7 in 1932. The richest tomb in the Americas at the time, Tomb 7 was not Zapotec; it was actually Mixtec. Mixtec people came in at a later date and put their own bodies in an originally Zapotec tomb.

- Many of the temples in the plaza are in the *talud-tablero* style of architecture—a sign that Teotihuacan influenced Monte Alban during the Classic period. The north end of the city is dominated by a large platform with houses, likely the residences of the royal family of Monte Alban. Three joined temples interrupt the open space in the center of Monte Alban's plaza. Two tombs were found underneath Building H, the central building.

Zenith Passage Tube

- Just south of the center temple is the most interesting building at Monte Alban: Building J. This structure is oriented differently than the rest of the buildings. It is 45 degrees off the center; it has an arrow shape; and it is not rectangular. It seems to be pointing to the southwest. It has been called an observatory because of its unusual orientation.

- It was been speculated that the building was pointing at the zenith passage at Monte Alban—the day on which the sun will appear directly overhead. If we visualize a line backward from the arrow tip to the edge of Monte Alban's plaza, it leads to Building P. Under Building P's staircase is a zenith passage tube, a specific chamber with a long tube so that astronomers could site and calculate zenith passage. This zenith passage tube is one of only three chambers like it found in all of Mesoamerica.

- If we stand above Building P, over the zenith passage tube, and look west, we see Buildings G, H, and I. Those three buildings could have been used to determine the solstices and equinoxes, just like the E-Groups located in the Maya areas.

Zapotec Writing System

- Archaeologists have two main sources for art forms in Monte Alban—carved stone monuments and offerings left in tombs. Over the decades, more than 170 tombs have been located within Monte Alban.

More than 300 Danzante figures have been found in and around the valley of Monte Alban.

- Monte Alban's most celebrated art pieces are the Danzantes, figures carved on irregularly shaped slabs. They are called Danzantes because the figures look as if they are dancing. However, they are not really dancing; they are naked and contorted, with obvious wounds. The images may have been a show of power by Monte Alban.

- Stelae 12 and 13 at Monte Alban are noteworthy because of their dates, estimated to be about 100 B.C. These stelae represent the earliest solar calendar glyphs in all of Mesoamerica. They are also proof that the Zapotec had a basic writing system in Preclassic times, perhaps as early as the Maya or Epi-Olmec systems.

- Monte Alban's Lisa Stela is significant because it depicts Teotihuacan-related images. It shows four men, bearing gifts and wearing Teotihuacan headdresses, heading to a fifth man, who is wearing a Zapotec headdress. Archaeologists suspect that this image implies that Teotihuacan elites started controlling Monte Alban's elite. Monte Alban is directly on the way to the Maya region; it would have been a logical stop for trade routes.

- Interesting carvings are embedded in the walls of Building J. About 40 slabs along its walls illustrate toponyms—meaning place names or name glyphs. Caso termed these *conquest slabs* and suggested that they were areas that were conquered by Monte Alban.

Zapotec Deities

- Art objects found in Monte Alban's tombs, such as ceramics, jewelry, and painted walls, provide insights into how the inhabitants dressed and how they worshipped. Tombs 103, 104, and 105, found under the palace structures, are ideal examples of Zapotec tombs.

- The tomb walls depict the elites and their rich clothing. Tomb 105 shows a scene of an elite procession, in which all are wearing headdresses of beautiful green quetzal feathers and green jade ear flares. The women's *huipiles* are woven with intricate geometric patterns, showing that the Zapotec were expert weavers. The men carry carved staffs and bundles. Out of their mouths are speech scrolls with flowers on them—which means that they were singing.

- The ceramics found in the tombs also provide images, especially of Zapotec deities. The most common Zapotec deity illustrated was Cocijo, God of Rain and Lightning. He is shown in a mask with a hooked nose, and he has a snake tongue. Because his image is found in nearly every tomb, Cocijo may actually have been the patron deity of Monte Alban.

- Another deity portrayed at Monte Alban is Xipe Totec, the "Flayed One"—a terrifying god who rips the skin off enemies and sacrificial victims. He is much better known from Aztec times, but Monte Alban ceramics prove that he was also in the Zapotec pantheon and probably in their practices.

Collapse of Monte Alban

- As it turns out, Monte Alban was not the sole authority on the mountain; it had a sister city, Atzompa. When Atzompa was opened up for excavations, many pyramids and plazas were discovered, as well as large elite residences and a very rich tomb. What's more, the site has three ball courts. The architecture at Atzompa is identical to the architecture at Monte Alban, but Atzompa's dates are all after 650 A.D.

- It seems that about 650, Monte Alban was beginning to lose its sole authority. In the east valley, Mitla began to grow; in the south valley, Zaachila expanded. Both those cities were still Zapotec, and they both survived up to the Spanish conquest, but Monte Alban did not.

- In 600, Monte Alban's population was 35,000, but it ceased building about that time. Atzompa and the other valley sites continued to grow, but by 750, Monte Alban was completely abandoned. Like the Maya sites, there was no sign of destruction at Monte Alban. Its people, apparently, just walked away.

- A few hundred years later, the site would be inhabited not by the Zapotec but by a closely related culture called the Mixtec. The Mixtec would reuse Monte Alban's tomb chambers, filling them with something that Monte Alban never had: gold.

Suggested Reading

Marcus and Flannery, *Zapotec Civilization.*

Miller, *The Art of Mesoamerica from Olmec to Aztec.*

Paddock, ed., *Ancient Oaxaca.*

1. The people of San Jose Mogote decided to move their population to Monte Alban. Why?

2. We have the names and portraits of rulers from nearly every Maya city. Why didn't Monte Alban provide us with similar names and portraits?

3. Do you think that the Danzantes represent tortured captives, ritual dancers, or something else?

Monte Alban and Zapotec Rule over Oaxaca
Lecture 25—Transcript

Monte Alban is one of the most beautiful ruins in all of Mesoamerica. Built on top of a mountain, it has a commanding view of the entire valley of Oaxaca in southern Mexico. From there, Zapotec rulers controlled a vast kingdom for over 1,000 years. This lecture will be a step back into the Preclassic and Classic periods to see what was happening in Oaxaca back then.

Today, Monte Alban can be seen from Oaxaca City. That's the beautiful colonial city that now controls the valley. It's also the starting point for visitors to visit the ruins. They're very close. They're really only about 10 minutes away by car. And the Convento de Santo Tomas in Oaxaca City displays many of Monte Alban's treasures. The valley of Oaxaca is in the highlands, and it's a very arid territory. It's at an elevation of about 6,400 feet above sea level. The region has cactuses, and stony buttes, and pine trees. Monte Alban is another 1,300 feet above the valley floor.

That valley has three arms. Together, they kind of look like a capital letter Y. The north arm is called the Etla Valley. The south arm is called the Valle Grande. And the east arm is the Tlacolula Valley. In the middle is a mountain right at the intersection, and on top of that mountain sits Monte Alban. It was a perfect location to control all three arms of the valley. The mountaintop was uninhabited before 500 B.C. At that time, the biggest city in the valley was San Jose Mogote; it was in the northern Etla branch. It lived from about 1,300 to 500 B.C. During its lifetime, it was trading with the Olmec and very influenced by the Olmec.

They were also having conflicts with other people in the valley, especially Tilcajete and Valle Grande, the south arm. In order for Monte Alban to have functioned by 500 B.C., a massive organized labor project must have preceded it. Leveling Monte Alban's mountaintop was a giant undertaking. It must have taken decades, and at least hundreds, if not thousands of people working on it all the time. It was almost certainly initiated by those people that were controlling San Jose Mogote. And that assertion is supported by a couple of facts.

Number one, San Jose Mogote's population drops as Monte Alban's rises, right about 500 B.C. Number two, Monte Alban's earliest architecture is very similar to San Jose Mogote. And number three, the people of Valle Grande resist Monte Alban, just as they were resisting and fighting with San Jose Mogote before Monte Alban.

By 500 B.C., Monte Alban's plaza was leveled and its first temples were erected. It seems to have been master planned. Below it, there were terraces covering the hillside below. Most of those had elite housing compounds on those terraces. There were discrete clusters around courtyards and some farming and irrigation, but not much. Most of those people on the terraces were not farmers; they appeared to be administrators, or artisans, or people controlling workshops.

By 300 B.C., there were 5,000 people there, and San Jose Mogote was completely gone. By 100 B.C., we believe that there were over 17,000 people living in and around Monte Alban. At that time, what other Mesoamerican city was larger? At 100 B.C., probably none. Kaminaljuyu was pretty big. Teotihuacan was starting. But it's really clear that Zapotec power was clear and present in that B.C. period.

As large as Monte Alban was, the city was only a fraction of the lands they controlled. It represented a new political and economic strategy, one that unified the entire valley of Oaxaca and bound them all in a new Zapotec cultural identity. The process of unification was probably a military conquest at first. Like San Jose Mogote, Monte Alban immediately erected monuments, displaying tortured prisoners. Some of them had name glyphs, indicating that those people were of some status.

Specifically, the site of Tilcajete held out until about 100 B.C., when they were finally subjugated by Monte Alban. By the B.C.-A.D. transition, Monte Alban had complete control of the valley. And it was a new strategy; it wasn't just control of trade, it was an organized division of labor. Each of the villages in the valley specialized in a different product, and Monte Alban was the administrative capital that kept all that an order. Goods were redistributed through a centralized government structure in the city of Monte Alban itself.

The capital was supplied by the valley. Some people call it the "disembedded capital" model of Oaxaca. Perhaps, it was some sort of proto-version of what would become tribute states in the Post-Classic. Monte Alban itself was not farming; they really had no access to dry-season water because they were so up high. We find evidence that even water itself was delivered to the city. All around Monte Alban, we find these very large water container vessels called Ollas.

A thing that I love about Oaxaca is the fact that all those craft villages are still there. The Zapotec pattern persists right up until today. Many of the villages in the valley are still specializing in certain crafts or activities; the only difference is that what Oaxaca City is the nexus of trade, not Monte Alban anymore. Tilcajete is a great example. Now it's called San Martin Tilcajete. It specializes in wooden figurines; they're beautiful things. They're painted very delicately, and there's a wide variety of them. That tradition is generally called Alebrijes. It's not actually traditionally Zapotec. It was adopted from forms that started in Mexico City. But still, it represents village specialization.

Another example is San Bartolo Coyotepec. They specialize in a black pottery called barro negro, and that is a traditional pottery for Oaxaca for almost 2,000 years. It used to be all over, broken pieces of it, at the site of Monte Alban. Tourists have picked up so much of it, there's not much of it left anymore, but it used to be everywhere; there were piles in the ruins in the 1990s.

Other areas of the valley specialized in farming. The Etla Valley specifically, was the most fertile. That's where modern San Jose Mogote is, and those ruins. That part of the valley is all corn farmers. Today, when you go visit those ruins, there's fields right up to the ancient platforms. And you can look off of it to see lots of irrigation canals and rivers, and I think it was very much like that 2,000 years ago.

And Monte Alban set this pattern. It's been working now for 2,000 years. Back then, it towered above the people. It had massive walls and terraces around it; some of those walls were nine meters tall and 20 meters thick in places. Were they for defense, or where they just to impress people? Well, probably both.

We've discussed the city's origins and the areas it controlled. Now, let's turn our attention to the city itself. At its peak, there wasn't another city for hundreds of miles that even came close to rivaling its sophistication or scale. At the heart of the city was its plaza. It's 300 by 200 meters; that's about six football fields. And around the plaza were all the temples and palaces. It's obviously master-planned. All of its buildings were in that final place by 300 B.C. They were built up on, after time, but they were always in the same places; they were rebuilt and rebuilt until they were in their largest form about 680 A.D. Other cities, like in the Maya area, were accretional; they built here, they built there, but not Monte Alban. It was a master-planned city from the beginning.

Today, tourists enter at the northeast end of the city. Right there is the museum, and the gift shop, and a nice little restaurant, and an entry path leads south past a statute. The statue is kind of funny; it reminds me of Han Solo in carbonite. But it's actually Alfonso Caso; he was the first excavator of Monte Alban and one of my personal heroes. Caso didn't come from an elite family. He got degrees in philosophy and law in 1919, but he loved archaeology. And so he got himself another degree in 1925, and he excavated Monte Alban for 18 seasons, from 1932 to 1953. And he was the founder of INAH, the Instituto Nacional de Antropologia e Historia, in 1939. He was its first director, from 1939 to 1944.

Now, Caso was most famous for discovering Monte Alban Tomb 7 in 1932. It was the richest tomb in the Americas at the time. But as it turns out, it wasn't Zapotec. It was actually Mixtec. Mixtec people came in at a later date and put their own bodies in an originally Zapotec tomb. So, for that reason, I'll leave Tomb 7 and more about amazing Alfonso Caso for my upcoming Mixtec lecture.

Walking past Dr. Caso at the site, visitors arrive first to the ball court. It's a classic I-shaped ball court with niches in its corner, and it's sunken into a platform, perhaps, again, it's underworld symbolism. Maybe, it's like Maya underworld symbolism. The thing is, though, we don't really understand much about Zapotec creation mythology.

From the ball court, visitors step down into the plaza. Again, this step down might be some sort of underworld symbolism; that plaza is surrounded by temples and palaces. Many of those temples have *talud-tablero* style architecture, and that's an outward sign that Teotihuacan also influenced this place during the Classic period. It seems, just like that Teotihuacan-Maya relationship, where they're putting their signature architecture in a capital to say they're having an influence there. The north end of the city is dominated by a large platform. On that platform are some temples, but mostly residences. They look like palaces, and they have many, many rooms. They have private courtyards and sunken patios in the middle, and they're obscured from view from the rest of the plaza, so they're private. They're likely the locations of the royal family of Monte Alban. But unlike the Maya, we don't have any depictions of the royals or the elites of Monte Alban, so we can't be sure who lived there.

There are three joined temples that interrupt the open space right in the center of Monte Alban's plaza. They're named Buildings G, H, and I. Caso was a creative guy, but he did not give many creative names to the temples of Monte Alban. These three temples, we're not sure what their function was, but the fact that they're right in the center made them obviously central to whatever activities were going on in there. Two tombs were found underneath H, the center of those three buildings.

Just south of the center temples lies the most interesting building at Monte Alban. It's called Building J, and it's oriented differently than the rest of the buildings. It's 45 degrees off of the rest of the center. And it's got an arrow shape; it's not perfectly rectangular. One side is kind of like a pointer, and it's pointing to the southwest. It's been called an observatory forever, because of its strange orientation, but the actual evidence of that identity is kind of shaky. Now, Anthony Aveni suggested that it was pointing at the star Capella. He said, specifically, it was looking at it on May 2. And he calculated its appearance there on May 2 back to 250 B.C.

That's when he estimated its first construction date was. Now, my problem with that is precessional drift. Stars move one degree every 72 years, and that's 13 degrees over a 900-year period. There were three phases of Building J, and the last one was 600 A.D. So, did they never adjust the building? The earlier phases say that it was in exactly the same orientation for each one of its phases. Now, Anthony Aveni picked May 2 for another reason. It's also because its zenith passage at Monte Alban, the day that the Sun will go directly over our head. So if we take a line backwards from the arrow tip and go back to the edge of Monte Alban's plaza, it leads us to Building P. And under Building P's staircase is a zenith passage tube; it's a specific chamber with a long tube so that people can sight and calculate zenith passage. It's actually one of only three chambers like that we found in all of Mesoamerica. And Aveni was seeking a connection between it and Building J.

The Capella argument, I think, is unclear, but the zenith passage tube, well, that's great. Standing above Building P, once, right over that zenith passage tube, my colleague and I, Alonso Mendez, came up with another idea. We were looking west, and on its center line, we could see Buildings G, H, and I, those ones that interrupt the plaza. Using our compasses, we determined that the three could be used to determine the solstices and equinoxes, just like E-Groups that we had seen in the Maya area. The zenith tube was the sighting location to use the three buildings in the middle as other solar reckoning points. This was something we did in an afternoon, and we walked away with our group. So, someday, I need to go back there and take photos and prove or disprove that. It's one of the many projects that I hope to get back to one of these days.

Astronomical alignments, such as those, teach us things about Monte Alban. But in general, we get a very limited view from an analysis of their architecture. For a better view into the mindset of ancient Zapotec, we need to look at their art. We have two main sources for art forms in Monte Alban. One, we have carved stone monuments, and there are hundreds of those found at the site. And two, we have the offerings left in tombs. And over the decades, over 170 tombs have been located within Monte Alban.

Monte Alban's most famous art pieces are the Danzante carvings. They're carved on irregular-shaped slabs. Each one is a single individual being depicted. Over 300 have been found in and around the valley. They're called Danzantes because the figures look kind of like they're dancing. But, they're not dancing. They're naked and contorted, and some of them have obvious wounds; they have their stomachs or guts coming out sometimes. Some of them have jewelry and name tags which probably marks them as elite captives; it was another one of these shows of power by Monte Alban.

All of Monte Alban's Danzantes are crowded into the plaza's southwest corner. They're lined up. And some of them were actually built over by subsequent building phases. It seems clear that they were moved there. So, there's a question. Were they no longer needed, or were they no longer valid messages at the end of Monte Alban's history? But there's more than just Danzantes that were piled up over in that southwest corner.

Also stacked there are Stelas 12 and 13. They are very famous because of their dates. There's not a long count there, but they're estimated to be about 100 B.C. They're the earliest solar calendar glyphs that we have in all of Mesoamerica. There's a proto version of the year bear symbol on those stelae. It's also proof that the Zapotecs had a basic writing system in Preclassic times. So their system seems to have been as early as the Maya or the Epi-Olmecs.

Not far from the Danzantes, along the base of the southern platform, sits the Lisa Stela. It's very important because it has Teotihuacan-related images. There are four men in procession, heading to a fifth, who's waiting for them. The four men wear Teotihuacan headdresses. And they appear to have gifts in their hands; the other is wearing a Zapotec headdress. The Lisa Stela reminds me of the arrivals pot at Tikal. It's the same sort of thing. It shows Teotihuacanos carrying gifts. But of course, in Tikal, we know how that worked out. Tikal's king was replaced, so, we can probably suspect the same sort of thing. The Teotihuacan came in, and they started controlling Monte Alban's elite. It makes sense. Monte Alban is directly on the way to the Maya region; it's a logical stop for trade routes.

One other interesting set of carvings are embedded into the walls of Building J. There are about 40 slabs along its walls, and they're all in random locations. They show toponyms, which are name places, name glyphs. They're very standard in the Mixtec and the Aztec codices that come later; we know what they are. Caso called these things *conquest slabs*. He suggested that they were all places that were conquered by Monte Alban. Some of them are identifiable by using the codices. One of them in particular is a place called Tututepec, which is south of the valley of Mexico.

I agree with Caso. They probably were conquest slabs, but I'm not sure about their context. I think they were reused, and they were probably hidden by stucco. They're not nicely placed. They're ugly fill stones of the building. And most buildings at Monte Alban were stuccoed. I assume that Building J was, too. So they were probably covered by stucco, and they couldn't be seen. They were covered like they were skeletons in the closet. They were things from their earlier history, when Monte Alban was on the warpath against its neighbors. Later on, they had a more peaceful, though dominant relationship, and these monuments were no longer necessary as public art, so they were reused in Building J.

The other context in which we get a chance to see the art of Monte Alban are the things that we found in its many tombs. Objects, like ceramics, and jewelry, and painted walls, provide insights into how they dressed and how they worshipped. As I mentioned before, there are over 170 tombs at Monte Alban; unfortunately, most of them were looted. Others were really deteriorated by the time archaeology got them. But there were a precious few that still have painted walls. Among them are Tombs 103, 104, and 105. They were found under the palace structures, and they're great examples of Zapotec tombs.

The walls show us elites and their rich clothing. Tomb 105 shows a scene of an elite procession, and all of them are wearing feathered headdresses of big, beautiful, green quetzal feathers. And they're wearing green ear flairs that have to be jade, probably also from the Maya area. The *huipiles* of women have these beautiful geometric patterns, showing that they were expert weavers. And the men carry carved staffs and bundles. Out of their mouths come these speech scrolls with flowers on them. A speech scroll alone is somebody speaking, but with flowers, it means they were singing, so this was a procession of elite people, singing as they went.

Some of the tombs also show hieroglyphs. And there are stelae that have entire texts at Monte Alban. There's been decades of work trying to decipher those glyphs. It's led mostly by a man named Javier Urcid. But, there's been very little progress. We don't have many symbols. Javier's been working on it, but I'm not sure he's going to get anywhere. In my opinion, I'm not exactly sure it's writing; there are too few symbols. It doesn't look or work like Maya or Olmec scripts. I think it's just a complex set of symbols. That's my opinion, at least.

The ceramics found in the tombs also provide images, especially of Zapotec deities. There are images in urns and incense burners that are elaborately modeled; it's expert work. There's a great variety of deities in the Zapotec pantheon, but they're kind of hard to ID. We got a list of Zapotec deities from colonial ethnographies; the Zapotec, at contact, told the Spanish all things about their gods, but it's really difficult to match them to the pieces we find in the tombs.

The most common one, we can identify; his name is Cocijo. He's a god of rain and lightning. And he's got this mask with a hooked nose, and he has a snake tongue. He's the image that we find in almost every tomb. And, because it's in such quantity, I suspect Cocijo is actually the patron deity of Monte Alban. Another easy to identify deity at Monte Alban is Xipe Totec. He's called the flayed one. He's a terrifying god, who represents ripping the skin off the enemies and sacrificial victims. He's much better known from Aztec times, but Monte Alban ceramics prove that he was also in their pantheon and probably in their practices.

I've been visiting Monte Alban for over 20 years, and I used to look off the ruins at another flattened hilltop and think, are those pyramids on top? Well, they were, and they were recently excavated. As it turns out, Monte Alban is not the lone authority on the mountain. It had a sister city. That sister city's name is Atzompa, and it's named after the nearby modern community. Caso did see it back in the 1930s. And in fact, he measured a large ball court over there, but he decided to focus on Monte Alban instead.

Nowadays, the current director of Monte Alban, Nelly Robles Garcia, has finally opened up excavations, and it was opened up to the public in

2012. She found many pyramids and plazas over there; she also found elite residences, very big ones. And she opened up a very rich tomb in 2011. It was clearly an elite person in that tomb. And the site over there has not one, but three ball courts. The architecture is identical to the architecture at Monte Alban. They are clearly related. But Atzompa's dates are very telling.

There are all after 650 A.D. We wonder what it is. Perhaps, it was a split at Monte Alban among the ruling class. At the same time, the valley sites are also showing changes. The population increases, and the autonomy of those villages seems to increase. They start building new temple complexes of their own. It seems that about 650, Monte Alban is beginning to lose its sole authority. In the east valley, the big city of Mitla grows. In the south valley, the big city of Zaachila grows. Both of those cities are still Zapotec, and they both survive right up into the contact period. The Spanish met people living in those cities. But Monte Alban did not survive. At 600, Monte Alban's population was 35,000 people. But, it stops building right about then. Instead, Atzompa and the valley sites are growing. By 750 A.D., Monte Alban is totally abandoned. Like the Maya sites, there's no sign of destruction. Its people, apparently, just walked away.

A few hundred years later, the site would be reused by not the Zapotecs, but a closely related culture called the Mixtecs. Primarily, they reused Monte Alban's tomb chambers, filling them with something that Monte Alban never had—gold. We're already in Oaxaca, so let's talk about the Mixtecs in my next lecture.

The Mixtec Rise—Gold and Epic Stories
Lecture 26

For millennia, people have inhabited the area known as La Mixteca, which covers western Oaxaca, Puebla, and parts of Guerrero. La Mixteca comprises three regions of Central Mexico: Mixteca Alta, the highlands; Mixteca Baja, the lowlands; and Mixteca de la Costa, along the Pacific coast. The Mixtec began to flourish just as the Classic period was ending. In this lecture, we'll study the Mixtec's history, archaeologist Alfonso Caso's fortuitous discovery of Tomb 7 at Monte Alban, his decipherment of the Mixtec codices, and a story about more gold than most archaeologists have ever seen.

The Mystery of Tomb 7

- In 1932, Mexican archaeologist Alfonso Caso discovered Tomb 7 at Monte Alban. That single tomb was filled with more gold than all previous excavations in Mesoamerica combined had ever found. The Zapotec had built Monte Alban, but the body buried in the grave was not Zapotec; it was Mixtec.

- The individual in Monte Alban's Tomb 7 was buried sometime during the 14th century; however, the Zapotec had abandoned the site 400 years earlier. The Mixtec did not re-inhabit Monte Alban; they just buried their kings there. The act was a connection to ancestral authority.

- During the Classic period, the Mixtec were eclipsed by their neighbors. Monte Alban was to the east; Teotihuacan was to the west. The Mixtec built urban centers in the typical city-state model. Their two main locations from the Classic period were Montenegro and Yucunudahui, both in the Mixteca Alta.

- A well-documented Mixtec Classic site was Huajuapan in the Mixteca Alta. The site was built in a style similar to Monte Alban's.

It produced a very distinctive orange-ware pottery that was also found at both Monte Alban and Teotihuacan.

- When the Classic period collapsed, Monte Alban and Teotihuacan were both abandoned, creating a massive power vacuum. That's when the Mixtec stepped in—forging a unique cultural identity.

A Wealth of Gold

- Howard Carter discovered the tomb of Tutankhamun in 1922 and captured the world's imagination. An ancient past of fabulously wealthy kings came to life. Then, just 10 years later, Caso discovered Monte Alban Tomb 7. Other tombs had been found in Mesoamerica, but this one had something that none other did: gold.

The Mixtec learned gold working from contact with Peru.

- Tomb 7 contained more gold than all the archaeologically obtained Aztec gold put together. In fact, the Aztecs mainly relied on the Mixtec to produce their golden jewelry and objects.

- Tomb 7 was constructed sometime in the 1300s. The proof that the Mixtec had mastered gold working was inside the tomb. There was also evidence of a South American influence in the gold work. There were three waves of definitive South American contact in Mexico: in the Preclassic, in the Classic, and with the Mixtec in the Post-Classic.

- Most of the designs on the gold in Tomb 7 are clearly Mesoamerican—the 260-day calendar signs, ball courts, solar motifs with volutes, and Mixtec deities. However, a few of the designs and images further hint at an influence from distant Peru. One is the South American tumi knife.

- Tomb 7 was filled with hundreds of beautifully crafted objects. In addition to gold and silver jewelry of all types, there were objects crafted in jade, pearls, turquoise, obsidian, and crystal. Gold objects included rings, earrings, bracelets, and necklaces, some with images of royalty, a ball court, or a sun symbol. Another beautiful, if macabre, object found in the tomb was a skull covered in a turquoise mosaic. This was an indication that the Mixtec practiced decapitation, like their neighbors—and their colleagues in South America.

Lady 9 Grass
- Objects carved in bone were also found in Tomb 7. Their elaborate carvings included place names, people, and dates. These were weaving battens, used in backstrap-loom weaving. In fact, some of the bodies found in Tomb 7 were identified as women.

- In the 1990s, a new interpretation of these finds was offered by archaeologists Sharisse and Geoffrey McCafferty. Looking at the entire collection of items in the tomb, they discovered spindle whorls, combs, and small bowls used for spinning cotton. Examining the placement of these objects, the pair determined that the objects were actually associated with the main body in the tomb.

- The McCaffertys suggested a radical reinterpretation: The main individual in the tomb was female. Weaving was a purely female activity. Elite women in codices were actually shown with battens. Further, the evidence suggested that the tomb was a shrine to the female deity Lady 9 Grass.

The Mixtec Codices

- Examining the carvings on the battens led to Alfonso Caso's discovery of the Mixtec codices. Today, we know of at least eight Mixtec codices in existence. Most recount the deeds of a culture hero named 8 Deer Jaguar Claw, who unified the Mixtec realm in the 11th century.

- Caso found the first Mixtec codex, later named the Zouche-Nuttall. That codex had been acquired by a man named Lord Zouche, a wealthy English bibliophile. Zelia Nuttall was an American archaeologist working for Harvard University's Peabody Museum. Lord Zouche gave her permission to make a copy of the codex in 1902.

- Nuttall commissioned the best artist she could find, who made a perfect copy of the codex, capturing all its brilliant colors and intricate details. Nuttall's conclusion was that the codex was Aztec.

- Caso, however, wrote a paper in 1949 identifying not only the Zouche-Nuttall Codex but also many other codices as a group that should be renamed the Mixtec codices. Caso used the Zouche-Nuttall Codex to prove that they all had a similar reading order.

- Unlike Maya or Aztec codices, the Mixtec codices had a continuous narrative. Much like the Greek *Odyssey* or *Iliad*, the Zouche-Nuttall Codex told a story of heroes. Other Mixtec codices told exactly the same story.

- There were two keys to Caso's decipherment of the Mixtec codices. He followed the red dividing lines through the pages, and he followed the date glyphs through those same red lines. Weaving through the red-line maze is how the reader navigates the narrative sequence. Each event is marked by a date showing the year and day in the typical 260-day glyphs. Caso used the dates to prove that the narrative moved logically forward through time.

- Once Caso knew the reading order, he tracked the heroes through the codices. He identified where they traveled using the location's toponym, or name glyph. Then, looking at Aztec tribute lists, Caso found the same toponyms.

- The Mixtec codices told Caso what excavations could not: who made Tomb 7 at Monte Alban. These people were the descendants of 8 Deer Jaguar Claw from Tilantongo, the capital city of the Mixteca Alta. Caso then studied the other seven codices, the ones written in the other Mixtec city-states, and put together a complete and fascinating account of Mixtec unification in the 11th century.

The Story of Mixtec Unification

- The man known as 8 Deer Jaguar Claw was born in 1063, the son of a priest of Tilantongo named 5 Alligator. During his young warrior days, 8 Deer Jaguar Claw conquers five places; then he reaches a significant moment in his life: He meets an oracle named Lady 9 Grass.

- After meeting the oracle, 8 Deer Jaguar Claw plays a ball game at Tututepec, a major city in the south near the coast. He becomes its ruler; now, the highlands and the lowlands are connected through him. Immediately after taking Tututepec, 8 Deer Jaguar Claw conquers another 24 places—they are all depicted as a toponym with a spear sticking into it.

- Going on a journey, 8 Deer Jaguar Claw meets a powerful lord named 4 Jaguar. Together, they perform some kind of bundle ritual. At the conclusion of that ritual, a priest comes out and pierces 8 Deer Jaguar Claw's nose. Some speculate that 4 Jaguar might have been the ruler of the Toltec capital of Tula at that time. Although that is debated by archaeologists, it is entirely possible that Tula was part of the Mixtec authority and right to rule.

- Once 8 Deer Jaguar Claw has 4 Jaguar's support, he seizes Tilantongo. The next 14 pages of the codex list 112 lords. Each one of them is shown seated with one finger pointing out. It is believed that they are all signaling their submission to 8 Deer Jaguar Claw. And with that, the Mixtec attained the largest, most unified empire in their history.

A Major Force in the Post-Classic Period

- Certain documents in the Mixtec codices say that 8 Deer Jaguar Claw was murdered in 1115, at exactly 52 years of age—which is one complete cycle of the Mesoamerican calendar. This seems to indicate that the story is part of a mythology.

- However, the epic stories written down by Homer were thought to be myth until Schliemann discovered Troy. In the 1960s, Caso's excavations began discovering the places in the Mixtec codices. Both colonial documents and modern town names helped Caso's search. He found modern-day Tilantongo—today called Santiago Tilantongo. Excavating under its colonial church, he found evidence of a palace and a temple complex. Caso also found evidence of a Classic period abandonment and a Post-Classic reestablishment of the site.

- The most recently discovered city from the Mixtec codices is Tututepec. Excavation showed that it had a Preclassic beginning and a large Classic period population. Between 800 and 1100, Tututepec was only 1 hectare in size, but then suddenly after 1100, its population surged again. All this evidence links to the story of 8 Deer Jaguar Claw.

- Thanks to the pioneering work of Alfonso Caso, the Mixtec have gone from an almost unknown culture to a major force in the Mesoamerican Post-Classic period landscape. It was the events during the Terminal Classic period that set the Mixtec on their path. We'll study those momentous events in our next lecture.

Suggested Reading

Byland and Pohl, *In the Realm of 8 Deer*.

Nuttall, ed., *The Codex Nuttall*.

Paddock, ed., *Ancient Oaxaca*.

Spores and Balkansky, *The Mixtecs of Oaxaca*.

Questions to Consider

1. Comparing Mixtec gold work with contemporary works from Peru, do you see stylistic similarities?

2. The typical Mesoamerican pattern is to leave abandoned cities alone. Why did the Mixtec decide to reuse old capitals, such as Tututepec or Monte Alban?

3. Do you think the Mixtec codices can lead us to the discovery of more Mixtec ruins?

The Mixtec Rise—Gold and Epic Stories
Lecture 26—Transcript

In 1932, Mexican archaeologist Alfonso Caso discovered Tomb 7 at Monte Alban. That single tomb was filled with more gold than all previous excavations in Mesoamerica combined had ever found. The Zapotec had built Monte Alban, but Caso was surprised to eventually learn that this was not a Zapotec grave; this person was a Mixtec.

The individual in Monte Alban's Tomb 7 was buried sometime during the 14th century. The Zapotec had abandoned the site 400 years earlier. They were still around in the Post-Classic, but they were at other sites. The Mixtec didn't actually re-inhabit Monte Alban; they were just burying their kings there. It was kind of connection to ancestral authority.

Now, I'll get back to Tomb 7. But first, let's talk a little bit about the Mixtecs' origins. The Mixtec are a people of central Mexico, located in between the Zapotecs in Oaxaca and the valley of Mexico. People had inhabited the area known as the Mixteca since the Archaic period, but their character always seemed defined by their neighbors, but as the Classic period fell apart, the Mixtec came into their own.

The Mixteca today spreads out over three states, and there are still 800,000 Mixtec people still living there. It covers western Oaxaca, Puebla, and parts of the state of Guerrero. And within it, there are three different regional parts. There's the Mixtec Alta, which is the highlands. There's the Mixteca Baja, which is the lowlands. And then there's the Mixteca Costa, which is along the Pacific coast.

As I said, the area was inhabited for millennia. The Tehuacan Valley is there. And that's where MacNeish found his dry caves, where he found some of the earliest domesticated corn, going back to 6000 B.C. It was also part of the Olmec revolution. There's a place called Etlatongo, and it's right there in the Mixteca, and it had a population explosion about 1150 B.C. It was kind of in a place that was a crossroads between the Olman and the Valley of Mexico's Tlatilco culture.

In the Classic period the Mixtec were eclipsed by their neighbors. They had Monte Alban to the east. They had Teotihuacan to the west. And they had the west Mexico culture on their coast. But still, the Mixtec had urban centers, and they were a typical city-state model; they were independent of the others.

They built hilltop cities, and they were fortified places. It appeared that they were worried about attack from someone. The two big places we know from the Classic period are Montenegro and Yucunudahui. They're both up in the Mixtec Alta, and they were their Classic period power base. The other regions at the time were less developed. Or, perhaps, they're just under studied. The truth is that, still today, we don't have near enough Mixtec archaeology.

One of the other well-documented classic sites was Huajuapan in the Mixteca Alta. It had many stone-carved monuments, and they looked a lot like Monte Alban style. That site was also producing a very distinct orange ware pottery, and that kind of pottery was found both in Monte Alban and Teotihuacan. So, it would appear, at least from that evidence, that they were trading with their neighbors; they weren't completely isolated. But then the Classic period collapsed. Monte Alban and Teotihuacan were both abandoned, and a huge power vacuum occurred on both sides if them. And that's when the Mixtec stepped into it. Where they were once blurred into their neighbors, now they forged a unique cultural identity.

The winds of Mixtec change started to blow in the 800s A.D. But it was around 1000 A.D., during the life of Mixtec culture hero 8 Deer Jaguar Claw, that things really changed. That story is documented in the Mixtec Codices, which we'll discuss shortly. But first, let's go back into Tomb 7. Howard Carter discovered the tomb of Tutankhamun in 1922, and captured the world's imagination. An ancient past of fabulously wealthy kings came to life. Then, just 10 years later, Caso found Monte Alban Tomb 7. Other tombs had been found in Mesoamerica, but this one had something that none other did, the gold. There were dozens of gold objects inside. There were always stories about Aztec gold for centuries. But where was it? In almost 50 years of archaeology, we had found almost nada, just ceramics and jade. And then, finally, we had this gold in Tomb 7. And it wasn't just gold—it was finely crafted.

Westerners are caught up in the legends of Aztec gold and the huge abundance it was found in. But the truth is, that really just wasn't true. First off, Mexico is really not that gold-rich; gold resources are in much more plenty in other parts of the world. Second, no one in Mesoamerica, but the West Coast culture, even knew about metallurgy until almost 1200 A.D. We'll discuss it more later, but briefly here, the Spanish told the Aztecs that they wanted gold. And so the Aztecs sent for it in the mines they knew. It wasn't just laying around; they had to go collect it for the Spanish. In fact, Aztec experts say that all of the known Aztec gold artifacts remaining today could fit into a pair of cupped hands. If that's true, and I believe it is, that means Tomb 7 contained more gold than all the archaeologically-obtained Aztec gold put together. In fact, the Aztecs mainly relied on the Mixtec to produce their golden jewelry and objects.

Tomb 7 was interred sometime in the 1300s. The proof that Mixtec had mastered gold working was inside there, and again, this was clearly South American influence. That's commonly known, but it's rarely discussed. The fact is, there were three waves of clear South American contact in Mexico, one in the Preclassic, one in the Classic, and another with the Mixtec in the Post-Classic. The first two waves were in the B.C. period, and then about 600 A.D., on the west coast; it was contacting that culture, and they were making tools and bells, probably connecting to Ecuador, Colombia, and maybe Peru. The third wave was about 1200. This time, it was the Chimu and the Sican cultures of Peru. And the sort of things they were making in jewelry and religious imagery were given to the Mixtec. The West Coast people at that time had already moved inland, and the Mixtec had moved down to populate more of the coast in the Mixteca Costa part.

Most of the designs on Tomb 7's gold are clearly Mesoamerican. There are 260-day calendar signs; there's ball courts; there's solar motifs with volutes; there's Mixtec deities, et cetera. However, a few of the designs and images are further evidence or hints that there was an influence from distant Peru. One of them is the South American tumi knife, again. One was actually found in Tomb 7, just like we found them in west Mexico in the 600s A.D. It's frequently overlooked in the museum collection, because it's a little thing, compared to all of the other beautiful objects. The marker calls it a copper ax, but it's not just a copper ax; it's South America's tool used to decapitate people.

There are other stylistic elements that point to South America, like elements in headdresses and nose pieces. But my point is that the Mixtec learned gold working from contact with Peru; that explains their sudden mastery. I'd like to see a lot more research on the coast, but for now, let's go back in to Tomb 7 at Monte Alban and talk about it a little more. Tomb 7 was filled with hundreds of beautifully crafted objects. In addition to gold and silver jewelry of all types, there were objects made in jade, and pearls, and turquoise, obsidian, and crystal. Some of the most fascinating objects, at least to me, were carved in bone. Let's talk about the contents of Tomb 7 next.

As I mentioned, there were many objects made in gold. They were rings, earrings, bracelets, necklaces; there was all sorts of pectorals, royal portraits on top of some of them; one of them had a ball court on top. There's another one with a sun symbol, just like on the Aztec sunstone. It's one of the things that show us that the Mixtec art inspired Aztec art.

Well, one of the under-appreciated objects is a crystal cup. It's carved like a goblet. It's hard to overstate how difficult it is to carve crystal without modern metal tools. This thing is like the fake crystal skulls. But, Tomb 7's chalice is real and very beautifully made. Another beautiful, if macabre, object found in the tomb was a skull covered in turquoise mosaic. Caso found it on a small altar inside the tomb. It had carved shale eyes in its sockets, and they were wide, like it was looking out at you. It was an indication that the Mixtec liked decapitation, like their neighbors, and, I point out, like South America.

Caso believed that this was a priest, perhaps dedicated to Xolotl, a dog-faced God of death. But there were clues to the individual's identity right under his nose, and he didn't see them. A set of objects carved in bone were also found in Tomb 7. There were beautiful, elaborate carvings on them. They had names, and place names, and people, and dates. Caso was caught up in all that information, and he overlooked the objects themselves. What were they? They were weaving tools. There were over 20 of the same object, bone battens, tapered on both ends. These were weaving battens. They were used in backstrap loom weaving. Caso did figure that out in the 1960s, but still, he attributed those artifacts to lesser bodies found in Tomb 7. There were actually another seven individuals in there, and some of them were identified as women.

In the 1990s, a new interpretation was offered by Charisse and Jeffrey McCaffrey. It wasn't just the battens in the tomb. Looking at the whole collection again, they also saw spindle whorls and combs, and they found small bowls that are made for spinning cotton. Examining the placement of these objects, they determined that they were actually associated with the main body in the tomb. So, they suggested the main individual was female. Weaving was a purely female activity. Elite women in codices are actually shown with battens, and further, this suggested the tomb was a shrine to the female deity Lady Nine Grass.

That's indeed a radical reinterpretation, and I believe it. It's important proof of the importance of women. And that's something we actually see reflected in the codices that we are going to talk about in a little bit. But it was actually the second time that those battens had led to important Mixtec discoveries. The carvings on them reminded Caso of things he had seen in codices that were branded Aztec, and that's what led his discovery of the actual Mixtec codices.

Today, we know that we have at least eight Mixtec codices still in existence. Most recount the deeds of a culture hero named 8 Deer Jaguar Claw, who unified the Mixtec realm in the 11th century A.D. But we didn't know these were Mixtec codices, or what they, said until Tomb 7 inspired Caso to study them.

Now, Caso knew that Tomb 7 was Mixtec, and there were colonial documents that spoke of the Mixtec. Aiding his studies was the fact that the Mixtec were still there; they still live in the Mixteca, but no archaeology had been done in that region. So he began excavating in the Mixteca. And he was also looking for clues anywhere he could find them. That's when he found the first Mixtec codex, the Zouche-Nuttall.

That codex had been acquired by a man named Lord Zouche. He was a rich English bookophile. Then comes into the picture Zelia Nuttall. She was an

American archaeologist, and at that time was working for Harvard's Peabody Museum. She met Lord Zouche, and he gave her permission to make a copy in 1902. So, she commissioned the best artist she could find, and they made a perfect copy. It captured all of its brilliant colors and details. But her conclusion was that this was an Aztec codex.

Nuttall recognized that it was about histories of real people. But again, she thought they were Aztec people. Other people that looked at her magnificent copy suggested maybe they were Zapotec people. Still other people noted that there was a narrative structure running through the codex. But it was Caso who put them all together. He wrote a very famous paper in 1949, where he identified not just the Zouche-Nuttall, but a whole bunch of other codices as a group that should be renamed the Mixtec Codices. And he used the Codex Nuttall to prove that they all had a similar reading order.

Unlike Maya or Aztec codices, These things had a continuous narrative, from beginning to end. The Codex Nuttall told a story of heroes. It was very much like the Greek *Odyssey* or the *Iliad*. Other Mixtec codices were telling the exact, same story. At first we didn't know that, because they were written in different cities, and they were written in their own town's perspective. So sometimes they highlighted some heroes and they de-emphasized others, based on their home-team perspective. The Codex Nuttall was written from our main hero's hometown of Tilantongo in the Mixteca Alta.

There were two keys to Caso's decipherment. First, he started following these red dividing lines through the pages. Number two, he followed the date glyphs through those same red lines. These were fan-fold books, like the Maya books. They were one huge page when you spread them out; you could spread them all the way out on the floor and just walk across the story. Each fold had these red dividing lines, and the arrangement was like a maze. The figures in the codex were walking through that red-line maze, and the reader follows them through the narrative. It gives the Mixtec Codices a very comic-book look. And a lot of scholars dismissed them as just being some sort of pictorial story, not really giving real information.

Weaving through the red-line maze is how the reader navigates the narrative sequence. Each event is marked by a date. It's the year and the day in the typical 260-day glyphs, and they had dots over them to tell us exactly what day within that glyph it was. Caso use the dates to prove that the narrative moved logically forward through time. Once Caso knew the reading order, he could track the heroes through the codices. He could also pick out the places they went. Each location had its own toponym. A toponym is a large but unique logo gram that names a place. For example, if we see the Hill of the Wasp. We know it's the Hill of the Wasp, because the symbol is a hill with a big wasp on top, really not that hard to read. Once you're oriented to the elements, anyone can read them relatively simply.

Then, looking at Aztec tribute lists, Caso found those same, exact toponyms. This time, there were Spanish notes scrawled under them, so we actually got their names, and he could ask people, where are these places? The Mixtec Codices told Caso what excavations couldn't. They told him who made the Tomb 7 at Monte Alban. These people were the descendants of Lord 8 Deer from Tilantongo, the capital city of the Mixteca Alta.

The Codex Nuttall told 8 Deer's story, but from a decidedly Tilantongo perspective. Caso then studied the other seven codices, the ones that were written in the other Mixtec city-states, and put together a very complete and fascinating account of Mixtec unification in the 11th century A.D. 8 Deer was born in the year 1063 A.D., in the year, in their reckoning, 12 Reed. He was the son of a priest of Tilantongo, a man named Five Alligator. On the front side of the Codex Nuttall, which we call the obverse, it tells all about his heritage. It tells the generations leading up to 8 Deer, and then it jumps over him, and it gives us another 11 generations, all the way up to 1458 A.D.

The back side of the Codex Nuttall is what we call the reverse. It's also titled the Saga of 8 Deer Jaguar Claw. It starts with his birth, on the day 8 Deer. The Jaguar Claw part is the distinguishing marker to name him separately from anyone else born on the day 8 Deer. Perhaps it was his family name, or perhaps it was something unique to him; we're really not sure about that.

But he starts as a young warrior. And during his young warrior days, he conquers five places, and we can see that he's conquered them because there are toponyms with arrows sticking out of them, or rather, spears sticking out of them. And then he reaches a very important moment in his life; he meets an Oracle named Lady Nine Grass. After meeting that Oracle, 8 Deer goes out immediately and conquers more places. He goes down to the south, and he plays a ball game at a place called Tututepec; that's a major city in the south near the coast. And he becomes the ruler of that place. Now the highlands and the lowlands are connected through him.

Immediately after taking Tututepec, he goes and conquers another 24 places. Again, it's shown each toponym with a spear sticking into it. Then 8 Deer goes on a journey. And he brings his brothers to accompany him. He has a brother named 12 Motion, who's a warrior. And he has another brother 9 Flower, who's a priest. Wherever they go, they end up meeting a very powerful lord, named Four Jaguar. And together, they perform some kind of bundle ritual. At the conclusion of that ritual, a priest comes out, and he pierces 8 Deer's nose. Some think that Four Jaguar might have been the ruler of the Toltec capital of Tula at that time. It's debated, but it's entirely possible that Tula is part of the Mixtec authority and right to rule.

Once 8 Deer has Jaguar's support, he attacks more places. His journeys lead him back to Tilantongo. And at this time, he seizes that city and becomes its ruler as well. Remember, he started out just as a son of a priest there; he did not have the right to rule. But with all of this authority, he comes back and he takes the rulership of Tilantongo. The next 14 pages of the codex list 112 lords. And each one of them are seated with one finger pointing out. We believe they're all signaling their submission to 8 Deer. And with that, the Mixtec reaches its largest, most unified empire in its entire history.

Then, 8 Deer meets Four Jaguar again. Together, they go off, and they conquer another 40 places. Then, they go on a journey together, an epic, perhaps mythic, journey. The codex shows them for three days crossing a large body of water. And when they get to the other side, they conquer supernatural places, and they meet gods. Upon their return, a whole line of people are shown surrendering. Each one of them are holding up a little white flag, which actually does mean their surrender, in that context.

8 Deer's kingdom and his success was set. But then, just like Greek tragic tales, tragedy struck. His brother, 12 Motion, is murdered in a sweat bath. Those responsible are tracked down, and they're brutally killed. One of them

is shown tied to a stone and beaten. The other one is nailed up to a scaffold, and he's shot with arrows. The Codex Nuttall ends there. But the other codices say that 8 Deer was murdered just a few years later, in 1115 A.D. At that time, he'd be exactly 52 years of age; that's one complete cycle. Perhaps that's saying that it's really mythologized. And that became the question. Like Greek epics, the question became, Are the Mixtec Codices myths, or are they real history?

The epic stories written down by Homer were thought to be myth until Schliemann discovered Troy. The Roman story of Masada was questioned until it's excavation in the 1960s. So, too, were the epics Caso discovered in the Mixtec Codices. They were names without places. That is, until Caso's excavations in the 1960s started finding them.

Both colonial documents and modern town names helped Caso's search. He found modern-day Tilantongo. Today, it's called Santiago Tilantongo. Excavating there in that town, he found evidence under its colonial church. He found evidence of a palace and a temple complex nearby. He also found evidence of a Classic abandonment of that site, and then, a Post-Classic reestablishment of that site. Was that 8 Deer coming in and revitalizing it? Perhaps so.

The most recently discovered city from the Mixtec Codices is Tututepec. It was really known since 1949, but we used to call it Yucu Dzaa. The first excavations really occurred in 2002. This was the southern city that 8 Deer took after visiting the Oracle Nine Grass. And there's an interesting match between the archaeology and the codices that we find there. Excavation showed that it had a Preclassic start and a large Classic period population. Then, Tututepec was mostly abandoned. Between 800 and 1100, it was only one full hectare in size, a very small place. But then suddenly, after 1100, its population surged again. By Spanish contact, it was a very powerful kingdom. It was actually independent and able to resist the Aztec empire on their own.

8 Deer's story links very nicely with that second population surge. Remember, he was a young warrior, the son of a priest. He had no right to Tilantongo's throne. So the Oracle Nine Wind sent him south. He does

some bird sacrifices in its ball court and becomes their King. Tututepec was reestablished peacefully, and 8 Deer goes back on his conquest trail.

Archaeological progress like this excites me. There are other projects finding out more cities that are involved in 8 Deer's saga right now. Mixtec expert John Pohl has been developing a map as each one of them is discovered, and it's growing. It's a unique case from Mesoamerica. Pre-Columbian historical documents are leading archaeologists to Mixtec cities. I think it's wonderful.

Thanks to the pioneering work of Alfonso Caso, the Mixtec have gone from an almost unknown culture to a major force in the Mesoamerican Post-Classic landscape. We've also learned that it was the events during the Terminal Classic that set them on their path. Next, let's look at how the Terminal Classic times also shook up central Mexico.

The Great Pyramid of Cholula and El Tajin
Lecture 27

In this lecture, we'll explore the region that encompasses the Gulf Coast state of Veracruz and the adjacent state of Puebla. During the Classic period, those areas were relatively quiet places under the control of Teotihuacan. But as Teotihuacan waned, Veracruz civilizations grew in size, power, and complexity. This lecture focuses on two unique cities that survived the Classic period collapse and prevailed into the Terminal Classic: Cholula and El Tajin.

Classic Veracruz Culture

- Veracruz has been occupied since the Archaic period. Archaeologists have found evidence of a hunter-gatherer culture; eventually, the Olmec civilization spread into Veracruz. The Epi-Olmec culture is theorized to have migrated north to become what archaeologists call Classic Veracruz culture, which flourished between 300 and 900.

© Daderot/Wikimedia Commons/Public Domain.

The well-known Sonrientes are remarkable because they depict smiling figures, which are otherwise quite rare in Mesoamerican art.

- Most of the known Classic Veracruz culture sites cluster around the modern-day city of Veracruz. The culture was probably inspired by Teotihuacan's vast trade network. The Classic Veracruz area outlived Teotihuacan, but the sites were abandoned before the Terminal Classic period ended.

- The Classic Veracruz people are most noted for their pottery, especially the Remojadas style. The best-known figures are called the Sonrientes, or the "Smilers." Sonrientes were mold-made and mass-produced. Classic Veracruz also produced marvelous terracotta figures that were hollow, with long arms and delicate appliques.

- When looking for precedents for these kinds of ceramics, western Mexico seems the best candidate. Another possible connection between the western coast of Mexico and Veracruz is Los Voladores, or "the flyers"—a tradition in which four men jump off the top of a pole attached to ropes. Today, it's said to come from Veracruz, but archaeology first finds evidence of those poles not in Veracruz but in west Mexico's Teuchitlan tradition as early as 200 B.C.—much earlier than Veracruz.

The World's Largest Pyramid

- Cholula is an archaeological site in Puebla containing the world's largest pyramid—larger than any in Egypt. Khufu in Egypt is the tallest, at 147 meters, but its base is only 230 meters on a side. Cholula's pyramid is only 66 meters tall, but it is 400 meters on a side.

- Cholula's massive structure was built in four major phases. The site sits under two towering volcanoes: Popocatepetl and Iztaccihuatl. The surrounding farmland is extremely rich, with deposits of clay and obsidian.

- The first-phase pyramid, started in 200 B.C., was Cholula's main temple for 400 years. The structure had rounded steps, like those at the site of Cuicuilco. Cuicuilco's temple was pre-Teotihuacan and was buried by repeated volcanic eruptions. The name *Cholula* actually means "Place of Retreat."

- The first-phase pyramid was constructed of adobe bricks, not stone, and the building itself was painted red and black. The temple contained many trade items from Teotihuacan. Around 280 A.D., the second phase of the pyramid was built, in *talud-tablero* style—

even more clearly influenced by Teotihuacan. This second phase was a combination of adobe and stone. Skulls were painted on the façades, perhaps an indication that the populace practiced ritual sacrifice, as did their neighbors in Teotihuacan.

Murals of the Drunkards

- Teotihuacan controlled Cholula, but the lesser city still maintained its own distinct character. One of the best examples of its unique character is the Murals of the Drunkards—a fascinating window into Cholula's life.

- The murals together represent the longest mural in all of Mesoamerica, a total of 57 meters. The murals depict people in a festival of sorts, not an austere ritual. All walks of life are involved in the mural—the young, the old, men, and women. And it seems that the gods are also intermingling.

- Everyone is drinking out of cups, dipping the cups in large basins. There are only 110 people in the scene, but there are 168 jars and cups—the drinks outnumber the people. The theory is that the people are drinking *pulque*, an ancient alcoholic drink made out of agave.

Cholula: A Powerful Capital City

- The third phase of Cholula's pyramid was built about 358 A.D. and illustrates even more Teotihuacan influence. Constructed of stone and stucco, this structure was larger than Teotihuacan's Pyramid of the Moon. This was a clear sign that Cholula was a powerful capital.

- But when Teotihuacan's power began to wane, Cholula's did not. By 400 A.D., Teotihuacan stopped growing, but Cholula did not. By 650, Teotihuacan burned to the ground; Cholula grew even stronger.

- After Teotihuacan was burned and abandoned, the inhabitants of Cholula responded by once again transforming their pyramid. In the fourth and final phase of construction, the builders went back to using adobe combined with packed earth to make the entire structure into a naturalistic, human-made mountain.

Symbolic Reenactment of the Creation Myth

- A complex called the Courtyard of the Altars was built on the south side of Cholula's pyramid. The Courtyard of the Altars is part of a set of clues that point to a mystic re-creation encoded in the new architecture.

- Popocatepetl is locally called Sustenance Mountain. There's a spring from the east side of the Cholula pyramid, from which water pours into a marshy area. In that marshy area are cattail reeds, or tollans. This is clearly symbolic of the mythical origin places. The courtyard is said to be the symbolic ball court; the marsh symbolizes the first maize crops; and the pyramid is the mountain. All the elements fit into the creation myth. And the same sort of mythology is repeated at El Tajin.

- Cholula's pyramid was finally abandoned in 1200; the Courtyard of the Altars was burned. Many sites in Central Mexico show the same evidence of burning. Scholars blame this destruction on a group called the Tolteca-Chichimeca, raiders from the northern deserts.

- In 1200, Cholula's people moved the center of their city to a new location and built a new temple, dedicated to Quetzalcoatl. At that same time, the inhabitants also made a major craft production switch, to making textiles. Cholula remained strong until the very end. When Cortes arrived, he estimated it was a city of 100,000 people.

El Tajin's Innovative and Unique Technology

- A site contemporary with Cholula was El Tajin, located in northern Veracruz. At first, it was simply another Teotihuacan underling, sending tobacco and vanilla to the powerful city. When the centralized control of Teotihuacan ended in the 600s, however, El Tajin grew quickly and became a regional capital.

- El Tajin had a very distinct style of architecture. The builders placed niches in each terrace. What's more, the site alone has 20 ball courts. El Tajin's most famous building is the Pyramid of the Niches. Styled in a variation of *talud-tablero*, the pyramid has square niches all around the sides; the *tableros* are what archaeologists call "flying cornices."

- The pyramid was painted mostly red, but the interior of the niches was painted black. It had seven terrace levels and exactly 365 niches; thus, the pyramid represented a kind of solar symbolism, as well.

- The pyramid had a perfect geometry based on combinations of the square root of 2 and the golden mean. The angles on the sides are perfect diagonals of square-root-2 rectangles. The staircase is constructed as two golden mean rectangles stacked on top of each other.

- One of the most impressive aspects of El Tajin was the use of poured cement slabs. This was an extraordinary technological development. Cement would not show up in Mesoamerica until the Europeans arrived—except at El Tajin.

The Ball Game as Warfare

- The most complex and beautiful art panels at El Tajin are found along the playing-field walls of certain ball courts. These panels provide remarkable insight into the connections among the ball games, warriors, sacrifice, and the favor of the gods.

- The imagery is clearest in the south ball court. The context is a ball game, but the images depict warriors carrying spear bundles. The warriors are clad in jaguar and eagle costumes. The illustrations also show victims being sacrificed and their hearts cut out. Skeletal gods look down on these sacrifices.

- The ball game is seen as a symbol of warfare. War is a political affair, driven in Mesoamerica by religion. Religion is driven by the fact that the gods need sacrifices. The warriors provide those sacrifices to the gods.

Connection between Cholula and El Tajin

- On another level of symbolism, the architecture tells us more. Underneath the south ball court is a water system, designed to flow from the temple into the ball court. Again, we are reminded of the Sustenance Mountain myth, just as in Cholula to the south.

- Portrayed in that ball court are people in costume sitting in vats of liquid, surrounded by deities drinking. Perhaps these are *pulque* rituals, like the ones depicted on Cholula's Murals of the Drunkards. It makes sense that there would be some sort of cultural association and connection between El Tajin and Cholula.

- Linguistically, there is a connection between the two. Today, the people around El Tajin are the Totonac people. They are not Maya, but the Huastec in the same area speak a Maya language. Perhaps these people were part of the migrations into the area during the Terminal Classic period. Although Cholula survived the radical changes of 1200, El Tajin did not. About 1230, El Tajin burned to the ground—most likely at the hands of the Tolteca-Chichimeca.

- El Tajin embodied the transitions of the Terminal Classic period. The city combined old symbols of authority and new strategies of political control and religion. Clearly, there was some Maya influence, which was backed up by the same local cultures at Cholula.

Suggested Reading

Koontz, *Lightning Gods and Feathered Serpents*.

Scarborough and Wilcox, eds., *The Mesoamerican Ballgame*.

1. Were Cholula and El Tajin the same culture, or did they just share certain religious ideas?

2. What was Cholula doing differently that it survived the 1200 A.D. transition and El Tajin didn't?

3. Do you think El Tajin and Cholula were responsible for Teotihuacan's demise?

The Great Pyramid of Cholula and El Tajin
Lecture 27—Transcript

In this lecture, we'll talk about an area we've spent very little time in thus far, the Gulf Coast state of Veracruz and the adjacent state of Puebla. During the Classic period, those areas were relatively quiet places under the control of Teotihuacan, but as Teotihuacan waned, Vera Cruz civilizations grew in size, power, and complexity.

Two big cities are going to be discussed during this lecture, Cholula and El Tajin. One is in Puebla, under the volcanoes. The other is in upper Veracruz, in the hills along the coast. Both survived the Classic period collapse, and both are unique and interesting Terminal Classic period sites.

Veracruz was occupied for a long time. We have evidence from the Archaic period and hunter-gatherer evidence. The Olmec civilization eventually spread into Veracruz. The Epi-Olmec culture is theorized to have migrated north to become what we call Classic Veracruz culture. Most of the known Classic Veracruz culture sites cluster around the modern-day city of Veracruz. None of them are very large, but they're a distinct group. They live up on hilltops with nice views of the gulf; 300 to 900 A.D. is about their time span. And they were probably inspired by Teotihuacan's vast trade network. They outlived Teotihuacan, but they were abandoned before the Terminal Classic period ended.

They're most famous for their pottery forms, especially a style called Remojadas. It's named after a site just northwest of the city of Veracruz; that's the same name for a subculture and that same pottery style. There were beautifully made figurines of all types, ranging from things that you could hold in the palm of your hand to life size. The best known of them are called the Sonrientes, or the smilers. Sonrientes were mold made and mass produced. They were very particular; they had triangular-shaped faces, and they had wide, open-smiling mouths. Smiles are really rare in Mesoamerican art. Their bodies were odd, too. They were toddler-like, chubby. They obviously weren't adult. And they had arms outstretched, like they're saying, pick me up, hold me. They look just like dolls, but they're creepy dolls. For that reason, sometimes I joke and I call them the Veracruz Chucky dolls, because they remind me of that movie character.

Classic Veracruz also produced marvelous terracotta figures. They were hollow, and they had long arms, and they had delicate applique attached. Most of them are human, and they're very, very lifelike. Some of them are small, but some of them were very big, life sized, as I say. And they were in very naturalistic poses. Those poses show us that they really had a mastery of the form at that time.

When looking for precedents for those kinds of ceramics, west Mexico seems like the best candidate. At the same time, they were also making figurines of varying forms, some odd little small ones, and some very realistic, larger terracotta ones. And the time frame is perfect for contact between the two.

And there's another odd connection between the west coast and Veracruz. It's the tradition of the Voladores, the flyers. It's a big pole in which four guys jump off the top of the pole attached to ropes. Today, it's said to come from Veracruz, and there are tourist places all around Veracruz that have these poles, where Voladores are still flying off of them. But, archaeology first finds evidence of those poles not in Veracruz, but in west Mexico's Teuchitlan tradition, and they find it as early as 200 B.C., which is much earlier than Veracruz.

To date, we still have very little archaeology for Classic Veracruz culture, and tempting connections, like these, to west Mexico intrigue me. I suspect there was some sort of cultural bridge we haven't teased out yet. We know much more about the region of Veracruz after the Classic Period collapse. So let's turn to those times now.

I suspect that when modern Westerners hear the name Cholula, they think of the hot sauce they see on the table at their local Mexican-food restaurant. But in fact, Cholula is an archaeological site in the Mexican state of Puebla containing the world's largest pyramid. That's right, larger than Egypt's. And by the way, Cholula hot sauce isn't even made in Puebla; it's made in Jalisco by the Jose Cuervo tequila producers. Now don't get me wrong; I love that hot sauce. I just think the amazing city of Cholula is more interesting.

As for Cholula's status as the world's largest ancient pyramid, here's why I can say that. Khufu in Giza, Egypt, is the tallest. It's 147 meters tall, but its base is only 230 meters on a side. Cholula's Great Pyramid is only 66 meters tall, but on each side, it's 400 meters. That means that Cholula's pyramid is 3.52 million cubic meters, while Khufu's is only 2.58 million cubic meters. I say "only"; they're both huge, but Cholula's is bigger.

Cholula's massive structure was built in 10 phases. There were four major phases and six minor, kind of remodeling phases. The site today stands less than an hour west of Puebla City. And it sits under two towering volcanoes. One is Popocatepetl, and the other one is Iztaccihuatl. And by the way, Popocatepetl sadly lost its glacial cap for good in 2001, due to global warming. Still, it's active and smoking today. So why would they build under an active volcano? Well, the reason is the soil. It's incredibly rich farmland. It also has great deposits of clay and obsidian. In the summer, they could depend on snowmelt for water. Perhaps it was dangerous to live there, but it was also beautiful and resource-rich. Still today millions of people live there and people have been living there almost continuously since Preclassic times.

Cholula's pyramid phase one started in 200 B.C., about the same time as Teotihuacan. And they're really not that far away from each other. Today, you can get between them in a three-hour car ride. That first phase had some interesting steps; they were rounded, like the site of Cuicuilco. Cuicuilco also had a rounded temple, but it was pre-Teotihuacan, and it was buried by repeated volcanic eruptions. The name Cholula actually means place of retreat, and looking at those rounded first steps, I've always wondered whether it wasn't that early retreat from Cuicuilco that gave Cholula its name.

That first-phase pyramid was odd in the regard that it was made of adobe bricks, not stone. Now, their neighbors had been building in stone for centuries. The building itself was painted red and black, and it was Cholula's main temple for 400 years. It shows a lot of trade items from Teotihuacan, so we know they were being influenced by that big city. Then, by about 280 A.D., they built the second phase of the pyramid, and it was even more clearly Teotihuacan; it had *talud-tablero* style architecture. The new temple was 120 meters on the side, but only 17 meters tall, so it was very wide, but not too tall yet. And this time, it was a combination of adobe and stone. And they painted skulls on the facades. Perhaps these were symbols telling us that they were now practicing sacrifice like their neighbors Teotihuacan.

Teotihuacan controlled Cholula, but they had their own character. One of the best examples of that is a set of murals that were found called the Murals of the Drunkards; they are a fascinating window into Cholula's life. They're very long murals, with people in a festival of sorts. In total, it's 57 meters long, which makes it the longest mural in all of Mesoamerica. It seems like it's some sort of party; it doesn't really look like some kind of ritual; it's not austere. All walks of life are involved in the mural; there's young people, old people, women. And it seems that gods are also intermingling. Everyone is drinking. They're drinking out of cups, and there's big basins that they're dipping their cups into. There's only 110 people in the scene, but there's 168 jars and cups. The drinks actually outnumber the people. We suspect it's pulque, an ancient drink made out of maguey. And in the scene, it's debaucherous. There are people vomiting. There are people pooping. They're stumbling around. It's a crazy scene.

Now, the third phase of the pyramid was built about 358 A.D. That one shows even more Teotihuacan influence. This time, it's both in stone and stucco, no longer adobe. And around it are carvings of jaguars and snakes. It's bigger than Teotihuacan's Pyramid of the Moon. And that really indicates that at that time, Cholula must have been a powerful capital; to be able to build something larger than Teotihuacan, right in their back yard, means something.

But when Teotihuacan's power begins to wane, Cholula's doesn't. By 400, Teotihuacan stops growing, but Cholula doesn't. By 650, Teotihuacan burns to the ground. Scholars wonder if Cholula had something to do with its demise. We're really not sure still. But what we do know is that Cholula grew yet stronger after the fall of Teotihuacan.

When Teotihuacan is burned and abandoned, the inhabitants of Cholula responded by once again transforming their Great Pyramid. This fourth and final phase of its construction went back to using adobe, and it did an odd thing; it used packed earth to make the entire structure into a naturalistic, man-made mountain. The archaeology proving that construction history is actually a little shaky. It was done back in the 1930s. Maybe it looked a little more polished than we've envisioned it, but it sure does look like they covered it with dirt, and a lot of dirt. It was 400 by 400 meters at its base and 66 meters high again. Again, that's 3.52 million cubic meters of fill. And then, they built a new complex on its south side. It was called the Courtyard of the Altars, and that one was made of stone and attached to the base of the Great Pyramid.

The Courtyard of the Altars is part of a set of clues that point to a mystic re-creation encoded in that new architecture. It's the symbols of the local creation myth; it's that story I've told before, with water coming down from a cave in Sustenance Mountain, and it comes out of a ball court and waters the first crops. Popocatepetl is locally called Sustenance Mountain. They call it other things, as well, but they're still calling it Sustenance Mountain; they did at contact, and they're still doing it. Modern farmers also call it El Gregorio. They envision it as a big, manly being with long, wavy hair. And some of them still go up to make offerings to him in a cave near the top. And they say that the pyramid is a man-made effigy mirroring the mountain.

Archaeology also finds mythic links. There's a spring from the side of the pyramid on its east side. Water comes down out of there into a marshy area, and in that marshy area are cattail reeds, tollans. It's like one of those mythical origin places. The courtyard is said to be the symbolic ball court. The marsh is the first maize crops. The pyramid is the mountain. It all fits into that myth. And, the same sort of thing is repeated at El Tajin that I'll speak about in a minute.

This form for Cholula's pyramid lasted for 500 years, from 780 A.D., all the way to 1,280 A.D. And during that time period, they seem to have reached a peak population of almost 50,000 people. And they became a huge trade center. They made beautiful pottery that they traded widely; they were chalices and plates, and very finely painted. They're found all the way down in the Maya area in plenty. And some of the Cholula burials have individuals that have obviously Maya skulls; they're shaped like Maya skulls. So maybe there was some sort of trade interchange between Cholula and the Maya area.

We actually have a lot of skulls from Cholula, and that's because Adolph Bandelier collected many of them in 1881 from the site. He wanted to measure their cranial capacity. He was following studies from a man named Samuel Morton, who created the study of craniometry in the 1840s. He was trying to prove that other races weren't as smart as white people because they had smaller heads. Now, that was racial foolishness, and it was eventually dismissed, but Adolph Bandelier really liked it.

Bandelier's studies did lead to increased interest in the site itself. The 1930s saw Ignacio Marquina start its first tunnels, and more and more and more were dug into the pyramid over the years. Now we have five miles of excavation tunnels within it. They're great tourist routes. You can go right through the belly of the pyramid. And, those tunnels taught us a lot about all the earlier building phases.

The tunnels also revealed that the pyramid was finally abandoned at 1200 A.D. The Courtyard of the Altars in front of it was burned. And the same thing happens all around central Mexico. All sorts of sites that have been living up to 1200 show signs of burning. Scholars blame it on a group called the Tolteca-Chichimeca; they were raiders from the northern deserts. And At Cholula, after this burning event, we go into what we call the Cholan phase that lasts from 1200 all the way up to 1521, which is Spanish contact.

So at 1200 A.D., Cholula moves the center of their city to a new location, and they build a new temple, dedicated this time to Quetzalcoatl. It was still there when Cortes arrived. The Spanish destroyed the temple, and now, that's where the *zocalo* of the modern town of Cholula stands. At that same time, they also made a major craft production switch, right around 1,200. They started making textiles, and they weren't making pottery much anymore. The evidence at that time shows us there were thousands of spindle whorls all over the residential places of Cholula.

Cholula remained strong until the very end. When Cortes arrived there, he estimated it was a city of 100,000 people. It was also the scene of a very infamous slaughter, and I'll talk more about that later. But for right now, let's move to Cholula's contemporary site, El Tajin.

El Tajin is a wonderful and underappreciated archaeological site in the rolling hills of northern Veracruz. It was long gone before the Spanish got there, and hence, it wasn't even located until 1785, when an inspector searching for illegal tobacco plantations stumbled across its amazing temples. El Tajin didn't last as long as Cholula, but its height overlaps nicely to a period of Cholula's history. At the beginning, it was just another Teotihuacan underlying; they were specializing in tobacco and vanilla and sending it to Teotihuacan. The region still specializes in those materials. But then, when the centralized control of Teotihuacan ended in the 600s, El Tajin grew fast and became a regional capital.

El Tajin grew into one of the most unique sites in all of Mesoamerica. It has very distinct architecture. It has a style of putting niches in each one of its terraces, and it has 20 ball courts in that single site, and three were just found in 2013, so there may be more. It's tightly clustered around a ceremonial center. UNESCO called it a World Heritage site in 1992, and since then, they've built up a beautiful visitor center and surrounded and protected it by a national park.

I used to drive down from Texas all the way down into Palenque, and I always stopped into the town of Poza Rica. It's a smelly oil town, but it's got very safe hotels. And I picked there also because I could take a break in my trip, and I could go visit El Tajin. The rolling, green hills and those amazing ruins makes for a nice, relaxing day. It's out of the way of everything, but I'd say it's well worth the effort to get to.

El Tajin's most famous building is the Pyramid of the Niches. It's elegant, unique architecture; it's a variation on *talud-tablero*. The *taluds* have inset square niches all around their sides, and the *tableros* are a kind of tablero we call a "flying cornice." The pyramid was painted mostly red, but the interior of the niches was painted black, so it probably really popped when you looked at it. It had seven terrace levels. And counting up the niches, there are exactly 365, so it had some sort of solar symbolism as well. It had a wide staircase going up the front, and that also had sections that had niches. It's aesthetically very pleasing to the eye, and that's because it's got perfect geometry.

When you look at it from a frontal view, you see combinations of the square root of two and the golden mean. The angles on the sides, as you watch it slope up, are perfect diagonals of square-root-two rectangles. If you look at the staircase, it's perfectly two golden-mean rectangles stacked on top of each other. There are still many other aspects of its geometry if you're looking at it from different angles. Chris Powell figured it out, and he put it as part of his 2010 dissertation.

The other sections of El Tajin also have niches, like the Great Enclosure. This is a big area, 12,000 square meters of space. It was large enough to have three ball courts inside. And it had a wall around it, and the wall has the niches. It was just northwest of what we call the Great Ball Court, and that's the largest one at the site; it's 60 meters long, quite a construction.

But to me, one of the most incredible aspects of El Tajin is their ability to make cement-form floors and ceilings. It's only seen in the elite residences of the city in the northwest part. It's a part called Tajin Chico. It's a private area enclosed with just elite housing. Tajin Chico has two-story homes, and the second-story floor levels are poured cement slabs. It's undeniable. We open them up, and we can see in the matrix there's pot shards and pumice stones. And the flat roof above the second story is the same. It's also cement pour. And this is amazing technology. Cement wouldn't show up until Europe arrived, except at El Tajin. We see it there and only there in Mesoamerica. I think it really needs more study and attention.

There are many amazing and unique aspects of El Tajin. As I've mentioned, it's got the niches and its many ball courts. But perhaps the most intriguing is the messages it conveys in its public art. And so for the last part of this lecture, let's talk about El Tajin's stone carvings.

The most complex and wonderful art panels at El Tajin are found along the playing field walls of certain ball courts. Other Mesoamerican cultures hint at it, but El Tajin provides great insight into the connections between the ball games, warriors, sacrifice, and the favor the gods. The imagery is clearest in the south ball court.

The context is a ball court, but the images aren't all about the game. Instead, they show us warriors carrying spear bundles. They show us jaguar- and eagle-costumed warriors. And that's very important when we get into the future and talk about the Aztecs. We also see victims being sacrificed. Their hearts are being cut out. And we see skeletal gods looking on at those activities.

So what does it all mean together? It means that the ball game is seen as a symbol of warfare. War is a political affair. It's driven in Mesoamerica by religion. Religion is driven by the fact that the gods need sacrifices. Who gets those sacrifices? The warriors, and then they bring them back to give them to the gods. So we can see this symbolism of war in their ball game. And is that really so different? Is that so alien? In American football, we're always talking about the players as warriors. It's the same sort of thing.

On another level of symbolism, we can see that the architecture is telling us something. The south ball court is just south of Building 5, and that's one of the big temples of the site; it's one of its main structures. And the ball court, just underneath there, has a drain built into it. There's a water system underneath designed to come from the temple and into the ball court. Again, that's that Sustenance Mountain myth. It's just like Cholula to the south of them.

And there's another possible connection between Cholula and that south ball court. There are eagle people in costume sitting in vats of liquid, and there are deities drinking something on these images. Maybe, like Cholula, these are pulque rituals, just like Cholula's drunkards. It makes sense that there'd be some sort of cultural association between the two. I believe that those are connections between those two cities, El Tajin and Cholula. The question is, are they the same people? Well, for at least until about 1200 A.D., that seems to make sense. Some scholars say they're both a group that's called the Olmeca-Xicalanca. They're people from the south. They're people that had intrusions of new, foreign ideas into that area. They had a local tradition that was already established, and these foreign ideas gave them new methods of rulership.

Linguistically, there are other reasons to believe that. Today, the people around El Tajin are the Totonac people; they're not Maya, but their neighbors are. The Huastecs, in the same area, speak a Maya language. How'd they get there? Well, perhaps they got there during these migrations into the area during the Terminal Classic period.

For El Tajin, whatever changed them could not sustain them. Cholula survived those big changes at 1200 A.D., but El Tajin didn't. About 1230 A.D., El Tajin burns to the ground. And it's commonly believed that that was at the hands of the Tolteca-Chichimeca. El Tajin was a perfect example of the Terminal Classic transitions. They had different ideas combining old symbols of authority and new strategies of political control and religion. Clearly, there was some Maya influence, and it was backed up by the same local cultures that we saw at Cholula.

Now, if it was just El Tajin and Cholula rising up in central Mexico during the Terminal Classic, the argument that the Maya influenced the entire region would be hard to make. But in our next lecture, we'll talk about two other Terminal Classic city-states that rose up in that same region at the same time with an undeniably Maya character.

Cacaxtla Murals and Xochicalco
Lecture 28

Mass abandonment and destruction of cities across Mesoamerica led to what scholars refer to as the Terminal Classic period. New cities emerged, experimenting with innovative strategies to legitimize their authority. In Central Mexico, certain cities were successful in blending cultural traits from all over Mesoamerica. In this lecture, we will study the two finest examples of cultural fusion: the cities of Cacaxtla and Xochicalco.

A New Militarization

- The Terminal Classic period was a time of transition. The Maya area saw population movements; in Central Mexico, Teotihuacan and Monte Alban were abandoned, as were many other cities. The old centers of power were gone. Boundary lines disappeared and trade was disrupted. Some of the newer cities that grew up had a decidedly military focus, seen in both their defensive works and their art.

- Teotihuacan had been the sole despotic authority, but now power had reverted back into the hands of numerous city-states. They scrapped for territory and power against one another. Most of these new cities militarized and fortified themselves on hilltops. The best examples of those hilltop cities are Cacaxtla and Xochicalco. Both were built very quickly and with walls surrounding them. And both, in their own way, honored Teotihuacan.

- Both Cacaxtla and Xochicalco adopted Maya traits and assumed the old trade routes. Both rose to prominence in exactly the same time frame, from 650 to 900. Scholars have suggested that they might have had something to do with Teotihuacan's demise.

- Both Cacaxtla and Xochicalco seem to be predecessors of the Toltec. Many Toltec art themes are seen in the two cities, and Toltec expansion began just as these two great cities fell.

Xochitecatl

- Cacaxtla was not a complete city but a large palace and ceremonial complex built on top of a hill. Its buildings were all located on a massive platform called Gran Basamento. These buildings are actually about a kilometer away from its associated ceremonial center, Xochitecatl.

- Xochitecatl was built atop a large lava dome; excavations in 1994 revealed that it dated back to almost 1000 B.C.—Olmec times. By 800 B.C., Xochitecatl's rulers had built the Pyramid of the Flowers in stone. At that same time, La Venta was building earthen mounds.

- Xochitecatl's peak Preclassic power extended from about 350 B.C. to about 150 A.D.; thus, it was contemporary with the Epi-Olmec site of Tres Zapotes. But in 150 A.D., the volcano Popocatepetl erupted, and Xochitecatl was abandoned.

- In a rare case, however, the city was actually re-inhabited during the Classic period. The inhabitants built a new temple called the Pyramid of the Volcanoes, and they rebuilt the Pyramid of the Flowers. The Pyramid of the Volcanoes was filled with female figurines and child sacrifices—most likely evidence of fertility rituals. The murals at Cacaxtla also were linked to fertility rituals.

The Jaguar and the Eagle

- The Cacaxtla murals are arguably the finest ever discovered in Mesoamerica. Their full-color beauty and skillful artistry are rivaled only by the enlightening nature of their content.

- Depictions of bird and jaguar warriors appear on the façade of Building B, which faces the plaza, the most public space of Cacaxtla. Called the Battle Mural, the paintings flank the central staircase and illustrate a narrative of two classes of warriors meeting in battle—the jaguars and the birds. After the battle, captures and sacrifices are shown. What is most interesting is that the faces in these Cacaxtla murals look very Maya.

The Cacaxtla murals are full of war imagery, such as this bird warrior; apparently, the city itself lived and died by the sword.

- Eagles and jaguars are shown together on the door jambs of Building A. These murals are called collectively the Priestly Attire Murals because everyone is clad in rich costumes. On the north jamb are men in jaguar costumes; on the south jamb are people in eagle costumes.

- Finding these two mythological symbols opposite each other is of undeniable significance. The juxtaposition is foundational for what would happen later in Mesoamerica. The Tula would use these jaguar and eagle warriors in their art, and those ideas would transfer all the way across Mesoamerica into Chichen Itza, a Maya site. Ultimately, the Aztecs would use those same symbols to dominate most of Mesoamerica.

Maya Influence

- Elements of the Priestly Attire Murals also indicate a cultural blending. A jaguar warrior stands on a serpent with legs. On the same column is the image of another jaguar warrior holding a coiled snake connected to the vision serpents. In his other hand, he holds a jar and is pouring water. Both these sections have a blue band around the scene, filled with aquatic imagery. The overall meaning seems to link sacrificial activities of warriors to fertility.

- The south jamb is also bordered by blue water with the same kind of fertility symbols. This time, an eagle warrior holds a double-headed-serpent bar at his chest—just like the Classic Maya kings. This eagle warrior is standing on a feathered serpent. What a telling image: a Maya who is an eagle warrior is standing on Quetzalcoatl, which is Teotihuacan's authority.

- Next to the eagle is a black shell from which a red-haired figure emerges. This is the Maya symbol of the old man who tweaked the moon goddess's breast. It is clear that Cacaxtla had Maya influence—perhaps even cultural domination.

The Red Temple

- At Cacaxtla, the murals at the Red Temple reveal both how and why the Maya arrived. The Red Temple's symbols are not about warfare; they are about fertility. They depict water flowing and a large toad hopping through it. At the base of the steps is God L, the Maya god who lives in the underworld.

- But God L is also a merchant god; we see this god abundantly in Maya Classic imagery. Inside his backpack are all sorts of particularly Maya items: quetzal feathers, cacao, and jaguar pelts. The merchant's name glyph is 4 Deer, which oddly, is neither a Maya nor a Teotihuacan name. It's more a tradition from Central Mexico.

- This merchant represents another important clue to the Terminal Classic transitions. The merchant is walking toward a group of warriors; in fact, merchants did reconnaissance missions for the Aztec before military conquests. But this merchant is a Maya. Cacaxtla demonstrates to us that the Maya were involved in creating an Aztec tradition.

Xochicalco: A Fortified City

- Xochicalco's dates are the same as those of Cacaxtla, 650 to 900, almost ensuring a link between the two. Xochicalco sits on a huge hill, with six smaller ones below. All three levels of the city are walled, and terraces connect each of the hillsides. It's a complex and well-fortified place. It has been estimated that its population was somewhere around 20,000.

- There was not much farming around Xochicalco; the city must have relied heavily on trade imports. The lowest level of the city was mostly residential compounds. In the middle level were the public ceremonial spaces. Also on the middle level is a ball court that is one of the three largest in all of Mesoamerica. The larger ones are found at Chichen Itza and Tula.

- A causeway leads up to the ball court, and another leads down from the top level. There are 21 altars lining the causeway, part of a theme at Xochicalco—calendars in time. Each altar relates to a different month in the calendar.

- On the upper level are the private ceremonial precincts. The hilltop was shaved off there and flattened. The platform on top of it was apparently built quickly. Building Xochicalco had to have been a massive effort. The inhabitants had to create large, safe places— and quickly. The city also had a large internal water system that would be useful if it were under siege.

- Xochitecatl also contains a cave with a zenith passage tube that is 8.7 meters long. Light through this long tube can strike the interior cave only on May 15 and July 29—the two times at Xochicalco when there is a zenith passage. This fits in with the calendrical theme of the city. Only two other zenith passage tubes are known in Mesoamerica—at Teotihuacan and Monte Alban.

Temple of the Feathered Serpent

- At the heart of the plaza on top of Xochicalco stands the Temple of the Feathered Serpent. Perhaps no other building in all of Mesoamerica is such a clear example of the blending of Teotihuacan and Classic Maya ideas—made after both faded away. Right in the center of the main top plaza are two temples that stand side by side—the Temple of the Feathered Serpent and the Twin Temple. The Feathered Serpent is covered with carvings and the Twin is absolutely blank. Both temples are in Classic Teotihuacan *talud-tablero* architecture.

- The Temple of the Feathered Serpent has the same iconography as the Temple of Quetzalcoatl in Teotihuacan itself. In the Xochicalco temple, feathered serpents move across the sides and shells float in the background. But there are Maya elements, too. A snake's body undulates throughout, and above and below are figures in Maya dress and headdresses. Some are priests and others are warriors. Calendar glyphs are seen along the *tablero* faces.

- One of the calendar glyphs has arms and is roping in another calendar glyph. The roper glyph is a Maya day name. The one being roped is the next day in sequence—but from the calendar of Central Mexico. The message is absolutely clear: The Maya calendar has captured that of Central Mexico.

- The Temple of the Feathered Serpent tells the story of the Terminal Classic in Central Mexico. Just like the Cacaxtla murals, it reveals that the elements of the old power players, such as Teotihuacan and the classic Maya cities of the south, were combined into a new form of political legitimacy. Cacaxtla and Xochicalco represent the intrusion of Maya culture and people into Central Mexico.

- Both Cacaxtla and Xochicalco were destroyed by 900. The cities represent the transition toward what would become the powerful Toltec domination of the entire region. In the next lecture, we'll examine the city and culture that arose out of Cacaxtla and Xochicalco: the Toltec and their capital at Tula.

Suggested Reading

Adams, *Prehistoric Mesoamerica*.

Coe and Koontz, *Mexico*.

Questions to Consider

1. Do you think Cacaxtla and Xochicalco should be considered the same culture group as the term *Olmeca Xicalanca* suggests?

2. Do you think the cities represent a Maya military entrada to Central Mexico or just a cultural exchange?

3. Who do you think burned these two cities down?

Cacaxtla Murals and Xochicalco
Lecture 28—Transcript

The mass abandonment and destruction of cities across Mesoamerica led to what we call the "terminal" or Epiclassic. New cities emerged, trying a whole new host of things to legitimize their authority. In central Mexico, a few became cultural blends, with traits from all over Mesoamerica. The two best examples are the cities of Cacaxtla and Xochicalco.

The Terminal Classic was a time of transition. In the Maya area, there were movements of populations. But in central Mexico, it was more profound. Teotihuacan and Monte Alban were gone. And with them, many other cities were abandoned. The area was once highly controlled, but now there was no control.

Boundary lines dropped and trade was disrupted. There were no more tributes to overlords. In Oaxaca, the Mixtec grows up to fill the gap. Other cities rose up in central Mexico. It was an opportunity, but it was also chaos. The old order and consequences for misbehavior were gone. It was a chance to take power by force. Some new cities had a decidedly military focus, seen in both their defensive works and their art. They needed sanctioned authority, but the old ways had failed. So they sought an infusion of new ideas. The Maya borrowed ideas from central Mexico, and Central Mexico, in turn, borrowed ideas from the Maya.

Teotihuacan was a sole, despotic authority, but now, power had reverted back into the hands of the many city-states, and each of them scrapped for territory against one another, and they used different strategies. Most of them militarized, and they sat up on hilltops. And perhaps, that was an influence from Oaxaca; Monte Alban and the Mixtec had been living on hilltops for a long time. The best examples of those hilltop cities are Cacaxtla and Xochicalco. Both were built very quickly and with walls surrounding them. And both, in ways, honor Teotihuacan. At the same time, both adapt many Maya traits. They were both very trade oriented. They got to assume the old trade routes. And they were both at about exactly the same time span, from 650 to 900 A.D. Because of that timeframe, some scholars have suggested they might have had something to do with Teotihuacan's demise, again, we really can't prove that.

And equally as important, both of them seem to be predecessors to the Toltec. Many of the Toltec art themes seem to begin in those two cities. Toltec expansion begins just as those two great cities fall. It's still a mystery in many ways, but somehow or another, their destinies seemed linked. Now Cacaxtla is not actually a whole city, but rather, a very large palace and ceremonial complex that was built on top of a hill in the present-day state of Tlaxcala. It was only found in 1974, revealed by some looters. The amazing murals it contained made it instantly one of Mexico's most celebrated archaeological sites.

For years, centuries, really, it sat camouflaged on a hilltop. It's all one big, massive platform that we call the Gran Basamento. It was a safe house, or a citadel, for an extended elite family. And we say that because there's no other little residential sectors around it; it's alone by itself. It's a palace structure associated to a few temples. And it's actually about a kilometer away from its associated ceremonial center.

The city center that it was actually associated with has another name. It's Xochitecatl. And that site has been known since contact. A Tlaxcalan historian recorded it in the 1500s. He was named Diego Muñoz Camargo, and he was actually of indigenous descent. And in his account, he said the people that lived there were called the Olmeca-Xicalanca. And that was a coincidentally apt name. That name Olmec in it is old, and the site turned out to be much older than he knew. Xochitecatl was built atop a large lava dome; 1994 excavations revealed just how old it was. Turned out, it dated back to almost 1000 B.C., into Olmec times. By 800 B.C., it had built a pyramid that we call the Pyramid of the Flowers. There were two other temples too, also built in stone. At the same time, La Venta was building earthen mounds to the south. And artifacts at Xochitecatl proved that it was trading with La Venta. But, they also outlived La Venta.

It's peak Preclassic extent went from about 350 B.C. to about 150 A.D. So at that time, it was contemporary with the Epi-Olmec site of Tres Zapotes. And also, by then, it seemed to control the entire area, which is now Tlaxcala.

But in 150 A.D., the volcano, Popocatepetl, erupted, and it landed on the city, and it was abandoned. In a rare case, though, that city was actually re-inhabited and reused in the Classic period. They build a new temple there that we call the Pyramid of the Volcanoes, and, they take time to rebuild the Pyramid of the Flowers.

Now, why did they do that? Well, my guess is that, in that classic period, they were trying to tap into ancient local authority. They were trying to find something earlier than Teotihuacan. They filled the Pyramid of the Volcanoes with female figurines and child sacrifices. They seem to be rituals that are promoting fertility. And over at Cacaxtla, their murals also seem heavily linked to fertility. Those 1994 excavations also revealed their end. At the Pyramid of the Flowers, we find it covered with 200 obsidian projectiles; there's evidence of attack and destruction. Cacaxtla's murals are full of war imagery. And apparently, the city itself lived and died by the sword.

Well, now let's talk about the Cacaxtla's fantastic murals. Arguably, they are the finest murals we've ever discovered in Mesoamerica. Their full-color beauty and skillful artistry are only rivaled by the incredibly enlightening nature of their content. If I had to choose the most significant thing about Cacaxtla's murals, I'd say it's their depictions of bird and jaguar warriors. Now, we saw those, originally, in Teotihuacan, so they're not first here. And we see an evolution of that into Aztec society. But Cacaxtla provides an important proof of transition between those two great cultures.

Those warriors are on the facade of what's called Building B. Building B faces into the plaza; it's the most public space of Cacaxtla. And it's a very long mural, going all the way across Building B. We call it the Battle Mural. It flanks the central staircase, and it displays a narrative. The narrative is two classes of warriors meeting. There are jaguars, and there are birds. And there's a battle that goes on. We also see what happens after the battle. There are captures and there are sacrifices.

The jaguars win the pitched battle, and their wielding spears, but they're never making any kill shots. They're intentionally wounding people to capture them. The capture and sacrifice scenes that we see in other parts of the mural support that idea. They're very much like the Bonampak murals down in the Maya area. It's the same sort of thing. Everyone's getting stabbed in the legs. They want to bring them back to sacrifice. So the scene is followed up by these captive sacrifices. And what's interesting is, the faces in these to Cacaxtla murals look very, very Maya.

Now the defeated warriors are the birds. We can see their entrails coming out; they're kneeled; they're humbled. And it's interesting that we're not really sure what kind of birds they are. They're not like Aztec; they're not eagles. John Paul says they might be Quetzals or Parrots. And that makes sense. Jaguars and eagles eventually are really on the same team; they're both Aztec sects of warriors. So in fact, there's another section of the murals that shows this same sort of thing, eagles and jaguars together this time, and that's on Building A's door jams.

Building A's murals are also really fantastic. Together, the building, we call it Los Vestidos de la Sacerdotes, or The Priestly Attire; that's what we call these murals that are inside Building A, and it's because they have these rich costumes. On the north jam, we see men in jaguar costumes. On the south jam, we see people in eagle costumes. Both of those places have two figures on separate walls. As you walk through that doorway, first they're on the front face, and then they're on the sides of the door as you walk through it.

Finding these two opposite each other is of incredible significance. It's foundational for what will happen later in Mesoamerica. Tula will use these jaguar and eagle warriors in their art. And those ideas transfer all the way across Mesoamerica into Chichen Itza, a Maya site. And then ultimately, the Aztecs are going to use those same symbols to dominate most of Mesoamerica.

And then back at the Teotihuacan murals, just like Cacaxtla, we see warrior classes. There seems to be the origin of this idea of warrior cults. We see it in compounds at Teotihuacan, like Tepantitla. Cacaxtla is the link between all of these things. There used to be a gap in the narrative. We had Teotihuacan and then blank, and then Tula, and then Aztecs. Cacaxtla's 1974 discovery filled that gap.

The elements of the priestly attire mural also indicate a cultural blending. A jaguar holds atlatl darts; he's clearly a warrior, not really a priest, as the name indicates. And he stands on a serpent with legs. People used to suggest that was a dragon. But now, the academic consensus is he's really just representing some sort of conflated animal, not an actual dragon. Around the corners of that same column is the image of another jaguar warrior; this one is holding a coiled snake that's connected to the vision serpents. In the other hand he has a jar and he's pouring water. Both of these sections have a blue band around the scene, and that blue band is filled with aquatic imagery. The overall meaning seems to link sacrificial activities of warriors to fertility.

The south jam is also bordered by blue water. It's that same kind of fertility symbols. But this time, it's an eagle warrior, but he's acting very Maya. He has a double-headed serpent bar at his chest, just like classic Maya kings. And he's standing, this time, on a feathered serpent. He's a Maya who is an eagle warrior standing on Quetzalcoatl, which is Teotihuacan's authority. What an interesting blend. Next to the eagle seen is a black painted figure. It's a big shell with a red-haired figure emerging. Now, that used to be suggested as the evidence of Viking contact. And, of course, that's not true. It's actually a very Maya symbol again. It's our old man coming out of the shell, the one the tweaks the moon goddess's breast. And also, what's abundantly true, is that Cacaxtla has Maya influence. Perhaps we could even argue that it was cultural domination in that area.

Even with just the iconographic evidence from the battle murals and the priestly attire frescoes, we could build a clear argument for the influence of Maya art at Cacaxtla. But the murals of a location called the Red Temple reveal both how and why the Maya arrived. The Red Temple is different. It's not showing any kind of warfare. It's on a level below the plaza that actually leads up to that big battle mural. The mural itself is actually painted along the side of a staircase that's going up into that main plaza. Its symbols are much more about fertility. It's got water flowing from the top, down to the bottom fret, and there's a big toad that's hopping through it. At the base of the steps we see a merchant resting. He's got his backpack off. And it's like he's just resting before his last push uphill into Cacaxtla. His face is clearly God L, who's the Maya god who lives in the underworld. And so hence, maybe that's why there's all water coming down the steps. But he's also a merchant god. And we see that merchant god abundantly in Maya Classic imagery.

So his backpack is at his side, and it's full of all sorts of particularly Maya things. You can see poking out of it that it has Quetzal feathers, and cacao, and jaguar pelts. The merchant's name glyph is above him. He's called Four Deer. And oddly, that's really not a Maya or a Teotihuacan name; that's more central Mexico. It's like Oaxaca and their tradition of giving birthday names to people's actual names. Along the path of the merchant are corn stocks and cacao trees. The stairs in that context look like agricultural terraces, and the corn cobs have little faces. Those faces represent the Maya maize god. The iconographic message of the Red Temple is like a sledgehammer—Maya traders come here.

This merchant represents another important clue to the Terminal Classic transitions. A merchant is walking towards a group of warriors. This may be a precursor to the Aztec *pochteca*. Those were merchants who were doing reconnaissance missions for the Aztecs before military conquests. But this guy is not an Aztec or a central Mexican, he's obviously a Maya. But it was, again, Teotihuacan who probably started that merchant warrior strategy. We saw it a long time ago. Traders entered with gifts to Tikal in 378 A.D. That entrada was shown on Yax Nuun Ayiin's pot inside his grave. Soon after that, we start seeing Teotihuacan war iconography at Tikal. So there was a transition from Teotihuacan, to Tula, and then the Aztecs. But now, Cacaxtla shows us an important addition, that Maya were also involved in creating that eventual Aztec tradition.

At the site of Xochicalco, located in the state of Morelos, about 40 kilometers south of Cuernavaca, we see the same kind of pattern, central Mexican people accepting a heavy amount of Maya influence and defending themselves on a fortified hilltop. It's dates are the same as Cacaxtla, 650 to 900 A.D., almost assuring a link between the two.

Some scholars call its people as well, Olmeca-Xicalanca, and they do so because it's so like Cacaxtla in its Maya influence. Those people are theorized to have come somewhere from between Tabasco and Campeche. Now, I'm not sure if that's exactly where they came from, but that is definitely the

Maya region. Now, the site of Xochicalco itself sits on one big, huge hill, with six smaller ones underneath it. There are three levels of the city, and each one of them are walled. There are terraces connecting each one of the hillsides. It's a complex and very well fortified place. Kenneth Herth did a survey there in the 1970s, and he found that its population was somewhere around 20,000 people, so a big city. But there weren't many farmers living there. The terraces really weren't about farming. So somehow or another, they must have relied heavily on trade imports.

The very bottom level of the city was mostly the residential compounds. They were living behind walls. There were some farming terraces, but as I say, not much. Those people at the bottom must have felt very threatened to live behind those walls. And, they probably were. Xochicalco was actually burned to the ground in 900 A.D., so they did have something to worry about. Now, the intermediate level of the city was where we find a lot of public ceremonial spaces. Perhaps that's also where trade and market activities went on. There's a plaza called the Plaza of the Stelae of two Glyphs; it's a wide, open area, a good candidate for a market.

Nearby was a palace with a sweat bath. But we're really not sure who exactly lived in that intermediate place. Also, on the intermediate level, we have the southern ball court. It's the largest of three at the site. In fact, it's one of the top three largest in all of Mesoamerica. The only other larger ones are founded at Chichen Itza and Tula. This one's dimensions and form are the same as the one at Tula. Tula is later, and Xochicalco might have been their model for how they build their ball court. We'll talk about that in a little bit.

A causeway leads up to that ball court, and there's another one that leads down from the top level. There are 21 altars that are lining that causeway, and they're part of an apparent theme at Xochicalco, which is calendars in time. Each one of those altars relates to a different month in the calendar. Now, on the uppermost level is where we find private ceremonial precincts. It's walled, too. In fact, there's only one portico that lets people in or out of that uppermost spot. It was built atop one huge, massive platform.

The hilltop was shaved off there and flattened. The platform on top of it was apparently built very quickly. Xochicalco had to have been a massive labor effort. They had to create big, safe places, and fast. There was some sort of large workforce and organizing authority that made Xochicalco happen. And if that was the case, they needed to be able to hold out inside the city. For that reason, we find a cistern on that very top of the city. It's the uppermost part of a very large water system going all the way through the city. It was an internal water supply apparently needed if they were threatened and had to hold out inside the city's walls for a long time.

There were other structures on top, as well. One of them was called the Ramp of the Animals, with various animal carvings on them. On top of it, it had columns with warriors. Again, they look very similar to what's going to happen in the later city of Tula, the Toltec capital. There were also a whole set of palaces up there, probably for the elite families of the city. Those were pretty much unknown when I first started visiting those ruins. In 1995, a mega archaeological project uncovered them.

Now, one of my favorite parts of Xochitecatl is a cave with a zenith passage tube inside. It's built up on top, but it's inside the walled enclosure, so it's included. It's a cave that they dug in an 8.7-meter-long tube, and they cut it down from above through natural rock. And light through that very long tube can only strike the interior cave on May 15 and July 29. Those are the two times at Xochicalco that you have a zenith passage. Again, I think it's part of their calendrical theme; it's probably a calibration of their calendar.

Only two other zenith passage tubes are known in Mesoamerica. One of them is at Teotihuacan, and the other one is at Monte Alban. Again, there are possible transitional links. Remember Monte Alban is on a hilltop, just liked Xochicalco. And the one at Teotihuacan is carved into a cave, just like Xochicalco. Xochicalco, perhaps, is trying to show a little of both. Especially Teotihuacan is shown at Xochicalco by its main temple, called the Temple of the Feathered Serpent.

At the heart of the plaza, on top of Xochicalco, stands the temple that it's most famous for, the Temple of the Feathered Serpent. Perhaps no other building in all of Mesoamerica is such a clear example of the blending of Teotihuacan and classic Maya ideas, made after both faded away. Right in the center of the main top plaza are two temples that stand side by side.

The Feathered Serpent is one of them, and the other one is called the Twin Temple. The Feathered Serpent is covered with carvings, and the Twin is absolutely blank. It's strange. But, it does beg a comparison, again, to later Aztec twin temple forms. I wonder if this wasn't a model in some ways for the Aztec forms.

Both of the temples are classic Teotihuacan *talud-tablero* style architecture. Undeniably, Teotihuacan-inspired in ways, not to mention the fact that it's a Temple of the Feathered Serpent. It has a different style, but it's the same iconography as we see on the temple of Quetzalcoatl in Teotihuacan itself. In this one, feathered serpents come across the sides, and there are shells floating around in the background. But then there are Maya elements, too. There's a snake body that undulates through, and above and below, we see seated, clearly Maya, figures. They're obviously Maya in their dress and the kind of headdresses they're wearing. Some of them are priests and others of them are warriors.

There are calendar glyphs along the tablero faces, and one of them repeats again and again, nine flaming eyebrow of a snake. There's a debate about whether that's a date, or maybe it's the name of someone who was a ruler there. The form of it, the glyphs themselves, look very Mixtec or Zapotec, which leads us to believe maybe it's a name. Now, Teotihuacan didn't have any calendar glyphs whatsoever, so, they are out of the picture there. But there's another dimension. Oaxaca had this, too. Is the temple trying to pull off old vestiges of power from all of these sites into one message? It sure seems so.

My favorite part of all the iconography on that building is a calendar glyph that has arms and he's roping another calendar glyph. The roper glyph is a Maya day name. The other one being roped is the next day in sequence, but it's from the central Mexican calendar. The message seems absolutely clear; it's saying, the Maya calendar has captured the central Mexican calendar here.

The Temple of the Feathered Serpent tells the story of the Terminal Classic in central Mexico. Just like Cacaxtla's murals, it's saying that elements of the old power players, like Teotihuacan and the classic Maya cities of the south, will be combined into a new form of political legitimacy. But remember where these two cities are; Cacaxtla and Xochicalco represent the intrusion of Maya culture and their people's into central Mexico. In the Classic—led by Teotihuacan, the stream was flowing the other way. At least for a time during the "Terminal Classic"—Maya culture was the more resilient and turned the flow of people and ideas back the other way.

The other enlightening thing that these cities tell us is that the Terminal Classic was a militarized and dangerous time. Neither Teotihuacan nor the classic Maya felt the need to live on hilltop citadels. And these were times where it was right to fear. Both of those cities ended up being destroyed by 900 A.D.

Finally, they represent the transition towards what will become the powerful Toltec domination of the entire region, or at least we think so. In our next lecture, let's talk about the city and culture that I said these two cities might have been the precursor to—the Toltecs and their capital at Tula.

The Toltecs—Role Models or Myth?
Lecture 29

A ccording to the Aztec, the Toltec were the greatest civilization on earth. To be civilized was to be Toltec. The Aztec kept lists of the Toltec kings and their mighty deeds. *Toltecatl* meant "master artist," and the Toltec were said to be the originators of numerous art forms and the masters of metalwork and jewelry. Strangely, however, archaeologists have found surprisingly little evidence of the Toltec civilization and culture. But archaeology has found their capital city: Tula. The Aztec called it Tollan, or Place of Reeds, a connection to the origin myth. In this lecture, we'll debate the evidence of the Toltec and determine whether they were a mighty power or a myth.

The Aztec Emulate the Toltec

- Just as American architects modeled public buildings after Greek temples, Aztec architects imitated Toltec temples. Toltec art forms are found all over Aztec public buildings. The Aztec excavated Tula and brought back ancient pieces for display in their own capital.

- The Aztec believed they shared cultural origins with the Toltec; both were a mixture of north and south people. The Toltec were part Chichimec, the savages from the north, but they were also part Nonoalca, the civilized people from the south. Not only the Aztec but also the Zapotec, Maya, and Tarascans were in awe of the Toltec. But archaeology cannot confirm the existence of a Toltec empire.

- It is possible that the legend of the Toltec was Aztec propaganda. We know that the Aztec rewrote their history. A generation before Spanish contact, an Aztec historian ordered all the history books burned, and he re-created a new pro-Aztec version of history. Even after the Aztec were defeated, legends of the Toltec's greatness persisted. In fact, one of those Toltec legends—the legend of Quetzalcoatl—was instrumental in the Spanish empire's defeat of the Aztec.

Legend of Quetzalcoatl

- The legend of Quetzalcoatl recounts an epic fight between two Toltec rulers—or perhaps gods—that resulted in the expulsion of Quetzalcoatl from the capital city of Tula. He sailed east but vowed to return some day and reclaim his throne. That legend was key to Cortes's success against the Aztec. The Aztec king Moctezuma was focused on it. Quetzalcoatl's return was prophesied to occur in the year 1519, and Cortes landed in that very same year.

- A few years earlier Moctezuma had received a prediction of the defeat of Aztec civilization. It was to be at the hands of foreign invaders from the east, and Moctezuma would lead them to the end. Moctezuma had his priests search the prophecies, and he found the legend of Quetzalcoatl.

- The legend of how Quetzalcoatl was expelled begins with two men co-ruling Tula. Quetzalcoatl was the head priest, and Huemac was the political leader. The god Tezcatlipoca plots to humiliate them and to destroy Tula.

- First, Tezcatlipoca tricks Quetzalcoatl into drinking; Quetzalcoatl gets so drunk that he sleeps with his own sister. This is a terrible scandal; the people reject him as impure, and he's shamed. To trick Huemac, Tezcatlipoca transforms himself into a naked chili salesman in the market. Huemac's daughter falls in love with him and they marry. The citizens, however, are upset that their princess would marry this merchant. Tezcatlipoca's final disguise is as an old woman roasting corn in the market. When any of the starving citizens try to enjoy the corn, they are killed.

- Both Quetzalcoatl and Huemac are in complete despair; they flee the city and abandon the people. Huemac goes to live in a cave for the rest of his life, in a place the Aztec knew well—Chapultepec, very near to the future Aztec capital. Quetzalcoatl and his followers go east to the ocean. There, they build a snake boat and sail away. But they vow that they will return in the year 1 Reed—or 1519.

And then, by coincidence, Hernan Cortes lands on the shores of Mesoamerica that very same year.

Similarities between Tula and Chichen Itza

- The first scholars to study Mesoamerica subscribed to the notion of an all-powerful Toltec empire. For quite some time, investigations supported that hypothesis. Desire Charnay was the first researcher to study the Toltec. Of French background but living in New Orleans, Charnay led expeditions for France to the Maya area and excavated at the site of Chichen Itza in the Yucatan.

- Charnay was the first to note striking similarities between Tula and Chichen Itza. Both cities had the same kind of art and used the same building styles. Charnay decided that these similarities fit the legend of Quetzalcoatl. He theorized that when Quetzalcoatl left in his snake boat to the east, he landed on the shore of Yucatan, went inland, and conquered Chichen Itza. He theorized that Chichen Itza was, in fact, the new capital of exiled Quetzalcoatl. This theory was also proof of Toltec supremacy and command of the region.

- Research in Tula continued in the early 1900s; archaeologists determined that the city flourished between 700 and 1200 and ended just about when the Aztec said it did. Studies indicated that Tula was the Toltec capital.

- Evidence of the existence of a large and powerful Toltec empire is still missing to this day, however. It may never have existed. There is no evidence of its control over Central Mexico. To the east was El Tajin; to the southeast was Cholula; and directly to the south was Xochicalco.

- In 2002, Aztec specialist Michael Smith suggested that historians should downgrade the Toltec from empire to simply kingdom. Other scholars have speculated that Chichen Itza in fact established Tula, not vice versa.

Tula Grande and Tula Chico

- There was no significant archaeological research at Tula until the 1960s. Two project teams, one led by INAH and one by the University of Missouri, discovered what Tula was—and was not. The INAH team focused on the public buildings and temples; the UMC project focused on the residential areas. Between the two project teams, archaeologists have a much better picture of Tula as a whole; but their findings do not support the idea that Tula was the capital of an empire.

- Tula's setting was similar to those of other Terminal Classic sites. It was located on top of a ridge, with two rivers below. The two different sections of the city are known as Tula Grande and Tula Chico. Tula's peak population may have reached 30,000.

- Tula Chico is the older part of the city and includes houses and a few small temples. Its start date—600—is significant; this is right after the fall of Teotihuacan. Tula Chico was abandoned by 900. Its end date is also telling; this is exactly the same end date as that of Cacaxtla and Xochicalco, which were also connected to Maya sites.

- Tula Grande is the city center, dating from 900 to 1200. In 1200, like a number of other cities in that area, Tula was burned. Tula reached its height during the Tula Grande phase. Tula's workshops were simple and small; craftspeople mainly worked in obsidian and made pottery. The pottery was not impressive; it was mainly utilitarian: bowls, plates, and jars. The serving dishes with three legs are very diagnostic of Tula.

- However, an unusual set of artifacts was discovered in Tula: ceramic toy dogs with wheels on axles through their feet. This was odd because Mesoamerica never created the wheel.

Toltec Architecture

- Excavations revealed Tula's population to be simple craftspeople. That does not support the Aztec description of a city full of master artists and civilized warriors. Archaeologists know that the Aztec re-inhabited Tula and excavated its ruins back in the 1400s. Perhaps they looted the city; those who subscribe to the Aztec version of the Toltec believe exactly that.

- Those who need more physical evidence of the Toltec can perhaps find it in Tula Grande. The grandest and most impressive part of Tula is the civic center of Tula Grande. It has the standard set of architectural features—pyramids, plazas, and ball courts—but in a style that's both an homage to the cultures that came before and a celebration of elements that are uniquely Toltec.

- The architecture of Tula's buildings seems to be influenced from all over Mesoamerica. There are hints of *talud-tablero* from Teotihuacan. There are colonnaded halls similar to those in sites far to the north. Tula's ball court looks just like the one at Xochicalco. At the same time, however, there are style elements that are distinctively Toltec.

A Warrior Culture

- Two pyramids stand in Tula's center. Pyramid B is 10 meters tall; the flat carved panels along its base and the statues on top have interesting features. The lower panels depict jaguars and eagles eating human hearts. This image conjures up both warrior cults and sacrifice—much like the images on the murals at Cacaxtla.

- On the top of Pyramid B are some of the most recognizable and celebrated pieces of ancient Mexican sculpture—the Atlanteans. These are four columns carved like warriors. At 15 feet tall, they once supported the temple roof. They have *atlatls* in their hands and wear loincloths and sandals. In the middle of their chests are butterfly pectorals; on their heads are feather headdresses.

- Other columns on the pyramid top also depict warriors. In fact, the temple is clearly dedicated to war. Below and in front are colonnades. Although those columns do not have any carvings, their equivalent in Chichen Itza does have carvings of warriors.

The Atlanteans—four columns carved in the image of warriors—probably represent soldiers in their formal uniforms, not dressed for combat.

An Idealized Heritage of the Aztec

- As it turns out, the Toltec were far more important as the idealized heritage of the Aztec than as a verifiable ancient empire. However, regardless of the true size and extent of the Toltec, it remains true that they were the ancestral connection that the Aztec used to validate their right to rule Mesoamerica.

- Archaeology finds that the Toltec were closed in by equally powerful neighbors, then finally defeated in 1200.

- In fact, the legend of the Toltec and Tollan as told by the Aztec would have been rejected long ago if it were not for the existence of Chichen Itza—the subject of the next lecture.

Suggested Reading

Carrasco, *Quetzalcoatl and the Irony of the Empire*.

Diehl, *Tula*.

Kowalski and Kristan-Graham, eds., *Twin Tollans*.

Questions to Consider

1. Why did the Aztecs choose Tula and the Toltecs for their rewritten ancestry? Wouldn't Cholula or Teotihuacan have been a better choice?

2. Do you think the Aztecs could have looted Tula of all of its riches, or was it really the simple city excavated by archaeologists in the 1970s?

3. Why was Tula sitting on the edge of the northern desert? There was better farmland not far south in unoccupied territory.

The Toltecs—Role Models or Myth?
Lecture 29—Transcript

The Aztecs said that the Toltecs were the greatest civilization to have ever graced the face of the Earth. They were exalted as superior artists and statesmen, both civilized and powerful warriors. But strangely, archaeology can't seem to confirm that. In fact, we find surprisingly little evidence of the Toltecs whatsoever.

The Aztecs went on and on about the Toltecs. It was like Westerners speak about Greece. It was the pinnacle of high culture, and they were remembered in great detail. They had lists of all their kings and the great deeds they performed. They were a model for civilized behavior.

Toltecatl meant "master artist," and they were said to be the originators of many different art forms. They were the masters of all mediums. They'd say lofty things like, they "taught the clay to lie." They were also said to be the masters of metal works and jewelry. But archaeology has found their capital city—Tula. The Aztecs called it Tollan. It's a place of reeds, like the origin myths we've been talking about. But the trouble is, Tula is really not that impressive.

Like the Greek temples we find in Washington, DC, the Aztec capital imitated Toltec temples. Toltec art forms are found all over their public buildings. The Aztecs even went as far as to excavate at Tula. They brought ancient pieces back for display in their own capital. They were clearly emulating the Toltecs. And like the U.S.A. fancies our democracy as modeled after Greek governance, so did the Aztec nobility model the Toltec. They said they were great speakers and orators and statesman. The name for an Aztec king was *Tlatoani*, which means "the spokesman." They were supposed to have manners, and they were supposed to be very clean, and very generous. To be civilized was to be Toltec.

They were also said to have similar culture origins. Like the Aztecs, they said that the Toltecs were a combination of north and south people. The Toltec were part Chichimec, the savages from the north. But they were also part Nonoala; that's the civilized people from the south. Now we're not really sure where in the south. Maybe they're talking about southern Vera Cruz, or maybe as far as Tabasco. Archaeology really can't determine either.

And it wasn't just the Aztecs. Other contact-period cultures said the same thing. They said that the Toltecs were the greatest empire ever. The Zapotecs, the Maya, the Tarascans, everywhere the Spanish went, it appeared a universal truth. However, there's a few problems.

As I mentioned, archaeology can't confirm the existence of a Toltec empire. It's possible that it really was all just Aztec propaganda. We know that the Aztecs rewrote their history. A man named Tlacaelel did so a generation before Spanish contact. He ordered all the history books burned, and he recreated a new pro-Aztec version of history, and, it worked.

Even after the Aztecs were defeated, the legends of the Toltec's greatness persisted. And archaeologists were hunting for it. Even today it survives. In New Age circles they talk about Toltec wisdom. There's a book called *The Four Agreements* by a man named Don Miguel Ruiz. Miguel Ruiz is a Mexican national, and he claims to be of Toltec ancestry. Oprah Winfrey and Ellen DeGeneres promoted his book, and as a result, it became a best seller. And once that was a best seller, it spawned a bunch of other books, until it hit its very lowest level. Looking on Amazon lately, I've seen a book called *The Idiot's Guide to Toltec Wisdom*. Sheesh.

You know, Ruiz's four agreements are actually pretty positive. They're, 1, Don't lie. 2, Don't take things personally. 3, Don't make assumptions, and 4, try your best. There's nothing wrong with those. But, to be clear, they have nothing to do with ancient Toltec philosophy. He's just riding the coattails of the Toltecs just like the Aztecs were.

The Aztecs, perhaps not unlike Ruiz, believed in Toltec philosophy. They also believed in Toltec legends, and one of those Toltec legends was key to how the Spanish managed to defeat them. The legend of Quetzalcoatl tells us of an epic fight between two Toltec rulers, or perhaps gods, which resulted in the expulsion of Quetzalcoatl from the capital city of Tula. He sailed east into the sea, but vowed to return some day and reclaim his throne. That legend was key to Cortes' success against the Aztecs. The king, Moctezuma, was focused upon it. Quetzalcoatl's return was prophesied to occur in the year Ce Acatl, or 1 Reed, that was 1519, and Cortes landed in that very same year.

A few years earlier Moctezuma had received a bad prediction from the philosopher king of Texcoco. He had a vision of Aztec defeat, the end of their civilization. It was to be at the hands of foreign invaders from the east, and Moctezuma would lead them to the end. He had his priests search the prophecies, and he found this legend of Quetzalcoatl. And he found that it matched. So he was braced for it when Cortes arrived.

So let me tell you about the legend and how Quetzalcoatl was expelled. But first, who are we going to believe about this? There's actually a lot of versions of this legend, and if you look into it yourself, you'll find these various versions. Some of them say that he was a god. Others say he was a man. So, we have to pick which one. I personally pick the version of priest and chronicler Sahagun, because he was very, very careful in his data collecting. So the story I'm talking about comes mostly from Sahagun.

So it starts off telling us that two men actually co-ruled Tula. There was Quetzalcoatl as the head priest. And then there was another named Huemac; he was the political leader. And the god Tezcatlipoca didn't like them, and he plotted to humiliate them and to destroy Tula. First he tricks Quetzalcoatl. He tricks him into drinking, and he claims that pulque is actually medicine that will make him feel better. Quetzalcoatl does so, and he gets very, very drunk, so incredibly drunk that he sleeps with his own sister. And this is a terrible scandal. He's shamed. He's a priest. He should never drink, and he should be celibate. So the people reject him as impure, and he's shamed.

Next it's Huemac's turn. Tezcatlipoca transforms himself. He becomes a naked chili salesman in the market. He looks like a Huastec from another area, and he's in Tula's market. His name is Tobeyo. And Huemac's daughter falls immediately in love with him, and she's so enamored with him that Huemac has no choice but allow her to marry him. And the citizens are very, very upset, because this is the princess of the town. How could the king let her be married to this weirdo, naked foreigner?

But Huemac has a plan. He decides, well, he's now my son-in-law, and he's got to be a warrior, too. So I'll send him to battle. But what I'll do is, I'll send him to battle with a bunch of dwarves and lame people so he has no support, and he'll die. And he also tells the other soldiers, look, when things get bad in battle, just leave him be. He's going to have his end. But somehow or another, because he's actually Tezcatlipoca, Tobeyo wins with that lame force, and he comes back as a hero. And Huemac has no choice but to honor him in a big festival. He's now the big hero of the town.

So, the victory celebration ensues, and Tobeyo's at the front of it. He's singing, and he's beating a drum. And all of the citizens are entranced. And they're dancing, and they're not even thinking of what they're doing. But then all of a sudden, these citizens start falling off cliffs in this trance. And the vibrations from his drum start wiggling the whole town, and entire bridges collapse. And it's panic, and it's mass death. So, Tezcatlipoca has caused this destruction. But, he still has more plans for the city.

The next thing he does, is he appears as a market performer, and he has this tiny little boy that he holds up his hand, and the boy is dancing in his hand. And the crowds are so excited to see this, they start trampling each other to get a view of this little boy dancing, and they crush each other. Then, they learn that it's a trick, and they kill that performer for lying. So there's Tezcatlipoca's body as this performer now, and he lies there in the middle of the market, and it starts to stink.

Then the stink becomes so terrible, that the smell itself actually starts to kill people; just smelling it is killing people. So they get together, and they try to drag that body out of the market. But it's supernaturally heavy; they can't move it. They put ropes around it, but it just keeps snapping. Finally, they all get together and a combination of both ropes and pulling and prayers help move it. But then, instantly, as he goes out, the entire city's food supply suddenly rots, and everyone's starving, and they're scared, and they're fighting.

Then, Tezcatlipoca takes his final disguise. He turns into an old woman. And he's again there in the market, and he's roasting corn, and it smells delicious. But any of the starving citizens that try to get close and enjoy this corn are instantly killed by this vicious old woman. That's all that they can take. Both Quetzalcoatl and Huemac are in complete despair. So they make the decision to just flee the city and to abandon the people. Huemac goes to live in a cave for the rest of his life, and the Aztecs know where that cave is. It's in a place called Chapoltepec, very near to the future Aztec capital.

Quetzalcoatl and his followers go east, and they go all the way to the shore of the ocean. There, they build a snake boat; it's a boat made out of snakes. And they sail away. But they vow that they're going to return in the year 1 Reed. And then, by crazy coincidence, Hernan Cortes lands on the shores of that very same year—1519.

The first explorers to study Mesoamerica started with those Aztec biases, the notion that the Toltecs where once an all-powerful empire who ruled the entire region. And for a while, actually, for a long while, investigations seem to support that sequence of events. Désiré Charnay was really the first researcher to study the Toltecs. He was a Frenchman who had moved to New Orleans, and while he was there, he read the book of John Lloyd Stephens that was written in the 1850s all about the Maya area.

He became very interested. So eventually, he started leading expeditions for France to the Maya area, and during those expeditions, he excavated and recorded things at the site of Chichen Itza in the Yucatan. Then, after a while away, he returned to Mexico in the 1880s. This time he went north, and he was actually the first to note Tula and its connection to Chichen Itza. He followed Sahagun's directions, and they brought him directly to Tula, just where Sahagun said it was. And when he got there, he immediately noticed its striking similarity to Chichen Itza. They have the same art, the same building styles. They were almost like carbon copies of each other. And he decided that this fit that legend of Quetzalcoatl like a glove.

So he's the first one to come up with this theory that when Quetzalcoatl left and he went in his snake boat to the east, that he landed on the shore of Yucatan. And that's where he went inland, and he conquered Chichen Itza; and that Chichen Itza was in fact the new capital of exiled Quetzalcoatl; and it was also proof of Toltec supremacy and command of the entire region.

There were more studies of Tula in the early 1900s. There were efforts to improve our chronology, and they confirmed the time that the Aztecs were talking about as well. They found that it was somewhere from around 700 to 1200 A.D. It ended just about when the Aztecs said it did, and, it conveniently started after Teotihuacan. And having seen that, it settled the debate. For a while people thought maybe Teotihuacan is Tula that the Aztecs are talking about. But these studies proved that Tula was the Toltec capital, and Teotihuacan was something earlier.

But where was that huge Toltec empire? The evidence of its existence is still missing to this day. It appears that it may have never really been. It should have controlled at least in central Mexico, but they didn't seem to even control that. Culture groups that we've spoken of already created borders around Tula's periphery. To the east, there was El Tajin; to the southeast, there was Cholula; directly to the south, there was Xochicalco. In 2002 Aztec specialist Michael Smith suggested that we should downgrade the Toltecs from empire to just kingdom. Others suggest that maybe Chichen Itza established Tula, not vice versa, as it has so long been believed. And why do we have sister cities that are over 1,000 miles apart like that? Well, maybe a closer look at Tula itself can tell us.

Aside from a few spot excavations here and there, no major projects took place at Tula until the 1960s. During that decade, and into the next, two projects ran concurrently, one led by INAH archaeologists, and the other, a team from the University of Missouri at Columbia. Together, they opened our eyes to what Tula really was, and wasn't. The INAH team focused on the center, and they were looking at the public buildings and the temples. The UMC project focused on the residential areas. Richard Diehl was in charge of that UMC team, and between the two areas of focus, we got a much better picture of Tula as a whole. In the end, it really did not support the idea that Tula was the capital of an empire.

Tula's setting was like that of other Terminal Classic states. It was located on the top of a ridge. There were two rivers below; they were the Tula and the Rosas rivers. And there were two sections of the city up on the hill; we call them Tula Grande and Tula Chico. They're separated by about a kilometer, and there are settlements scattered between the two of them. Looking over the whole city, its peak population was maybe as many as 30,000 people.

Tula Chico is the older part of the city. It's mostly housing, and there are a few small temples. Dates came back for Tula Chico at 600 to 900 A.D. It was abandoned by 900 A.D. And that left a big blank space in the city from then on. Now its start dates are very telling; it's right after Teotihuacan falls. Its end dates are also very telling; they're exactly the same end dates as Cacaxtla and Xochicalco, also connected to Maya sites. And it's also interesting that Cholula and El Tajin, our other Terminal Classic sites, didn't even skip a beat at 900; they kept going.

Tula Grande is the city center. It lives from 900 to 1200 A.D. And at 1200 A.D., like a number of other cities in that area, Tula is burned, just like El Tajin. Cholula, if you'll remember, changes, but it lives on. These are interesting clues to a still poorly-understood sequence of historical events. We're honestly still not sure what was going on at that time period. And in some regards, I as an archaeologist just look at that as job security.

Tula really reached their height during the Tula Grande phase. That time between 900 and 1200 is what we call really the Early Post-Classic, and they were a large civic center at that time. It was surrounded by thousands of houses. They were all single story houses, though, stone with flat roofs; and they were arranged in little patio groups. We can tell there were extended families living together within those groups, and within them, were many workshops inside those houses.

Tula is very close to the northern deserts, and it's not particularly good farming land. For that reason, they had to irrigate from the rivers; that was vital to their survival. And they really just grew enough food to feed their population. They were eating mainly corn; we could see that from house trash bins, and corn was in every one of their meals.

We can see it was ground-in with burnt lime on their metates. That's how you actually pull out the nutrients of corn when you're grounding them on metates; you use a little bit of burnt lime, and it activates it. Tortillas are made with that on comals. But they were eating in very simple bowls. They were just tableware bowls in the average house.

Tula's workshops were simple and small. They were mostly working things in obsidian, and they were making pottery. The obsidian came from area mines, and it also came as cores, perhaps from places that were giving tribute to Tula as a regional capital. The pottery they made was not particularly impressive. It was mostly utilitarian; it was common wares, bowls and plates. There were jars and serving dishes as well. The serving dishes are very diagnostic of Tula; they have three little pointy legs.

There was one very odd artifact type there. They found a couple of examples of ceramic toy dogs with wheels that connected through their little legs. There were axles through their feet and wheels on the outside. I've always been very skeptical of those artifacts. I see them in museum exhibits, and I think that's got to be a fake, because, Mesoamerica never created the wheel. But here they are on these little toys. But looking into it, especially for this course, I absolutely confirmed that these were found in context in Tula. And so, we have these weird, enigmatic wheeled objects that we've only really found in Tula, but they really did exist in Mesoamerica.

So, excavations found Tula's population to be a bunch of simple craftsmen. They were in their houses eating mostly corn, and they were creating tools for use in daily life. It certainly didn't support the Aztec description of a city full of master artists and their fancy noblemen. Of course, we know that the Aztecs re-inhabited Tula, and they excavated its ruins back in the 1400s. Maybe, they pulled all the good stuff out. Those who choose to believe the Aztec version of the Toltecs believe exactly that. But for those of us, like myself, who need some more physical evidence, well, at least we still have the evidence in the center of Tula Grande.

The most grand and impressive part of Tula is the civic center of Tula Grande. It has the standard set of architectural features. It's got pyramids and plazas and ball courts, but in a style that's both an homage to the cultures that came before them and a few elements that are uniquely their own. Arranged around a large central plaza, Tula's architecture seems influenced from all over. There's hints of *talud-tablero* from Teotihuacan. There's colonnaded halls, like sites far to the north of them. Their ball court looks just like Xochicalco's; it's the same dimensions and style. But at the same time, there were other elements that seemed to be uniquely Toltec.

There are two pyramids in Tula's center. They have boring names; they're Pyramid B and Pyramid C. Pyramid C is the main one, and it's on the east side of the plaza. Unfortunately, it was completely looted before archaeologists got there. All of its art panels were removed. Now, Richard Diehl blames the Aztecs. He said they pulled them off long ago. In any event, luckily, Pyramid B was much better preserved. Pyramid B is 10 meters tall. That's really not a very big or impressive building, but the flat carved panels along its base and the statues up top are very interesting features. The lower panels depict jaguars and eagles, and they're eating human hearts; they're actually removed, and you can see them in their claws as they're eating them. That conjures both warrior cults and sacrifice. And where did we see that before? The same sort of thing is on the murals at Cacaxtla.

On the top of Pyramid B are some of the most recognizable and famous pieces of ancient Mexican sculpture, the Atlanteans. There are four of them. They are columns carved like warriors. They're 15 feet tall, and they once were columns that held the temple roof. They have atlatls in their hands, and loin cloths, and they're wearing nice sandals. And right in the middle of their chests are beautiful butterfly pectorals. And they're wearing feather headdresses. They're so nicely dressed that I think they're probably soldiers in their formal uniform, but not actually in the act of combat.

Other columns on the top also depict warriors. The whole temple is clearly dedicated to war. Below and in front, there are these colonnades; there are dozens of columns. None of them have any carving, but their equivalent over in Chichen Itza in the same kind of building does have carving. Those in Chichen Itza are carved with warriors. So it's a good bet that Tula's columns were the same, perhaps just painted.

Connected at the west end of the colonnade is the Palacio Quemado, or the burned palace. It's another colonnade, even bigger. It was named that because Acosta found it burned. In fact, it's our primary evidence that Tula was burned at 1200. It probably wasn't even really a palace. It had no areas for kitchens or for sleeping. It was more likely a council house, very much like the council house we see in the Aztec capital.

Colonnades like this are also not from anywhere south of Tula. The earliest examples we can find are in Alta Vista, way north of Tula. That was a site that was established by Teotihuacan; we talked about it in earlier lectures. It was thriving as a Tula trade partner during this time. It had huge mining operations; there are thousands of mines found around Alta Vista. Those colonnades that are there and at Tula indicate very strong ties between the two of them, probably even stronger ties than Tula had going south.

So, as it turns out, the Toltec were actually far more important as the idealized heritage of the Aztecs than a verifiable ancient empire. However, regardless of their true size, it remains true that they were the ancestral connection that the Aztecs used to validate their right to rule Mesoamerica. In fact, the Aztecs emulated Tula to a T. We can see that in their art and architecture. The Aztec capital emulated Tula's features in three important ways. Number one, all of the eagles and jaguars, the cult is present in Tula in their carved panels, and it becomes a signature Aztec war symbolism.

Two, the chacmool statues. These are unique statues of men lying on their backs and holding bowls on their chest. We're not sure what or who they are, but they're found on the tops of the temples of Tula, and Aztec sites have them as well. Most people believe them be sacrificial altars. The name actually comes from the chacmools found at Chichen Itza, and that's a very interesting story that I'll tell you in my next lecture. Here, what I'm highlighting is the Aztec-Tula connection as seen by both of them holding these chacmools.

Third is the association of ball courts and skull racks. Tula has our oldest tzompantli, a skull rack. It's right in front of their ball court, and it's across from the main temple, Pyramid C. The Aztec capital had the same, a skull rack between a temple and a ball court. There were thousands of skulls on long poles, and these horrified the Spanish when they saw them. So the Aztec story is, in at least, part, true. They're clearly connecting their art to Tula. But the size of the Toltec empire was grossly exaggerated. Archaeology finds them closed-in by equally powerful neighbors, and then finally defeated in

1200. There's really no evidence that they were master artists. In truth, their art could be criticized as sub-par in Mesoamerica.

In fact, the entire legend of the Toltecs and Tollan, as told by the Aztecs, would have been thrown out a long time ago if it were not for the existence of the city that's the subject of my next lecture—Chichen Itza.

Chichen Itza—Maya Capital of the Yucatan
Lecture 30

V isited by about 3 million tourists every year, Chichen Itza is the best known of all ancient Maya sites. For archaeologists, Chichen Itza is a great mystery. Despite more than 100 years of study, scholars still debate who ruled Chichen Itza and where its inhabitants came from. In this lecture, we will discover the history of Chichen Itza; explore the two distinct sections of the city, separated by time and architectural style; and examine the Maya influence on Toltec Chichen Itza.

Remade in Tula's Image

- Chichen Itza was clearly the capital of Post-Classic Yucatan; no other site has come near to its size or grandeur. Before it reached its peak population, however, it had a Terminal Classic phase. The difference between those two times is stark.

- There are two main time periods assigned to Chichen Itza. The period from 800 to 1000 is called Maya or Old Chichen. The second period, from 1000 to 1200, is called Toltec or New Chichen. Small populations remained after the Itza people left, but Chichen Itza's history spans about 400 years. It was at its height during the 10th *bak'tun*: 830 through 1224. In this lecture, we'll start with the later phase of Chichen Itza, 1000 to 1200, which is the time of the Toltec Chichen.

- Around the year 1000, Chichen Itza's art and public architecture changed radically. It seems to have been remade in Tula's image. About that time, its population soared to nearly 40,000. The Temple of the Warriors, constructed during that phase, looks very much like Tula's Pyramid B.

- The Temple of the Warriors has the same flat-roof design found at Tula. Although the flat roof was appropriate for Tula because it was in an arid location, it does not make sense in Yucatan, which gets much more rain. The roof was in obvious imitation of the ones in Tula. On a bench in Chichen Itza were smaller illustrations of the same Atlanteans seen in Tula.

- The Temple of the Warriors also depicts images of jaguars and eagles eating hearts—images that were most likely influences from Central Mexico. The temple was connected to a colonnade in a complex called the Temple of a Thousand Columns. The colonnade columns at Chichen Itza are carved with images of warriors carrying *atlatls*. Just like Tula's Pyramid B, this building was clearly connected to war.

The Largest Ball Court in Mesoamerica
- Multiple low platforms are placed around Chichen Itza's main plaza. Called Venus platforms, each has an image of the Venus deity from Central Mexico, as well as eagles and jaguars eating hearts. A line of Venus platforms leads from the Temple of the Warriors to another Toltec feature—a skull rack. The skull rack is next to Chichen Itza's ball court, as it was in Tula.

- At 150 meters long, Chichen Itza's ball court is the largest in all of Mesoamerica. Themes in its carved stone images and painted murals focus on conquest and foundation. Interestingly, these images may help us understand exactly what happened at Chichen Itza.

- Panels along the walls in the ball court show ball teams meeting each other. The ball is in the center with a skull inside—an image of sacrifice. Two team captains—Captain Sun Disk and Captain Serpent—stand around the center ball, and one has lost his head. Seven snakes are spurting out of his head like blood. This has been interpreted as a Toltec team versus a Maya team.

- Captain Sun Disk and Captain Serpent also meet in battle on another mural in the ball court area. This mural is located in the Temple of the Bearded Man. The mural depicts a battle scene and an arrival by sea. Again, Captain Sun Disk is defeated.

- Traditionally, this has been seen as proof that the Toltec arrived by sea and took Chichen Itza. In this scenario, Captain Serpent is Quetzalcoatl. But there are those who disagree with this hypothesis. There is contradictory evidence, especially in terms of dating. For example, Chichen Itza's ball court marker actually says it was established in 864.

Maya Influence in Toltec Chichen Itza

- In fact, archaeologists have identified a great deal of Maya cultural influence in what has been called Toltec Chichen Itza. This could have several interpretations: There was a Toltec tolerance of Maya tradition; there may not have been a clear Toltec domination; or the Maya placed their stamp on Tula, not vice versa.

© Gizelka/iStock/Thinkstock.

El Castillo sits at the heart of Chichen Itza's ceremonial precinct; it is a beautifully ornate structure with staircases on all four sides.

- There's no doubt that Quetzalcoatl was especially honored at Chichen Itza. He's everywhere in the Toltec section. Nowhere is Quetzalcoatl's importance seen more clearly than on Chichen Itza's main temple, El Castillo.

- On the top of El Castillo and down its north balustrade are feathered serpents, marking it as a temple of Quetzalcoatl. Although it shows both Toltec and Maya influences, it is much more Maya. In its construction, it resembles buildings at Tula. It also has feathered serpent columns at its doorway, but those are not seen in the Toltec capital at Tula.

- The measurements and details of the pyramid base are inspired by numerology and astronomy—a purely Maya approach. The pyramid's four staircases have 91 steps each. If the top platform is added, that's 365 steps—one for each day of the solar year. The pyramid also has nine terraces—another peculiarly Maya number. What's more, there are 52 shallow niches in each one of the terraces. By contrast, there is no sign of calendrical numerology at Tula.

Cenote of Sacrifice
- El Castillo's northern staircase points to Chichen Itza's primary cenote—the cenote of sacrifice. That cenote is actually what gives the city its name. *Chichen Itza* means "at the mouth of the well of the Itzas." A raised causeway leads 400 meters from El Castillo all the way to this cenote. By contrast, Tula has no causeways. Human sacrifices were thrown into the well—a practice that continued up to the Spanish contact.

- The cenote at Chichen Itza is called the Well of the Itza (not the Well of the Toltec). Dredging projects at the cenote have produced human bones and some surprising items. The first and longest dredging project was conducted by Edward Thompson from 1903 through 1910. He discovered bones and pottery through dredging; then, during a dive, he found a golden disk that was actually made in Oaxaca. He also found turquoise and copper bells—which were from Chaco Canyon in New Mexico.

- Here was clear evidence of a long-distance trade network. Since Tula had no metal, this was Chichen Itza's network alone. One particular object found in the cenote is puzzling: a stucco bust from Palenque. Either this was a Post-Classic excavation by Chichen Itza in Palenque, or it was an offering actually thrown in the cenote in the 8th century. Some sections of Chichen Itza suggest that the cenote was indeed that old.

Maya Chichen Itza

- A section of the city just south of the Toltec area is much older and more purely Maya. In fact, the city's ceremonial core is really split into two distinct parts—north and south. The south section is often referred to as Maya or Old Chichen. Its architecture is built in Puuc Maya style, like Uxmal and the Terminal Classic cities just to the southwest of Chichen Itza.

- The dates of this section are from 800 to 1000—and possibly earlier. The architecture is undeniably Puuc Maya; the corners are covered with Chaac masks. There is latticework on the façades just like that at Uxmal. Just the fact that this section remained standing is telling. If the Toltec really came to dominate the place, they would not have left a trace of manifestly Maya architecture.

- The most famous structure in the south section of Chichen Itza is El Caracol, or the Observatory. Its cylindrical form is unique at Chichen Itza. There is nothing Toltec about it; it is Maya in design and located in the Maya section of the city. It was so important that Mayapan—Yucatan's next capital—would erect an imitation of it.

A More Nuanced History of Chichen Itza

- Temple hieroglyphs at Chichen Itza dating from 832 to 950 are in a style from the Peten, not Yucatan. Around 950, texts become more Yucatan in wording and style. The Peten-influenced texts speak mostly of gods, not men. They tell of an early leader, perhaps a founder. His name is Kaku Pakal, meaning "fire is his shield."

- Kaku Pakal is first mentioned in 869. He is also called a western tree lord, which is a title from the Peten. The theory is that Kaku Pakal's father was from the Peten, and he married into the local Chichen royalty, Kaku Pakal's mother. Her bloodline was the important one to emphasize, not his. Despite how clearly the story of Quetzalcoatl's exile from Tula seems to fit the Toltec art and architecture, a much more nuanced history is now coming into focus.

- Here's how the story of Chichen Itza might read: Around the year 800, Maya refugee elites from the Classic period collapse of the Peten migrated up into Yucatan and intermarried. Then, a council form of government of the Yucatan was established, with Chichen Itza as its capital. The 980 shakeup in Central Mexico shifted trade networks, and Chichen Itza became a point of contact—taking on a more international identity and, hence, Toltec art and architecture.

- Although archaeologists do not know when Chichen Itza began, we know when it ended. According to Maya documents, the year was 1224—also the end of the 10th $bak\,'tun$ and the start of the 11th. In that year, everything changed, and the Itza simply walked away. As we'll discuss in the next lecture, a new capital of Yucatan then emerged: Mayapan.

Suggested Reading

Andrews, *Maya Cities.*

Coggins, *Cenote of Sacrifice.*

Edmonson, trans., *The Ancient Future of the Itza.*

Kowalski and Kristan-Graham, eds., *Twin Tollans.*

Schele and Friedel, *A Forest of Kings.*

Schele and Mathews, *The Code of Kings.*

1. Despite the problems, the elements of the Toltec myth of Quetzalcoatl seem to fit Chichen Itza nicely. Do you think it could be true?

2. Why, after hundreds of years of a kingship system, would the Maya choose to shift into a council system of government?

3. Do you think it was right to dredge the Sacred Cenote, or should such religious objects be left alone?

Chichen Itza—Maya Capital of the Yucatan
Lecture 30—Transcript

Visited by about three million tourists every year, Chichen Itza is the best known of all ancient Maya sites. Tourists love it for its violent art and its imposing temples. But archaeologists love it for the mystery it represents. Despite over 100 years of study, we're still debating who ruled Chichen Itza and where they came from.

Chichen Itza is actually the second most-visited ruins in Mexico. It's just after Teotihuacan. And Teotihuacan sits next to Mexico City, of 25 million people. So the amount of people that go to Chichen Itza is impressive. It's 2.5 hours from either Cancun or Mérida by car. It's right in the middle of the Yucatan Peninsula. People have to want to see it, and they do, or, at least until the Sun gets them. Most people that visit are asleep on the bus back to their cruise ship when they're done.

In 2007, Chichen Itza was voted as one of the new Seven Wonders of the World. That very same year, actually about a week after they were elected that, I was leading a tour of professors to Chichen Itza, and, I had the director himself, Eduardo Pérez, as our host that year. So, I had the opportunity to ask Eduardo what he thought of this new honor. And he looked at me and he said, "Great, look what happened to the last seven." Now, that's a funny story. But it's actually a serious problem. Tourism really does endanger the ruins. But, I think that history is everyone's property. We need to protect the ruins, but the main reason we're doing it is for people to appreciate and enjoy them. And Chichen Itza is a perfect case in point.

Back in 2007, Eduardo told me that at that time about 12,000 people a day were visiting. He had 24 guards total, and only 12 were on duty at any one time. That's a 1 to 1,000 ratio. How can one man watch 1,000 people? So, his only solution was to restrict access. He made sure that no one could climb the temples, because he just couldn't protect them. And I've watched this happen. I've watched all of them shut down one after another during my lifetime.

Now you might say, well, what about all those tourist dollars? Chichen Itza does make millions of dollars every year, but that money goes to the state. And really, only a fraction of it comes back to Chichen Itza itself. Most of it goes to support lesser-known ruins. It goes to research and further tourism development. Now, that seems unfair. But it's actually also very practical. It's a complicated situation. Institutions like UNESCO and World Monument Foundation try to help. They raise global awareness of great ancient sites. But still, their funds are filtered through the state and the government.

The ruins are national patrimony. And, ultimately, it's the decision of those nations. There are pros and cons to both of them. On the pro side, we can say, there's so much more to find. It's good the tourism dollars are helping that. The more ruins we know, the more tourist dollars can fund further research. So the tourism in that form helps drive an increase in knowledge. The cons are that that that seems very unfair for Chichen Itza. It needs more staff. And it's also that in this system, it's very non-transparent; it's unclear accounting. Are we sure that that money's going to its best use? It's a growing problem, and not just in the Yucatan, but everywhere. Big sites suffer while toeing the line for smaller sites. I wonder whether that's not all that different than what was happening in ancient times. Today, it's an ethical and logistical problem. But, for now, let's go back to ancient Chichen Itza.

Chichen Itza was clearly the capital of post-Classic Yucatan, or at least early post-Classic Yucatan. No other site came near to its size or grandeur. And colonial counts confirmed its supremacy. But it also had a Terminal Classic phase. Before it reached its peak population, it was in that phase. The difference between those two times is stark.

There are two main time periods we assign to Chichen Itza. One is from 800 to 1,000, and we call that Maya or old Chichen. The second one is 1,000 to 1,200. We call that Toltec or new Chichen. There were probably minor occupations before those periods, and there were small populations that remained after the Itza people left. But mostly, we have its history within about 400 years. More or less, it's the 10th Baton. It's 830 through 1224 A.D.

Now, this time I'm going to switch my lecture. Normally, I follow chronology from early to late. But this time, I'm going to start with the later phase, 1,000 to 1,200, that Toltec Maya time. In my last lecture, we spoke about Tula. It's the Toltec capital in northern Mexico. And we talked about its similarities to Chichen Itza. Now, let's look at that picture from the Chichen side.

About 1,000 A.D., Chichen got a big makeover. Its art and public architecture totally changed. It seems to have been remade in Tula's image. Tula's center, called Tula Grande, seems to have started about 900, so that was earlier than Chichen's changes. Whatever happened, it made Chichen Itza more popular and more powerful. About that time, its population soars to almost 40,000 people.

The Temple of the Warriors was constructed during that phase. It looks very much like Tula's Pyramid B. On its top, it has a Chac Mool on the top of the stairs. It doesn't have any Atlantean columns, but it had that same flat roof design that we find at Tula. And that flat roof was very appropriate for Tula, because it was up in a more arid desert location. But a flat roof doesn't really make sense in Yucatan. They got a lot more rain there. They weren't worried about collecting rain water; they were worried about draining it. So, it's interesting to that flat-roof design even exists there. It's non-functional in the Yucatan, and obviously, an imitation of Tula. In the top of that room, in the back, was a room with a bench, and that bench had dwarf versions of the Atlanteans we see in Tula holding up the seat of the bench.

Last lecture, I said I'd explain chacmool. It's really a strange story, revolving around a man named Augustus Le Plongeon. He was digging there in the 1880s at Chichen Itza. And one night he said he had a dream of a guy named Prince Chac Mool. And he wrote this story about Prince Chac Mool and his queen mother, who were the rulers of Chichen Itza. But then they were ousted, and they went across the sea to establish the first kingdoms at Egypt.

So when he woke up the next day, he found this statue. And he said, that's the statue in my dream. I know what his name is. His name is Prince Chac Mool. And that's how it got its name. It's funny. It sounds very much like a Mesoamerican name, but actually, it's just out of the imagination of a semi-madman.

So enough about Plongeon. Let's get back to Chichen Itza. The Temple of the Warriors, as I said, was the same as Temples at Tula. It also had the same images of jaguars and eagles eating hearts. They run flat facades, just like Tula. There were really no Maya precedents in the area before that, so we have every reason to believe those images were influences from central Mexico.

The temple was also connected to a colonnade. We call it The Temple of a Thousand Columns. And it's L-shaped, wrapping around the temple. Again, that's just like what we saw at Tula. But unlike Tula, the colonnade columns at Chichen Itza are carved. The carvings mostly depict warriors, with atlatls, just like the Atlanteans from Tula. Just as with Tula's Pyramid B, that building is clearly connected to war. Then, there are the multiple small platforms. They're in various places around Chichen's main plaza. We call them Venus platforms. They're very low platforms, only standing about two meters in height. And each one of them have four staircases, one on each side of the building. And there's a big, central Mexican Venus symbol on the sides of each one of these. It's central Mexican, not the Maya, who have their own version of that symbol. It also displays eagles and jaguars eating hearts. So those are definitely associated as well with this Tula-Chichen Itza complex.

A line of Venus platforms lead from The Temple of the Warriors to another Toltec feature, a skull rack. Chichen Itza clearly has one of these tzompantlis. It's carved with skulls all around its base, and those skulls are actually shown stacked up on stakes, just like the Spanish saw in the Aztec capital. Again, there's no Maya precedent for that anywhere that was something that was happening only in central Mexico at the time, before we see it in Chichen Itza.

The skull rack is right next to Chichen Itza's ball court, just like Tula, again. But Chichen Itza's court is even bigger, in fact, it's the biggest ball court in all of Mesoamerica. In length, it's 150 meters long. And it's a fantastic structure. It's full of all sorts of different art panels, and it's big enough to have multiple temples on this one, single building. There's both carved stone images and there's painted murals. It's themes focus on conquest and foundation. And they are possibly holding the keys to understanding exactly what happened at Chichen Itza.

Along the walls of the ball field center lane are long, carved panels showing ballgame teams meeting each other. The ball is in the center, with the skull inside that ball. Clearly, it's relating itself to sacrifice. There are two captains around that center ball. And the right one has lost his head, and where his head was, seven snakes are spurting out like blood. We've identified these two, or named them, I should say, Captain Sun Disk and Captain Serpent. And they've been interpreted as a Toltec team versus a Maya team. Captain Sun Disk and Captain Serpent also meet in battle on another mural, also in the ball court area. It's called the Temple of the Bearded Man, and it's the temple on the north end of the court. Within that mural, there's a bearded man, hence its name. But, overall, it's a battle scene. It shows an arrival by sea. Again, Captain Sun Disk is defeated in this picture.

Traditionally, this has been seen as proof that the Toltecs arrive by sea and took Chichen Itza. In this scenario, Captain Serpent is Quetzalcoatl. But, there are those who disagree with this hypothesis. There is contradictory evidence, especially in terms of dating. For example, Chichen Itza's ball court marker actually says it's established in 864 A.D. So, now let's talk about the competing perspectives on Chichen Itza.

Taking a critical look at what for decades has been called Toltec Chichen Itza, one actually finds a lot of Maya culture there. The question is, how should we interpret it? I see three primary options. One, we could say, well, that's to be expected; it's just Toltec tolerance of Maya tradition. Two, we could see it as proof that it was not a clear domination as traditionally thought. Or three, we could go even further and suggest it was Maya Chichen who placed their stamp on Tula, not vice versa.

The last option is hard for old school scholars to even contemplate. But it's becoming a growing possibility. If nothing else, option two is almost certainly proving true. This was not a complete dominance, as once believed. Let's look back at some of those Toltec elements. I believe there's room to rethink some of them. Let's start by returning to the Temple of the Warriors.

It has all of the Toltec elements we described. But it also has some purely Maya ones. For example, the corners of the upper temple have Chac faces, the masks stacked up, just like we saw in Puuc-style temples in the Maya

Terminal Classic. On the side wall of the upper temples, there are full-figured snake heads protruding off the walls. Their mouths are open, and there's a men's faces emerging out of them. That is classic Maya. It's the ancestors coming out of the vision serpent, the Butz Chan. It's the classic version of ancestor worship. So the Temple of the Warriors is a Toltec/Maya combo, not a purely Toltec building.

How about the conquest an arrival scenes in the ball court? Early studies clearly concluded that that was the Toltec invasion. But, it's just as easy to suggest that it's the arrival of the Itza Maya. The Itza arrived up the East Coast, not on the West Coast. Captain Serpent could be in Itza Maya. It's not necessarily Toltec. Another published alternative is the idea that Captain Serpent could be a Patung Maya. He could be from the Tabasco Coast area. That would be the same people that we were talking about called the Olmeca-Xicalanca, the people that some scholars said forged north into central Mexico and influenced places like the Cacaxtla and Xochicalco. That would neatly explain Toltec ideas coming along for the ride through the trade network that these people in Tabasco had established.

Landa's Chronicle speaks about Chichen, and it clearly says that the Itza Maya established it. It also speaks of a person called Kukulcan, a man from the west who came there to rule. But he wasn't sure if he came before, after, or with the Itza. In any event, there was no talk of him coming over and conquering the area. Now, the name Kukulcan is the Maya way that you say the word Quetzalcoatl, so it's the same person; they are talking about Quetzalcoatl. Traditionally, this was yet further Toltec proof.

But, there are at least two problems with that. One, the feathered serpent was everywhere at Chichen. But, actually, he's almost nowhere back at Tula; we really don't see his image there. Number two, the chronology is foggy and sometimes all wrong. Landa goes on to say Kukulcan established Mayapan in the 15th century. It's a myth, like the Aztec stories of the Toltecs, and it can't be confirmed archaeologically.

There's no doubt that Quetzalcoatl, or Kukulcan, was especially honored at Chichen Itza. He's everywhere in that Toltec section. But is he a purely Toltec addition? Nowhere has Quetzalcoatl's importance seen more clearly than on the city's main temple, El Castillo. At the heart of Chichen Itza's ceremonial precinct, stands its most famous temple, El Castillo. It's beautiful, ornate, and it has staircases coming down on all four sides. On its top and down its north balustrade are feathered serpents, marking it clearly as a temple of Kukulcan. It's a wonderfully-preserved structure, because it was still a living temple when the Spanish arrived. Landa, in fact, saw it and mentions it.

It's both Toltec and Maya, but I think it's much more Maya. On the Toltec side, it's got that top temple form, the flat temple, just like we see at Tula; that's its construction. It's also got feathered serpent columns at its doorway. People have always said that's Toltec. But really, again, is that really Toltec? We don't see that in the Toltec Capital of Tula.

The pyramid base is full of numerology and astronomy, Maya-style things. Those four staircases have 91 steps each. If you add that top platform, that's 365, one for each day of the solar year. It's also got nine terraces, another Mayan number. There are shallow niches in each one of the terraces. When you count them up, there are 52. Now, there's no sign of calendrical numerology at Tula; that's something that the Maya loved to do.

The Castillo's northern staircase points to Chichen's primary cenote, the cenote of sacrifice. That cenote is actually what gives the city its name; *Chichen Itza* means "at the mouth of the well of the Itzas." A raised causeway leads from the Castillo all the way to that cenote. It's 400 meters to the edge of the cenote. Landa reported human sacrifices were thrown into the well, and that it was still happening at the time of contact.

And just to mention, Tula has no causeways. And, at Chichen Itza, it's called the Well of the Itza, not the well of the Toltecs. Landa's account of sacrifices was confirmed in archaeology. There were multiple dredging projects at the cenote, and they produced human bones and much more, some very surprising things.

The first and longest dredging project was conducted by Edward Thompson in 1903 through 1910. He came down and he bought all of the land around Chichen Itza. He rebuilt an old hacienda there. Today, it's a nice hotel you can still stay at. Then, he mounted a huge iron crane at the edge of the cenote.

And he used that to scrape the bottom of the cenote looking for treasures. It was a very destructive process. He did that for two seasons, and he scraped up a bunch of mud. And then finally, bone and pottery started coming up.

By season five, he got even more desperate to find something special down there, and he decided to dive the cenote. He got that really old school diving equipment, with that bulb helmet. And he went down there himself in this big equipment. But it was way too murky. He couldn't see a thing. He was down there feeling around with his hands. But then, finally, doing that, he found a golden disk that was actually made in Oaxaca. He also found some turquoise, and he found some copper bells. Those turned out to be all the way from Chaco Canyon in New Mexico.

So he had proven a huge, long-distance trade network had occurred there. And remember, Tula had no metal. So, this had to be Chichen's network, not Tula's. Thompson's discoveries were big news. T.A. Willard's book, *City of the Sacred Well*, said that he had found immense wealth. And that really upset the new Mexican government.

They sued him in 1926 for $1.3 million pesos. So he never returned. In fact, he sold Chichen Itza to the Barbachano family. They were the descendants of Miguel Barbachano, who I am going to talk about when we talk about the Caste Wars in the Yucatan. Chichen Itza was actually just recently sold back to the government in 2011. Finally, it's in the hands of the government. But for a long time, it was Barbachano property.

One particular object found in the cenote really captures my imagination. It was a stucco bust of Kan B'alam from Palenque. Now, either this was a Post-Classic excavation by Chichen over in Palenque, or, it was an offering actually thrown in there in the 8th century. Was the cenote really in use that early? Well, some sections of Chichen Itza suggest yes.

So far we've talked about Chichen Itza's city during the 1,000 to 1,200 time period. But there's an older section of the city, just south of the Toltec, or new Chichen. That section is much more purely Maya, and earlier than the section with all of the Toltec influence. The city's ceremonial core is really split into two distinct parts, north and south. The south section is often referred to as old, or Maya, Chichen Itza. Its architecture is built in Puuc Maya style, like Uxmal and the Terminal Classic cities just to the southwest of Chichen Itza.

Its dates are older, 800 to 1,000 A.D., maybe even earlier. And the architecture is undeniably Puuc. The corners are covered with those Chac masks, and it has rounded corners. The main structure is called The Nunnery. Again, just because it looked like nunneries to European eyes, not because there were any nuns in there. On the outside, was lattice work, on the façade, just like Uxmal. Just the fact that it still stood there is telling. If the Toltecs really came to dominate the place, why would they leave such blatantly Maya architecture out in the open? The most famous structure in the south is El Caracol, or The Observatory. I've discussed it more in my astronomy lecture. Its cylindrical form is unique at Chichen. It's definitely an observatory, and it's nothing Toltec. It's Maya, and in the Maya section of the city. It's so important that Mayapan, Yucatan's next capital, would erect an imitation of it.

Other temples in the area have hieroglyphs. No hieroglyphs have really been found in the new Chichen section. The dates of the hieroglyphs range from 832 to 950 A.D. Casa Colorada and the Temple of the Hieroglyphic Jambs both have very long texts. And the writing style is the style from the Peten, not from the Yucatan. Towards about 950 A.D., texts become more Yucatan in wording and style, but these early ones seem connected to the Peten.

The text speaks mostly of gods, not men. Fire drilling ceremonies are another major topic. But they do tell us of an early leader, maybe a founder. His name is Kaku Pakal; "fire is his shield." He's first mentioned in 869 A.D. And he's not alone. He co-rules with a brother, a man named Kamil Kopo. He's also called a colom te, a western tree lord, which is a title, again, from the Peten. Kaku Pakal is mentioned along with other lords as well. In one text he's mentioned with the Lord of Ek Balam, a nearby major city. The Akab Dzib structure has glyphs that mention the divine Kokom. Kokom is an elite Yucatan family known from the contact period. So the evidence points to a council of Lords over Chichen, not despotic kings, like the Classic period. Kaku Pakal's parentage is also telling. His mother is named many times. She has a wonderful name; she's Lady Kayim, Lady Singer. His father, Jawbone, is barely mentioned. So, the theory goes that Kaku Pakal's father was from the Peten, and he married into the local Chichen royalty, their mother. So her bloodline was the important one to emphasize, not his.

So, despite how clearly the story of Quetzalcoatl's exile from Tula seems to fit the Toltec art and architecture at Chichen, a much more nuanced history is coming into focus. Here's how I see the story of Chichen Itza shaping up. Step one, around 800 A.D., Maya refugee elite from the Classic collapse of the Peten migrate up into Yucatan and intermarry. Step two, a council-form government of the Yucatan is established with Chichen Itza as its capital. Step three, the 980 shakeup in central Mexico shifts trade networks, and Chichen Itza becomes a point of contact, taking on a more international identity, and hence, Toltec art and architecture.

There's still one question in my mind. Why Chichen Itza? Who was there for the Peten elites to intermarry with? The answer may be coming soon. In just 2013, new excavations began at Chichen Itza. Rafael Cobos found Classic-period architecture underneath El Castillo's plaza. That's underneath new Chichen. What he found underneath there might just be old, old Chichen.

We still don't know when Chichen Itza started. But we do know when it ended. Maya contact documents say that kak tun a'thow was the moment. That's 1224 A.D., and it happens to be the very same year of the end of the 10th *bak'tun* and the start of the 11th. In that year, the Itza walked away; they just returned to the South. And again, there was no sign of destruction. It was a peaceful abandonment.

But that was not the end of the Maya or council forms of government in Yucatan. As we'll discuss in my next lecture, a new capital of Yucatan emerged. It still had a council form of government, but not one that was dominated by the Itza or the Toltecs. That city was called Mayapan.

League of Mayapan—Maya New World Order
Lecture 31

As Chichen Itza declined, Mayapan rose to power. This city was the seat of a more representative government that heralded in an era of prosperity that lasted for more than 200 years. But in the end, that new form of government did not succeed; the city was sacked and burned in the mid-1400s. Mayapan was an obvious imitation of Chichen Itza but not as large or as finely built. In this lecture, we'll explore the establishment of this new capital of the Yucatan, examine the innovative form of government practiced by the League of Mayapan, discuss Mayapan's social structure and eventual adoption of slavery, and record the city's demise at the hands of the Xiu family.

Books of Chilam Balam

- There are two primary sources for the history of Mayapan. One is Diego de Landa's chronicle *Relation of Things in Yucatan*. The second source is the Books of Chilam Balam, documents written by Maya priests in European script accompanied by Maya drawings. *Chilam Balam* means "jaguar prophecy." There are at least nine Chilam Balam books, named for the villages in which they were written.

- The Books of Chilam Balam address a variety of topics, such as ritual songs, calendar rites, and stories, but the history of the region is one of their major themes. They have been called prophecy books because they refer to the *k'atun* cycle. The Books of Chilam Balam do predict the future but in a repeating, cyclical way, not as literal, linear time.

- The *k'atun* cycle was in 13 sets of 20 years—260 years total. Each of the 13 *k'atuns* was called Ahau for the 260-day name on which it mathematically occurred—the cycle would go from 1 Ahau to 13 Ahau. Chichen Itza fell from power during 8 Ahau, and according

to the Books of Chilam Balam, Mayapan fell in 8 Ahau, as well—
but 260 years later.

League of Mayapan

- Based on the archaeological evidence, the end of Chichen Itza was not a violent one; no structures were burned or destroyed. However, both Landa's account and the Books of Chilam Balam report that the establishment of the new capital at Mayapan was brought on by a rebellion.

- The Books of Chilam Balam indicate that the Yucatan Maya rebelled against Toltec and Itza Maya rule. The rebellion was led by the Cocoms, a powerful family in Yucatan. The Cocom family was part of Chichen Itza's council. In the 800s, the name *Divine Cocom* was written in the hieroglyphs on Chichen Itza's Akab Dzib building.

- The Cocom family established Mayapan and invited families from all over Yucatan to participate in a new government—an improved, more representative version of Chichen Itza's council, called the League of Mayapan.

An Imitation of Chichen Itza

- Mayapan looks like a replica of Chichen Itza; its major structures are blatant copies of those first built at Chichen Itza. However, closer inspection also finds some telling differences. The two major buildings, El Castillo and the Observatory, are clear copies. The fact that the Observatory was reproduced suggests the importance that Mayapan placed on that structure. However, Mayapan's version of the Observatory is neither as large nor as well built as the one at Chichen Itza. The Observatory sits right next to the primary temple, El Castillo.

- Mayapan's El Castillo is also a lesser replica of the original at Chichen Itza; it is only 15 meters tall, not 24 meters, as is the one at Chichen Itza. On the sides of El Castillo are stucco art panels that reveal Mayapan's focus on sacrifice. The panels show skeletal human bodies with bee wings. The niches in the terraces are places

In Mayapan, the Observatory was given prominence as an established symbol of political authority.

to put real skulls. Even though the League of Mayapan was a council to represent everyone, the city still had enemies to sacrifice. It was not the harmonious region it was reported to be.

Lack of Urban Planning

- Although Mayapan's two main structures were copies of those at Chichen Itza, the overall city plan was new. A significant addition was dozens of long structures with many columns located in the city center. Archaeologists believe that these were the council houses, where the representative families stayed while they were participating in the government.

- Mayapan also has a clearly different aesthetic. Chichen Itza looks as if it was master planned; all the architecture is unified and cohesive. That's not the case at Mayapan, which looks disorganized and lacks a harmony of orientation and building style. Mayapan is clearly accretional, built without an overarching plan.

- That lack of urban planning was likely the result of the council form of government. There was no unified vision for the city; each family had rights to a certain part of the city, and each put its own stamp on that part alone.

The Walls of Mayapan

- In one aspect, however, the city was united: the need for defense. The most impressive feature of the entire city is the walls of Mayapan. Mayapan had two sets of massive walls—one surrounding the civic center, where the League of Mayapan met, and another around the entire city. These walls not only indicate that Mayapan was concerned with defense, but they reveal important clues about class distinctions within the city's population.

- The city's elite lived in the inner section. The middle and lower classes lived in the outer sections but still within the walls. There were 9.5 kilometers of walls surrounding an area of 4.2 square kilometers. Within those walls, there were 4,000 buildings—which works out to about 982 structures per square kilometer. In fact, Mayapan was the most densely populated city in Maya history.

- Archaeologist Bradley Russell conducted a wide-reaching survey of Mayapan in the 2000s and found settlements outside the walls of the city. In total, Russell estimated that there were 15,000 to 17,000 people living in Mayapan—but that was still less than half of Chichen Itza's population of 40,000.

- Archaeological research revealed a marketplace in Mayapan containing many workshops for ceramics and stucco. Trash pits next to houses were excavated to find out what the populace ate. Interestingly, there was much more meat being consumed in the inner section. Three times as much deer and twice as much turkey was consumed in the elites' inner section. In the end, those kinds of social inequalities may have been the demise of Mayapan.

The Cocom Practice Slavery

- Eventually, the Xiu family rose up and led a rebellion against the Cocom, killing the entire family and effectively ending Mayapan. Archaeological evidence appears to confirm this story. Landa's account starts out with a peaceful and prosperous Mayapan council led by two main positions, a ruler and a high priest. The League of Mayapan was dedicated to the common people, leading missions to assist those in need.

- Then, a group of wanderers, the Tutul Xiu clan, came to Mayapan and settled near Uxmal. They were excellent farmers and made tributes to Mayapan. Eventually, the family gained respect, and its members were allowed to intermarry with the elites of Mayapan. They found themselves a place in the League of Mayapan.

- Without consulting the council, the Cocom family made new trade deals with people from Central Mexico who were stationed in Tabasco. The Cocom allowed the Mexicans outposts within the city. The Cocom family grew very rich from these deals and allowed more Mexicans to stay. The Mexicans brought along armed guards to protect their interests.

- Then, the Cocoms started allowing the poorest in their community to become slaves to the Mexicans. What's more, they started using slaves for themselves. It seems as if the Mexican presence had caused shifts in Mayapan's social structure.

Influence from Central Mexico

- Proof of the entrada from Central Mexico is also found in the archaeology of the city. An annex attached to the base of El Castillo contains murals in Mixteca-Puebla style. The murals depict large sun disks, a symbol that was clearly from Central Mexico. The murals also illustrate warriors from Central Mexico—which would become signature Aztec iconography.

- A later addition to Mayapan was a group of circular temples built in the middle of Mayapan's plaza, interrupting the public space. Circular temples in Central Mexico were erected in honor of Ehecatl, the Wind God. Ehecatl was also the protector of the Aztec trader warriors.

- As the practice of slavery expanded, the other council lords grew enraged at the Cocom. But the people from Central Mexico were very well armed. Slowly, however, the local Maya learned the ways of the Mexicans; they learned to use their weapons and craft their armor. Then, when the situation reached a crisis point, the Xiu family led the rebellion against the Cocom.

Dissolution of the League
- According to the Books of Chilam Balam, a large force of Xiu attacked in 1441. Every single Cocom was killed, even the women and children. Archaeology seems to confirm this event. Carbon-14 samples from the burned council houses put the date of destruction between 1400 and 1450. Following this, there are no new constructions or ceramics found in the city.

- The chronicles report that the Xiu took Mayapan, but then pestilence began, and the League of Mayapan was dissolved. Everyone returned to their own territories in 1441. The peninsula was once again fragmented into independent city-states. The Xiu blamed the Cocom family; the Cocom blamed the Xiu. As for the people from Central Mexico, the Maya forgave them. They were allowed to continue living in the Yucatan.

- That was a grave mistake. Those Mexicans were not just trading partners; they were the Aztec, and the Aztec Empire would use its military trade outposts to dominate numerous cultures. The Maya were next in their sights when the Spanish arrived.

Bricker, *The Indian Christ, the Indian King.*

Edmonson, trans., *The Ancient Future of the Itza.*

Landa, *Yucatan before and after the Conquest.*

Shook, *The Great Wall of Mayapan.*

Questions to Consider

1. Why did Mayapan have such extensive walls? Do you think the walls were primarily for defense or more about socioeconomic order?

2. If Mayapan rejected what Chichen Itza stood for, why did it imitate the larger city's architecture?

3. Do you think the Chilam Balams should be considered valid historical documents or stories?

League of Mayapan—Maya New World Order
Lecture 31—Transcript

As Chichen Itza declined, a city named Mayapan rose to power. It was the seat of a new, more representative government that heralded in an era of prosperity that lasted for over 200 years. But in the end, that government form did not succeed, and Mayapan was sacked and burned in the mid-1400s.

Mayapan is 100 kilometers west of Chichen Itza. It's far enough away to be separate, but it's close enough to control the same region. It really wasn't the best farmland, but there were lots of cenotes for water. It was an obvious copy of Chichen Itza, but not as finely built or as large. Its principal temple was also an El Castillo. It had four staircases, and it had feathered serpents. And nearby it was a copy of El Caracol, the Observatory; it was that same circular design, and it had four doorways, just like Chichen Itza's.

By the time the Spanish arrived, it had been abandoned for more than 100 years. The city core had been burned, and it was in ruins. But all the Maya remembered it. They knew where it was and what it was. Maya peasants were still living there, farming in the periphery. Without those accounts, archaeologists probably wouldn't have recognized it for the capital it was. It was smaller, and frankly, ugly, compared to Chichen Itza or Uxmal. Stevens visited it in 1841, but only for two days. Catherwood made a few nice drawings of it. Then, in the 1950s, there was a big Carnegie Institution project. They were pointed there by those colonial chronicles.

There are two primary historical sources for Mayapan. One, is Diego de Landa's chronicle, *Relation of Things in Yucatan*. And the second is the Chilam Balams; those were books written by the Maya at contact. They were written in European script, but they had Maya drawings along with them. They were written by Maya priests. They were the very first literate generation, the ones that could write in European alphabet.

Chilam Balam means "jaguar prophecy." *Chilam* also means "Maya priest." There are at least nine Chilam Balam books. They're named for the villages they were written in. Some of them are longer than others. The Chumayel and the Tzimin both have English translations now. The Books of Chilam

Balam contain a variety of topics. They talk about ritual songs and calendar rites and stories. But the history of the region is one of their major themes, and there's significant overlap in their historical sections. There's also some contradictions from book to book, as well. And that's not surprising, because they were written from, again, their home-team perspectives. And they were, after all, still independent city-states.

They've been called prophecy books, because they talk a lot about the *k'atun* cycle. That's the main source of the Maya prophecy misunderstanding around the year 2012. People misunderstood it and said the Maya are predicting the end of the world. And those do predict the future. The Chilam Balams do predict the future, but in a repeating, cyclical way, not as linear time. The *k'atun* cycle was 13 sets of 20 years, 260 total. Each of the 13 *k'atuns* was called Ahau, for the 260-day name that it mathematically occurred on. We'd go through 1 Ahau, 2 Ahau, 3 Ahau, et cetera, to 13 Ahau. Each one of them were a 20-year period.

And the Maya said that, in each one of those 20-year periods, basically, the same thing was going to happen. Sadly, most of the *k'atun* predictions were bad. They'd say there'll be failing crops this year or there'll be corrupt government or we'll be beset by enemies. In fact, *k'atun* 12 Ahau was one of the only positive ones. Chichen Itza fell from power during 8 Ahau. The Chilam Balams say so did Mayapan; it fell in the 8 Ahau, 260 years later. Stories of how and why differ. The facts don't always match up, but it's fun to finally have historical sources to compare to archaeological data.

Archaeology doesn't find any evidence of Chichen Itza's end as a violent one. None of the structures were burned or destroyed. However, both Landa's account and the stories of the Chilam Balams say it was a rebellion, one that ended in the establishment of the new capital at Mayapan.

The Chilam Balams say it was a rebellion, that Yucatan Maya got tired of Toltec and Itza Maya role. And all sources agree that it was led by the Cocoms, a powerful old family in Yucatan. They were part of Chichen Itza's council. The name *Divine Cocom* was written in the hieroglyphs there. It was in the 800s on Chichen Itza's Akab Dzib building.

Some Chilam Balams gloss over the fight, and they go straight to the establishment of Mayapan. Others tell detailed stories of how and why. Multiple tell of a Cocom war captain. His name was Hunac Ceel, and he led the rebellion. Either he or another Cocom eventually become Mayapan's first ruler. The Chilam Balam of Chumayel gives a reason. They say that Chichen Itza stole a royal bride from the town of Izamal. Her name was Lady Ah Ulil, and she was stolen by a king named Ah Mex Cuc. That's an interesting name, because Mex is like Mexica, or the name of the Aztecs. Cuc is a quetzal bird; it's a Maya word. So it really denotes a Toltec-Maya combo name in and of itself. Mex is because it's written in the 1500s.

Hunac Ceel fights for his ally, Izamal's, honor. Some accounts just say he won. Others say he was captured, and when he was captured, he was thrown into Chichen Itza's cenote of sacrifice. But, he survives the night, swimming around in there. And during that time, he receives a prophecy; it's a prophecy from Chac about the upcoming harvest. Ah Mex Cuc forgives him, and he pulls him out, and he appoints him the next ruler of Mayapan.

Landa's version is significantly different. He says the legendary Kukulcan established Mayapan. He was part man and part god. He was the same figure who co-ruled Chichen Itza with the Itzas. And when he sees Chichen Itza is not working, he creates a better system at Mayapan. Then, he departs peacefully to the West, going back where he came from. But Landa's account also conflicts with archaeology. If Toltec influence at Chichen Itza started with the arrival of Kukulcan, it was 200 years before Mayapan. It couldn't be the same individual. It also states that Uxmal, Chichen Itza, and Mayapan were contemporaries. And archaeology denies that. We see little or no overlap. Aside from these contradictions, all the stories converge on the same result. The Cocom family started Mayapan, and it invites families from all over Yucatan to participate in a new government, an improved, more representative version of Chichen Itza's council. It was called the League of Mayapan.

Let's now turn to the city itself. Even when one walks into the ruins today, their first impression validates what the Chilam Balams say. It looks like an imitation of Chichen Itza. Its major structures are blatant copies of ones first built at Chichen. However, closer inspection also finds some telling differences. The two major buildings are copies, the Castillo and the Observatory. Why they're there makes good sense; they were established symbols of political authority. They were what the public expected to see. Now, a good analogy is that United States capitals are modeled after the architecture in Washington, DC. People expect to see things, and that's what they get.

I like that the Observatory was copied. It supports its importance at Chichen Itza. At Chichen, it wasn't in the very center, and it wasn't clear that it was central to the city's governance. But in Mayapan, they give it great importance; it sits right next to the primary temple, El Castillo. Mayapan's version of the Observatory is neither as large or as finely built. It had four doorways and the circular shape. But it had none of the windows up on the upper level than Chichen's did.

Catherwood drew a drawing a long time ago, when it was much more complete, and it definitely showed there were no windows. There were no stone-carved sculptures on it, either. And its doors are oriented differently. They really weren't functional in the same way that Chichen Itza's were. Mayapan's El Castillo is the same case. It's not as big or as finely built. It's only 15 meters tall, not Chichen Itza's 24 meters tall.

There's really not much left of its upper temple. It was either destroyed during the rebellion, or it wasn't built well enough to last. Now we only have the stub walls, and we have the basic floor plan. But even with that, we can see that it didn't have the four rooms and doors, like Chichen Itza's version.

On the sides of the Castillo are stucco art panels that reveal Mayapan's focus on sacrifice. They show skeletal human bodies with bee wings. And there's niches in the terraces right where the skulls of those skeletons should be. It seems clear that those niches were places to put real skulls in. If that was true, what a gruesome sight this temple must have been. Clearly, even though they were a council of everyone, they still had enemies to sacrifice. It was not the harmonious region it was said to be.

Those two main structures were copies. But the overall city plan was new. There was a major new addition. There were long structures with many columns. There were dozens of them in the city center. We believe those were the council houses; those were the places that each one of those representative families stayed in while they were participating in the government. That part, at least, fits perfectly with the historical documents. There's also a clearly different aesthetic. Chichen Itza, at least its old part, looks very much master planned; all of the architecture works nicely together. That's not the case at Mayapan. It looks very, very disorganized. It seems like there's no unity of orientation or building style. It's clearly accretional. It was built here and there, without an overarching plan. Late structures are actually even built in the middle of plazas, like they're interrupting space that was open in the past.

That lack of urban planning is likely the result of the council form of government. There was no unified vision for the city. Each family had rights to a certain part of the city, and they did their own thing with it. But one thing they were unified about was their need for defense, and that was indicated by the most impressive feature of the entire city, the walls of Mayapan. Mayapan had two sets of massive walls, one surrounding the civic center, where the League of Mayapan met and they resided. The other one was around the entire city. These walls not only indicate that Mayapan was concerned with defense, but they reveal the important clues about class distinctions within the city's population.

The city's elite lived in the inner section. The middle and lower classes lived in the outer sections, but they were still within the walls. There were 9.5 kilometers of walls surrounding an area of 4.2 square kilometers. Within that, there were 4,000 buildings. That was the most densely populated Maya city ever. That works out to basically 982 structures per square kilometer. Bradley Russell conducted a wide-reaching survey in the 2000s. And he actually found settlement outside the walls of the city for another half-kilometer more in every direction, and that added to the total buildings. Russell estimates that there were 15,000 to 17,000 total people living in Mayapan. That's really big, but that's still less than half of Chichen Itza's 40,000 people.

Russell's survey called the function of the walls into question. Were they purely defensive? If they were, what were all those people doing living outside of them? He also points out that there are 12 gates in the walls, some of them very wide with corbelled arches. Perhaps it was something like Tulum, its contemporary, in that the walls were delineating a space. They were for social stratification and trade control, rather than for defense.

Now, Russell's survey was part of a larger project called the Economic Foundations of Mayapan. It was directed by my friend Dr. Marilyn Masson. She was doing surface collections and test pits. It's not really glamorous work, but it gives us a lot of information. They discovered a marketplace in the north sector in that way. And they found many, many workshops. Most of them were ceramics. They also found a whole lot of stucco workshops.

Trash pits next to houses were excavated to find what they were eating. And Masson found some really big differences. There was much, much more meat being consumed in the inner section. There was three times as much white-tailed deer there as in the outside. And there was twice as much turkey. Those elites were eating a lot better than the commoners.

Both the inner and the outer populations were eating iguanas. Of course, the ratio was 10% in one versus 14% of the bones in another. The modern Maya joke, and they call iguanas Maya chickens. Everyone says that they eat them today. But I have asked multiple times for someone to cook me one, and nobody ever takes me up on it. They always say, oh, we don't do it. It's the people over in there, in that village. So I think maybe the small percentage in the past might indicate the same thing, that people were really only eating them in times of need, just like today. They always say, no, it's always the poorer people that are eating the iguanas, not us. You'll have to go over to them. Masson's simple, non-glamorous study is the real archaeology. It revealed important evidence of social stratification. It showed us the haves and the have-nots. And in the end, those kind of social inequalities may have been the demise of Mayapan.

I've said that all the historical sources agree that the Cocom family founded Mayapan. There's another point upon which they all agree, that the Xiu family rose up and led a rebellion against the Cocom, killing their entire family and effectively ending Mayapan. Again, the Chilam Balam accounts vary a bit; there are different renditions of this story. But the overall story is always the same. And in the case of the demise, Landa's account is similar as well. At this point, archaeology also comes into play. It seemingly confirms that same story.

Landa's account starts out with a peaceful, prosperous, and loving Mayapan, a council led by two main positions. One was a higher ruler named the Helach Unic; that translates "real man" in Maya. The other was a high priest called the Ah K'in, "he of the days," the exact same day that Maya day keeper priests in Guatemala are called.

Both positions were hereditary. They were passed from father to son. Both were within the Cocom family. And by the way, Landa's informant, his name was Nachi Cocom. So maybe we have a little bit of bias there. Those are the people that taught the other leaders and priests. And they'd send them out to the outer communities. And they were supposed to be models of behavior and ethics for the entire peninsula.

The League of Mayapan was dedicated to the common people, and they actually led missions to help those in need. They would go out and help the sick and the lame and the old and the blind. They were all cared for by the state. Mayapan was a benevolent and accepting state. And then, a group of wanderers entered their lands. They were the Tutul Xiu clan, and they were wandering around for 40 years. Landa thought maybe they were down from Chiapas. But eventually, they came, and they asked to settle in Mayapan's kingdom. And they were accepted. And they settled somewhere near Uxmal. They were excellent farmers. And they gave good tribute to Mayapan. Eventually, they gained respect, and they were allowed to intermarry into Mayapan's league. And they found themselves a place in the League of Mayapan.

Then the Cocom made new trade deals with central Mexicans who were stationed in Tabasco. They allowed these Mexicans to have outposts within the city. And that was done without consulting the entire council. The Cocom family ends up getting very rich from this deal. And they allow more and more Mexicans to stay, and those Mexicans come along with armed guards to protect their interests. Then, the Cocoms start allowing the poorest in their community to become slaves. They trade them to the Mexicans. And then, they start using slaves for themselves. And archaeology does find late evidence for slavery. We find a tiny, little living quarters next to fancy, elite homes. It seems like the Mexican presence has shifted Mayapan's social structure.

The proof of the Mexican entrada is also found in the archaeology of the city. There's an annex attached to the base of El Castillo, late. And there are murals inside, and they are Mixteca-Puebla style. They have these big sun disc symbols that are definitely central Mexican. And they also depict central Mexican warriors. That was signature Aztec iconography later. Also, a few circular temples were built right into the middle of Mayapan's plaza. They were probably later additions, because they interrupted the plaza space. Circular temples in central Mexico are to Ehecatl, the wind god. Ehecatl is also the protector of the Aztec trader warriors, called the *pochteca*.

Slavery begins to expand into capturing common people, as well. The other council lords become very, very angry. They're blaming the Cocom. But they can't do anything about it. They're scared of the Mexicans, because the Mexicans are very, very well armed. And this situation continues for several years. But slowly, the local Maya learn the ways of the Mexicans. They learn to use their weapons and craft their armor. Then, when the situation had become nearly unbearable, the Xiu family led the rebellion against the Cocom.

History is unclear of how they got through Mayapan's walls. But a large force of Xiu attacked. The Chilam Balams say it was the year 1441; every single Cocom was killed, even the women and children. Only one son that was away on a trading mission was spared. Archaeology seems to confirm this event. Multiple of the council houses were burned. The carbon-14 samples from those burned beams come back right about between 1400 and 1450 A.D. There are no more constructions or ceramics in the city. The city, at least in its core, was abandoned right about then.

The chronicles say that the Xiu took Mayapan and that they stayed for a while, but then pestilence began, and the league totally dissolved. Everyone returned back to their own territories in 1441 A.D. Many Mayapan residents followed the Ah Kin, the high priest. And he said to move on and establish the city of Tiho, which would become the modern city of Mérida. The peninsula was once again fragmented into independent city-states. The Xiu blamed the Cocom family. The Cocom blamed the Xiu, called them foreigners. Other families blamed both or other factors. The Yucatec families remain to this day. All of those names are still around there. I have friends in the Yucatan whose last names are Cocom, or Xiu, or Canul, or Pech.

As for the Mexicans, the Maya forgave them. They were viewed as just misled by the Cocom, and they were allowed to continue living in the Yucatan. They had to live in their own communities, and they weren't allowed to intermarry, but they could stay. And that was a mistake. These Mexicans weren't just new trade partners; they were the Aztecs. The Maya didn't know it then, but the Aztec empire used military trade outposts to dominate culture after culture. The Maya were next in their sights when the Spanish arrived. We'll discuss the Aztecs soon. But in my next lecture, I want to pull together some of what we know about Mesoamerican religion.

Mesoamerican Religion
Lecture 32

Mesoamerican religion is a labyrinth of belief systems—polytheism, ancestor worship, animism, shamanism, and time veneration—interconnected with one another to create one of the most complex and poorly understood religions in the world. In this lecture, we'll explore the evolution of the multilayered system of religion in Mesoamerica, examine the sacred calendar, and focus on the religious practices and deities of the Maya, Teotihuacan, and the Aztec.

Layered Belief Systems
- All Mesoamerican cultures are polytheistic; the people believe in multiple gods envisoned in a kind of pantheon. Mesoamericans also practice ancestor worship, the veneration of deceased ancestors. The practice is more than simply veneration, however; descendants make contact with the spirits of their ancestors and seek their help in the living world.

- Layered on top of the worship of gods and ancestors is animism: the belief that everything has a living spirit—not only humans but also animals, plants, rivers, mountains, and so on.

- Contact with the supernatural world is done through another aspect of religion: shamanism. A shaman has the ability to travel by dream or trance into the land of the dead and the supernatural and to see and speak to spirits on the earthly plane.

- A final element of Mesoamerican religions is the use of ritual calendars and the concept of a mystical sense of time. Individual days are living beings with spirits. Mesoamericans consider time as a force of nature and pray to the days themselves.

Olmec Religion

- Mesoamerica's first great civilization, the Olmec, produced public art in the form of massive stone sculptures. Although gods and spirits are not evident in Olmec art, there are depictions of Olmec shamanism, which is the main display of religion in their art. For example, humans are shown transforming into jaguars.

- In their art, the Olmec show themselves emerging from caves with figures floating above them. Those images are similar to later Maya scenes of ancestor worship. A common theme in Olmec sculpture is a man emerging from a cave. In some examples, a rope leads out of that cave, and it connects to the sides. On the sides are human figures who are protecting babies who, in turn, are in the process of transforming into jaguars.

- La Venta Altar 5 shows this sort of imagery. The message is that the ancestors are living in caves in the underworld and that they come out to communicate with the living. They are connecting to and protecting their descendants. The fact that the ancestors are floating in the air is telling; it signifies that the ancestors are returning from an ethereal place back to the earth.

- Humans are the main themes of Olmec art. In certain cases, however, there are depictions of animals or abstract monsters. Although some archaeologists interpret those images as Olmec gods, they may be general forces of nature. In fact, the concept of gods first developed in the cultures that followed the Olmec—especially the Maya.

Izapa

- As the Olmec fade and the Maya rise in the mountains to the south, two new elements of Mesoamerican religion take shape—namely, the clear appearance of deities and the development of a sacred calendar. This revolution in religion can best be seen at Izapa, in southwest Chiapas on the Guatemalan border.

- At Izapa are many carved stelae with images from the creation story, the *Popol Vuh*. In these images are multiple references to the hero twins and their journey into the underworld. This story is a metaphor for a human's ability to pass back and forth between the worlds. The twins' father actually becomes the Maize God at the end of the story.

- Maya gods shown at Izapa that are not mentioned in the *Popol Vuh* include an early version of the Rain God, named Chaac, who becomes a core member of the Maya pantheon. Stela 3 depicts K'awiil, a god of shamanic magic. His most diagnostic characteristic is displayed—his right foot is turning into a snake. Each of these gods became prominent in the Classic period cities.

- As Izapa was celebrating the *Popol Vuh*, other early Maya cities were celebrating the creation of a new calendar, the Long Count. Chiapa de Corzo contains a stela with nothing on it but a date: 36 B.C. The date itself is celebrated; it is a religious icon. The Long Count and the *Popol Vuh* emerged in Maya art about the same time. That is no coincidence: The start of the Long Count is linked to the fourth creation and the *Popol Vuh*.

Main Maya Gods

- Although there are a number of Maya gods, only the major ones are depicted on stone monuments. More appear in the contexts of painted ceramics and in the codices. There is no clear ruler of the gods, however. Like the Maya city-states themselves, the gods share power, and each rules over an independent realm.

- Of the gods depicted on monuments, K'awiil is the most commonly seen. Rulers are shown on monuments carrying staffs with K'awiil on top or holding tiny K'awiil statues. The god of shamanic magic, he is connected to conjuring the ancestors. K'awiil had a different name in the Post-Classic period: Itzamna (*itz* means "magical stuff"). He is frequently depicted in the few codices that remain.

- Chaac, the Rain God, was important to farming. In images, he holds a stone ax, which he uses to crack open the clouds and let the rain out. Equally important to farmers was the Maize God, Hunal Ye. He is not often depicted on stelae, but rulers are frequently shown wearing his jade lattice skirt. With this, the rulers put themselves in the guise of the Maize God. Their message is: "I am the embodiment of what gives you sustenance, and I am your father" (because the Maize God was the father of the twins).

- One other god comes to light during the Maya Classic period: the Sun God, K'inich Ahau. In the late Classic period, his name actually became a title of kings. He is connected to farming and astronomy.

Gods of Teotihuacan

- The Maya were not the only civilization flourishing in Mesoamerica during the Classic period. The Classic period superpower, Teotihuacan, had a religious tradition and a pantheon of gods that was distinct from the Maya. It is somewhat surprising that Teotihuacan's gods were so different because, in fact, they lived close to the Maya area and most likely shared some sort of Olmec heritage.

- There are three main gods of Teotihuacan: Tlaloc, the Rain God; the great goddess, a kind of Mother Earth; and Quetzalcoatl, the Feathered Serpent. Tlaloc is much like the Maya Chaac. He is associated with the rain but also with warfare and conquest. As discussed earlier, Teotihuacan dominated Mesoamerica for centuries—and did so at the point of a sword. Its power lay in their Venus-Tlaloc cult of warriors.

- Quetzalcoatl is pictured as a giant snake with long, green feathers. By the Post-Classic period, he was everywhere—Cholula, Xochicalco, even Chichen Itza. At Teotihuacan, we see the first temple dedicated solely to Quetzalcoatl.

- The great goddess was a female deity—rare in Mesoamerican pantheons. She is depicted on many murals in Teotihuacan. A goddess of fertility, she is shown in images with Sustenance Mountain, from the origin myth. This goddess is unique to Teotihuacan; she did not make her way into any future pantheons.

- When Teotihuacan fell and new cities emerged, Quetzalcoatl and Tlaloc persisted in public art. Toltec ideas dominated Mesoamerica for centuries, honoring both those deities. Then everything gave way to Mesoamerica's last great civilization, the Aztec.

The Sun God, K'inich Ahau, is depicted frequently on Maya temples, as on the huge stucco masks found at the Terminal Classic site of Kohunlich.

© Aguilardo/Wikimedia Commons/CC BY-SA 3.0.

Aztec Religion

- Because the Aztec were at their height when the Spanish made contact with the New World, archaeologists have more information about the Aztec gods than those of any other Mesoamerican culture. More than 200 gods were recorded in the chronicles, identifying their domains and the ritual offerings they received. However, the information is at times as confusing as it is detailed.

- In some ways, Aztec religion is different than all other Mesoamerican religions. Ancestor worship, so core to Maya religion, was apparently not an Aztec practice. Most dead souls went downward, to Mictlan, which had nine levels. When the souls reached the bottom, they were ruled by Mictlantecuhtli, the Lord of Mictlan.

- Aztec heaven had 13 levels. Warriors who died in battle or sacrifice went there and were privileged to accompany the sun through its daily route. Women who died in childbirth also were permitted to accompany the sun.

Human Sacrifice

- Based on the gods honored in Aztec temples, the following is a short list of the main gods: Quetzalcoatl was a god of wisdom. Tezcatlipoca, which the Aztec say came from the Toltec, had a strong connection to the Maya K'awiil. He has a mirror on his right foot, just like the snake of K'awiil. Both the snake and the mirror are symbols of viewing into the other world. Huitzilopochtli, the War God, was unique to the Aztecs. Aztec mythology states that he led the people south and drove them to war and domination.

- Chronicles record hundreds of Aztec gods. However, each main god has many aspects. For example, the Wind God, Ehecatl, is actually an aspect of the primary god Quetzalcoatl. Thus, there may not be hundreds of gods but simply a few gods with many aspects.

- Of one point we are sure: Aztec religion was sacrifice-oriented. Human sacrifices were needed almost daily. As the Aztec dominated their neighbors, the practice of human sacrifice spread everywhere. By the time Cortes arrived, it was ubiquitous. Human sacrifices appalled the Spanish, and they did everything they could to annihilate the religion. This is one of the reasons we know so little about Mesoamerican religions today.

Suggested Reading

Carrasco, *Quetzalcoatl and the Irony of the Empire.*

Duran, *Book of the Gods and Rites and the Ancient Calendar.*

Miller and Taube, *The Gods and Symbols of Ancient Mexico and the Maya.*

Schele and Miller, *Blood of Kings.*

1. Why do you think the Classic Maya used ancestor worship to contact the gods? Why didn't they do it directly?

2. Is it more likely that Mesoamerican religion sprouted from one culture, such as the Olmec, or from multiple locations in the wider region?

3. Why didn't the pantheons of Mesoamerica have a clear king of the gods, as other ancient religions did?

Mesoamerican Religion
Lecture 32—Transcript

Understanding Mesoamerican religions and the gods they worshipped is not an easy task. Aside from the multiple cultures and substantial time depth, there are different layers of Mesoamerican religious beliefs. Those layers interconnect with each other in ways that create one of the most complex and poorly understood religions in our world.

In terms of deities, all Mesoamerican cultures are polytheistic. That's a belief in multiple gods, like a pantheon. That's opposed to monotheism, which is only one God. Polytheism is actually the more common pattern in the world. Monotheisms, like Christianity, are actually in the minority, not by population, but by religion type in the world.

But there's also ancestor worship, the veneration of our deceased ancestors. It's done in shrines, and they give offerings. But it's more than that. It's actually contact with their spirits. Ancestors come back down to Earth, and they assist their descendants with knowledge.

In many parts of the world, often before a belief in the gods, there was animism. That's the belief that all things have a living spirit, not just humans, but plants and animals and rivers and mountains and rocks, et cetera. This also seems to be present in Mesoamerica, right alongside a belief in deities and ancestors.

Contact with the supernatural world, sometimes called the other world, is done through yet another aspect of religion, and that's shamanism. That's the ability to travel by dream or trance into the land of the dead and the supernatural. It's also the ability to see and speak to spirits on the earthly plane. In many cultures, shamans have an animal spirit. It's their counterpart in the spirit world. Sometimes, they go to the spirit world and it guides them. Sometimes, they see it on Earth, and it guides them to places or tells them things. And other times, they actually channel that animal spirit, turning into that animal on Earth.

Shamanism is actually all over the world, not just Mesoamerica. It's called different things in different places. American Indians called it medicine men. They're called witch doctors in Africa. In Europe, we call them wizards or sorcerers. The term *shaman* actually comes from Siberia, where they also have the same sort of characters in religion.

A final element of Mesoamerican religions is time and ritual calendars. On one level, it's just a ritual schedule. But, to them, it's more than that. Individual days can actually have spirits and be living beings. The days themselves are sometimes prayed to. It's like animism. They consider them a force of nature.

So, we have all these different religious systems working together in Mesoamerica. We have deity worship, we have ancestor worship, we have animism, we have shamanism, and we have time worship. All of these exist in other places in the world in one form or another. But in Mesoamerica, they all occur together, and that's unique. Of course, it didn't always start out that way in Mesoamerica; it developed and evolved over time.

In order to better understand the evolution of religion in Mesoamerica, let's review the major time periods through time. We'll start out with Mesoamerica's first great civilization, the Olmec. Now, the Olmec give us our first public art in the form of massive stone sculptures. But when we look at those sculptures, gods and spirits are hard to find within the messages. Most of them are depicting what seem to be clearly men, and those men seem to be of political and perhaps religious power. One of the things that's always interested me in Olmec art is the striking absence of violence; in those early depictions of men performing activities, you almost never, ever see anyone in an act of violence.

Now, looking at Olmec shamanism, I think that's our main display of religion in their art. We clearly see humans transforming into jaguars, and that is clearly shamanism. From all over the world, it's a commonality that when we see ancient art showing people transforming, that's got to be part of a shamanic complex.

In the Olmec area, there's an interesting focus on babies transforming. There are adults, as well, transforming, but mostly babies. I think, at least in my theory, that that focus on babies is telling us further that shamanism isn't only a power, but it's an inherited power. When they're showing babies transforming, they're telling us this is an innate power that this thing was born with. It didn't develop it. A shaman's main job is to contact the supernatural. But in the case of the Olmec, who exactly are they contacting? Well, I would argue they're contacting their ancestors, perhaps the supernatural world. And I base that on later Maya depictions that we can interpret more clearly.

Now, that frequently happens in studies of Mesoamerican religions. Sometimes we run into art that's just inscrutable. And we can either say, "Well, I give up," or we can look for next-step examples that try to inform us of things that look confusing in their own contexts. So, in this case, we have later religions that can inform us about earlier ones. The Olmec show themselves frequently emerging from caves, and we see figures floating above them. And those are very similar to later Maya ancestor worship scenes.

The Olmec have these frequent altar-thrown stones; it's a very common theme within Olmec sculpture. On the front of these, almost always there's a man emerging from a cave. In some examples, there's a rope leading out of that cave, and it connects to the sides. And on the sides, there are human figures that are protecting babies. Those babies are in the process of transforming into jaguars. Especially, La Venta Altar 5 shows this sort of imagery. In that one, the man is actually emerging with another one of these jaguar babies. The message is telling us that the ancestors are living in the underworld, in caves, and that they come out to communicate with us. They're connecting to their descendants and protecting them.

La Venta Stela 2 shows floating spirits around who's obviously an elite person. They're almost certainly his ancestors. The elite is holding a baton in front of him, and all of the floating figures around him are holding that same baton. I think the message is that they are the same. There's a sameness depicted there. The fact that they're floating in the air is very important, too. This tells us that they are coming back from an ethereal place back to the Earth. Those are the core elements of ancestor worship.

Humans are the main themes of Olmec art, but they're not the only depictions there. Sometimes, we do get animals or abstract monsters. And some people interpret those as the Olmec gods. I myself am not completely sure of that. I think they might also be general forces of nature, things that we see in more animism-like religions. The Olmec dragon is one of those. It's a giant, crocodilian creature. The Maya have a correlate creature that we call the Earth monster. The Maya tell us a lot more about who that thing is, and they don't describe it as a god. It's more of a force of nature.

The Maya also have another creature that we call the celestial monster; we have an Earth monster, and we have a sky monster, called the celestial monster. That one is a combination of reptile and bird elements. The Olmec have something that we call the bird monster, and it's just like that. Some people think it's a god, but I tend to think it's a force of nature, not particularly a god. There seem to be elements of later gods, too. But it's really hard to say with confidence. Again, myself, I can't be completely confident those are gods. We see things like corn imagery, corn sprouting from the headdress of someone who's in the process of jaguar transformation. Is that the corn god? Well, it might be related, but it's hard to say. We also see things like feathered serpents. But, I have to ask, is every snake body with feathers the god Quetzalcoatl? There's a lot of rain and water imagery, too. Is every being associated that a rain god?

Personally, I tend to see these Olmec depictions as elements of their natural, animate world. I see Olmec religion working like this. Number one, Olmec shamans connect to their ancestors. And then, step two, the ancestors commune with the forces of nature, like they were liaisons to the people. So in my opinion, the concept of gods first develops in the next culture, especially the Maya.

As the Olmec fade and the Maya rise in the mountains to the south, we start seeing two new elements of Mesoamerican religion take shape, namely, the clear appearance of deities and the development of a sacred calendar. The revolution can best be seen at Izapa. It's in southwest Chiapas, on the Guatemalan border. We've discussed it in previous lectures. There, we have many, many carved stelae with images from the story of the *Popol Vuh*. That's where we get our first gods on stone, as part of their creation story.

There we see multiple references to the hero twins. We also see death gods that are the people they interact with in the story, clearly represented. Still, I think these elements are entwined with the concepts of ancestor worship and shamanism. The twins' journey down into the underworld is a metaphor for a human's ability to pass back and forth between the worlds.

The *Popol Vuh* has gods in it. And so by proxy, so did Izapa. The twins' father actually becomes the maize god at the end of the story. And he is almost very clearly depicted on Stela 67 there. There are other Maya gods shown at Izapa, too, ones not mentioned in the *Popol Vuh*. Stela 1 almost certainly depicts an early version of the rain god. His name's Chac, and he becomes a core member of the Maya pantheon. Stela 3 shows us Kahuil. He's a god of shamanic magic, and he's especially connected to royal families. This one, again, doesn't exactly look like Kahuil later but he has his most diagnostic characteristic, which is that his right foot is turning into a snake. Each of those gods become a prominent god in the Classic-period cities. That's one of the reasons we identify them, who they are in Izapa, because we know who they are later.

As Izapa is celebrating the *Popol Vuh*, other early Maya cities are celebrating the creation of a new calendar, that calendar being the famous Maya Long Count. Chiapa de Corzo, not that far from Izapa, writes a date at 36 B.C.. And that stela has nothing but that date on it; it's celebrating a date. It's historical, yes. But it's in a religious context. It itself is religious. By the Classic Period, all stelae have dates. In fact, stelae have mostly dates in their inscriptions. That's why Eric Thompson, way back when, called the Maya esoteric time worshipers.

But there's a key connection here. And it goes all the way back to the Preclassic. The Long Count and the *Popol Vuh* emerge in Maya art about the same time. And that's no coincidence. The start of the Long Count is linked to the fourth creation and the *Popol Vuh*. That was always hinted at, but then it was proved when we translated the stelae at the site of Quirigua that talked about that moment of creation and linked 3114 B.C. to the deeds of the hero twins when they brought their father up into the sky.

Classic Maya monuments speak of gods more clearly than ever before. Still, we always see them connected to ancestor worship. Now, most Maya souls went down, into Xibalba. But royal, magic souls eventually went up, into the world of the gods. That put them in a position to be liaisons between the gods and the humans on Earth. Humans down on Earth, only their blood descendants, could do bloodletting ceremonies to conjure the contact to their ancestors and bring them down to speak to the living and return with messages and praise.

Classic Maya cities also have another religious concept that they publicly revere, something much more akin to the Olmec animism. That Earth monster I spoke about, they put his face on masks all over temples, especially in the Preclassic Period, and they believed that Earth is a living force. You can talk to modern Maya today that say the same thing. And caves are the Earth's symbolic mouth. A *witz* is a mountain, and mountains are also living forces. The ancient Maya called their pyramids *tuun witz*, "stone mountains." They were making effigies to honor the spirits of the mountains.

So, by Classic Maya times, we have a very complex religious system. We have shamanism and animism and ancestor worship and sacred cycles of time. All of those are weaved together under a pantheon of gods. But who were these gods? Let's talk about that next.

There are a number of Maya gods, but only the major ones are mentioned or depicted on stone monuments. More appear in the contexts of painted ceramics and in the codices. But even with those, it's notable that there's not a clear ruler of the gods. Like the Maya city-states themselves, they share power, each with their own independent realm.

Of the gods on the monuments, Kahuil is the most commonly seen. He's humanoid, but he has an odd monster face; it's not really like any animal I can place. He has a long, beak-like nose. But he also has reptilian features. And of course, his most diagnostic trait, as I said, is his right foot is turning into a snake. He's always associated with rulers. Rulers are shown on monuments carrying staffs with Kahuil on top. And sometimes they're holding tiny Kahuil statues. There are many depictions of him at Palenque, along with kings. And a beautiful set of Kahuil statues, very small and green, were found in a Tikal tomb. He's the god of shamanic magic, and he's connected to conjuring the ancestors.

Now, Kahuil had a different name in the post-Classic. He becomes Itzamna, and *itz* means "magical stuff." He's very frequently depicted in the few codices we have. His name, some scholars say, is connected to the name Itzamna; that's the Post-Classic name for the bird Seven-Macaw out of the *Popol Vuh*. And that may explain how why sometimes he's shown with bird features, as well. But that's still a debate. And I'm personally not sure if there's a true connection there. Honestly, it confuses me. I'm not sure how a bad guy out of the *Popol Vuh* turns into a good, major god of their pantheon. I'm not sure we have the story right there, but a lot of scholars believe there's a connection.

Chac is another monster-faced god. He's green, like Kahuil. And he has an upturned nose. He's the rain god, and he's very, very important to farming. He's often involved in rituals or sometimes even kings' names. In image, he holds a stone ax, and he uses that ax to crack the clouds and let the rain out. The water pours out, and as he hits it, that's a thunder clap.

Equally important to farmers was the maize god, Hunal Ye. He's always seen as a young man, And his head is often topped with corn. He's not often depicted on stelae. But, rulers wear his jade lattice skirt often. The rulers are putting themselves in the guise of the maize god. They're saying, I am the embodiment of the thing that gives you sustenance. And I am also your father, as he was the father of the twins.

One other god literally comes to light during the Maya Classic Period, and that's the sun god, K'inich Ahau, the sun-faced lord. He's depicted all over temples, like the huge stucco masks we talked about in the Terminal Classic site of Kohunlich. His features are goggle eyes, like sunglasses, and he has a single pointy tooth. And oftentimes, he has three dots on his cheek. The sun god mask actually begins way back in the Preclassic. But by the Classic Period, he's all over the art. I worked for years at the site of Palenque, and I was part of the excavations at the cross group.

All over the temples of the cross group, we found incense burners, hundreds of them, and they had these huge stands. And on those stands were almost always the face of the sun god. In the late Classic, his name actually becomes a title of kings. Kings at Palenque have a title K'inich Ahau, sun-faced lord. Again, he's connected to farming. This time, he's connected to astronomy, too. It's the cycles of the seasons, when to plant. Watching the Sun is essential to farmers.

So, from an Olmec foundation of animism and ancestor worship, a pantheon of Maya gods emerged. Now, why don't I believe there are Olmec gods? Well, it's because other Mesoamerican cultures also developed gods in the Classic Period. But theirs, while related, were different than the Maya.

As we've discussed in previous lectures, the Maya were not the only civilization flourishing in Mesoamerica during the Classic Period. The Classic Period superpower, Teotihuacan, had a religious tradition and a pantheon of gods very distinct from the Maya. Teotihuacan's gods were very different, so much so, it surprises me. You know, they really weren't that far from the Maya area. And they seemingly shared the same sort of Olmec influence as their beginnings. But in terms of religion, they must have had some sort of other influence, too. Perhaps, it was from the poorly understood basin of Mexico origins, that Tlatilco culture that the urban sprawl of Mexico City wiped out before we could properly study it.

We see essentially three main gods at Teotihuacan. We see Tlaloc, the rain god. We see the great goddess, who's kind of a Mother Earth. And we see Quetzalcoatl, the feathered serpent. There were other gods present, but they were much less prominent. For example, an old fire god, we found a statue of him up on top of the Pyramid of the Sun. Tlaloc is the rain god. He's very much like Maya Chac. But he's different in look and association. He has goggle eyes and fangs, and his mouth curls at the end, a little bit like a handlebar mustache. He's associated with the rain, but he's also associated with warfare and conquest.

As we've discussed, Teotihuacan dominated Mesoamerica for centuries, and they did so with the tip of their sword, with warriors. A Venus-Tlaloc cult of warriors was their sword. Tlaloc and Venus obviously were the emblems of those warriors. So the face of Tlaloc in places that were dominated by Teotihuacan was the symbol of their military prowess and probably the god who gave it to them. Then we have Quetzalcoatl, a giant snake with long, green feathers. By the Post-Classic, he's everywhere. He's at Cholula, at Xochicalco, even Chichen Itza. At Teotihuacan, we see our first temple of Quetzalcoatl; that's the first known temple really dedicated to him.

Scholars argue he's earlier, from the south. And there are indeed hints of Quetzalcoatl all the way back to Olmec art. There are snakes with feathers in Classic Maya art. But it's so prominent at Teotihuacan. I do see the clues from the other cultures, but you really have to argue their presence there. That's not the case in Teotihuacan. So to me, I argue that he first really evolved as a god there, at Teotihuacan.

Third, we have the great goddess. She's clearly a woman; she wears a huipil. And that's kind of rare. We don't have many women in any of the Mesoamerican pantheons. She's depicted on many murals in Teotihuacan. She's obviously a god of fertility. She's shown in a few images next to something we believe to be Sustenance Mountain, out of their origin myth. That same myth, we see in Cholula and El Tajin. Strangely, though, the great goddess never goes beyond the walls of Teotihuacan. I've never seen her in any other context, and she doesn't make her way into any future pantheons.

When Teotihuacan falls, new cities emerge. And Quetzalcoatl and Tlaloc persist in the public art. Toltec ideas rule Mesoamerica for centuries, honoring both of those deities. Then it all gives way to Mesoamerica's last great civilization, the Aztec. Because they were in full swing at contact, we have more information about the Aztec gods than for any other Mesoamerican culture. Over 200 gods were recorded in the chronicles, what their domains were and the ritual offerings they received. However, the information is at times as confusing as it is detailed.

In some ways, Aztec religion is different than all the other Mesoamerican religions. But then, in other regards, there's a lot of overlap. And that makes sense, considering their origins. They're actually a people from the north looking to fit in with and relate to southern traditions. Ancestor worship, so core to Maya religion, was apparently not an Aztec practice. Their dead souls could go up or down. Most of them went down, to a place called Mictlan.

There were nine levels of Mictlan. And it was a very perilous journey for a soul. They had trials at each one of those levels to get to the bottom. They had to cross rivers, they had to run from jaguars, sometimes there was lava. When they got to the bottom, they were ruled by a person called Mictlantecuhtli. He's the Lord of Mictlan. There are many other underworld gods that live there, too, but he's the lord.

Aztec heaven had 13 different levels. Warriors who died in battle or sacrifice got to go up there and accompany the Sun through its daily route. Women who died in childbirth also got to accompany the Sun. Drowning victims went to a special place called Tlalocan. It was a paradise. But none of these souls ever came back. The Maya used their ancestors as liaisons to the gods. But apparently, the Aztecs implored them directly.

Based on the gods that Aztec temples were dedicated to, there's a short list of a few main gods. Quetzalcoatl is there; he's a god of wisdom. Another is named Tezcatlipoca. Aztecs say he came from the Toltecs. He has a strong connection to Maya's Kahuil, because if you look at him, he's got a mirror on his right foot, just like the snake of Kahuil. Both of them are symbols of viewing into the other world.

The Templo Mayor has two main temples on top, one to Tlaloc with roots in Teotihuacan, and the other one is Huitzilopochtli, the war god; he's the hummingbird on the left is the translation. This is a new god, unique to the Aztecs. They say that it was him that led them south and him that drove them to war and domination.

Chronicles record hundreds of gods, to hunting, to weaving, flowers, mage. But there's a concept of aspects of different gods that may be the root of our misunderstanding. Each god has many aspects, for example, there's a god called Ehecatl, the wind god. But he's actually an aspect of the primary god Quetzalcoatl. So, in my opinion, we probably actually have many less than those hundreds of gods. It's a few gods with many different aspects. And this is a confusion that perhaps we're never going to be able to unravel.

One thing we do know for sure, Aztec religion was sacrifice-oriented. Almost daily human sacrifices were needed. As they dominated their neighbors, the practice of human sacrifice spread everywhere. By the time Cortes arrived, it was everywhere he traveled. Those sacrifices appalled the Spanish. It painted a bloody face on all of the native religions, and it was a validation for stomping them out. They had to convert them to Christianity. It was a priority. But at the same time, it was one of the reasons that we know so little about Mesoamerican religions today.

As I've said, we know the most about Aztec religion. A priest named Sahagun recorded 12 volumes of information, virtually all aspects of Aztec life. In our next lecture, let's start talking about the Aztecs by discussing what Sahagun and others recorded about their origins and how they arrived to the Valley of Mexico.

Aztec Origins—Arrival and Rise of the Mexica
Lecture 33

At the time of Spanish contact, the Aztec were the most powerful civilization in all of North America. The Aztec Empire was centered in the Valley of Mexico. The early Tlatilco culture had flourished there, but starting about 1427, it was the Aztec's turn to dominate. Tenochtitlan, the Aztec capital, was a magnificent city situated in the middle of a lake. At its peak, it had at least 200,000 people. The Spanish called it the "Venice of the New World." In this lecture, we'll study the history of the Aztec from their beginnings in Aztlan to the north, describe Aztec daily life and warrior culture, and chart Aztec domination of the Valley of Mexico.

The Aztec World

- The Aztec Empire was not an empire in the traditional sense—it was more like a massive collection system for tribute. Other world powers, such as the Roman, Inca, or British empires, reshaped the world in their image. They put their stamp on architecture, politics, religion, and language. They imposed their culture directly on others. The Aztec required tribute but not a change in culture.

- At the time of European contact, the Aztec area of domination was growing quickly. They controlled most of Central Mexico from coast to coast, and their language, Nahuatl, spread widely throughout Central Mexico. The Nahuatl language is not Mexican; linguistically, it is an Uto-Aztecan language from the southwestern United States.

- The Aztec warrior class was huge. All commoner boys were trained to be warriors. They defended the capital, and they were quickly dispatched if other cultures did not provide their proper tribute. There were two classes of warriors: eagles and jaguars.

- Aztec wealth was based on a commercial economy. Merchants called *pochteca* traveled to source exotic goods. Common folk traded in the market on a daily basis; 60,000 people were recorded in Tenochtitlan's market every day. Warriors protected the transport of tribute. It was an extremely orderly system.

- Aztec elites were statesmen. Well-mannered and well-spoken, they were lovers of art and literature. Poems and songs were exalted in Aztec society. It was a society that aspired to higher ideals. The Aztec envisioned themselves as having a Toltec heritage. History knows the Aztec as brutal; however, beauty and blood went hand in hand. That was the Aztec world from the mid-1300s up until contact in 1519.

Aztec Origins in Aztlan

- The Aztec did not start out in the Valley of Mexico; they were foreigners who migrated there. Although they were not immediately welcome to the area, the Aztec eventually went from interlopers to overlords of the region.

- Accounts of Aztec origins vary, but all agree that the Aztec came from a place called Aztlan to the north. Chances are that the original Aztlan was actually somewhere near the American Southwest.

- An important historical side note is that a man named Tlacaelel, the brother of Moctezuma I, completely rewrote Aztec history. He ordered every history book in the region burned, and in the mid-1400s, he recast the story of Aztec origins, probably into a new, more complimentary story.

- *Aztlan* means "Place of Herons" and was depicted as an island on a lake—as was Tenochtitlan. The mythological message seems to be that the gods wanted the Aztec to re-create Aztlan in the Valley of Mexico. The name *Aztec* comes from the word *Aztlan*. *Aztecatl* means "person from Aztlan."

- However, the Aztec actually referred to themselves as Mexica, which is the origin of the name of the country Mexico. The name *Aztec* in the literature was a modern invention from Alexander von Humboldt. He first used it in 1810 to distinguish the ancient Aztec from their modern descendants, the Nahuatl people.

- Aztec legends speak of a location before Aztlan—a mythic place of human origins called Chicomoztoc, the "Place of 7 Caves." All Nahuatl speakers were supposed to have come from those caves. The seven groups from those caves are the original groups in the Valley of Mexico.

Settlement at Coatepec

- Some speculate that the Aztec were driven out of Aztlan. Other accounts note that they were forced to leave because of a drought. Climate studies support the timing of the exodus. There was a huge drought in the southwestern United States from about 1100 to about 1300; the Aztec report that they left about 1200. Archaeology sees mass migrations in the American Southwest at the same time.

- All accounts agree that the Aztec left Aztlan and traveled south, becoming nomadic wanderers. The chronicles name the year 1 Flint as the beginning of their journey. Given that 1 Flint is a day in a 52-year cycle, it is unclear which 52-year cycle is meant. The year 1272 seems to make the most sense.

- The Aztec stopped many times along their way and briefly settled in certain places. Legend has it that the Aztec stopped for a time at a place called Coatepec, or Snake Mountain. Coatepec is another name for Sustenance Mountain—the mythic place of origin. For the Aztec, however, Coatepec took on an extra significance: It was also the birthplace of Huitzilopochtli, the Aztec god of the sun and war.

- Legends say that the Aztec were divided; some wanted to stay in Coatepec, but the priests of Huitzilopochtli said that they had to move on. The crisis came to a head during a night raid, and all those who wanted to stay were killed; the rest of the Aztec moved on. Somewhere around 1300, the Aztec arrived at Lake Texcoco.

Mercenaries for the Culhuacan

- When the Aztec arrived in the Valley of Mexico, the valley was already full of people—descendants of the highly cultured Toltec. The Aztec were outnumbered, outranked, and outclassed. Two groups in the valley were larger than the rest: the Tepanec of Azcapotzalco, who held the northwest shore of Lake Texcoco, and the Culhuacan, who controlled the area south of the lake. The Tepanec allowed the Aztec to settle in Chapultepec, or Grasshopper Hill.

- The city of Azcapotzalco was actually part of Teotihuacan's kingdom; when Teotihuacan fell, it became part of the Toltec Empire. When the Toltec fell around 1200, the Tepanec rose to power in the Valley of Mexico. In less than a year, however, the Tepanec forced the Aztec out of Chapultepec because they were savage and uncultured, and—worst of all—they refused to pay proper tribute.

- The Aztec were forced south, into Culhuacan-controlled land. Culhuacan allowed them to settle in a barren area called Tizapan. That was perhaps the turning point in Aztec history. Because the Aztec had nothing to trade, the priests of Huitzilopochtli ordered them to become mercenaries, to use their skills and honor the War God with their deeds. Thus, they fought for Culhuacan.

- As the Aztec honed their skills as warriors, they gained in strength and respect. What's more, they were rewarded and intermarried with the Culhuacan people. Then, they were given a great gift: a king's daughter was presented to the ruler of the Aztec as a wife—officially inviting the Aztec into the royal dynasty. But then the Aztec did something unexpected: They sacrificed her. The Culhuacan people were furious, and in 1323, the Aztec were expelled.

Capital City of Tenochtitlan

- The Aztec ended up settling in Tepanec lands, but this time, they paid their tribute. They became mercenaries for the Tepanec and stirred up a great deal of trouble in the region. The Aztec began to search for the sign indicating where their new capital should be. Then the priests saw the sign: an eagle perched on a cactus on a lake on a tiny island. That is where Huitzilopochtli told them to settle.

- The area was shallow, marshy swampland. Using a local farming technique called *chinampa*, the Aztec created usable land from the marsh. The top surface was fertile for planting, and the lake's waters perpetually replenished the nutrients for the fields. Although the Aztec were still officially in Tepanec territory and paying tribute, little by little, they transferred themselves from the lake shore out to the pieces of land they were creating.

- The Aztec named the place Tenochtitlan. The new city was officially established in 1325. By then, there was enough land to live on. And the city grew larger. The capital was easily defensible, and the people could live there autonomously because, along with the land they built, they could create *chinampas* that supplied them their food. Through this method, the Aztec population grew.

- Although their leaders were statesmen, not savages, the Aztec still, at heart, were warriors. They grew their army so large that it began to rival their neighbors' forces. A hundred years passed in this way.

- With the Aztec as their mercenaries, the Tepanec widely expanded their territory. The Tepanec controlled the entire valley and started to control areas beyond the valley. The other cities in the valley that were once Tepanec allies were all now forced to pay tribute. Tepanec dominion increased greatly, but so did Aztec wealth and power.

Birth of the Aztec Empire

- Then, in 1427, the Aztec finally made their move. Itzcoatl, the Aztec ruler at the time, forged an alliance with two smaller local kingdoms, Texcoco and Tlacopan. The three cities, in what was called the Triple Alliance, turned on the Tepanec, and Azcapotzalco was conquered. With the Tepanec gone, the alliance eliminated Culhuacan to the south. The entire valley belonged to the Aztec and their allies.

- The Aztec had gone from a vagabond group of wanderers to the dominant power controlling the entire Valley of Mexico. Itzcoatl took the spoils of war and expanded Tenochtitlan exponentially.

- In 1440, Moctezuma I took the Aztec throne. Moctezuma and his brother Tlacaelel then recast the Aztec public image. All the old history was burned and a new age began. Tenochtitlan became Aztlan reborn. The age of the Aztec Empire had officially begun.

Suggested Reading

Carrasco, *Quetzalcoatl and the Irony of the Empire.*

———, *The Aztecs: A Very Short Introduction.*

Gruzinski, *The Aztecs: Rise and Fall of an Empire.*

Smith, *The Aztecs.*

Stuart, *The Mighty Aztecs.*

Questions to Consider

1. Where do you think the Aztecs came from? Is their migration story fiction or fact?

2. What made the Valley of Mexico such a desirable place to live?

3. Are the Aztecs unique, or did any other ancient civilization migrate into a foreign territory and eventually come to dominate it?

Aztec Origins—Arrival and Rise of the Mexica
Lecture 33—Transcript

At long last, we finally come to the Aztecs, perhaps the most famous and well known of all Mesoamerican cultures. At the time of Spanish contact, they were the most powerful civilization in all of North America. But they didn't start out that way. In this lecture we'll talk about their origins, who they were, and where they came from.

The Aztecs were an empire centered in the Valley of Mexico. It was a highlands valley around Lake Texcoco. The area had been inhabited for thousands of years. The early Tlatilco culture flourished there. But starting at about 1427, it was the Aztecs' turn to dominate. Its capital was a city called Tenochtitlan. It was an amazing city sitting in the middle of the lake. There were causeways leading from the mainland to the city. There were canals with canoe traffic running all through it. At its peak it had at least 200,000 people. The Spanish called it the Venice of the New World.

Today it's underneath Mexico City. The Aztec Empire was not really an empire in the traditional sense. It was more like a massive collection system for tribute. Other world empires acted slightly differently. The Romans, the Inca, even the English Empire, what they did is they went out and they reshaped the world in their image. They put architecture and politics and religion and language; they imposed their culture directly on other cultures. The Aztecs required tribute, but not a change in customs. The old leaders were left in place and most people could continue their own ways. Life continued as separate cultures. But the new thing they had to do was to send trade goods to the Aztec capital. That was a big boom, actually, for the elites, who got a bunch of new connections and accolades. But it was harder work for the commoners, who had to produce more to support the Aztecs.

At European contact, the Aztec area of domination was growing quickly. They controlled most of central Mexico, from coast to coast, and they did make most of those people start speaking their language, Nahuatl. In a few places, they actually rebuilt temples, and they oftentimes occupied places with Aztec warriors. They might have actually grown into a true empire had not the Spanish destructed everything.

Their language was Nahuatl, and it's actually not from Mexico. Linguistically, it comes from the north. It's an Uto-Aztecan language from the southwest of the United States, and it was imposed on most of central Mexico. Today, there are still 1.5 million speakers of Nahuatl in Mexico. Where the speakers live today is an echo of the Aztec Empire's extent.

The Aztec warrior class was huge. All commoner boys were trained to be warriors. They defended the capital, and they were quickly dispatched if other cultures didn't provide their tribute. There were two classes of warriors; there were the Eagle and the Jaguar warriors.

Aztec wealth was based on a commercial economy. Merchants, called *pochteca*, traveled to find exotic things. Common folk traded in the market on a daily basis. Most families were trading goods on a daily basis; 60,000 people were recorded in Tenochtitlan's market every day. Warriors protected the transport of tribute. It was a very, very orderly system. Aztec elites were statesman. They were well-mannered and well-spoken. They always had to be very clean and nicely dressed. They were lovers of art and literature. Poems and songs were exalted in Aztec society. It was a society that aspired to higher ideals. They envisioned themselves as having a Toltec heritage.

History knows the Aztecs as brutal, but there was both beauty and blood; those two went hand in hand. That was the Aztec world from the mid-1300s up to contact in 1519. That was to end, but about how it started? The Aztecs didn't start out in the Valley of Mexico. They were foreigners who migrated there. There were people already there, and the Aztecs were not immediately welcome. It took a few generations, but they eventually went from interlopers to overlords of the region.

The accounts of Aztec origins vary, but they all agree that they came from the north, a place called Aztlan. The question is, is it mythical or real? We still don't have an actual location for Aztlan. If you search the Internet for Aztlan, you'll find the modern Chicano movement in the United States, mostly in the southwest of the United States. That was actually Chicano land before it was the United States. So Aztlan is a national-pride movement. And it's not anti-U.S, it's just pro-Chicano. And in my opinion, it's a perfect name, because chances are the original Aztlan was actually somewhere near the American Southwest.

Archaeologists and historians have various ideas. Some of them say they came just from the northwest Mexico, maybe Nayarit. Others say they came much closer in, just straight north of the Valley of Mexico. Some Aztec calculations seem to say it was only about 150 kilometers north. Cerro Culiacan, near Lake Yuriria, is a place that looks very much like drawings made by the Aztecs of Aztlan. The trouble is that the chronicles contradict each other. It's also important to know that a man named Tlacaelel made a huge revision to history. He was the half-brother of Moctezuma I, and he totally rewrote Aztec history. He ordered that every history book in the region was to be burned, and in the mid-1400s, he recast the story of Aztec origins, probably into a new, more complimentary story.

Aztlan means "Place of Herons." It's envisioned as a white, marshy place. It's depicted as an island on a lake. But, so is Tenochtitlan, their capital. So I suspect that Tlacaelel created a parallel, something that said, we weren't forced into the lake; the gods wanted us to go there and recreate Aztlan in the Valley of Mexico.

The name *Aztec* actually comes from the word *Aztlan. Aztecatl* means a "person from Aztlan." It's a general term for the people of the Valley of Mexico. The Aztecs actually referred to themselves as Mexica, and that's where we get the name of the country, Mexico. I'm going to continue calling them Aztecs, but please note that the real, correct name of that culture is the Mexica; that's what they called themselves.

The name Aztec in the literature was actually a modern invention. It came from Alexander Von Humboldt. He published it first in 1810 to distinguish the ancient Aztecs from their modern descendants, the Nahuatl people. And by the way, while I was researching Humboldt, I found that that man had over a dozen portraits made of himself. What a ham.

Myths speak of a place before Aztlan, a mythic place of human origins. It's called Chicomoztoc. It's the Place of 7 Caves. All Nahuatl speakers were supposed to have come from those caves. There were seven different groups named that came out of those caves, and they're all the original groups in the Valley of Mexico. The Mexica alone stayed up in that area, and they settled nearby Aztlan. The other six groups, after they departed the cave, headed directly south, and they settled in central Mexico. So the Mexica said that they were actually the last ones to arrive down into central Mexico. I suspect this is more of Tlacaelel's propaganda. He was saying, hey, you know, we're late to the party, but we're all family, right?

Is Aztlan real or mythical? Well, I myself am not sure. The priest Diego Duran recorded a story about it. He said that Moctezuma I sent a mission to find Aztlan. Reportedly it did, but then the maps were burned in a siege. But hey, does that mean that they didn't know where it was either? They had only left about a century or so before, not thousands of years. That in and of itself makes me suspicious if Aztlan ever really existed.

Duran wrote that the location sounded like a place in the American Southwest. The myth inspired expeditions to go up to the Southwest and as far as California. Now, I have a theory that Aztlan might be the site of Paquime, a large city near the U.S.-Mexico border. But I'll talk about that more in my lecture that I dedicate to that big site.

So, all sources agree that the Aztecs were foreigners from the north, originating from a place called Aztlan. But if it was such a great place, why did they leave? And what made them choose the already crowded Valley of Mexico? Some say the Aztecs were driven out of Aztlan, that they were mistreated. They were the commoners of the city, and the cruel elites, the Aztec Chicomoztoca, were the people that kicked them out. They decided to leave for a better life, and that they were inspired by visions of a patron God. Huitzilopochtli is the God of War and the God of the Aztecs.

Other accounts say it might have been drought, that there was no rainfall up there, and that they were forced to leave because they couldn't farm. And climatic studies actually do support the timing. There was a huge drought in the southwest of the United States from about 1100 to about 1300 A.D. And the Aztecs say they left about 1200. Archaeology sees mass migrations in the American Southwest at that same time. So it works archaeologically, at least that story. Regardless of why, all accounts agree that they left Aztlan and they traveled south. The chronicles record many stops along the way, and hardships. Some of them say that they traveled for 50 years. Some of them say they traveled up to 200 years. Either way, they became nomadic wanderers.

The chronicles name the year 1 Flint as the beginning of their journey. But again, there's a debate on exactly what year that is. Since 1 Flint is a day in a 52-year cycle, which 52-year cycle were we talking about? Some say it was 1064, but I think that's way too early. Personally, I think 1272 makes more sense. But again, we're not even sure of that 1 Flint date, because Tlacaelel tried to make their arrival earlier because it was a better foundation story.

The Aztec stopped many times along their way. They rested, and sometimes they briefly settled in places. The priests of Huitzilopochtli urged continuing, always. But legends say they stopped for a while at a place called Coatepec, Snake Mountain. If you've been watching this lecture series in order, you should already know the problem with that part. Every culture talks about Coatepec. It's another name for Sustenance Mountain. It's a mythic place of origin. It's the place where first corn showed up and water sprung from a ball court. This really smacks of being more Aztec propaganda.

But for the Aztecs, Coatepec takes on an extra importance in their story. Coatepec is also the birthplace of Huitzilopochtli. He was born in full war gear up on top of that mountain. And his sister and his siblings are trying to attack his mother, so he chops up his sister as they're trying to kill his mother, and he throws her body down the mountain.

Legends say that the Aztecs were really divided. Some of them wanted to stay in Coatepec and just stay there. But the priests of Huitzilopochtli said no, we have to move on. So it came to a head during a night raid, and all of the rebels that wanted to stay were killed. And the rest of the Aztecs moved on to Lake Texcoco. Finally, somewhere around 1300 A.D., the Aztecs arrived to Lake Texcoco. It's a beautiful region, full of cities. They're all Toltec descendants, so they're very cultured. The Aztecs were dirty, uncivilized vagrants, and they weren't welcome.

As I've said, when the Aztecs arrived around 1300 A.D., the Valley of Mexico was already full of people. They were outnumbered, outranked, and outclassed. The Aztecs began their life in the Valley as the lowest of the low. The lake was surrounded by rival cities, and there were more in the wider valley. There was a tenuous alliance between them.

Two groups were larger than the rest, the Tepanecs of Azcapotzalco, who held the northwest shore of Lake Texcoco. The other group was Culhuacan, and they were in the south of the lake. The Tepanecs allowed the Aztecs to settle. At first, they gave them Chapultepec, Grasshopper Hill. Now, that's in Mexico City, and it's their Central Park. Around it are some of the richest homes. Azcapotzalco is also in Mexico City. Now, it's a stop along their subway. Their subway has icons for people who are illiterate, and its icon is a hill with an ant on it.

The city of Azcapotzalco was old. It was actually part of Teotihuacan's kingdom, and when Teotihuacan fell, it became part of the Toltec Empire. When the Toltec fell around 1200, the Tepanec society rose to power in the Valley, and they became the dominant force. All the other cities around also considered themselves of Toltec descendancy, but the Tepanecs were the top of the pile.

In less than a year, the Tepanecs kicked the Aztecs out of Chapultepec. They did so because they were savage, they were uncultured, and worst of all, they refused to pay their proper tribute. But in truth, they had nothing to give. So they were forced south, and they wandered the shore, and they entered Culhuacan's controlled land. Culhuacan accepted them, well, sort of. They gave them this horrible, barren land called Tizapan. It was very hard to farm, and there was very little water. And they say that the Aztecs, during that time, lived off of eating rodents and lizards. But all that time, they prayed to Huitzilopochtli for guidance.

That was perhaps the turning point in Aztec history, at least as they tell the story. They had nothing but to trade themselves. The priests of Huitzilopochtli said that they were to become mercenaries, to use their skills and honor their war god with their deeds. So, they fought for Culhuacan. They did the dirty jobs not for the civilized people, and they honed their skills as warriors, and they made sacrifices to their god. They gained strength and respect.

And they were rewarded. They intermarried with the Culhuacan people. Aztec children learned culture. Twenty years went by, and a new generation of Aztecs emerged. They were no longer uncivilized savages, but they were still following Huitzilopochtli. Then they were given a great gift, the princess. King Achicometl's daughter was given to the ruler of the Aztecs as a wife. That was officially inviting them into the royal dynasty. But then they did something very unexpected. They sacrificed her. They gave her as a precious gift to Huitzilopochtli, and Culhuacan was furious. In 1323, the Aztecs were repelled from their lands, and once again they were forced to wander the lake.

On their forced journey, their high priest had a vision; he saw the place of their new home. He said it would be marked by an eagle on a cactus with a snake in its mouth. That today, is the symbol on Mexico's flag. They didn't find it right then, but they ended up settling back in Tepanec lands. They were smarter this time, and they paid their tribute. They became mercenaries for the Tepanecs now, and they stirred up lots of trouble in the region. All the Valley cities were fighting back and forth, and the Aztecs were in the middle of it, like a hornet's nest stirring up everyone in the area. Once they fought for Culhuacan. Now, they were fighting against them, and this caused strife everywhere. They had settled in Tepanec lands, and they started a search for the sign where their new capital would be.

About two years after Culhuacan had them on the run for sacrificing their princess, the priests saw the sign, the eagle on the cactus. But, it wasn't on land; it was out in the lake on a tiny island. Well, so be it. That's where Huitzilopochtli told them to settle. So they waded out into the lake. It was shallow. It was marshy swampland. And to build their capital, they used a local farming technique, something called *chinampa*. It was a process in which they piled up lake muck. And you'd pile it up, and that's where you'd farm.

For the Aztecs, they took this to a new level. They'd put pole enclosures inside the shallow lake, and then in those pole enclosures, they'd put the muck on the inside to make a much more sturdy, usable piece of land. The top surface, for farming, was very fertile for planting. And it was good because the lake's waters were always replenishing the nutrients for those fields.

So they used this *chinampa* method to make land that they could actually live on, and they slowly expanded the habitable sections. They were still officially in Tepanec territory and they were still paying their tribute. But little by little, they transferred themselves from the lake shore out to these pieces of land they were making.

They named this new place Tenochtitlan. That name probably comes from an Aztec leader back then named Tenoch. Tenochtitlan was officially established in the year 1325. By then, they had enough land where they could live on it. And from there, it grew larger and larger. And it was very practical. It was actually very defensible. It was out there in the middle of the lake. And, they could live out there autonomously, because along with the land they built, they could build *chinampas* that supplied them their food.

Through this method, the Aztec population grew. And the leaders were now not savages, but they were statesmen. But the Aztecs still, at their heart, were warriors. And one of the things they did the most there is they grew their army. And it grew so large that it really began to rival their neighbors.

One hundred years passed like this. And with Aztecs as their mercenaries, the Tepanecs expanded their territory widely. They controlled the entire valley, and, they started to control areas beyond the valley. The other cities in the valley that were once their allies were all now forced to pay tribute. And Tepanec wealth increased greatly. But along with it, so did Aztec wealth and power.

Then, in 1427, the Aztecs finally made their move. Itzcoatl became the Aztec ruler at that time, and he, on the sly, forged an alliance with two smaller local kingdoms, Texcoco and Tlacopan. Together with those two, they suddenly turned on the Tepanecs, and Azcapotzalco was conquered. Their empire and their wealth suddenly transferred to the Aztecs and their allies.

Those three cities became what was called the famous Triple Alliance. The Aztecs couldn't do this all on their own still, so, they partnered with these two other groups. But with the Tepanecs gone, those cultures were next on the list. First, though, they took out Culhuacan to the south, on the end of the lake. With those defeated as well, now the entire valley was theirs.

Itzcoatl needed to co-rule. Texcoco and Tlacopan had great regional support. And even though the Aztecs had made big headway in the area, the other local groups still had a great amount of distrust; they were still considered foreigners. But, the Aztecs had done it. They went from a vagabond group of wanderers to controlling the entire valley. Itzcoatl took the spoils of war, and he expanded Tenochtitlan exponentially. In 1440, Montezuma I took the Aztec throne. Along with him came Tlacaelel. That's when they took the next step. They recast the Aztec public image. All of the old history was burned, and a new age began. Tenochtitlan became Aztlan reborn.

The age of the Aztec empire had officially begun. Ruling over an ever-expanding area, the heart of their empire was the city of Tenochtitlan. For our next lecture, let's take a closer look at why many say it was the most magnificent city ever built in the pre-Columbian new world.

The Aztec Capital of Tenochtitlan
Lecture 34

Tenochtitlan, the Aztec capital, was the most magnificent city in the pre-Columbian New World. It dwarfed every other city not only in Mesoamerica but also in the entire New World. Its amenities and quality of life were unrivaled virtually anywhere on the planet. Built on an island in the middle of Lake Texcoco, Tenochtitlan covered 13.5 square kilometers and housed more than 200,000 people. In this lecture, we will explore the wonders of the Aztec capital, its impressive public works projects and amenities, and its architectural marvels.

Largest City in the New World

- Tenochtitlan was not only the largest city in the New World, but it was created using a unique construction method. The island it sits on was literally created layer by layer, using a farming technique called *chinampa*. It took two years of work to build the city. Little by little, the Aztec people would lash poles together in a pen, then fill up the pens with dirt and mud from the lake. By 1325, the Aztec had enough land to live on and to keep building the city.

- They named the city Tenochtitlan. Some speculate that it was named after Tenoch, the Aztec leader at the time. Others believe that the word *Tenochtitlan* translates to "among stone cactus fruit." The toponym, or name glyph, for Tenochtitlan shows cactuses sitting among stones.

- Tenochtitlan actually comprised two cities. The second part of the city, Tlatelolco, was started about 1358. Although it was Aztec, it was ruled by a Tepanec prince. In 1473, Tenochtitlan officially absorbed Tlatelolco into itself.

- The city had a grid pattern of both canals and streets. Nearly every house, even the poorer ones, had water access. The city did not originally have a grid pattern, however. In 1427, the Aztec redesigned the city to look more like the city of Teotihuacan to the north. According to Aztec mythology, Teotihuacan was where the Aztec gods were located. In fact, the name *Teotihuacan* means "city of the gods" in Nahuatl.

- Tenochtitlan was divided into four zones called *campans*; the ceremonial center was at the heart of those four zones. The *campans* were further divided into a number of *calpullis*—a neighborhood associated with a certain clan. Each *calpulli* had its own temple, school, and marketplace.

- Three long causeways connected Tenochtitlan to the mainland. Islands surrounded the city, where the Aztec grew food and flowers. Aztec farmers also used terraces on the mainland to produce food.

Massive Public Works Projects

- Tenochtitlan's public works were astonishing; they were absolutely massive projects that required not only a well-organized labor force, but also a sophisticated knowledge of engineering. The causeways to the island were about 40 feet wide. Each causeway had multiple drawbridges, used for defense. Gaps in the causeways also had an engineering function: They allowed the lake water to flow in a normal fashion.

- Inside the main causeway were aqueducts. Because the lake was actually brackish water, the Aztec created two wide pipelines of stone and terracotta to carry water from springs on the mainland. Once the aqueduct reached the city, the system fanned out into the neighborhoods. Many structures in the city had running water, used for washing and cleaning. Drinking water came directly from the springs, and it was sold it in the local market. The Aztec may have been the first in Mesoamerica to drink bottled water.

- Another massive hydraulic engineering project was the levee built by the king Nezahualcoyotl in 1453 after a lake flood. The levee, 16 kilometers long, held back the brackish water, and the aqueducts pumped in more spring water. This helped purify the water, and it made the *chinampas* grow even more vibrantly.

- To permit canoe traffic, Nezahualcoyotl had the entire wall built out of wooden poles. Between the poles were rocks and earth. Then, floodgates were built along the length, enabling city planners to open them during times when the lake was low.

An Orderly and Civilized Society

- Tenochtitlan also possessed a significant city infrastructure. Public schooling was offered to all citizens. Each *calpulli* had its own school, called a Telpochcalli, or "house of youth." Elite children went to a school called the Calmecac, whose patron was Quetzalcoatl. These children were taught reading and writing and the rituals and calendar cycles. Children entered at the age of 5 and, at age 15, began the military portion of their training there.

- Teams of public service workers kept the city clean and maintained the public lands. A police force patrolled the city and kept the peace.

- The Aztec were lovers of beauty and art. Poets were remembered for generations, and people could recite their works from memory. Artists were exalted as national treasures. Throughout the city were gardens, statues, and works of art. In the center of the city was the Cuicacalli, or "house of song"—an opera house and a music school for youth.

- The Aztec also had a fondness for flowers and plants. Moctezuma himself had a botanical garden with plants from everywhere in Mesoamerica. Cortes's men were amazed by the city zoo. It had two vast sections. The first was devoted purely to birds. A second, larger section held mammals, reptiles, and more exotic birds, such as quetzals. Europe had no zoos at that time. Tenochtitlan also maintained an aquarium, with 10 saltwater ponds and 10 freshwater ponds.

- The Aztec were archaeologists themselves and had a museum of ancient cultures, filled with artifacts. The museum held objects from Teotihuacan, Tula, and the Olmec.

Templo Mayor and Human Sacrifice

- The most impressive sight of Tenochtitlan was undoubtedly its downtown, with the Templo Mayor rising from it like a modern-day skyscraper. The very center of Tenochtitlan was a walled precinct, 300 by 300 meters. Today, it is Mexico City's *zocalo*, or main plaza.

- The largest building within the enclosure was the Templo Mayor. It had one base, but there were two staircases leading up, and on top were two temples. The red temple was dedicated to Huitzilopochtli; the blue temple was dedicated to Tlaloc. Daily sacrifices were made at the top of Templo Mayor.

- To the Aztec, the Templo Mayor was actually a symbolic model of Coatepec, Huizilopochtli's birthplace. Anywhere from 10,000 to as

© Fuse/iStock/Thinkstock.

According to Cortes, the tzompantli, or skull rack, in front of the Templo Mayor held more skulls than could be counted.

many as 80,000 people were sacrificed in the inauguration of the seventh phase of the Templo Mayor. Reports note that for three days, priests were ankle deep in blood. Proof of the many sacrifices was the skull rack, or *tzompantli*, in front of the Templo Mayor.

- Directly in front of the Templo Mayor was the Temple of Quetzalcoatl. Opposite the Temple of Quetzalcoatl was the ball court, a huge, lavish arena. To the right and left of the Templo Mayor stood the houses of the warriors. The eagles were housed to the left and the jaguars, to the right. They brought the sacrifices from war and were honored as the Aztec power foundation.

- Another great temple within the compound was the Temple of Tezcatlipoca. Tezcatlipoca means "Smoking Mirror," and he is depicted with a mirror on his right foot. Tezcatlipoca, the god of magic and the night, was part of Toltec mythology. And he, like the other gods, demanded many sacrifices. Almost the entire precinct was dedicated to sacrifice.

Palace of Moctezuma

- In stark contrast to the central precinct—the location for the practice of human sacrifice and the glorification of war—was the Palace of Moctezuma. The two areas together demonstrate that both beauty and savagery coexisted in the Aztec world.

- Moctezuma's palace had hundreds of rooms. On the second story were the lodgings for visiting nobles or ambassadors; each room had its own private bath. There were hundreds more rooms just for the palace staff. This was a place where Moctezuma's generosity was displayed.

- The bottom floor held meeting halls and tribute chambers, piled with the riches of tribute. The ceilings had beautifully carved cedar beams; on the walls were tapestries and murals. Today, in the same spot, stands the Palacio Nacional.

- The Palace of Moctezuma had a massive dining hall, and there was a feast almost every day. There were 300 plates just on Moctezuma's table alone. Women washed his hands after he touched food, and in front of him were dwarves, jesters, and singers playing for his entertainment.

Aztec Capitalism

- Commerce was at the heart of everyday life in Tenochtitlan. Every *calpulli* had its own market, and trade was the center of social life. Cortes's men toured the main market of Tlatelolco and estimated that 60,000 people were trading there.

- Every imaginable item was sold. There were streets just for pottery and others for cloth. Another section was for gold and jewelry, and yet another where slaves were sold. At certain restaurants, one could eat food from anywhere in Mesoamerica.

- The government did not control the market; that was the responsibility of the powerful *pochteca* traders. The *pochteca* forged far-flung trade arrangements and presided over the market. The market was a free-trade zone—a kind of Aztec capitalism.

The Sack of Tenochtitlan

- Imagine Tenochtitlan, a magnificent city of more than 200,000 people living in prosperity, enjoying economic opportunities, and surrounded in beauty. Then, imagine the entire city on fire, the people fleeing in horror. That's what happened in 1521 when Cortes sacked Tenochtitlan.

- When Cortes took the city, many Aztec chose to stay. But he immediately rebuilt it in the image of Spain. The Spanish ripped down the Temple Mayor and used the materials to build the cathedral, using local labor forces. This act sent a powerful message to the Aztec—in the words of Cortes, using the rubble of an old religion to build the temple of a new one.

- Houses were torn down and the materials were used to build Spanish palaces for the conquistadors. It was reported just 10 years later that only 20,000 people were visiting the market in Tenochtitlan every day. Within 100 years, Tenochtitlan was little more than a corpse buried under a Spanish city.

Suggested Reading

Carrasco, *The Aztecs: A Very Short Introduction*.

Diaz, *The Conquest of New Spain*.

Gruzinski, *The Aztecs: Rise and Fall of an Empire*.

Smith, *The Aztecs*.

Stuart, *The Mighty Aztecs*.

Questions to Consider

1. How do you think the Aztecs reconciled their love of the arts and beauty with their gods' needs for brutal human sacrifice?

2. If the Aztec had not been conquered, what do you think the city of Tenochtitlan would be like today?

3. Where else on the planet at A.D. 1500 were so many people enjoying such a high standard of living?

The Aztec Capital of Tenochtitlan
Lecture 34—Transcript

The Aztec capital of Tenochtitlan was an amazing city. It dwarfed every other city, not just in Mesoamerica, but the entire new world. And as we'll discuss in this lecture, its amenities and quality of life were unrivaled virtually anywhere on the planet.

It was a massive city built inside Lake Texcoco. In area it covered 13.5 square kilometers, and on that area lived over 200,000 people. There was absolutely nothing as large as that in Europe at the time. Paris was maybe 150,000 people at the time. If we expand out to the rest of the world, there were a few larger cities. One of them was Cairo, which was probably 400,000 people at the time. And the biggest one was probably Beijing with 650,000 people. But Tenochtitlan certainly was one of the largest in the world, and perhaps even larger than we know. The shame of it is that we never actually found a proper Aztec census. These were estimates.

So, as I said, Tenochtitlan was the largest city in the New World. And it was also a very unique construction in world history. Before it started, the very land it sat on was not there. The Aztecs made it; they used a farming technique to make their land. That technique was called *chinampa*, and it's still being used today around Mexico City.

It took them two years of work to establish the city. Little by little they would lash poles together in a pen and then fill those up with dirt and mud from the lake. That's how they created the islands for the city. By 1325, they had enough to live on and to keep building the city. They named it Tenochtitlan. Some people say that it was named after their leader at the time, Tenoch. Other folks look at that whole word, Tenochtitlan, and they think it translates "among stone cactus fruit." And that idea has some validation, because we have the actual toponym, or name glyph, for Tenochtitlan. And that glyph shows us cactuses sitting among stones. So, either one of them might be right; we're really not sure how it got its name.

And it was actually two cities. The second part of the city was called Tlatelolco, and it started about 1358. It was another island being made separately. It was Aztec, but it was actually ruled by a Tepanec prince. And on that island was the huge marketplace. Both of the islands grew and grew and grew until finally they joined together, and in 1473, Tenochtitlan officially absorbed Tlatelolco into the city itself.

The city had a grid pattern. There were both canals and streets. Most of the traffic in the city went by canoe, but there were also lots of little foot paths. And there were small bridges over each one of the canals, so you could walk or use a canoe. And near every single house, even the poor ones, there was water access.

Now, the city actually did not start out with that grid pattern. It was a little more loose until 1427, when they started redesigning it. At that point, the Aztecs were looking at the city of Teotihuacan to the north of them. And then they mythologized that that's where their gods were, and since Teotihuacan had a grid pattern, they reordered the city to look like Teotihuacan. In fact, the name Teotihuacan means "city of the gods" in Nahuatl. We got that name from the Aztecs, who were emulating it in their own city's design.

The city itself was divided into four zones called *campans*, and the ceremonial center was right at the heart of those four zones. The *campans* were further divided into *calpullis*. Each *calpulli* was a neighborhood that was associated with a certain clan. And each one of those *calpullis* had its own temple, and it had schools for their children, and it had a number of little small markets. In that regard, it kind of reminds me of modern-day London's concept of high streets, where each little neighborhood was kind of a city or a village in and of itself.

Long causeways connected the city to the mainland. There were three of these causeways, a north one, a south one, and a west one, and off those were a few more smaller chutes. There were drawbridges along each one of the causeways so they could open them up and let canoe traffic through. They could also be removed in the case of needing defense of the city.

There were also a number of smaller islands surrounding the city, and those are the places that they put their *chinampa* farms. They were planting food and lots of flowers there. Those were also protected by water. It was a very neat system. They could protect their food supply and themselves by living out on the lake like this. There was also terracing on the mainland as well that fed the Aztec. Because remember, there were 200,000 of them. That was a massive population to feed.

And the Aztec were planners. They built that city up slowly over a 100-year period. During that time, they were living quietly under Tepanec rule. They were paying their tribute, and they slowly made allies around the lake. But then finally, in 1427, they beat the Tepanecs, and that's when some of the most beautiful parts of the city began emerging.

All of the features of Tenochtitlan impress me, but I find none more amazing than the public works they put in place. They completed simply massive projects that took not only well-organized labor forces, but a sophisticated knowledge of engineering. Those causeways were fantastic. Bernal Diaz, a soldier with Cortes, said that they were 10 horses wide; that's about 40 feet. And each of them stretched for kilometers. And they were lined on either side with gardens that were made from the *chinampas*. They were beautiful.

Each causeway also had multiple drawbridges. As I said, they let through canoe traffic, but they were also good for defense; they could pull them up. Of course, they never, ever needed to do that before the Spanish showed up. Those gaps also had an engineering function; they allowed the lake water to flow. If they bottled up the currents of the lake, it would have had ill effects. But being able to open that up and let it through the various causeways allowed the lake's currents to continue in a normal fashion.

Inside the main causeway, dividing it into two different traffic lanes, were the Aztec aqueducts. The lake was actually brackish water, so they created two wide pipelines from springs on the mainland. They made them of stone and terra cotta, and they went all the way to Chapultepec Hill, four kilometers away. And they had two, so that one could be emptied and cleaned while the other one was still functioning.

Once the aqueduct reached the city, the system fanned out into the neighborhoods. Many, many structures in the city had running water. That was providing them washing water and cleaning water. The Aztec were a very clean people, so, they actually only used that water for washing and cleaning. Drinking water came directly from the springs, and they sold it in the local market. Can you believe it? The Aztecs were actually drinking bottled water.

The other huge hydraulic engineering project was the levee of Nezahualcoyotl. He was a brilliant king of Texcoco. He built, in 1453, that huge levee. It was after a lake flood. When he built it, it turned out to be 16 kilometers of walls, and it held back the brackish water of the rest of the lake. From there, they used the aqueducts to pump in more spring water into their part of the lake, and that helped purify the water, and it made their chinampas grow even more vibrantly.

But one of his challenges was, how to still let canoe traffic into their part from the other part of the lake. So, Nezahualcoyotl built this entire wall out of wooden poles. They were parallel to each other, about 30 feet wide, and it was 16 kilometers long. Between the poles, he filled it with rocks and earth. And then he designed floodgates along the length so they could open them up in low times of the lake. They were sturdy enough to close and open and hold back floodwaters if that was necessary.

In addition to these great public works, there was also other significant city infrastructure. There were things like public services. Schools were in every single neighborhood and offered to all citizens. Each *calpulli* had its own school; they were called Telpochcallis, House of Youth. There, they taught basic skills. All boys were taught to fight; even the most common of children were taught to be part of the Army.

Elite children went to another school. It was called the Calmecac, and its patron was Quetzalcoatl. They were taught reading and writing and songs, and they were also taught all the rituals and the calendar cycles. The art of speaking and poetry was a big part of the Calmecac. It was kind of an Aztec charm school. Children entered it at the age of five, and at 15 they began the military portion of their training there.

Not only were the people themselves very clean, so was the city. There were teams of public service workers. There was a whole group of gardeners that were just dedicated to tending public landscapes. There were street sweepers, and there were garbage collectors; there wasn't a speck of trash around the entire city. There was also an entire police force that patrolled the city and kept the peace. It was a truly orderly and civilized place. In addition to these kinds of public works, city work forces, and access to public education, there were even more benefits to living in Tenochtitlan. Some of the most amazing were the public amenities, things rivaling even modern cities today.

The Aztecs were lovers of beauty and art. Songs and poems thrilled them. Poets were remembered for generations for their poems, and people could recite them by memory. Artists were exalted as public treasures. Throughout the city there were gardens, and even those were works of art. Everywhere you walked in the city, you'd see public statues and works of art. Things about famous poets and artists stood alongside famous warriors or kings.

And just like modern cities, there was public theater. In the center of the city there was the Cuicacalli; that was the "house of song." It was really an opera house. It was also a school of music for youth. Certain children that showed a talent for music could gain entry into that school to learn more. They learned how to play drums and flutes and trumpets and gongs. It was also a place where children learned to dance, and dances were performed for the public in that same spot. The Aztec called dancing singing with your feet.

The city, as I said, had gardens everywhere, and Moctezuma himself had a true botanical garden. Within his palace complex was a garden that had plants from everywhere in Mesoamerica. Tropical plants that really shouldn't have been able to live in that highland environment were kept alive by expert gardeners on his staff. Constant care was given to that garden to make sure that nothing died and that it all flowered. If something fell apart, *pochteca* were sent out to get more samples of that kind of plant to replace them in the king's garden. There was a staff of 300 to 500 people just for his gardens. There was a general love of the Aztec in regards to flowers and plants.

Cortes's men were amazed by the city zoo. It had two vast sections. The first was devoted purely to birds. Specifically, they loved birds of prey. There were all manners of them kept in separate aviaries, and they were bred in captivity. That's really not very easy to do. Even modern zoos have a hard time doing that. A second, larger section, held the rest of the animals. There were mammals, reptiles, and more exotic birds. They had Quetzals kept in captivity, and no zoo in the world today actually can do that. I don't know how the Aztecs did it.

The Spanish didn't know the names of the various felines of the New World, so their report said they had many lions and tigers. They also saw for the first time rattlesnakes, and they called those snakes with music in their tails. Europe had no zoos at the time. The idea of a zoo amazed the Spaniards. However, the cat house actually also scared them. It was full of idols, and the cats were often fed parts of sacrificial victims. Diaz actually said upon seeing it that it felt like seeing hell. Not only did they have a zoo, but they also had an aquarium. They had 10 ponds that were salt water and 10 ponds that were fresh water. Diaz noted all kinds of fish within them. There was really no explanation of their construction. I wish we had more written about these aquariums, but they were there.

To me, one of the most exciting features was the city's museum of ancient cultures. They actually had a building full of artifacts, and it was dedicated to displaying their history. They had objects within it from Teotihuacan, from Tula. They even had Olmec objects inside there. The Aztecs were actually archaeologists themselves.

Well, so far we've talked about a lot of amazing aspects of Tenochtitlan. Most of these, however, were not what drew the eye of a first-time visitor to the city. The most impressive sight of the city was undoubtedly its downtown, with the Templo Mayor rising, like a modern day skyscraper from its center. The very center of Tenochtitlan was a walled, enclosed precinct. It was 300 by 300 meters on its sides. Today, it's modern Mexico City's *zocalo*, its main plaza. Back then, there were 78 structures inside. Most of them were temples to various gods. The Aztecs called that complex Tecpan.

The largest building within the enclosure was the Templo Mayor. It was 50, maybe 60 meters tall. It had one base, but there were two staircases leading up, and on top there were two temples. One of them was to Huitzilopochtli, and it was red. The other one was to Tlaloc, and it was blue. Daily sacrifices occurred on top. Parts were ripped out, and people were bent over a stone so they could better get that heart out. The Spanish were invited to watch this, and they were horrified; they said it was evil. They said the Aztec gods were evil, too, and Moctezuma's priests were furious about that. Cortes was told to never say that again.

To the Aztecs, the Templo Mayor was actually a symbolic model of Coatepec. It was built on that very same spot where they saw the eagle on the cactus. Coatepec was Huitzilopochtli's birthplace. It was the place where he first came out of his mother with the weapons in hand. He saved his mother from his bad siblings, and he chopped up his sister and threw her down the temple.

They say anywhere from 10,000 to as much as 80,000 people were sacrificed in the inauguration of the seventh phase of that same temple. Reports say that for three days, priests were ankle deep in blood up on top. Some scholars say that's an exaggeration; they say it was meant to vilify Aztec religion. But, it's a fact that at least thousands of people were sacrificed up there every year. The proof of the many sacrifices was the skull rack, or the *tzompantli*. It was right in front of the Templo Mayor. It was a huge platform with posts and poles, and on those poles were skulls. It held thousands of skulls. Cortes said that there were so many that it was impossible to count.

Directly in front of the Temple Mayor or was the temple of Quetzalcoatl. Opposite the temple of Quetzalcoatl was the ball court; it was a huge arena and lavishly built. The ball court under the mountain next to the skull rack was just like Tula's arrangement, and probably, once again, alluding to the myth of Sustenance Mountain. To the right and left of the temple Mayor stood the houses of the warriors. The Eagles were to the left and the Jaguars to the right. They brought the sacrifices from war, and they were honored as the Aztec power foundation.

The other temple of good size within that compound was the Temple of Tezcatlipoca. His name means "Smoking Mirror," and he has that mirror on his right foot. He was the god of magic and the night. He was part of that Toltec mythology, where he was responsible for kicking Quetzalcoatl off the continent. And he, like the other gods, demanded many sacrifices.

There were many other temples and platforms there. Most of them were devoted to one sacrifice or another. Each god had their own requirements. Sometimes it was children, sometimes it was foreigners, sometimes they needed people who were willing to be sacrificed. Some of the platforms within there were meant for ritual fights so people could watch, mock, or really, real battles. But almost the entire precinct was dedicated to sacrifice. And again, that horrified the Spanish.

In stark contrast to the central precinct of violent sacrifice and the glorification of war was the palace of Montezuma. Standing right next to the center, the two together were a perfect example of how both beauty and savagery existed hand in hand in the Aztec world. Montezuma's palace had hundreds of rooms. There was a second story for lodging, and each of them had their own private bath. They were for visiting nobles or ambassadors. There were hundreds more rooms just for the palace staff. It was a place of formality and good graces. It was a place where Moctezuma's generosity was displayed.

The bottom floor was full of meeting halls and tribute chambers. It was piled with riches of people bringing in their tribute. The ceilings were all cedar beams and beautifully carved, and on the walls there were tapestries and murals. Today, in the same spot, stands the Palacio Nacional. There was a huge dining hall, and there was a feast almost every day. There were 300 plates just on Moctezuma's table alone, and they wore brassieres to keep them warm. There were women who were always washing his hands after every time he touched food, and in front of him there were dwarves and jesters and singers playing for his entertainment. And there were also hundreds of guards and the servants. And they were allowed to eat in the same hall, but only after the king was done.

All of that food came from the city market. More than anything, commerce was at the heart of everyday life Tenochtitlan. Every *calpulli* had their own market, and trade was the center of social life. Tlatelolco had the main market. Cortes's men got a tour of Tlatelolco. It was the largest market they had ever seen. They estimated 60,000 people were there and trading in a very orderly fashion. At that time, all of the city of London was only 40,000 people, so this market was bigger than London; it was unrivaled in the world. Well, maybe Beijing had a larger one.

Every imaginable item was sold there. There was every kind of product, and each one had its own section of the market. There were streets just for pottery, others for cloth. There was a rich section that held gold and jewelry. There was also another section where slaves were sold. And there were always police there to prevent theft. And in the middle of the market were judges who were meant to settle disputes. There were other services, too. You could go in there and you could get your hair cut, or you could get your fortune read. There were doctors there prescribing cures. And, like a modern market, there were restaurants of all kinds. You could get food from anywhere in Mesoamerica at a certain kind of restaurant there.

And there was lots of entertainment; there were always singers and dancers in the market. And there were acrobats; there was one particular kind of juggler where people would lay down on their back and they would juggle huge logs on their feet. There were also Voladores; the Spanish saw those tall poles with people swinging off of them with ropes attached to their legs. It was a place for a family outing.

And the government actually didn't control the market. That was the responsibility of the powerful *pochteca* traders. They were diplomats and warriors. They're the ones who forged those far-flung trade arrangements. And they were the ones that presided over the market. They were the judges.

The market was a free-trade zone. Other cities also had huge markets like this. And the *pochteca* had a self-regulated network. The markets had daily circuits and agreed cooperation. One day would be Tenochtitlan's market day; the next day would be Texcoco's market day. It was a kind of Aztec capitalism that existed.

Imagine, if you will, this magnificent city of over 200,000 people living in prosperity, enjoying economic opportunities, and surrounded in beauty. Then imagine the entire city on fire, the people fleeing in horror. That's what happened in 1521 when Cortes finally sacked Tenochtitlan. When Cortes took the city, many Aztec chose to stay. But he immediately rebuilt it like Spain.

They ripped down the Temple Mayor, and they used those materials to build the cathedral. They used all local labor forces to do it. It was a very powerful message to the Aztec. Cortes said, use the rubble of your old religion to build the temple of your new one. Houses were torn down, and the materials were used to build Spanish palaces for the Conquistadors. Sahagun reported, just 10 years later, that only 20,000 people were inhabiting the market every day. Within 100 years, Tenochtitlan was little more than a corpse buried under a Spanish city.

Echoes of the city remain only in name. Many neighborhoods of Mexico City still retain their original names. When they built the subway in the 1960s, they found remains of the Old City everywhere. Today, you see them in glass cases as you whiz by on the subway. One of the subway stations actually holds one of the old temples. It's the Temple of Ehecatl in the station called Pino Suarez.

There was a big find in the 1970s. They found the Templo Mayor's base under the modern-day *zocalo*. They did five years of excavations, and they uncovered all of its early phases. Now there's a museum on the site. There's a growing collection of city artifacts. Finally, there's a renewed interest in Aztec archaeology. I hope it's not too late to salvage what's left of the city.

It's my hope that as Mexico City's development continues, it will happen with an eye out for what still remains of the ancient Aztec capital. For now, let's devote our next lecture to the city as well, but this time, to the people who lived there.

Life in the Aztec World
Lecture 35

D aily life for an Aztec citizen in Tenochtitlan was steeped in religious ritual, strict codes of behavior, and obligations to the community. In this lecture, we'll examine many different accounts of Aztec life—some of which were witnessed and recorded by soldiers at the point of contact and others that were written later by priests who understood the Aztec people and spoke their language. These accounts serve as our sources for understanding what it was to be Aztec.

Witnesses at the Point of Spanish Contact
- Historians draw on a number of sources to learn about Aztec life. Some accounts were written by soldiers, others by priests, and others by the Aztec themselves. All have different perspectives. Some were written during the period of Spanish contact; others were written much later.

- Hernan Cortes, the captain who defeated Moctezuma and took Tenochtitlan, wrote letters to King Charles V of Spain from 1519 to 1521 recording his experiences with the Aztec. These letters include detailed descriptions of events, people, and places. They are significant because they reflect Aztec life before the Spanish influence.

- After the conquest, Cortes commissioned his biography to be written by Lopez de Gomara. This document inspired other conquest accounts—one in particular was by Bernal Diaz, a soldier under Cortes. Diaz wrote his account years later as a response to Gomara's account, which he called "the lies of Gomara." Diaz was in the Yucatan in 1517 and 1518, and he joined Cortes in 1519. He subsequently wrote *The True History of the Conquest of New Spain* as a great adventure story.

Accounts of Spanish Priests

- Although the accounts of Cortes and Diaz are significant because they come from the moment of contact, the authors were soldiers who did not know the people or understand the language. But the priests who came later learned the language.

- Bernardino de Sahagun was a Franciscan who arrived in Mexico City in 1529. He learned Nahuatl and traveled widely in the region. Sahagun spent 50 years of his life chronicling Aztec life. In the end, he wrote a 12-volume series that today is known as the Florentine Codex. Comprising 2,400 pages with illustrations, the Florentine Codex is like an encyclopedia of everything Aztec.

- Sahagun had respect for the indigenous people and a distinct dislike for the conquistadors. He credited all his sources by name, and he recorded all aspects of life that he could view. He was a scrupulous journalist: He would not include an account in his book until he could independently prove it through three different chroniclers. Some call him the father of American ethnography.

- Diego Duran moved to Mexico as a child in the 1540s; he was a Spaniard who grew up Aztec. Duran wrote three books: *History of the Indies of New Spain*, the *Book of Gods and Rites*, and the *Ancient Calendar*. Duran joined the Dominican order in 1556 and wrote his books to alert his fellow priests to Aztec practices and religion.

Experiences of Slaves

- In Aztec society, at the very bottom of the social hierarchy were the slaves. Some were captured in foreign lands and brought into the city. Others were sentenced to slavery for crimes. Still others actually sold themselves into slavery because of debts. Poor families sometimes sold their children into slavery to support the rest.

- The loss of someone's freedom, though, had to be recorded in official documents and decrees. Slaves could still use money, and they could have wives and children. What's more, their children were born free. Slaves could also be bought specifically to be sacrificed.

Experiences of Commoners

- The vast majority of Aztec people were commoners—farmers, craftspeople, laborers, or warriors on a campaign. Common women did the cleaning, cooking, and weaving, and they traded and bought in the marketplace.

- Aztec commoners lived in simple, one-room houses, made of reeds or adobe, with a hearth inside. A number of houses would be grouped around a central patio. Usually, four to five related families shared a patio.

- Although commoners could not become nobles, they could elevate their status by becoming warriors or priests.

Experiences of the *Pochteca*

- Within the middle class were the *pochteca*, or traveling merchants. The *pochteca* sold exotic trade items in the market. Often, they

Each group of commoner houses had a *temazcal*, or sweat bath, that was central to domestic and social life.

would go on diplomatic missions for the king or act as spies to assess new lands for conquest.

- Trade missions took months and involved teams of *pochteca*, their apprentices, and professional carriers. The carriers and the *pochteca* were also trained warriors and were always armed.

- The profession of *pochteca* was hereditary. The 12 guilds of *pochteca* in Tenochtitlan controlled all the trade routes and acted as judges in the markets. The *pochteca* could become fabulously wealthy—even richer than the nobles.

Experiences of the Nobility

- The nobles made up only 5 percent of society, but they owned everything. Certain capes and jewelry could be worn only by nobles. The children of nobles attended a special school, called the Calmecac. The Calmecac was mainly for government officials— those who would lead the armies or become high priests. The nobles lived in grand homes built of stone with flat roofs and cedar beams.

- Nobles, however, were held to a higher standard; they were expected to be model citizens. Penalties were greater for nobles than for commoners. Nobles planned the feasts and organized labor teams. In times of war, they led the armies.

Experiences of Royalty

- At the top of society was the king, or Tlatoani, the "Speaker." In the Toltec fashion, the king was first and foremost a statesman. He was also the commander in chief. The kingship of the Aztec was not hereditary, however; the king was elected by a group of nobles.

- The Tlatoani had vast privileges and enormous power. He had a huge palace, many wives, and thousands of servants. All the city lands were his property; nobles were granted land by him; and all taxes and laws were his to decide.

- The Tlatoani also had tremendous responsibility. Technically, he was the high priest, and he oversaw the daily sacrifices. He also served as the general of the army. Political relationships with other kings were led by the Tlatoani. He was the father figure and spiritual leader of everyone in Aztec society.

Children and Home Life
- The official name of an Aztec baby was given by the priests. Although nobles were given elaborate names (for example, *Moctezuma* means "Angry Lord"), most commoners were given the day of their birth as their name. If a baby was born on 5 Eagle, that was his name—and his destiny.

- School was mandatory for children. Boys and girls learned basic skills. Boys were trained as warriors, and every Aztec male had to serve in the army. The number of captives he caught in a lifetime was the measure of a man's worth in society.

- Marriages were arranged by the relatives and teachers of children. Men were to marry by the age of 20, but girls were married much earlier, about age 10 or 12. Soothsayers would pick the day for the wedding.

- As adults, women did the weaving, cooked, cleaned, and shopped in the marketplace. Men farmed, built, and fought battles. Some men were artisans, but they were still required to be warriors when needed. All activities were done by order of the calendar. There were good days and bad days for certain activities. No farmer could harvest unless the priest said it was the right day to do so.

- The raising of children was of the utmost importance. Parents were supposed to be focused on the upbringing of their children and act as proper role models. Most of their income was to be spent on their children and to help support their elders. Adults had responsibilities, both to the old and the young.

Yearly Cycle

- As a society, all Aztec participated in the monthly festivals. There were 18 months of 20 days each, then a 5-day month. Each month had its own theme and activities. Some of those festivals were quite picturesque, and others were downright macabre.

- The first day of every month was a feast day. Any day that started with the number 1 was a day that the Aztec would honor all the people of that day sign. For example, if the first day was 1 Crocodile, every person with the name Crocodile in the Aztec capital would be honored.

- The 1st month was March. Called Touch the Bouquets, on this month people went around touching plants, and they offered food to the gods. The goal was to ask for a fruitful year. The 2nd month occurred 20 days later, on March 21, the spring equinox. This month honored the god Xipe Totec, otherwise known as the Flayed One.

- The 8th month, when corn was ripe, was July. During that time, a virgin was sacrificed, along with four men. The 11th month was the Day of Sweeping; everywhere, everything was cleaned: homes, streets, even the rivers and streams.

- The 12th and the 15th months were in honor of Tlacaxipehualiztli. The 12th month was about his birth; when the priests announced it, everyone rejoiced. But the celebration involved severe bloodletting. Everyone in the party would cut themselves many times and rub the blood over themselves. The 13th month was called Great Moss, when the volcanoes were honored, especially Popocatepetl.

- The 18th and final month was Growth. The planting season began then, and the Aztec ate special foods—amaranth leaves and corn. That same month, a boy and a girl were sacrificed to Tlaloc, to ask for rain for the newly planted crops. At the end of the solar year cycle were five extra days. Then, the next year began again with 1 Crocodile, and the festival of the year renewed itself.

Suggested Reading

Carrasco, *The Aztecs: A Very Short Introduction.*

Coe, *America's First Cuisines.*

Duran, *Book of the Gods and Rites and the Ancient Calendar.*

Gruzinski, *The Aztecs: Rise and Fall of an Empire.*

Leon-Portilla, *Fifteen Poets of the Aztec World.*

Smith, *The Aztecs.*

Stuart, *The Mighty Aztecs.*

Questions to Consider

1. How could the Aztecs willingly sacrifice children on an annual basis?

2. What would you do if you were an Aztec born on one of the days considered bad or evil?

3. In balance, could we say there was gender equality in Aztec society?

Life in the Aztec World
Lecture 35—Transcript

Life in the Aztec world was full of traditions, some beautiful, and others quite macabre from the perspective of modern society. Daily life for a citizen in Tenochtitlan was steeped in religious ritual, strict codes of behavior, and obligations to their community. Let's take a look at what it was like to be an Aztec.

To start out, how do we know about Aztec life? Well, there were many chronicles from the contact period. Some of them were written by soldiers, others by priests, and others by literate Aztec people. They were different perspectives, and some of them disagreed with each other. Some of them were made right at contact, and others were made well after the fact.

I'll list my favorite sources here first. First, there's Hernan Cortes himself. He was the captain who defeated Tenochtitlan, and he wrote letters to the King of Spain all along the way. We have a number of letters from 1519 to 1521 chronicling his experience with the Aztecs. They are detailed descriptions of events, and they describe people and places. And they're really important, because life was still fully Aztec at that time; there was almost no Spanish influence in what they did. However, his motivations are suspect. His expedition was actually a mutiny. Cuba's governor had forbidden him to go. And he actually sent a force to try to stop Cortes, but Cortes defeated them. So all of his letters were justifying himself to King Charles V. And he might have exaggerated a number of things. He might have justified the destruction of the Aztec capital by emphasizing Aztec savagery.

After the conquest, Cortes wrote his biography. He actually had a writer named Lopez de Gomara write it. And it inspired other conquest accounts. One in particular was by Bernal Diaz. He was a soldier with Cortes, and he wrote his years and years later as a response to what Gomara had written. He didn't like that account; he specifically called it "the lies of Gomara," and he wanted to counteract them with his own version of events.

Bernal Diaz was born in Spain, and at that time, he was poor and uneducated. But he was on one of the first missions sent to the Yucatan. He was there in

1517 and 1518, and then he joined Cortes in 1519, and he saw every bit of it with his own eyes. After the conquest, he was given certain privileges. He became the governor of Guatemala and Chiapas. So about 30 years after the conquest, he got offended by all these other books, especially the one from Gomara, but others, too. So he wrote *The True History of The Conquest of New Spain*, and he explained the Aztec cities and their people. And he wrote it as a great adventure story; it's one of my favorite accounts of the conquest.

Both of those accounts, though, are important because they were witnessed at the moment of contact. However, remember, they were soldiers. They really didn't take the time to understand the people. And they didn't speak the language. The priests that came later did learn the language, and in my opinion, the best of them was Sahagun.

Bernardino de Sahagun was a Franciscan who arrived to Mexico City in 1529. He learned Nahuatl, and he traveled the region widely. He actually spent 50 years of his life chronicling Aztec life. In the end, he wrote a 12-volume series that together, today, we call the Florentine Codex. It was 2,400 pages with illustrations. It's like an encyclopedia of everything Aztec. And Sahagun had a respect for the indigenous people, and, a distinct dislike for the conquistadors. He credited all of his sources by name, and he recorded all aspects of life that he could view. One of the things I really like about his account is that everything was verified. He wouldn't write it in his book until he could independently prove it through three different chroniclers. So three different people had to tell him the same thing before he put it in his book. Some people call him the father of American ethnography.

My other favorite chronicler is Diego Duran. He moved to Mexico as a child in the 1540s. At the start of his book, he says he got his second teeth in Texcoco, which means his baby teeth fell out then. He was a Spaniard who basically grew up Aztec; all of his playmates were Aztec children. And he wrote three books. One of them was *The History of the Indies of New Spain*. Another one was the *Book of Gods and Rights*, and a third one was the *Ancient Calendar*.

Duran joined the Dominican Order in 1556. And he wrote his books to alert his fellow priests of what was happening; he knew that Aztec religion was still very much alive. He had grown up an Aztec, and people trusted him. So they told him all sorts of things they didn't tell other priests. And he was able to witness and record many, many brutal rituals that were still going on. And in part of his book, he rants at the other priests that they don't know what the Aztecs were doing. The Aztecs were actually holding off doing Saint Day festivals until it was their pagan patron deity's day. So they were having the priests fund their own Aztec rituals. And Duran knew it, but the other priests didn't. It's amazing what was still happening then. Much of Aztec life went on uninterrupted. And thanks to these chronicles, I can now tell you about Aztec life.

Aztec society had many different roles and occupations. But there were two very clear-cut tiers; there were commoners, and there were nobles. Let's talk about the shades of those two broad groups, working up from the lowest to the highest ranks of society. At the very, very bottom were slaves, and there were many. Anyone could actually end up a slave. They were sold in the markets. The owners were obligated to feed and house them. And many of the houses of the nobles had multiple servants who were actually their slaves.

People could become slaves in different ways. Some of them were just captured in foreign lands and brought into the city. Others could be sentenced to slavery for crimes. Some people actually sold themselves into slavery because of debts they owed. Gamblers hit that fate often; they would bet themselves and then lose. Poor families oftentimes sold their children into slavery to support the rest.

The loss of someone's freedom, though, had to be recorded. There were official documents and decrees. Slaves could still have money, and they could have time off. They could also have wives and children of their own. And their children were born free; they weren't slaves. But if you think that wasn't so bad, well, listen to this; they could also be bought specifically to be sacrificed.

The vast majority of people were commoners. They were simple farmers or craftsmen. And most men were tending the land of nobles. They farmed during the rainy season, which was about May to November. And otherwise, they would work as taxation for the state. They'd end up as construction laborers or warriors on a campaign.

Common women stayed home. They did the cleaning and the cooking and the weaving. They also did all the shopping in the market. The market was mostly women buying things. If they made excess textiles, they could actually sell those in the market. There were certain men who were craftsmen who stayed home, too. They'd make pottery, or woodworking, or et cetera. And children stayed at the home learning their parents' trade.

Aztec lived in simple, one-room houses. They were usually made of reed walls or wattle and daub, or sometimes adobe. They'd have a thatched roof and no windows around, and just one doorway. Inside, they'd sleep on reed mat beds, and they'd have a little hearth inside there to keep them warm at night. There'd be a number of these little houses around a central patio, and usually four to five families shared a patio. They were often blood related, so they were part of a larger clan of that neighborhood.

And each house, or at least each group of houses, had a *temazcal*, a sweat bath. This was central to home life. Families gathered inside of their temazcal. Children were actually born inside the temazcals. And this is still common in Mesoamerica today. In fact, when I lived in Palenque, my neighbor Alonso built a sweat bath. And every week, our survey team would go in there and gather together. When I first did it, I thought, it's so horribly hot here; why would I get into a sweat bath? But actually, when you live without air conditioning, going into one of those sweat baths and then coming back out is the coolest you feel the entire week.

House groups were within calpullis, or neighborhoods. They were neighborhoods that were usually owned by a specific noble. And labor within that neighborhood was assigned by that noble. The calpullis also had temples and schools and markets. Some of them even had small ball courts. The noble would always have a larger palace within that calpulli, and he would organize everyone.

Commoners couldn't become nobles. But, they could elevate their status. They could do that by becoming a warrior or a priest. If they did that, they could maybe go live in one of the other city compounds. Maybe they could even become a royal guard and live in the palace. That got them greater respect in the community, but it still did not make them a noble.

There was a kind of middle class, and that was *pochteca*; those where those traveling merchants. They sold exotic trade items in the market. They were the ones that brought all the finery that the nobles bought. And they often served the king. Oftentimes, they would go on missions that were diplomatic, or they were spies looking at new places to conquer. They assessed those new lands for conquest for the king.

Their trade missions took months and months sometimes. There'd be teams of *pochteca* and their apprentices, and they would hire professional carriers to come along and carry all the things they bought or they brought. Those carriers and the *pochteca* were also trained warriors, and they were always armed. *Pochteca* was a hereditary thing. And there were really only 12 guilds of *pochteca* within Tenochtitlan. They were the ones that controlled all the trade routes, and they were also the judges in the markets.

They could become very, very rich. Some of them were even richer than the nobles. All of those quetzal feathers and the cacao made them rich, but they weren't nobles, and they couldn't show their wealth. So typically, they'd return to the city at night. Sometimes, they would purposely dress in rags to disguise themselves. They had to hide all that wealth they brought back.

Then there were the nobles. They were actually only five percent of society, but they owned everything. They could wear capes and jewelry that only they could wear. Commoners couldn't wear what they were wearing, so you could really see them in the street walking down. And their kids went to a special school, the Calmecac. That was for mostly government officials. They were people who were going to lead the armies, or they were the high priests.

And those people lived in much nicer homes. Some of them were fully palaces. They were all built of stone walls, not adobe or waddle and dob. Oftentimes, those stones were beautiful volcanic stones they brought from somewhere else. They would have flat roofs and those beautiful cedar beams.

And inside, they had very finely crafted furniture, and they had plate ware that was beautiful. And in there, there were many rooms, and sometimes they'd have their own servants' quarters that were always there serving them.

But they were also expected to be model citizens. Penalties .were worse for nobles than commoners. They had more public responsibilities. They had to lead and organize all the feasts, and they had to organize successful labor teams. In times of war, they were the ones that had to lead the armies.

Then finally on the top, there was the king, the Tlatoani. He was the speaker. He was a statesman first and foremost in a Toltec manner. He was also the head of the army. He was the commander in chief. It wasn't actually hereditary; the kingship of the Aztecs wasn't hereditary. They were elected by a group of nobles. It might be the son of the king, but it was always merit-based.

The Tlatoani had great privileges. He had a huge palace, and many, many wives. He also had thousands of servants. All the city lands were actually his property. Nobles were granted land by him. And all taxes and laws were his to decide. The Tlatoani also had a lot of responsibilities. Technically, he was the high priest, and he oversaw the daily sacrifices. He was also the general of the army; he had to lead it. All battle strategies were made by him. And also, political relationships with other kings were led by the Tlatoani. Other city-states also had their own Tlatoanis. It was their jobs to work together with each other. Everyone, from slave to noble, depended on the Tlatoani to provide security and a good life. The Tlatoani was the father figure and the spiritual leader of everyone in Aztec society.

So now we've talked about the Aztec social hierarchy. Essentially, 95 percent regular people and 5 percent nobles. So, it really hasn't changed much in modern times, has it? But now, let's talk more generally about everyday life in the Aztec Empire. Aztec babies were born at home. They were born with the help of a midwife in the temazcal, the sweat bath. And the midwife stayed on to help for a couple of days. On the fourth day, they would bring that baby out into the courtyard, and they would bathe it in a tub of lake reeds. Three boys would stand there and call out the baby's name. And that was a name that the midwife would give it, and it was a temporary name.

The baby's umbilicus was buried right there. If it was a boy, it was buried under a little shield and bow. If it was a girl, it was buried under a grinding stone. Burying it there connected them to their home forever. Even today in the Guatemalan highlands, if a Maya wants to talk to another Maya and ask him where he was born, he says, where is your umbilicus buried?

Their official name was given in a May festival. Priests in the temple gave it to that child. Nobles could get really cool names, like *Moctezuma* means "angry lord." But most commoners were just given the day of their birth. So, if you were born on 5 Eagle, that was your name, and your destiny. What day you were born on was a serious matter. Some of them were good, and other of them were bad. But that was going to be your destiny. There are 20 possible day names. So for example, the day wind, that one had a bad connotation. If you were born on wind, you were likely going to be negligent, lazy, and probably a drifter. But if you were born on lizard, that was a good day; you were probably going to be wealthy without even trying.

Aztec birthday celebrations were very different, too, very different from Western society. On your birthday, your friends woke you up, and they immediately threw you in a river. And then you had to get out of there, and you had to throw them a party. You had to say thank you to everyone that helped you through your life. And if you didn't, you were scorned the next year.

And even though they accounted their birthdays as 260 days, funny enough, they only had one per solar year. If it so happened that their 260-day birthday happened twice in a solar year, they only celebrated the first one. The next one was a bye.

All children had to help at home. By five, boys were hauling wood and girls were cleaning. School was also mandatory for them. They all had to go to schools called the Telpochcalli. Boys and girls learned basic skills. Boys were trained as warriors. And every Aztec had to serve in the army, at least all the males. How many captives you had caught in your lifetime was the measure of a man's worth society.

Marriages were arranged. It was decided by the relatives and the teachers of children. Men were to marry by the age of 20. But girls got married much earlier, about 10 or 12. Soothsayers would pick the day for the wedding. And the wedding ceremony would occur in two parts. The party began at the bride's home. There would be a feast for the wedding guests. There was tamales and flowers and tobacco and pulque. And the guests were served in order of their importance, so the mother and father to be served first, and the grandparents, and so on.

At sunset, the bride was bathed and dressed. And then she'd get the typical lecture from the groom's family, who would chide her and say, there's no more childishness or girly behavior. You're now going to be a wife, and you've got to be a wife. So it's time for you to grow up. Then the bride was carried to the groom's house. The family followed in procession with torchlight. The couple then sat on a mat together, and their robes were tied together. Elders fed them, and they burned incense around them. From then on, they were adults. And they were to begin their adult responsibilities. Mats are still in bridal shops today. I still see them in the typical bride shop in Mexico City as I walk down the street.

As adults, they had to begin their jobs. Women weaved, and cooked, and cleaned, and shopped. Men farmed, and built, and they fought battles. Some men were artisans, but they were still required to be warriors when needed. All activities were done by order of the calendar. There were good days and bad days to do things. So for example, no farmer would harvest unless the priest said it was the right day to do so.

The raising of children was of the utmost importance. Parents were supposed to be focused on the upbringing of their children. They were supposed to be proper social role models the entire time. And most of their income was supposed to be spent on their children. It was also to support their elders. Adults had responsibilities, both to the old and the young. And they had to allow their elders to live in their home; it was part of what was the idea of being a good Aztec.

But upon old age, one could relax a bit. You didn't have to be a good example anymore. If your kids were raised, your social contract was done. So old people were frequently in the street publicly drunk. And, old men didn't have to go to war anymore; they were free. They had crossed the finish line of Aztec society.

As a society, all Aztecs participated in the monthly festivals. There were 18 months of 20 days each, and then a five-day useless month. Each month had its own theme and activities. And as we'll discuss now, some of those festivals were quite beautiful, and others were downright scary.

Diego Duran recorded each of those festivals, sometimes in gory detail. He was truly upset by most of them. And he wrote it down in such great detail with the goal of telling the other priests what was really going on in Aztec society. Aztec religion was alive and well, well into the 1570s. Now, I don't have time to tell you about each one of the months in this lecture. But, let's talk about a few of them and see what kind of interesting events happened in these festivals.

First off, the first day of every month was a feast day. And any day that started with the number one was a day that you'd honor all the people of that sign. So for example, if day one was one crocodile, that would be a day that every person with the name Crocodile in the Aztec capital was going to be honored. And so, as you learned in the calendar lecture, that meant that as we went through the month, day 14 would actually be a one day again. In this case, it would be 1 Jaguar. And all the jaguars would be honored on that day. So every one day was a party for all those people that had jaguar in their name.

The first month was March 1, at least in Duran's time. And it was called Touch the Bouquets. People went around touching plants, and they offered food to the gods. And the goal was to ask for a fruitful year. The second month occurred 20 days later, so that would be March 21, and that's spring equinox. It had a very different name. It was called skinning of men. It was honoring the God Xipe Totec, otherwise known as the Flayed One. During this month, priests wore the dried skin of their enemies, and they danced through the neighborhoods wearing these skins. And boys would come out of their homes with fake little wooden swords to defend their home and slash them against these priests that were in the guise of these skinned enemies.

The eighth month, when corn was ripe, was July. During that time, a virgin was sacrificed. And she was sacrificed on top of four men. She was lying on top of them like they were a table. And they were sacrificed as well. This same month was the time for midwives to give their sacrifice. In their case, they would lead a girl to Chapultepec, and then they'd run her all the way back to the Temple Mayor. On top of the temple, she'd dance for a while, and then they'd sacrifice her. And then her blood was rubbed all over the idols on top of the temple. The 11th month was called the Day of Sweeping. This honored grandmother, heart of the Earth. At that time, everything was cleaned everywhere. Families cleaned their homes. Communities cleaned the streets. Even the rivers and the streams were cleaned. Duran actually had a negative opinion of this month, too. He thought that this big cleaning festival promoted sloth for the rest of the year.

The 12th and the 15th months were to Huitzilopochtli. The 12th month was about his birth. A sign of his birth was waited for all night, and when the priests announced it, everyone rejoiced. But that was done by severe bloodletting, the worse the better. Everyone in the party would cut themselves many times, and then they'd rub the blood all over themselves and everywhere.

The 13th month was called Great Moss. And it was a month where they honored the volcanoes, especially Popocatepetl. They made little bitty volcanoes, models out of amaranth, and they gave them paper clothes and faces. The family honored them in a feast, and then, they chopped their heads off with a flint knife.

The 18th and last month was Growth. The planting season began then, and they only ate special foods, amaranth leaves and corn. And children's limbs were stretched. They believed it promoted their growth. At that same month, a boy and a girl were sacrificed to Tlaloc. The sacrifice was to ask for rain for the newly-planted crops.

Finally, we had the extra days to complete that 365-day cycle. These were useless or profitless days. There was fasting, no sex, and more bloodletting. They didn't actually count those days. Thus, the next year began again with one crocodile, and the cycle renewed itself.

As you can tell from these descriptions, the cycle of festivals was a driving force in everyday Aztec life. You can also see that Aztec life was an almost constant mix of happy feasting and solemn sacrifices. Such was life in the Aztec Empire. This lifestyle went on not just at the capital of Tenochtitlan, but everywhere in the valley of Mexico and the culture regions beyond.

In my next lecture, we'll discuss just how far away the Aztec life spread, and how they were able to expand their empire.

How the Aztecs Expanded Their Empire
Lecture 36

By the time of European contact, the extensive Aztec Empire had conquered more of Mesoamerica than any other civilization. Their empire was not a traditional one, however, and its shortcomings made control of the empire tenuous at best. In this lecture, we'll discuss how the Aztec dominated their world and debate whether or not it was a true empire.

A True Empire?

- The Aztec Empire extended from coast to coast in Central Mexico; it reached into Oaxaca and dominated Mixtec lands; and it encompassed a large area of the Soconusco, as well. Aztec dominion was commercial, not cultural. The Aztec demanded tribute but not assimilation. The conquered lands were left to their own leaders, politics, and religion. For that reason, some scholars assert that theirs was not a true empire.

- Traditionally, when we think of empires, we consider such cultures as ancient Rome civilization. The Romans imposed a new world order; they created a new infrastructure; they built roads, temples, and administrative buildings; and they sent government officials to regulate their lands and garrisons of soldiers to maintain control. What's more, they imposed their language and religion on conquered peoples.

- An example of a traditional empire from the New World is the Inca, an empire of 10 million people under the same rule. Every territory was connected by roads, and every community was outfitted with new buildings. Language and religion were uniform—everyone had to follow the Inca way. Tax collectors were in every city, and everything was administered from a single capital, Cuzco.

- In contrast, all the Aztec wanted was tribute. They dominated cities but only to acquire taxes. They built no new roads, fortresses, or temples. Religion and local leaders were left alone.

- The Aztecs were not the only conquerors to function in this way. Consider Alexander the Great. Greece controlled wide areas but left local cultures alone. For example, the Greeks conquered Egypt but left its religion intact. Perhaps the connection here is the city-state model both in Greece and in Mesoamerica. Although the Aztec did not impose their culture, just as the Greeks, theirs should be considered an empire.

- Some scholars identify two kinds of empires—territorial and hegemonic. Rome controlled a territorial empire. Athens and Tenochtitlan maintained hegemonic empires. The Aztec did not invade the Valley of Mexico as an empire; rather, they were a group of ruffians following a cult of war. Empire building was a trick they learned from the already established cultures of the valley.

The Triple Alliance

- When the Aztec arrived, the Valley of Mexico—at that time called Anahuac—comprised a group of city-states called *altepetls*. Each controlled its own territory, and each had a capital city and a Tlatoani, or king. Tenuous alliances were maintained through trade, intermarriage, and border control. Settling in the Valley of Mexico, the Aztec learned that their skills in battle could be leveraged to create a steady stream of wealth. Together with the Tepanec, the Aztec created a network of dominated tribute payers—in other words, an empire.

- In 1425, the Tepanec ruler, Tezozomac, died, and his son Maxtla took over. Maxtla was too forceful in his control, however; he attacked the city of Texcoco for rebelling and forced its king, Nezahualcoyotl, into exile. Maxtla also assassinated the Aztec leader, Chimalpopoca, which infuriated the Aztec.

- The new Aztec leader, Itzcoatl, teamed up with Nezahualcoyotl and the city of Tlacopan, and together, they overthrew Maxtla. They took over the entire valley and formed what became the Triple Alliance in 1427.

- Moctezuma I became the Tlatoani of the Aztec in 1440. He and Nezahualcoyotl inherited the Tepanec tribute system and divided up the wealth between themselves and Tlacopan (which received a smaller portion).

From Raiders to Rulers

- For the Aztec, the next step was to change their public image, which they did by rewriting history. They portrayed themselves as a chosen people. They claimed that they were the lost tribe of Aztlan and were brothers with every other culture in the valley. Although they were the Mexica, everyone was an Aztec—meaning a person from Aztlan. That story was created by Tlacaelel, the brother of Moctezuma.

- Tlacaelel was the archetypal "power behind the throne." He devised the Triple Alliance and created a new code of laws and public behavior. Nobles were afforded new rights according to those laws. He increased their military presence and the frequency of their sacrifices. He also established new standards for tribute, increasing it significantly.

- But most important, Tlacaelel rewrote history. He ordered all the old history books burned, especially the histories about tribute states. There was no memory of who the Aztec used to be. He set the stage for Mesoamerica to accept the Aztec as the divinely chosen leaders of the new empire.

- The Aztec had gone from raiders to rulers. Along with their partners in the Triple Alliance, they had broken the yoke of Tepanec dominance. Now their task was to take the Tepanec's place as leaders of the Valley of Mexico. Many cities were already in the Tepanec sphere of influence, and many others submitted readily. But if they did not comply, they were attacked.

The Flowery Wars

- Under the Aztec, a new system of tax collection was established, territory boundaries were reformed, and alliances were reset. One by one, the Anahuac city-states were absorbed into the empire. Chalco on the lake shore was the last, largest, and most resistant. It suffered repeated attacks by the Aztec.

Tlacaelel claimed that he maintained hostilities with the people of Tlaxcala on purpose—because they provided sacrifices for the Flowery Wars.

- Then, beginning in 1446, a terrible drought came to the Valley of Mexico. People were starving, and many migrated out of the valley. Tlacaelel maintained that the gods needed more sacrifices, and he inspired—or invented—the so-called Flowery Wars to capture warriors for sacrifice. Of course, the Aztec took this opportunity to wage those ritual wars against Chalco.

- After two decades of Flowery Wars, Chalco finally fell to the Aztec in 1465. With Chalco under control, the valley was finally unified. Endemic war, at least in that area, was over. And, as promised, economic prosperity followed.

Empire-Building Strategies

- Moctezuma I and the Triple Alliance had even bigger plans for expansion and domination of foreign lands. The first step to expansion was assessment. In this mission, the *pochteca* were key. A group of international traders very loyal to the Aztec, the *pochteca* established permanent trading outposts, which they used to assess the resources of an area.

- Eventually, those trading outposts became garrisons, and the local leaders would be invited to the Aztec capital of Tenochtitlan. At that impressive capital city, they would witness the sacrifice ceremonies and observe the might of the Aztec army. Then, after these displays of Aztec power, the local leaders were invited to join the empire. The only payment was tribute two to four times a year.

- Many cultures initially resisted, but the Aztec forces would immediately attack their cities and take their warriors as sacrifices. The mission of the Aztec soldiers was not to kill but to capture warriors for sacrifice.

- Moctezuma I subdued the cultures of the Veracruz area, the Huastec and the Totonac, who controlled tropical lands with significant resources: cocoa, rubber, feathers, and seafood. These were luxury items craved by the Aztec nobles.

Expansion beyond Control

- Moctezuma's reign set the empire-building strategy. As Tenochtitlan grew, Aztec control of the Triple Alliance increased. The next four kings would further expand the Aztec Empire, which eventually reached all the way into Guatemala. There were over 450 different tribute states within the empire. But the larger the empire grew, the harder it was to control.

- Moctezuma I died in 1469, and his grandson Axayacatl became the next king. He spent much of his 12-year reign putting down various rebellions in the empire. Axayacatl was best known for conquering Tlatelolco, the island city next to Tenochtitlan. Because the *pochteca* leaders in control of it had become too powerful, they posed a threat to Tenochtitlan's authority.

- Both Axayacatl and the next Aztec ruler encountered groups they could not conquer. To the west were the Tarascans, with armies as large as the Aztec's. The Tlaxcalans were to the east; although they were small, they refused to submit.

Tributary and Client States

- In the face of resistance, the Aztec devised a new strategy. At that time, there were two kinds of vassal states: tributary states and client states. Tributary states paid taxes and tribute to Tenochtitlan. Tributary states also established new trading relationships to set the ground for the expansion of the Aztec Empire. Client states were set up on hostile borders. Although they were not required to pay tribute, they had to house and supply Aztec garrisons. These client states created a kind of a buffer zone that protected the empire.

- The Aztec Empire continued to expand, especially to the south and east. Moctezuma II, the king at Spanish contact, had grown up as a general of one of the conquering armies. The Tarascans remained a threat during his reign. Moctezuma set up Aztec garrisons all along the border.

- To the south, Moctezuma's predecessor had subjugated the Soconusco along Guatemala's Pacific coast. Eventually, when the Spanish arrived, the Aztec led them down to that same area through their pre-established trade routes. The Aztec were also mounting an assault against Yucatan.

Implosion of the Empire

- In retrospect, the Aztec's greatest mistake was in not conquering Tlaxcala. Those people were supposedly from Aztlan, and they had been an independent state since Tepanec times. Tlaxcala reported that even if surrounded on all sides, it would never submit to Aztec authority.

- The Aztec now had a hostile enemy far too close to their capital. When Cortes landed in Veracruz, he first met the Tlaxcalans. He had only a couple hundred men, but the Tlaxcalan army had tens of thousands. And those men were ready and willing to destroy the Aztec. This was the Aztec Empire's Achilles heel.

- Using the Tlaxcalans as his army, Cortes brought down the city of Tenochtitlan in a matter of months. Without the threat of Aztec punishment, the tribute states quickly broke away, and Mesoamerica's largest empire imploded.

Suggested Reading

Carrasco, *The Aztecs: A Very Short Introduction.*

Smith, *The Aztecs.*

1. What other ancient empire is most similar to the Aztec Empire?

2. Would the conquest have gone differently if Tlaxcala hadn't remained independent?

3. Would there have been less rebellion if the Aztecs had imposed their religion on conquered peoples?

How the Aztecs Expanded Their Empire
Lecture 36—Transcript

By the time of European contact, the Aztec Empire covered more of Mesoamerica than any culture had ever managed to dominate. But their empire was not a traditional one, and its shortcomings made their control of it tenuous at best. In this lecture, we'll discuss how they did it and whether or not it was a true empire.

Not since the days of Teotihuacan had any culture had such a wide influence. And really, we're still unsure of the nature of Teotihuacan's control, or how much they really influence them. Tula was also said to have had a wide influence. But as we've discussed, archaeology can't really detect it.

The Aztec empire was expansive. It went from coast to coast in central Mexico, and it went down into Oaxaca and dominated the Mixtec lands. There was also a large pocket of the Soconusco that was under their control. Its frontiers were really the resistors at their borders. But at the time of contact, they were still pushing their way into those lands as well.

Aztec control was commercial, not cultural. They demanded tribute, but not assimilation. Leaders, politics, and religion were pretty much left alone. And for that reason, some people say it wasn't really an empire. Of course, that depends on how you define the term *empire*. The textbook definition of *empire* from Webster's dictionary says, "it's a major political unit having a territory of great extent or a number of territories or peoples under a single sovereign authority."

Traditionally, when we think of empire, we think of cultures like ancient Rome. The Romans imposed a new world order. They built new infrastructure. They built roads and temples and new administrative buildings. They sent new government officials to regulate things. They also sent garrisons of soldiers. They imposed their language and their religion on the new peoples. And of course, they demanded tribute and taxes.

A good new-world example is the Inca. That was an empire of 10 million people, all under the same rules. Every territory was connected by roads; and every community was outfitted with brand new buildings. Again, language and religion had to be uniform. They all had to follow the Inca way. And there were tax collectors from the capital in every little city. Everything was administered from a single capital, Cusco.

Now, the Aztecs were a little different. All they really wanted was the tribute. They dominated cities but only to get the taxes. They didn't build any big new roads to them, and there were really very few fortresses or temples they put within their dominated areas. Religion was also left alone. Local leaders could remain in charge and conduct their business. As long as tribute was sent, there wasn't anything else for them to do.

But they weren't the only empire in world history to function like that. Consider Alexander the Great. Greece controlled wide areas. And they brought prosperity into those areas, but they left culture alone. For example, they controlled Egypt, but they left the religion intact. In fact, Alexander was crowned the pharaoh, and they loved him there. So, maybe it's about the city-state model that was present both in Greece and in Mesoamerica. There were independent city-states that co-existed. So perhaps it was ingrained in the minds of the people that forced assimilation wasn't something that they really thought of, because they had always lived these independent lives.

And by the way, I know that Alexander did build cities. And after his death, a lot of Greek ways took hold. It was just a rough analogy, so, please don't send me any emails about that. My point is that though the Aztecs didn't impose their culture, I think what they did should be considered an empire. Some scholars say there are two different kinds of empires, territorial and hegemonic. Rome controlled a territorial empire. But Athens and Tenochtitlan had hegemonic empires. The Aztecs did not enter the valley of Mexico as an empire. Rather, they were a group of ruffians following a cult of war. Empire building was a trick they learned from the already established cultures of the valley.

The Aztecs, or Machida, were a displaced people; they were wanderers. We're really still not quite sure of the reasons of why they were wandering. But eventually, they arrived to the valley of Mexico, which at that time was called Anahuac. In that valley was a group of city-states. City-states were called *altepetls*. And each of them had their own territory. And each of them had a capital city and a Tlatoani, or a King, a ruler.

A tenuous alliance existed, maintained through trade, intermarriage, and borders. There were a few large *altepetls*, and then there were many small ones. And within them, there were little groups and towns. The Aztec had to settle within one of them. And their taxes to the people that were under their control were their fighting skills. Eventually, they were upsetting the balance of the valley.

As we discussed in the Aztec origins lecture, they were with Culhuacan for a while. And then, when they sacrificed their princess, that pretty much ended that. They moved on and they lived with Tepanecs for a while. And they fought battles for them. As they were fighting, they built their own capital called Tenochtitlan. And both cultures during that time period learned something. The Tepanecs learned that they could make smaller city-states pay them tribute by force. The Aztecs learned how their skills in battle could be used to create a steady stream of wealth. Together, they created a network of dominated tribute payers, in other words, an empire.

In 1425, the Tepanec ruler, Tezozomac, died. And his son, Maxtla, took over. And his son was really too forceful in controlling the empire. He attacked the city of Texcoco for rebelling. And it was the second largest city in the entire valley. Their King, Nezahualcoyotl, was forced into exile. Maxtla also assassinated the Aztec leader, Chimalpopoca, and the Aztecs were furious about this. The new Aztec leader was Itzcoatl, and he made a deal with Nezahualcoyotl. They teamed up together, along with one other small city called Tlacopan. And the three together overthrew Maxtla. Together, they took over the entire valley, and they formed what became the Triple Alliance and 1427.

Moctezuma I became the Tlatoani of the Aztecs in 1440. And he and Nezahualcoyotl were in control of the valley. They inherited the Tepanec tribute system, and they divided up the wealth, $2/_5$, $2/_5$, and $1/_5$. Tlacopan got a little smaller; they got the $1/_5$, because they were the smaller of the three cities. Texcoco at the time was really in the lead, because Nezahualcoyotl was a beloved statesman. Everyone in the valley trusted him. The Aztecs, not so much.

But Aztec circumstances had changed. Their next step was to change their public image. So, they re-wrote history. They painted themselves a chosen people. They said they were the lost tribe of Aztlan and they were brothers with every other culture in the valley. They were the Mexica, but everyone was an Aztec, meaning someone from Aztlan. That story was created by a man named Tlacaelel, who was the brother of the King, Moctezuma.

Tlacaelel was the classic man behind the throne. He was actually the person who invented and thought up the Triple Alliance. He was an adviser to Itzcoatl and the next three kings. They say he lived for 90 years, from 1397 to 1487. He's the man who created their new code of laws. There were new codes of public behavior, especially when it came to the nobles. Nobles also got brand new rights according to those laws. He increased their military presence and the frequency of their sacrifices. He also established brand new tribute standards, specifically that there was going to be a lot more of it. But most importantly, Tlacaelel re-wrote history. He ordered all the old history books burned, especially the histories about tribute states. There was no memory of who the Aztec used to be. He set the stage for Mesoamerica to accept them as the divinely chosen leaders of the new empire.

So the Aztecs had gone from raiders to rulers. Along with their partners in the Triple Alliance, they had broken the yoke of Tepanec dominance. Now their task was to take the Tepanec's place in Anahuac as the leaders of the valley of Mexico. With Tlacaelel's new image, the Aztec went around the valley trying to convince the other *altepetls* to join forces with the Triple Alliance. The deal was going to be taxes in tribute in exchange for security and economic prosperity.

Texcoco's established authority advocated Tlacaelel's new world order. They said, we're all people from Aztlan. So the strategy was at first to be kind and to offer gifts in order to come into the Triple Alliance. If that wasn't accepted, then there were threats. If they were still defiant, there was destruction, attack, and ultimately higher taxes than the original deal. Many cities were already in the Tepanec empire. Many others submitted pretty readily. But if they didn't comply, they were attacked. Unfriendly Tlatoanis were just replaced with more compliant ones. As long as they sent their tribute, those cities were left alone, and they could conduct their business as usual.

A new system of tax collection was established. Territory boundaries were reformed. And this was a political strategy. They reset alliances in the valley. They'd break up big blocks of alliances, and they'd have groups that weren't allies before work together to present their taxes. Taxes were collected directly the main *altepetls*. Each of them had an imperial tax collector there judging everything. They also put in laws against adultery, theft, and drunkenness to create order and prosperity in the valley.

Most Anahuac city-states were east or south of the lake. And one by one, they were absorbed. Chalco, on the lake shore, was the last, biggest, and most resistant. They suffered repeated attacks by the Aztecs. Then starting in 1446, a terrible drought set into the valley of Mexico. People were starving; a lot of people migrated out of the valley. Tlacaelel stood up and said, this is because the gods need more sacrifices. And he inspired, or invented, what was called the Flowery Wars. These were ritual wars in order to capture warriors. And of course, the Aztecs took this opportunity to put most of those ritual wars against Chalco, that was their primary target.

After two decades of Flowery Wars and fighting, Chalco finally fell to the Aztecs in 1465. Their Tlatoani was exiled. And the Chalco region was forced to pay more taxes than any other place in the valley. They had very rich crop land, so they could do it. But really, it was more about punishing them and making them an example. With Chalco under their control, the valley was finally unified. Endemic war, at least in that area, was over. And, as they promised, economic prosperity took over. The valley's leaders became very wealthy; they were all showered with gifts from Moctezuma, and each of them were given their own residence within the capital city, Tenochtitlan.

Anahuac was secured, and trade around the valley created a network of economic prosperity. But Moctezuma I and the Triple Alliance had even bigger plans. Following the lead of the Tepanecs, the Aztecs started to dominate foreign lands. The first step to expansion was assessment. Which areas were rich in what products? The *pochteca* traders were key; they paved the way. They were a group of international traders. They worked for themselves, but they were very loyal to Aztecs. They were the people that made first contact. They were also the people that established the trade relationships, and they were welcomed into communities for all the rich things they brought. They were wealthy, and they came to buy things, as well as sell things. And they established permanent trading outposts. But from those outposts, they were assessing the resources of an area, and they were taking inventories of their holdings, and they were learning about the local politics.

Then the *pochteca* would come back, and they'd report to the king. Eventually, those trading outposts would become garrisons. And the newly contacted local leaders would be invited to Tenochtitlan. At that big capital city, they would witness the sacrifice ceremonies, and they would see the grandeur or the city. And they would also see the huge size of the Aztec army. Then, after they had witnessed these shows of Aztec power, they were invited to join the empire. The King said, you just need to pay us tribute two to four times a year. Many cultures did initially resist. And the Aztec forces would immediately attack their cities. They would take their warriors back as sacrifices, and they would actually target rebel leaders, specifically, to bring back for sacrifices. Once that was done, that community would have to pay higher taxes than if they had just originally taken the deal.

The Aztec armies were very well organized. They had a range of weapons. Some of them were spears and slings that could go a long distance. Others of them were hand-to-hand combat weapons, like the Aztec sword. It wasn't like a European sword; instead, it was a wooden bat with obsidian blades running up either side. Multiple Spanish accounts said that those swords were so sharp that they could cut the head off a horse. But that wasn't the Aztec goal; they weren't trying to kill people. They were trying to capture them. They needed many warriors to come back to Tenochtitlan and be sacrificed. Tlacaelel's sacrifice laws increased that demand even further.

Moctezuma I subdued the cultures of the Vera Cruz Gulf Coast, the Oaxtecs and the Totonacs. These were tropical lands, and they had really important resources. They had cocoa, rubber, feathers, and seafood. A lot of these things were luxury items that Aztec nobles wanted. And they became gifts for loyalty to other royal people from dominated states. Moctezuma also invaded the Mixtec lands. He went down into Oaxaca and raided one of their big cities called Coixtlahuaca.

It was actually done on a pretext. Reports had come in that *pochteca* traders were being abused. And so the Aztec empire responded by attacking. It was a very hard-fought battle, because it was a huge population. But they won, and eventually, the Mixtec lords of Coixtlahuaca were strangled, and their royal family was turned into slaves. They were given a huge tax burden. They were made an example of.

Moctezuma's reign set the empire building strategy. They were ever going to be expanding their boundaries, and tribute always came directly into the capital. As Tenochtitlan became larger, Aztec control of the Triple Alliance increased. The next four kings would further expand the empire. Eventually, it reached all the way down into Guatemala. There were over 450 different tribute states within the Aztec empire. But the larger the empire grew, the harder it was to control.

Moctezuma I died in 1469. But his brother, Tlacaelel, would live on to be the adviser for the next three Aztec kings. His advice was the same always— iron-fist control and constant sacrifice of captured warriors. Rebellions started almost immediately. Moctezuma I had lived a long life. Axayacatl, his grandson, was the next king. He spent much of his 12 years of reign putting down various rebellions in the empire. Both gulf coast people and the Mixtec made repeated attempts to break away.

Axayacatl was best known for conquering Tlatelolco; that was the island city right next to Tenochtitlan in the lake. It was their sister city. It was actually the home of the main Aztec market, and all of their tribute went there to be this distributed to the Triple Alliance. The *pochteca* leaders were really in control of it and had become too powerful, so they posed a threat to Tenochtitlan's authority. So they conquered Tlatelolco in 1473, and they killed its Tlatoani, and they set up a military governance. Soon after, they absorbed it officially into Tenochtitlan, actually building islands that connected the two. They let the *pochteca* still control commerce, but now, it answered only to Tenochtitlan.

Both Axayacatl and the next Aztec ruler, his brother Tizoc, ran into groups that they couldn't conquer. To the west, there were the Tarascans. They had armies as large as the Aztecs. The Tlaxcalans were to the east, and they were small but refused to submit. The Aztec said that that was on purpose, that they needed someone close by to conduct the Flowery Wars with, so they on purpose never took out the Tlaxcalans.

So, with these borders that they couldn't surmount, they started a new strategy. There were two different kinds of vassal states at that point. There were tributary states, and then there were client states. Tributary states paid their taxes. And one capital was picked in each one of the regions. All the smaller cities delivered their goods to that one capital, and from that capital, it was all sent to Tenochtitlan.

Client states were set up on hostile borders. They did not have to pay tribute. Instead, they had to allow Aztec garrisons to stay there. And they had to provide the warriors with housing and supplies. They were partners, allies, in the defense of these borders. And they created a kind of a buffer zone that protected the empire. Tributary states owed not just local goods, but they were also, on purpose, asked to provide exotic goods, things that weren't from within their territory. And this was another Aztec strategy. The benefit for the Aztec was, it promoted trade and commerce; these tributary states had to go establish new relationships, and those new relationships were setting the grounds for the next place that the Aztec empire could move out to and expand.

Tribute was delivered to Tenochtitlan two to four times a year and distributed in a number of contexts. It could be used for feasting days and religious rituals. It could feed administrative and city workers. It could also be food for people during construction projects. A lot of it ended up being just for sale in Tlatelolco's market, or, it could become gifts for nobles or citizens that had done good deeds. The Codex Mendoza lists all the different tribute states. It names all the items owned by each and owed by each. It's our absolutely best document for the empire's extent. That's the document that tells us that there were over 450 different tax-paying areas.

The Aztec Empire continued to expand, especially to the south and east. First *pochteca*, then garrisons of warriors, then demands of tribute. They ruled through fear, not kindness. And that was eventually to be their undoing. Moctezuma II was the king at Spanish contact. He had grown up being a general of one of the armies, and much of his early life and reign was spent in war. He's the king who conquered the Zapotec lands completely.

The Tarascans remained a threat during his reign. He set up Aztec garrisons all along the border. There's a place called Oztuma that we've excavated a bit, and it shows that there was actually evidence of Aztec settlers; they were moving Aztec out there to try to establish themselves along that border. It also shows us that there was constant fighting. And recent surveys in the area show us that there were lots of small, hilltop forts along the way.

To the south, Moctezuma's predecessor, an uncle, Ahuitzotl, had subjugated the Soconusco along Guatemala's Pacific coast. That had increased Moctezuma's control as well. He, at the time, was working to get from there up into the Guatemalan highlands. Eventually, when the Spanish got there, the Aztecs led them down to that same area through their pre-established trade routes. The Aztec were also mounting for an assault against Yucatan. Cortes learned of the Aztecs from Maya people. He had picked up La Malinche, his translator, near Champoton, and she knew Nahuatl from trade contact. As I'll explain in another lecture, even Tulum on the east coast of Yucatan showed signs of Aztec control. So, they were into step one, control trade ports with the *pochteca*.

In retrospect, the Aztec's greatest mistake was not conquering Tlaxcala. Those people were supposedly from Aztlan, too. And they were an independent state since Tepanec times. Tlacaelel said that he left them hostile on purpose, because they needed sacrifices for the Flowery Wars, and that was a close-by enemy they could always rely on. He said he left them unconquered for ritual warfare, like cattle. Tlaxcala had another story. They said that they were surrounded on all sides but that they were never going to submit to Aztec authority, that they remembered the lowly dogs they were when they came into the valley.

Whoever was correct, the Aztec had a hostile enemy way too close to their capital. When Cortes landed in Vera Cruz, he first met the Tlaxcalans. He only had a couple hundred men, but the Tlaxcalans had tens of thousands of men, and those men were all ready and willing to destroy the Aztecs. And that was the Aztec Empire's Achilles heel. Using the Tlaxcalans as his army, Cortes brought down the city of Tenochtitlan in a matter of months. Without the threat of Aztec punishment, the tribute states quickly broke away, and Mesoamerica's largest empire imploded.

In the end, the Aztec were a perfect example of the old saying, he who lives by the sword, dies by the sword. Could Cortes have done it without the Tlaxcalans? Probably not. Perhaps he would have teamed up with another enemy of the Aztecs. Maybe, a people like the subject of my next lecture, the Tarascans.

Independent Tarascans—Desert Warriors
Lecture 37

Just 50 miles to the west of Tenochtitlan was a line that the Aztec could not cross—the border of the Tarascan Empire. In many ways, the Tarascans were like their Aztec counterparts: fierce warriors, lovers of the arts, and devoted worshippers. Also like the Aztec, the Tarascans were all about conquest and tribute. But in other ways, the Tarascans were aliens on the Mesoamerican landscape. In this lecture, we'll demonstrate that the Tarascans represented a unique cultural blend: desert warriors with a South American heritage.

Beginnings of the Tarascan Empire

- The Tarascans were second only to the Aztec in the size of their empire. Like the Aztec, the Tarascans controlled a tributary empire. They maintained a highly centralized trading system; all goods went through the capital of Tzintzuntzan. Tarascan territory today is in Michoacan, an ancient Aztec name that means "place of fishermen."

- In that area were many highland lakes, and Lake Patzcuaro was the heart of the Tarascan Empire. Between Patzcuaro and Tenochtitlan was a large buffer zone. According to Tarascan history, the Tarascans arrived at Patzcuaro somewhere around 1250, which was when the Aztec say that they entered the Valley of Mexico. The Tarascans expanded their empire during the 1300s, just like the Aztec. The two cultures clashed in the river basins between their two empires until the time of Spanish contact.

- Tzintzuntzan had a massive temple complex inhabited by nobles and priests. At the top of the social hierarchy was the Tarascan king, a *cazonci*. He was the head priest, the head warrior, and the head administrator. All the vast land holdings were his property. At its peak, Tzintzuntzan's population was about 35,000. The capital was surrounded by smaller cities, tightly bound together in a social network. In total, archaeologists estimate that there might have been as many as 100,000 people in the surrounding areas.

- By the Tarascans' own account, they were not originally from Patzcuaro. Chronicles of the Tarascans were not compiled until the 1530s. A priest named Jeronimo de Alcala studied the Tarascans and wrote *Relacion de Michoacan*, which was divided into three parts: religion, society, and history.

- The Tarascans' first warrior king was Tariacuri; Patzcuaro was his capital in 1325. The Purepecha people blended with the local population. Then, after Tariacuri died, his nephews spread out into the basin and conquered the entire area. They established two new towns: Ihuatzio and Tzintzuntzan. Tzintzuntzan grew in population, and by 1440, it was the new capital.

A Unique Culture
- Although the history of the Tarascans sounds similar to the Aztec origin story, there was an important difference—these people did not speak Nahuatl. Analysis of the Purepecha language concludes that it is closest to Quechua, the Inca language in South America.

- The Tarascans were clearly a culture distinct from the Aztec: They spoke a different language and had different customs, artifacts, and architecture. The origin of their culture was most likely the people from western Mexico who migrated inland. Those people were definitely influenced by South America.

- Evidence that the Tarascans were influenced by South America is supported by three points.
  - The Tarascans were experts in metallurgy, a craft that originated in South America.

  - Archaeologists have found Tarascan stirrup vessels that are similar to some found in South America. The odd forms of these vessels are too distinct to have been created independently in both areas.

○ The Purepecha language is derived from Quechua—which could not have happened independently.

- Although the evidence is not definitive, the Tarascans were most likely a cultural blend of people connected to South America and the Chichimec, who came from the north about 1250. The Tarascan Empire was essentially a new socioeconomic strategy exerted over an already established resource base.

Expansion of the Empire

- The Tarascans conquered the Patzcuaro basin and imposed a new order of tax collection. Tribute poured into Tzintzuntzan from 90 communities under Tarascan control. Every 80 days, vast storehouses of wealth were owed to the capital—mostly food, cotton, and clothing.

- An aggressive expansion of the empire began in the 1400s. The *Relacion de Michoacan* notes that there was a specific month dedicated to conquest, and men were enlisted into service at that time. The Purepecha armies expanded their borders all the way to the coast—where they ran up against the Aztec trying to do exactly the same thing.

- Different kinds of tributes were taken from different places. On the Aztec frontier, the Tarascans collected slaves and people to sacrifice. Like Tenochtitlan with its bloodthirsty gods, Tzintzuntzan needed constant sacrificial victims to appease Curicaueri, the Fire God.

- Also like the Aztec, all the tribute to the Tarascans went directly to the capital city. From the south and west came metal products. Metals were the exclusive possessions of the nobles; commoners were not permitted to own metal. Metals were in the form of tools made of copper alloys, as well as needles, fishhooks, tweezers, axe heads, and spear points. There was also a great deal of gold and silver jewelry.

- The tribute lists also included items not available locally, such as cacao, quetzal feathers, and tropical fruits. Much like the Aztec, the Tarascans built trade relations with people who would eventually become part of the Tarascan Empire.

The elites and honored warriors of the Tarascan wore ear plugs and lip plugs, but commoners could not.

Life in Tzintzuntzan

- Consumer products in the Tarascan Empire were acquired in three ways: by market trading, through state merchants directly, or from state lands. Markets were the only places where common people could acquire goods and services. There were notably fewer exotic goods in the Tarascan markets compared to the market at Tenochtitlan.

- The elite Tarascan society lived a completely different life than that of the common people. Their sources of income, lifestyle, and range of responsibilities were like night and day. However, like two sides of the same coin, they were connected.

- General tribute was stored and used for festival feasts, to feed state labor teams, and to outfit the Tarascan army. State merchants were similar to Aztec *pochteca*, but they had no independent wealth; they worked for the king. These state merchants accompanied gold and silver shipments to the capital.

- Most of the food for royals came from the king's estate lands. People worked those lands as labor taxation. The king owned huge areas of forest, a source of deer and rabbit meat.

- Tarascan royalty were direct liaisons to the Fire God. They kept an ever-burning fire in the main temple, and when they were buried, an entire entourage joined them. The *Relacion de Michoacan* records that dozens of servants and wives were killed and sent to the other world with the king when he died.

- Community identity in the Patzcuaro basin was centered on an annual cycle of festivals. Like the Aztec, each month had a theme. In a certain month, evildoers were punished—killed in gladiatorial matches in the public squares, then flayed. Other months were devoted to conquest—a short month to prepare for war and a longer month to go to war.

- As with the Aztec, monthly festivals and preparation for them dominated most of the average Tarascan's life—both commoner and noble. But unlike the Aztec, Tarascan festivals seemed to place greater emphasis on the capital city and, thereby, increased its centralized control.

The Great Platform
- The capital at Tzintzuntzan had one central ceremonial complex, surrounded by residential neighborhoods. A massive platform called the Great Platform dominated city life. It had five circular temples on top and was embedded into a hillside overlooking the lake. In the back end on the top were palaces and storehouses.

- The Great Platform was an impressive 400 by 250 meters—almost 30 football fields. An entire royal city once stood on top of it. It dwarfed the Aztec Templo Mayor.

- The circular temples on top of the Great Platform were called *yacatas*. These were the places of public ceremony. An eternal fire was kept in the main one. The architecture is unique in Mesoamerica; the temples are keyhole shaped. The stonework of the temples is also different; it consists of large stones fitted together without stucco. In fact, it looks very much like Inca-style architecture.

- Unfortunately, much of the architecture at Tzintzuntzan was destroyed by the Spanish in their search for gold and silver. The Spanish noted that there massive storehouses inscribed with spirals and geometric shapes, containing quantities of wealth. The first Spanish to arrive in Tzintzuntzan in the 1520s reported that they found 40 chests—20 of gold and 20 of silver. And they found a few more chests in other cities around the basin.

End of an Empire

- When the end came for the Tarascan Empire, it was like a storm cloud moving over them from the east. Their scouts came back with reports that the Aztec had abandoned their frontier forts because the conquistadors were laying siege to Tenochtitlan. All the Tarascans could do was wait and see what would come.

- In 1520, the Aztec were so desperate that they sent a plea for aid to the Tarascans. The emperor rejected the plea and, shortly afterward, died of smallpox. The next emperor of the Tarascans sent his brothers on a reconnaissance mission: They witnessed the Aztec defeat. When they came back, they urged immediate surrender to the Spanish, which the Tarascans did.

- The Spanish arrived in force to Tzintzuntzan in 1522 and immediately demanded all the gold and silver. When that was gone, the Spanish demanded more. Temples were ripped down and churches built from the rubble. The two mighty empires of people from the north—the Aztec and the Tarascans—had fallen to the Spanish in less than a decade. Mesoamerica would never be the same.

Suggested Reading

Foster, *Tzintzuntzan*.

Coe and Koontz, *Mexico*.

1. Why were the Tarascans so different? Do you believe the South American influence hypothesis?

2. Do you think it's possible, as the origin stories claim, that the Aztecs and the Tarascans held common ancestry?

3. If the Tarascans had answered the Aztec call for help, do you think Cortes would have still taken Tenochtitlan?

Independent Tarascans—Desert Warriors
Lecture 37—Transcript

Just 50 miles to the west of Tenochtitlan stood a line that the Aztecs could not cross, the border of the Tarascan empire. In many ways, the Tarascans were like their Aztec counterparts, fierce warriors, lovers of the arts, and devoted worshippers. But in other ways, they were aliens on the Mesoamerican landscape.

Like the Aztecs, the Tarascans controlled a tributary empire. They widely subjugated areas that had to pay their taxes. They were actually only second to the Aztecs in the size of their empire, and year after year they expanded out. It was a very highly centralized trading system, and everything went through their capital, called Tzintzuntzan.

Tarascan territory today is within the state of Michoacan, and that's actually an ancient Aztec name that means, place of fishermen. In that area, there were many highland lakes, and Lake Patzcuaro was the heart of their empire. Between Patzcuaro and Tenochtitlan, there was a large buffer zone. According to Tarascan history, they arrived to Patzcuaro somewhere around 1250 A.D., just like the Aztec say their entry into the valley of Mexico. And they expanded their empire during the 1300s, just like the Aztecs.

The two clashed together in the fertile river basins between their two empires, and they both built fortresses and dug in along the line. It remained that way right up until Spanish contact. So the Patzcuaro basin was their heartland. It was volcanic country, so the soil was very, very good. Those highland lakes provided good fishing, and there were thick forests that were great for hunting. And because they were such hunters and fishermen, some viewed them as less advanced than other cultures, like the Aztecs.

The capital city in the basin was called Tzintzuntzan, and it was right on the shores of Lake Patzcuaro. It had a massive temple complex, and that complex was inhabited by nobles and priests; those are the people that controlled the highly controlled administration. There were worship schedules and trade distribution networks that were controlled from that capital.

At the top of the social hierarchy was the Tarascan king, a *cazonci*. And he ruled like an emperor. He lived on the great platform in Tzintzuntzan. He was the head priest, the head warrior, and the head administrator. The empire's wealth came directly to him. And all of the vast land holdings were actually his property. At a single word from him, the entire empire went to war. Tzintzuntzan's peak population was maybe about 35,000 people, and within the basin there was another 90 cities. Most of them were very small, and few of them had any temples. But they were tightly bound together in a social network. There were market and religious circuits that went through each one of these smaller areas, and all of the citizens in the basin owed their taxes. In total, around the basin, we estimate there might have been as many as 100,000 people.

The Tarascan Empire was much wider than just the Patzcuaro basin. In total, we estimate it was about 75,000 square kilometers. But the other areas were tribute states. Just like the Aztecs, those people were not considered by the Tarascans as part of us, they were just people who gave their taxes. So, as the Aztecs controlled the Lake Texcoco basin, and that was the us, the Aztecs, the Tarascans controlled the Lake Patzcuaro basin. In that regard, both empires were quite similar. By the Tarascan's own account, they were not originally from Patzcuaro. Unfortunately, and as usual, the Spanish didn't ask a lot of questions. Luckily, a combination of contact period chronicles, later ethnographies, and archaeology allows us to make some good guesses.

The Spanish arrived to that area quickly, as early as 1520. They were chasing stories of gold and silver. They founded at Tzintzuntzan; they took it; and they didn't ask questions. During that first visit, they gave them the name the Tarascans. That's probably from their word, that's *tarhaskua*, father-in-law. It appears that it was some sort of sad attempt to garner peace by offering them their daughters.

They actually call themselves the *Purepecha*. That translates, "the late arrivals." Now real chronicles of them weren't made until the 1530s, and by that time, the named Tarascan had stuck. A priest named Jeronimo de Alcala was the first one to study them, and he wrote a wonderful document called *Relacion de Michoacan*. And it was broken up into three parts: religion, society, and history. He collected his information mostly from elders. They explained this name, the late arrivals. They said that they had come from the north, from Chichimeca lands, just like the Aztec, and that they had arrived at roughly 1250, again, like the Aztec. They also said that 1325 was the year that they first established their capital. Again, that was just like the Aztec. And to me, the stories are so close, that sounds fishy. I'm not sure whether that was the real story.

But, taking that on face value and continuing, they said that the first warrior king was named Tariacuri, and Patzcuaro was his capital in 1325. And that the Purepecha people had blended with the local population. Then, after his lifetime, his nephews spread out into the basin and conquered the entire area. They established two new towns, Ihuatzio and Tzintzuntzan. Tzintzuntzan, especially, swelled in population. It became five times larger than all the other cities. And by 1440, it became the new capital. Tariacuri's family became the royal dynasty. Now, again, this sounds a lot like Aztec origins, but there was an important difference; these people didn't speak Nahuatl.

Analysis of Purepecha language concludes that it's closest to Quechua. That's the Inca language way down in South America. And recall from my earlier lectures, the early west coast Mexico cultures had connections with South America. And it makes logical sense, since they're so close by, that that was the most likely population that these new Tarascans had blended with.

There were other Tarascan origin stories, too. Some of them say they came from the seven caves of Chicomoztoc, that they wandered along with the Aztecs, and that they split off somewhere in Chichimec lands. Again, this makes me wonder whether the Aztecs hadn't imposed that on them. But they say they settled at a lake under a volcano, Coatepeque, and then at that point they fight and split and they became the two cultures. I wonder, are they implying that Patzcuaro, with its lake and volcano, was that space of Coatepeque? We'll probably never be sure.

But as you can see, these stories are somewhat dubious. However, the Tarascans are clearly different people. They speak a different language, they have different customs, crafts, and temples. And the base of their population is most likely the people from west Mexico that migrated inland. And those people were definitely influenced by South America. If that was true, so were the Tarascans.

Further evidence supports that. In fact, we have three points. One, metallurgy, the Tarascans were experts, and that knowledge entered the west coast from South America. That much is incontrovertible. Number two, stirrup vessels. These are odd forms from South America that are too distinct to have been created independently in both areas; we find those among the Tarascans, as well. And three, the Purepecha language. It's Quechua derived. There's no way that that happened independently. Further, Cortez's accounts reported that there were traders on the Pacific coast in 1525. They saw them at the mouth of the Balsa River. They arrived in massive dugout canoes, and they stayed for five to six months; then they returned south. Even further, in 1531 Pedro de Alvarado guided from Guatemala to Ecuador on established navigation routes.

Now, the evidence is admittedly a little shaky, but I believe that the Tarascans were a cultural blend. South America-connected people were already there. Then the Chichimecs came down from the north about 1250, and those two populations blended together. Presto. Tarascan culture is born, desert warriors with South American cultural influence. So, the Tarascan empire was essentially a new socioeconomic strategy exerted over an already established resource base. What was a vast region of independent city-states, like the rest of Mesoamerica, came under the control of a new, highly centralized political unit.

The Tarascans were all about conquest and tribute. Like the Aztecs, step one was local control, so they conquered the Patzcuaro basin, and they imposed a new order, especially in terms of tax collection. Ninety communities came under their control, and all of their tribute poured into the capital city of Tzintzuntzan. Nobles of Tzintzuntzan became very wealthy, and they requested tribute actually much more frequently than the Aztecs. Every 80 days vast storehouses of wealth were owed to the capital. It was mostly food, cotton, and clothes from the basin. There were labor for state projects, as well; everyone had to participate in state constructions. But the Nobles wanted even more than that; they wanted exotic goods. So an aggressive expansion of their empire began in the 1400s. "The Relation of Michoacan" says there was actually a specific month dedicated to conquest. They don't say which one it is, but everybody was enlisted into service at that time. The Purepecha armies expanded their borders all the way to the coast, and then they ran up against the Aztecs trying to do exactly the same thing.

Different kinds of tributes were taken from different places. On the Aztec frontier, they mainly wanted slaves and people to sacrifice. Like Tenochtitlan, Tzintzuntzan needed constant sacrificial victims to appease their god. In this case, it was a fire god named Curicaueri. Also, like Tenochtitlan, all of their tribute went directly to the capital city. From the south and west they got metal products. They established many shaft mines in that area, and there were state smelting operations. Local farmers were sometimes enlisted to go and work in those mines. People had to work wherever they were told.

Metals were purely noble possessions. Commoners were not allowed to have anything made of metal. Many of those noble tools were made of copper alloys; they were stronger, harder metals in that way. There were things like needles and fish hooks and tweezers. There were also axe heads and spear points. There was also a lot of jewelry made of gold and silver in that case. And the elites would wear these ear plugs and lip plugs. Honored warriors could have ear plugs too, but commoners couldn't have such things. The tribute lists also included things that they could not have acquired locally, things like a cacao, and Quetzal feathers, and tropical fruits. Taxpaying regions had to trade outside of their borders. Tarascans asked them to go collect those things. It appears that it's the same technique as the Aztecs. Getting people to build further trade relations that would eventually become part of the Tarascan empire. It was a technique to stimulate trade and commerce.

Consumer products in the Tarascan empire were acquired in three different ways. They were either done through market trading, through state merchants directly, or taken from the royaled estate lands. Markets were the only places where common people could acquire goods and services. There were many, many small markets in all the towns, and a few big, large ones that everybody participated in. Tzintzuntzan had one, and another three cities had these large markets. They were very, very orderly, like the Aztec markets. The stalls were all run by women, and they would keep their materials in baskets in front of them, each one grouped in a different sector of the market. There were also fun things, like restaurants and services for hire.

But there were notably less exotic goods in those markets as compared to the market at Tenochtitlan. There was a little bit, but that stuff really wasn't for the commoners. The Tarascan state had tight control over exotic items. Medals and luxury goods were things that only the nobles could have. So when you went to the markets, those things weren't there. Those things went directly to the palace storehouses.

The elite Tarascan society were living an almost completely different life than those of the common people. Their sources of income and how they lived and the range of responsibilities they had were night and day. However, like two sides of the same coin, they were connected. Food and other commodities for nobles, priests, and the royal family came from two sources, either directly from state merchants or from the royaled estate land holdings. General tribute was stored and used for festival feasts, feeding state labor teams, and outfitting the Tarascan army.

State merchants were like Aztec *pochteca*, but they were different. They didn't have any independent wealth; they worked for the king. They also traveled widely, though, just *pochteca*. Some of them actually went outside the empire trying to establish new relationships. Others oversaw luxury tribute payments. These state merchants accompanied gold and silver shipments all the way to the capital. Most of the royal food came from the king's estate lands. There were vast holdings, Patzcuaro's best land. On that land there were vast fields of corn and maguey. And people worked those lands as labor taxation. It was completely private land, only royaled use. Anyone who was caught stealing from it, the penalty was death.

The king owned huge areas of forest, as well. Within those forests, they got tons of deer and rabbit meat. And they actually had state hunters who went out there to capture that off the king's land. They hunted for the king. But the king also enjoyed hunting, and he would go out with big hunting parties, an entourage would accompany him. I envision it as the European kings, how they used to go out into the king's forest on these hunting expeditions. Sadly, most of those forests are gone today. The wood has been cut down, and now it's cattle land.

Tarascan royalty were almost godlike. They were direct liaisons to the fire god. They kept an ever-burning fire in the main temple. And when they were buried, an entire entourage joined them. "The Relation of Michoacan" records that dozens of servants and wives were killed and sent to the other world with the king when they died. And as an interesting side note, when I was studying for this, I remembered the Natchez Indians of Louisiana. They were found by Frenchmen in the 16th century, and they did things very much like the Tarascans. They had this eternal fire, and the king was buried with his servants and his wives. They were also people who were big sacrificers, which was not common in the United States area. They also spoke a language which was called a language isolate. A man named Le Page du Pratz learned some of it, but it was never fully recorded. And it obviously wasn't like the languages around it.

Their own myths say that they had migrated from way to the south. I wonder, are those Natchez Indians connected to the Tarascans? Well, that's a story for another lecture series, I suppose. Tarascan commoners lived pretty simply, very basic. They lived in one-room houses. The houses had thatched roofs and wattle and daub walls. Men were typically farmers or fishermen. Women worked at home and in the local markets. They bought and sold things for the family, but they rarely left their own communities.

Every one owed taxes for tribute. But products could still be made at home and used. They could have personal, small farming plots, as well. Most people gave not materials, but their labor. And we're really not sure how often they owed that labor, but when they were called to duty, they had to work. Otherwise, they could work for themselves.

Community identity in the Patzcuaro basin was very, very strong. It was centered around an annual cycle of festivals. Like the Aztecs, each month had a theme. They were following basically the same calendar, but the Tarascan months had different themes. In general, they were much more war and conquest focused. Everyone participated in these festivals, and they bonded society.

Alfonso Caso studied their festival cycle in the 1940s. He didn't get it all, but he saw a few of them. One month in particular he noticed was a month in which evildoers were punished. They were killed in gladiatorial matches in the public squares. And after that, they were flayed and their skins were worn. There were other months that were devoted to conquest. There was one little month that was to prepare for war, and there was a big month to go to war. And all men participated in this on an annual basis. Like the Aztecs, monthly festivals and preparation for them dominated most of the average Tarascan's life, both commoner and noble. But unlike the Aztec, Tarascan festivals seemed to place greater emphasis on the capital city and thereby increasing its centralized control. For example, in one month every citizen in the basin was expected to bring wood for the fires that eternally burned in the main temples.

As I've been saying, the Tarascan empire was strongly centralized, focused around the capital at Tzintzuntzan. Now, let's turn to a focus on that capital and discuss what we knew about it. Unfortunately, we don't know a lot about it. The Spanish destroyed most of its temples. The common houses were easily leveled. And there was gold and silver fever. They ripped up the place looking for it. No one bothered to chronicle until a decade after contact.

The city had one central ceremonial complex, and it was surrounded by residential neighborhoods. The chronicles say there were 40 wards with about 25 houses each. And they also said there were about 35,000 inhabitants, but I don't really trust that data. It doesn't add up; 40 wards times 25 houses, that equals 1,000 houses in the area. Were there 35 people a house? I wish we had more info in that regard.

There was one huge platform that dominated city life. Now it's called the Great Platform. It had five circular temples up on top, and it was embedded into a hillside overlooking the lake. In the back end on the top were palaces and storehouses. The Great Platform is impressive. It's 400 by 250 meters in size. That's almost 30 football fields. An entire royal city once stood on top of it. It dwarfed the Aztec temple, Mayor. If you put the Aztec temple Mayor inside, it covers just one little area of the Great Platform.

At the top of the platform, along its front face, stood five circular temples called *yacatas*. They were connected in the back, so they were joined together. And they were keyhole shaped when you looked at them from above. They were the places of public ceremony. An eternal fire was kept in the main one. The architecture is unique in Mesoamerica. It's rounded, yes, and we've seen rounded things. But these are keyhole shaped, and we hadn't seen that before. It's stone work is also different. It's fitted very large stones and there's no stucco. In fact, it looks much more like Inca-style architecture. This may be yet another connection to South America. Unfortunately, again, most of those temples were ripped down from the Spanish, so we don't have a good idea of what they looked like originally.

Behind the *yacata* line stood the palaces and storehouses. Royals, nobles, and priests lived there as well. That architecture, again, was ripped out at contact looking for gold and silver. And still, we've had no serious excavations at it at their bases. The Spanish told us they were massive storehouses, and they also said they were inscribed with spirals and geometric shapes. Quantities of gold and silver were kept in these palaces. In the 1520s, the first Spanish that arrived found it. They reported that they found 40 chests of it, 20 of gold and 20 of silver. And they found a few more chests in other cities around the basin. And the Spanish went crazy looking for it. They tortured nobles for the locations of the gold.

The description of one room caught my eye and imagination. The Spanish said it was full of enemy heads, maybe like an Aztec skull rack, or, maybe like Peruvian trophy heads. I wish I could have seen it or had a better description. When the end came for the Tarascan Empire, it was like a storm cloud moving over them from the east. Their scouts came back with reports that the Aztec had abandoned their frontier forts because the conquistadors were laying siege to Tenochtitlan. All they could do was wait and see.

In 1520, the Aztec were so desperate that they sent a plea for aid to the Tarascans. The emperor, Zuangua, said no. Then shortly after, he died of smallpox in that same year. The new, young emperor, Tangaxoan, sent his brothers to take a look, and they looked at the Aztec defeat. When they came back, they said, we need to immediately surrender to the Spanish; let's not give a fight, and that's what they did.

The Spanish arrived in force to Tzintzuntzan in 1522 and immediately demanded all their gold. When all the gold and silver was gone, they demanded more from the mines. And eventually, Tangaxoan resisted. Cristobal de Olid, one of Cortez's soldiers, was sent to subdue him. Tangaxoan hid with his family, but eventually he was found, captured, and tortured.

On February 14, 1530, he was dragged by horses, strangled, and burned at the stake. The temples were ripped down, and they built churches out of the rubble. The Tarascan empire ended that year. The two mighty empires of people from the north, the Aztecs and the Tarascans, had fallen to the Spanish in less than a decade. Mesoamerica would never be the same.

In our next lecture, let's take a step back and look at the possible place these northern warriors could have come from—Paquime.

Paquime—Northernmost Mesoamerican City?
Lecture 38

Paquime, in northern Mexico's state of Chihuahua, is an enigma. It stands at the frontier between Mesoamerica and the American Southwest. Archaeology at the site suggests that Mesoamerican elites were controlling a Pueblo population there. In this lecture, we'll discuss Paquime's divided nature—with both Mesoamerican and Pueblo influences—and examine its architectural and engineering achievements, as well as its extensive trading network. With the end of Paquime in 1450, a unique way of life in the northern deserts of Mexico disappeared. The end for the rest of Mesoamerica was not far behind.

A Time of Transition

- The site of Paquime, or Casas Grandes, is the largest ruins for hundreds of miles in its area. Architecturally, Paquime is half Pueblo and half Mesoamerican. On the west side are temples and Mesoamerican-style ball courts. On the east side are pit houses and adobe structures. Paquime ceramics are primarily Pueblo forms, but there are also ceramics that resemble those from western Mexico.

- Some archaeologists connect Paquime to the American Southwest, specifically to the cultures at Chaco Canyon. However, Chaco Canyon was abandoned in 1150, and Paquime seems to have originated about 1250. Other scholars link Paquime to the Aztec, suggesting that the city may have been an outpost of *pochteca* traders.

- In any event, the Mesoamerican influence is very clear at Paquime. Paquime was burned, then rebuilt about 1340; when it was rebuilt, it was even more Mesoamerican in style. The Aztec were still under Tepanec control in 1340; their empire and its expansion did not begin until 1427. Paquime was abandoned about 1450. In fact, Paquime's dates—between 1250 and 1450—fall in a transitional period for both the American Southwest and Mesoamerica.

The site of Paquime is near the San Miguel River and is surrounded by abundant farm land; the city also constructed reservoirs and a water system that further aided farming.

- Paquime has been known since the 1500s. A Spanish explorer named Francisco de Ibarra, following trade routes from Mexico up north, first reported the ruins in 1565. At that time, a people called the Opata were farming in the region, organized into small, typically Mesoamerican city-states.

Joint Casas Grandes Project

- Little professional archaeological work was done at Paquime until 1958, with the inauguration of the Joint Casas Grandes Project, led by Charles Di Peso. Di Peso excavated the ceremonial architecture in the west part of Paquime and left the east side almost completely intact.

- After Di Peso's project, Paquime sat untouched by archaeology for almost 50 years, although the areas surrounding Paquime have been further studied. There have been extensive surveys, most of which took place in the 2000s by Michael Whalen and Paul Minnis. These two archaeologists focused on issues of trade, politics, and local farming.

- Much of what we know about Paquime, however, comes from Di Peso's excavations, his reports, and the subsequent studies of the artifacts he collected. It sounds as if we don't have much evidence to work with, but thankfully, Di Peso's work was exceptional.

East and West Paquime
- Paquime's layout reflects its divided nature. There are two distinct sections, east and west, divided by a wall and a water channel feeding both sides. Every housing zone had its own running water.

- The west side has Mesoamerican-style architecture, with stone buildings. The east side is in the Pueblo style, with adobe buildings. On the east side—almost purely residential—are a couple of circular house pits, but most of the dwellings are rectangular adobe houses of one to two stories, arranged around patios.

- The west side held the public buildings and three ball courts, which were I-shaped, like Mesoamerican ball courts, and built in stone. Hohokam ball courts, which are in Arizona, are ovals. To confirm the Mesoamerican influence, underneath those ball courts were sacrificial victims, with men in the center and women on the ends. Each was dismembered—definitely not Pueblo behavior.

- There are 18 platform mounds at the site, of varying shapes and sizes. Some are more circular; others are rectangular. One large circular mound is connected to the city reservoir; a rectangular mound is attached to the main ball court. Some of the mounds are effigies, in the shape of a bird or a cross. Those mounds are not Mesoamerican forms, nor are they Pueblo. If anything, they look like mound structures built by the native cultures in the Midwest United States.

- Perhaps the strongest Mesoamerican connection at the site is the House of the Macaws—apparently a breeding site for macaws used in rituals. This may be connected to an odd find in archaeological digs in the Southwest. In a cache there was found the left wing of a macaw of about a year old. Perhaps Paquime provided the birds for such rituals.

- A strangely absent feature at Paquime is the *kiva*. Kivas—circular, subterranean temples—are at the core of Pueblo religious life. There is a roof on the surface level, with an access hole and a ladder leading down. Inside are fire pits and benches.

Architectural and Engineering Achievements

- The most impressive section of Paquime is its huge apartment complex, at least three stories tall, with hundreds of rooms and patio areas connected together. Underneath were subterranean wells for water and sweat baths.

- The complex itself had space for more than 1,000 people. Architecturally, that complex is particularly Pueblo. It is made of adobe and has T-shaped doorways—exactly like those seen in Chaco Canyon. Its stories are in a step form; ladders serve as to provide access between floors.

- From an engineering perspective, the most remarkable construction at the site is the city's water system. It contains reservoirs and channels, all of them plaster-lined, leading to the houses and temples. There were also silting ponds outside the reservoirs, indicating the activity of organized labor crews and routine maintenance.

Heart of a Network

- Although Paquime was a cosmopolitan city whose rulers led with a complex blend of multicultural ideas, the estimated population of Paquime is surprisingly small—perhaps only 2,500 people. A possible explanation is that Paquime was a disembedded capital, like Monte Alban in Oaxaca.

- Whalen's studies in the area found 128 contemporary sites, all within 30 kilometers of Paquime. Most of them are small, but some of them are almost as large as Paquime itself. Whalen's studies indicate that Paquime was not an isolated city; rather, it was the heart of some kind of network.

- Whalen's research also found fire signals on hills in the area. An analysis demonstrated that Paquime could signal the entire network with this system. The Tarascans also had a network of fire signals for the Patzcuaro basin.

- The villages surrounding Paquime are from the Viejo period, which began between 1200 and 1250. Paquime was very small at that time, with only about 20 house clusters and a small water system. This suggests that Paquime started local, then amplified through trade into a larger and more international system.

Connections to the American Southwest

- Artifacts found at Paquime indicate that its people traded far and wide. What's more, the city's blended architecture styles are neatly reflected in the objects found in Di Peso's excavation. The largest single category of trade item was shells imported from the Gulf of California and perhaps as far away as the coast of western Mexico. Di Peso found more than 4 million shells.

- Paquime produced and exported excellent pottery, very much in the Pueblo style: bowls and jars painted red on brown with geometric bands. Some ceramics resembled those of the Mogollon culture, as well.

- Paquime imported many items from the south but exported almost exclusively to the north. Items from Paquime have been found in Arizona, New Mexico, and Texas.

- Archaeologist Stephen Lekson interprets this northern trade as evidence that the people of Paquime were part of the American Southwest, not Mesoamerica. He sees the north–south line between Paquime, Chaco Canyon, and the Southwest ruins of the Aztec as a continuum of culture. The discovery of fragments of a Pueblo road toward Paquime also supports Lekson's theory of a connection.

South American Influence

- The majority of Paquime's imports from western Mexico, aside from tons of shells, are copper bells and jewelry. The best sources of those were Colima, Nayarit, and Jalisco. These western coast people, after the fall of the Teuchitlan tradition and before the Tarascans, might have been Paquime's trade partners.

- Although most of Paquime's pottery was Pueblo, not all of it was. Some of it was in the form of human figurines, like those in western Mexico; as we've said, western Mexico was influenced by South America.

- One of the items Di Peso found was a stirrup vessel with a portrait head, just like those found in South America. This discovery adds yet another layer to the mystery that is Paquime.

A Curious Theory

- We conclude this lecture with a unique theory of the origin of Paquime: The timing and the evidence may suggest that Paquime was Aztlan—the Aztec mythic place of origin.

- Paquime was burned about 1340, then rebuilt as a Mesoamerican city. It also has a water system very much like the Aztec capital's water system: Both were masterpieces of hydraulic engineering. There are also hints of Tarascan influence at Paquime, such as the fire signals. A trader would have to travel through Tarascan territory to reach western Mexico trade routes.

- Paquime may have been a capital of an Aztec tribute state. Both the Aztec and the Tarascans say that they came from Aztlan in the north, and the clues seem to be pointing to Paquime.

- Aztlan was said to be a place of herons, a marshy place. *Chihuahua* is a Nahuatl word, meaning "the place where river waters meet." And it just so happens that today, that is a migratory bird destination for herons.

- The people of Aztlan came from Chicomoztoc, the Place of 7 Caves. There are a number of caves in the Paquime area, and they were inhabited by pre-Paquime people. The drawings of those caves look very much like the Aztec drawings of Chicomoztoc.

The End of Paquime
- Paquime met its end in 1450 A.D. That, too, might have been related to cultures in the south. The Pueblo area experienced a drought in the 1300s, as well as a lack of trade partners. At the same time, the Aztec and the Tarascan empires arose, changing and dominating the tribute networks.

- The people that Paquime could have been trading with earlier were now under the control of either the Tarascans or the Aztecs. By 1400, there were no more west Mexico trade goods at Paquime, probably because those routes had been cut off to them.

- Paquime's last few decades were bad ones. A lack of centralized leadership is apparent in the archaeology. People started building inside the plazas, and the water system fell into disrepair. In the end, people were actually buried in the water channels.

- We're not sure how Paquime ended, but the locals in the area have a myth that it was an uprising, a protest of slavery practices. Whatever happened to Paquime, it was the end of a unique way of life in the northern deserts of Mexico. The end for the rest of Mesoamerica was not far behind.

Suggested Reading

Powell, ed., *Secrets of Casas Grandes*.

Schaafsma and Riley, eds., *The Casas Grandes World*.

1. Who were the leaders of Paquime? Were they locals or foreigners who took over?

2. Why did so few people live in Paquime, given that it had enough water for many more people?

3. Why was Paquime burned around 1340? Who was responsible?

Paquime—Northernmost Mesoamerican City?
Lecture 38—Transcript

The site of Paquime in way Northern Mexico is an enigma. It stands at the frontier between Mesoamerica and the American Southwest, belonging to both and neither at the same time. In this lecture we'll discuss what we do and don't know about Paquime, and I'll conclude with some of my own outlandish theories.

Paquime, or Casas Grandes, as we call it in the U.S., is the largest ruins for hundreds of miles around. It's in the northwest part of Chihuahua state, just south of the New Mexico border. About 140 miles to the northeast is the modern city of El Paso. The site itself is near the San Miguel river, and there there's abundant farming land around there. The City made reservoirs and water systems that further aided their farming.

Architecturally, it's half-Pueblo and half-Mesoamerican. On the west side, we have temples and Mesoamerican-style ball courts. On the east side we have pit houses and adobe structures. Their ceramics were primarily Pueblo forms, but there's also forms that look more like West Mexico-culture ceramics. Tons of shells were found at the site, all from the Gulf of California. And Mesoamerican elite people seem to be controlling a Pueblo population there.

Regionally, it's part of the American Southwest. And some people want to connect it to the cultures at Chaco Canyon. That's the amazing Anasazi ruins that lie to the North. But Chaco Canyon was abandoned in 1150 A.D., and Paquime seems to start about 1250 A.D. We have the same trouble trying to connect them to the Mogollon culture. They were also in the Southwest, but just like the Anasazi, there was a big upheaval about 1150 A.D. that caused them to move. It was a massive drought, and it even got worse around 1300 A.D.

Others have tried to link Paquime to the Aztecs, or more generally, Central Mexico. There are suggestions that maybe it was an outpost of *pochteca* traders. But again, the dates really are wrong; 1250 is really too early for the Aztecs, and, it's too late for the Toltecs that came before them. But, in any event, the Mesoamerican influence is very clear at Paquime. Paquime was burned and then rebuilt about 1340 A.D., and when it was rebuilt, it looked even more Mesoamerican in form. And at that point, maybe it was connected to the Aztecs. But no, that doesn't exactly work either, because the Aztecs are still under Tepanec control at 1340. Their empire and its expansion really didn't begin until 1427. Paquime is abandoned about 1450, so, the chronology, again, doesn't really work out.

In fact, Paquime's dates are in a perfect gap. They're in a place where both the Southwest and Mesoamerica are kind of in a slump. It's between 1250 and 1450; that's a transitional period for both of those areas. There were really no thriving neighbors through most of that time period. But Paquime is definitely thriving. If anything, it seems that they're the ones doing the influencing, not outside forces influencing them.

But even the chronology is part of our problem. There's a lot a debate and revisions on Paquime itself's dates. Some want to push it back to make it work with Choco times. Others want to push it forward to make it work with Aztec times. But when we look at all the evidence, neither of them really work. It's a push and pull. Archaeology really can't support either movement either way. And actually, it's the archaeology that's the problem. Specifically, there hasn't been enough. Personally, I'm shocked how little archaeology has actually been done at Paquime. Despite its size an obvious importance, most projects there have been little more than surface observations.

Paquime has been known since the 1500s. A Spanish explorer named Francisco de Ibarra first reported the ruins in 1565. He was following trade routes from Mexico up to the north. At that time, there was a people called the Opata. They were living in the region, and they were farming, and they were organized into small, typically Mesoamerican city-states.

Settlement of the area was tried in the 1600s by Spanish colonies. But they were repeatedly attacked, and their communities were burned. At that time, it was Apache country, and had been since the late 1500s. The Apaches were on both sides of the border at that time, and they controlled that area up through the 1800s. The United States pretty much gave them free reign if they stayed in Mexico. But then finally, in 1886, Geronimo was defeated in Arizona.

Just one year before Geronimo's death in 1885, Adolph Bandelier visited Paquime, and he made our first map and he took some samples. He was one of over a half-dozen explorers that poked through the area over the next 50 years. But each expedition only lasted for a few days, and again, they did about the same thing. They made a few maps. They took a few surface collections. And they left.

Now, Bandelier was actually aware of Paquime through an odd story. In 1866, someone had found a 5,000-pound meteorite within the site. It was a bureaucrat from the State of Chihuahua. And they were exploring around Paquime, which means, basically, they were out there looting. His group was camping out and exploring the ruins. And then one of them walked into a room in an apartment complex, and he found this meteorite. He said it was in some sort of tomb made of bricks, and it was covered with some kind of linen. Word of it got to William Pearson, a U.S. Vice Console, and he decided to buy it from these guys. And he gets it back to El Paso at some difficult trouble. He actually had to hire a 10,000-pound-capacity wagon to drag this meteorite back to El Paso. From there, it went by train all the way up to Philadelphia. And now, it's in the Smithsonian Museum. I was asked, actually, by the show Ancient Aliens what in the world that thing was. And I had to say, I have no idea. How did those ancient people move it? And why did they have it? They really weren't used to carrying things that big in Paquime. I have no idea what it was doing there.

Aside from looting and mapping, little professional work was done there until 1958. That's when something called the Joint Casas Grandes Project happened. It was led by Charles Di Peso; he was one of the most famous archaeologists in the American Southwest at the time. And he did two seasons of excavations. It was the biggest project ever or since. And luckily, he wrote a very complete report.

Now, Di Peso mostly excavated in the west part. He excavated the ceremonial architecture, and he left the east side almost completely intact. To get his dates he used dendrochronology, which is looking at tree rings and things like roof beams. He was also using some carbon-14 dating, but it was very, very new, and it wasn't a very good technique; dendrochronology was better. Even with that, most of his dates today have been overturned. He said that the site lived about 1150. But today, with revised techniques, we're looking at more like 1250 as a start. With 1150, he hypothesized that it was Choco and perhaps early *pochteca* connections that had built the site.

After Di Peso's project, Paquime sat there untouched by archaeology for almost 50 years. Then finally in the 1990s, a super fund for tourism was developed in Central America and Mexico. And a lot of money went to Paquime for this, but it was mostly consolidation and repair of buildings. The buildings that had been exposed by Di Peso's project were in pretty bad shape. So, INA cleaned that up and did a little archaeology, too. But, to date, very little of it has been published. In 1998, UNESCO made it a World Heritage site, so at least it's being further protected nowadays.

What has been further studied are the areas surrounding Paquime. There have been extensive surveys, most of them taking place in the 2000s. Michael Whalen and Paul Minnis have been doing most of that work. And they were focused on looking at issues of trade, and politics, and local farming. They also took a moment to reanalyze Di Peso's work from his notes and from his artifact collections. But at Paquime itself, there's been nothing done in decades, and as far as I can see, there are no plans for further excavations. So most of what we know about Paquime comes from Di Peso's excavations, his reports, and the subsequent studies of the artifacts he collected. It sounds like not much to go on, but thankfully, Di Peso actually did a lot of fine and thorough work.

The City's layout reflects its nature. There are two distinct sections, east and west. They're divided by a wall and a water channel, and that water channel fed to both sides. Apparently, every housing zone had its own running water. The west side was the Mesoamerican style, and there were a lot of things built in stone there. The east side was Pueblo culture style, and there were a lot of adobe buildings there.

That east Pueblo side seemed almost purely residential. There were a couple of circular house pits, but most of them were rectangular adobe houses on the surface. Those Adobe houses were one to two stories and arranged around patios. Di Peso estimated there were probably about 1,200 of them, but he never really excavated them. Looking back through his notes, Whalen has revised that number to only about 500 houses, much less.

Now, the west side held the public buildings. Within it there are three ball courts, I-shaped ball courts, like Mesoamerica, and built in stone. They're definitely Mesoamerican in style. Hohokam ball courts, which aren't that far away in Arizona, are ovals; they're not I-shaped, so they're distinct. To add to the Mesoamerican flavor, underneath those ball courts they found sacrificial victims. There were men in the center and females on the ends. Each of them were dismembered; there were arms and skulls in odd places. That was definitely not Pueblo behavior.

There were also platform mounds. Not just one or two, but there were 18 mounds at the site, and they were of varying shapes and sizes. Some of them more circular, others were rectangular. It's hard to say if there was one main temple there. There is one circular mound that's larger and connected to the city reservoir. There's another one that's rectangular and attached to its main ball court.

Some of the mounds are effigies, meaning they're shaped to resemble something. One collection of mounds looks like a bird, a headless bird, that is. Another one is the mound of the cross. It has a cross, and then on each end of the cross there are mounds that look like dots. Those aren't really Mesoamerican forms either; we don't see them in Mesoamerica; we don't see them in the Pueblo area. If anything, they look a lot like the Midwest United States, the mound-builder cultures there. So maybe we're seeing yet more cultural blending in the guise of these effigy mounds.

Perhaps the strongest Mesoamerican connection at the site is the House of the Macaws. There, they actually found macaw breeding pens. There are 122 macaws buried there, and they found egg shells. They were definitely breeding them there, we believe for ritual use. And that was quite a feat to breed a tropical bird that far north. In the Southwest, in other studies that I've been part of, I remembered an odd ritual there. In caches there, we'd find the left wing of a macaw that had reached the age of one. So perhaps, Paquime was the place that was providing these birds for those rituals.

An oddly absent feature at Paquime is the kiva. Kivas are the core of Pueblo religious life. They're circular, subterranean temples. They have a roof that's on the surface level and then an access hole and the ladder where people go down in. Inside, there are fire pits and benches. They're a very particular form. And if Paquime is Pueblo, where are all the kivas? Well, I guess perhaps they're hiding over there in the east side that Di Peso never excavated, but no one's seen them yet.

The most impressive section of the city is its huge apartment complex. There are hundreds of rooms and patio areas all interconnected together. And it's at least three stories tall. Some people used to say six or seven, but conservatively, we know it was three stories tall. And underneath, there were subterranean wells for water. In that same area we found sweat baths.

The complex, just in and of itself, had space for over 1,000 people. Architecturally, that complex is very, very Pueblo. It's made of adobe, though it has very thick walls for an adobe, 70 centimeters on average. It has t-shaped doorways, which are exactly like what we see in Chaco Canyon. It also has the same kind of Pueblo form where it's stepped, in regards to the multi-story look. The roof of this first floor is the patio of the second floor, so it kind of steps up. And the roof of the second floor is the patio of the third floor. Ladders would access between those two floors. From an engineering perspective, the most impressive construction at the site is the City's water system. There are reservoirs and channels, all of them are plaster-lined. They lead to all the houses and the temples. There were also silting ponds outside the reservoirs. This indicates organized labor crews and probably required perpetual maintenance.

So we have this very cosmopolitan city. The leaders are obviously ruling with a complex blend of multicultural ideas. But who were the City's general population? Who supported it? And who were they trading with? The estimated population of Paquime is surprisingly small. Di Peso said only 5,000 people. Now Whalen is saying 2,500. All of that for 2,500 people? Something's wrong. We're missing something. Perhaps there were a bunch of perishable houses that are now gone? But probably no; we would have at least found the bases.

Another possible explanation is that Paquime was a disembedded capital, like Monte Alban down in Oaxaca, that villages supported a relatively small capital. Recent surveys in the area support that idea. Whalen's studies found 128 contemporary sites, all within 30 kilometers of Paquime. Most of them are small, but some of them are almost as large as Paquime itself.

Thanks to studies like Whalen's, we're learning that Paquime was not an isolated city. Rather, it was the heart of some kind of network. His studies found that there were fire signals on hills. An analysis showed that Paquime could signal the entire network with this system. And who does that remind us of? The Tarascans. The Tarascans also had a network of fire signals for the Patzcuaro Basin.

What's more, those surrounding village sites are pretty old. Much of the evidence there comes from the Viejo period, which is 1200 to 1250, the start. Paquime was very small back in that period, too. In that Viejo period, we suspect that there were only about 20 house clusters and a small water system at Paquime. And the other villages were also there at that same time. So that's important new evidence. That means that Paquime started local. Early explanations were always trying to find some kind of foreign migration explanation for Paquime. Di Peso suggested it was a *pochteca* outpost. Lekson, up in the Southwest, says it was part of a Pueblo continuum. But Whalen's survey suggests that the local people amplified trade into a larger and more international system on their very own. So if that's right, they were locals. But they were definitely trading. The question becomes with who? And how far? The artifact record there says from all over the place. Perhaps with the artifacts came these international ideas. The City's blended architecture styles are neatly reflected in the objects found in Di Peso's excavation.

The largest single trade item we find there is shells. They're imported from the Gulf of California, maybe as far as the coast of West Mexico. Di Peso found more than four million shells. They were all over the workshops. They were traded north and locally, but not south. Paquime produced excellent pottery. And they exported a lot of it. It was a very Pueblo-style pottery. It was bowls and jars. It was a specific red-on-brown painted style. There were also some black on whites, just like Mogollon types to the north of them. But all of them had very Pueblo designs, geometric bands. Sometimes there were animal forms mixed in, too, which again, was very Mogollon in style.

Paquime imported lots of items from the south. But they exported almost exclusively north. In Arizona, New Mexico, and Texas, we find all sorts of things that we know came from Paquime. But going south, we find almost nothing from Paquime, neither to Central Mexico or even to West Mexico that we know they're connected to. It's seemingly a very one-sided relationship.

Steve Lekson takes that northern trade as evidence that they were part of the American Southwest, not Mesoamerica. His best evidence, which he calls incontrovertible, is a perfect north-south line between Paquime, Chaco Canyon, and the Southwest ruins named Aztec. He sees it as a continuum of culture. He says Chaco Canyon was from 900 to 1125; that the ruins of Aztec up there in the American Southwest were 1110 to 1275; and then finally Paquime was 1250 to 1450, a nice, neat overlap. And there are lidar studies now that are finding fragments of a Pueblo road that the system is heading straight down towards Paquime. We haven't found all of it, but the more we're finding these roads, the more his idea of their connection is supported.

The majority of imports from West Mexico, aside from tons of shell, are copper bells and jewelry. The best sources of that were Colima, Nayarit, and Jalisco. Those West Coast people, after the fall of the Teuchitlan tradition and before the Tarascans, might have been the trade partners. But it's another odd gap in the chronology. We're really not sure what was going on down there.

Most of Paquime's pottery was Pueblo, but not all of it. There were also some human figurines, like West Mexico. It might have been another sign of that influence. And remember, West Mexico was influenced by South America. And surprisingly enough, one of the things that Di Peso found was a stirrup vessel with a portrait head, just like what we find in South America; that adds yet another layer to the mystery that is Paquime.

That brief discussion of Paquime's foreign connections leads me to the final part of our discussion, and another one of my kind of lunatic-fringe theories. I think the timing and the evidence is just about right to suggest that Paquime was Aztlan, the Aztec mythic place of origin. Let me start by acknowledging a problem. We have chronology problems on both ends of the question. There's constant debate on Paquime's dates. Di Peso said it was 1100s; now we're saying it's 1200; 1200s don't make a likely Chaco Canyon origin, nor Toltec, Aztec, or Tarascan.

Then there's Aztec chronology. Archaeology can actually only confirm it in the 1400s. But we know that early history was burned. It was rewritten by Tlacaelel in the 1430s. His goal was to make the Aztecs seemed more established. So there's a good chance that they arrived later than the 1200s, as they say. They say that Tenochtitlan was established in the year 1325. The Tarascans say their capital was the same year, 1325. Patzcuaro in the same year? I think that's propaganda. They know it's a capital at Tenochtitlan by 1428. The Aztecs say they wandered for about 50 years. And they're very clear about coming from the north.

Now, Paquime was burned about 1340, that's what dendrochronology says. And then it was rebuilt as a Mesoamerican city, with sacrificial victims and ball courts and macaws. It also has a water system very much like the Aztec capital's water system. Both of them were master hydraulic engineering cultures, and both were building water systems about the 1300s.

There's also hints of Tarascan influence. There are clear West Mexico trade routes, and they had to go through Tarascan territory to get there. So Paquime is a capital of a tribute state. Think also of those systems of fire signals; those are just like Tarascans. And also, Di Peso found the same sort of thing we found in Tzintzuntzan; he found one chamber full of trophy heads. Both the Aztecs and the Tarascans say they came from Aztlan in the north, and the clues seem to be pointing to Paquime. So, where could Aztlan be out there in the desert? What are the other candidates? There's none for hundreds of miles. There's an expanse of Chichimeca desert. Northwest Chihuahua is actually the most habitable place between Central Mexico and New Mexico.

Aztlan is said to be a place of herons, a marshy place. Tlacaelel said it was an island, like Tenochtitlan. He was probably making an attempt to connect the two. Chihuahua is a Nahuatl word, meaning, the place where river waters meet. And it just so happens that today, that is a migratory bird place that a lot of herons migrate to. Today, birders go out specifically to Chihuahua to look for herons.

The people of Aztlan came from the seven caves. So does anything up there look like Chicomoztoc? Well, as a matter of fact, yes. There are a number of caves in the Paquime area, and they were inhabited by pre-Paquime people. There were big granaries, and they had adobe constructions inside. And when we look at them in profile, they have odd little pockets that they carved out. And the drawings of those caves look very much like the Aztec drawings of Chicomoztoc, especially a place called Coral Cave. It has multiple little pockets just like the Aztec drawings.

The only other guess could be Cerro Culiacan in Guanajuato. And that doesn't have ruins or herons, and it's very close to the valley of Mexico. I may well be wrong; there's really not enough to strongly say. But, remember, every idea is crazy, until it's not.

Paquime met its end in 1450 A.D. That, too, might have been related to cultures in the south. The Pueblo area was experiencing a drought in the 1300s. They really didn't have any more trade partners up there. And then the Aztec and the Tarascan empires rise, and they change and dominate the tribute networks. People that Paquime could have been trading with earlier, now those folks were under the control of either the Tarascans or the Aztecs. So by 1400, there were no more West Mexico trade goods at Paquime, probably because those routes were cut off to them.

Paquime's last few decades were bad. There was a lack of centralized leadership, and it's apparent in the archaeology. People start building buildings inside the plazas, and the water system falls into disrepair. At the end, we see people actually being buried in those water channels. We're not actually sure how it ended, but the locals in the area have a myth that it was an uprising, a protest for slavery practices.

Whatever happened to Paquime, it was the end of a unique way of life in the northern deserts of Mexico. The end for the rest of Mesoamerica was not far behind. In our next lecture, let's return to the Aztecs and talk about some of their finest art.

Illuminating Works of Aztec Art
Lecture 39

Aztec civilization was a fascinating combination of brutality and beauty—a culture that combined the practice of human sacrifice with a deep appreciation for art, music, and philosophy. For the Aztec, life was a series of paired dualities: male and female, darkness and light, life and death. Nowhere is this dichotomy more evident than in Aztec art. This lecture examines the intricate symbolism in Aztec art, details its depiction of time and mythology, and considers the phenomenon of the dually created Codex Mendoza—an Aztec piece of literature with Spanish intent.

Calendar Stone

- The most famous piece of Aztec art is the Calendar Stone, also called the Sun Stone. A beautifully carved stone disk fabricated from 12 tons of solid basalt, this artwork has come to represent all of Mesoamerica. Originally, it sat on top of the Templo Mayor in Tenochtitlan.

- In the 1500s, Spanish priest Diego Duran spotted it in the rubble, buried under the cathedral's foundation. It was then rediscovered in the 1790s during repairs on the cathedral. At that point, the Spanish mounted it into the cathedral's facade, where it was known as Moctezuma's Clock.

Images of Venus and flint knives encircling the side of the Calendar Stone may make the symbolic point that the Aztec universe was surrounded by war.

- Although the artwork was all about time, it was not a clock. The Calendar Stone was a representation of

Aztec time and history. Overall, it symbolizes the sun. Arrow symbols on the exterior of the disk represent the rays of the sun.

- The inner ring bands hold calendar glyphs. In the very center of the stone is the face of the Sun God, Tonatiuh. Tonatiuh is shown with a flint knife as his tongue. According to the Aztec, sacrifices were needed to keep the sun moving; that flint-knife tongue is said to be Tonatiuh's thirst for blood.

The Aztec Dichotomy
- Four glyph blocks around the innermost circle of the Calendar Stone represent the four previous creations: 4 Jaguar, 4 Wind, 4 Rain, and 4 Water. Today's people are living in the fifth creation, known as 4 Motion. Although we do not have an Aztec estimation of how long the fifth creation will last, there is a prediction that it will be destroyed by earthquakes—hence, the motion.

- The dates in the four blocks are days, not years. Interestingly, each starts with 4—the same as the Maya creation day. On the next band out from those blocks is a list of 20 day names in the sacred calendar, in a circle all the way around. Depicted here are the five mythological eras of time enfolded by the sacred calendar.

- The outermost band is a double-headed snake wrapping all the way around the stone. The faces meet together at the bottom; from the mouths come two deities: the Sun God and the Fire God. The snake's body has fire signs along it—symbolizing Xiuhcoatl, the Fire Serpent.

- Very near the top of the stone is a date cartouche that reads 13 Reed. Many scholars believe that denotes the year 1479, during Itzcoatl's reign. Others believe that it was Moctezuma II's work. Images of Venus and flint knives are found around the sides of the Calendar Stone. Both Venus and flint knives are symbols of war. The Calendar Stone may have been a gladiatorial ring, where sacrificial victims would be made to fight to the death.

- The Calendar Stone typifies the Aztec dichotomy. It was an elegantly combined statement of mythological history, time, astronomy, philosophy, and religion all carved into a single stone—a stone that was used to kill sacrificial victims.

Symbolic Re-Creation of Myth

- Two other major carvings were found at the same time as the Calendar Stone: the stone of Tizoc and the statue of Coatlicue.

- The stone of Tizoc is somewhat like the Calendar Stone. A large disk 10 feet in diameter and 3 feet thick, it has beautiful carvings on the top and the sides. The stone of Tizoc is clearly a sacrificial stone. A bowl and channel are carved into the top. Hearts of the victims were placed in the bowl, and the channel allowed the blood to drain off. On the side are 15 different scenes of domination. Aztec warriors are wearing costumes of Huitzilopochtli and Tezcatlipoca. King Tizoc, who reigned from 1481 to 1486, is said to be one of those images.

- The statue of Coatlicue weighs 3 tons and is 8 feet tall. A monstrous figure, it depicts a human with snake heads and snakes on its skirt. It has a necklace of human hearts and hands, and skulls hang from its belt.
  - Coatlicue was the mother of Huitzilopochtli. This statue was most likely on the top of Templo Mayor.

  - Coatlicue's story is well-known. She was living at Coatepec with her daughter, Coyolxauhqui, and her 400 sons. The daughter rallied the sons to murder the mother; they chopped her head off, and blood spewed out like snakes. But then, Huitzilopochtli killed all 400 boys and Coyolxauhqui.

- Another important find was made in 1978. During street repairs near the cathedral, workers found the base of the Templo Mayor. Attached to the base was another disk showing the dismembered body of Coyolxauhqui, whose name means "face painted with bells."

- With that find, archaeologists can definitively say that the Templo Mayor is a symbolic re-creation of a mythical moment on Coatepec mountain. The Templo Mayor's right side was dedicated to Huitzilopochtli. His mother was on top, beheaded. His half-sister was in pieces below.

Codex Mendoza

- Altogether, there are nearly 500 Aztec documents—some written by Europeans and others by Aztec people. The Codex Mendoza has particular credence because it was written by Aztec people at Spanish contact.

- The Codex Mendoza was commissioned in 1535 by Antonio de Mendoza, the first viceroy of New Spain. He had the book created for Charles V as an assessment and explanation of the Aztec Empire. Aztec scholars worked along with the Spanish to create the book.

- The Codex Mendoza never actually made it to the court of Charles V. The ships carrying the book were attacked by French privateers, and the book was taken to France about 1553. It ended up in Oxford, and Lord Kingsborough made the first copy of it in 1831.
  - Section 1 covers Aztec history from 1325 to 1521. It records the founding of Tenochtitlan and provides a list of Aztec rulers and their conquered cities.

  - Section 2 is a list of the conquered cities within the Triple Alliance territories and the tribute that was demanded from each.

  - Section 3 is a description of Aztec life, complete with drawings. Lives of priests and warriors are covered in great detail, as are descriptions of clothing, battle methods, and the establishment of tribute.

- In that single picture book, the Aztec told their history, detailed the specifics of their wealth base, and described the daily lives of their people. In an ironic twist, the Spanish led the Aztec to create a document that preserved their culture. And in crafting the Codex Mendoza as an Aztec piece of literature with Spanish intent, the two cultures together created a piece of cultural patrimony that remains invaluable today.

Nezahualcoyotl: Poet King

- We know that the Aztec were fierce warriors, ruthless conquerors, and bloodthirsty practitioners of human sacrifice. They also loved poetry. All across the Triple Alliance, the ability to create a beautiful poem was respected as much as prowess in battle.

- The Aztec memorized songs and poems and handed them down from generation to generation. There were songs for each one of the festivals. The Aztec called poems "flower songs." Poetry was spoken rhythmically and often accompanied by a drum or flute.

- Nezahualcoyotl—the king of Texcoco and one of the founders of the Triple Alliance—was the most famous of all Aztec poets. He was a true Renaissance man in the spirit of Thomas Jefferson or Imhotep: architect, engineer, artist, orator, seer of the future, and reluctant warrior-king.

- The oldest poem we have from Nezahualcoyotl was from before the creation of the Triple Alliance. The Tepanec had driven Nezahualcoyotl from Texcoco. In exile, he was inspired to create a poem, called "Song of the Flight," about his sorrow and the fleeting nature of human existence.

- For the Aztec, life was a series of paired dualities: men and women, darkness and light, life and death. Through their arts and actions, we can see that the Aztec also saw beauty and horror as paired dualities—two sides of the same coin.

Suggested Reading

Duran, *Book of the Gods and Rites and the Ancient Calendar.*

Leon-Portilla, *Fifteen Poets of the Aztec World.*

Miller, *The Art of Mesoamerica from Olmec to Aztec.*

Questions to Consider

1. Is it hard to understand how a culture as the Aztec could be so violent and such lovers of the arts at the same time?

2. Do you think the average Aztec citizen lived in fear of the religion, or did religion give Aztecs peace?

3. Why was the main Aztec temple filled with the story of Huitzilopochtli's violent birth?

Illuminating Works of Aztec Art
Lecture 39—Transcript

Aztec civilization was a fascinating combination of brutality and beauty. Their penchant for human sacrifice, coupled with their love of art, music, and philosophy boggles the Western mind. Nowhere is this dichotomy better seen than in Aztec art.

To start off with, let's talk about the most famous piece of Aztec art, the Calendar Stone. It's also called the Sun Stone. It's a beautifully carved stone disk, and it's known worldwide. It's become more than an Aztec object; it's come to represent all of Mesoamerica.

It's 12 feet in diameter and 8 inches thick. It was 24 tons of solid basalt, very, very hard stone. Originally, it sat on top of the Templo Mayor. We're not sure exactly where, but probably somewhere on the top. It was actually broken out of the floor there and thrown down the stairs. It landed somewhere at the base. Duran saw it laying there in the rubble in the 1500s. It was buried under the cathedral's foundation, like rubble fill, along with a bunch of other carvings. And then it was found again, though, in the 1790s while they were doing repairs on the cathedral.

At that point, they took it and they mounted it into the cathedral's facade. It sat there for 100 years, and they called it Moctezuma's Clock. In 1885, they moved it to the new National Museum. And then finally in 1964 it got moved to the new anthropology museum, and now, again, it's mounted up on the wall, like it's a clock. But it was originally set into the floor, not the wall. It wasn't a clock.

So it wasn't a clock, but it actually was about time. It was a representation of Aztec time and history. Overall, it represents the Sun. There are arrow symbols, like Vs, on the exterior of the disk, and those are representing the rays of the Sun. The inner-ring bands hold calendar glyphs. In the very center of the stone is the face of the sun god, Tonatiuh. He's shown with a flint knife as his tongue. Aztecs said that they needed to sacrifice to keep the Sun moving along, and that flint-knife tongue is said to be his thirst for blood. And sacrifices were more than likely made on top of that stone.

Four glyph blocks around the innermost circle represent the four previous creations. The first one was 4 Jaguar. That was the first world, and it lasted 676 years. At the end, people were eaten by Jaguars. The second one is 4 Wind, it's the second world, and it lasted 364 years. People were destroyed by hurricanes and wind at the end. The third one is 4 Rain, lasting 312 years, and a rain of fire burned everything at the end of that creation. Finally, we have 4 Water, and it was, again, 676 years, and people were destroyed by floods that time.

We are people who are living in the fifth creation, and this one is known as 4 Motion. And we don't have an Aztec description of how long it's going to last. We have a prediction that we're going to be destroyed by earthquakes, hence that motion. And that motion sign is called Ollin. And that symbol is elegantly worked into the center. It uses those four blocks in the center to create the symbol Ollin. It's such a nice symbol that actually INAH uses it as their logo today.

The dates in the four blocks are days, not years, actually. The year signs are house, rabbit, reed, flint. These were other ones. These were symbols of the different types of destruction. And an interesting parallel note here is that each one of them start with the number four; that's the same as the Maya creation day. It starts in 4 Ajaw. I'm not sure what to make of it, but for some reason, a 4 day is a proper day to begin a creation.

On the next band out from those blocks, the ones that show us the five creations, are a list of 20 day names in the sacred calendar, in their order. So we start off with Crocodile is the 1st, Flower is the 20th, and they meet in a circle going all the way around. So we have the five mythological eras of time wrapped by their sacred calendar. It's a very poetic statement in and of itself. Now, just outside that day-glyph band is a more simple band of repeating elements. They're blocks with five dots inside. It kind of looks like the five-side of a dice. That's the Aztec symbol for turquoise. So, maybe if it was painted, they'd have actually made that a turquoise color. We're not sure. I'm not sure whether that's turquoise, or maybe it's the five dots for the five eras.

The outermost band is a double-headed snake wrapping all the way around the stone. The faces meet together at the bottom, and they're burping out two deities. It's Tonatiuh and Xiuhtecuhtli, the sun god and the fire god. It's very much like one of those Maya serpent bars, and it might symbolize, in the same way it symbolizes for the Maya, the ecliptic path of the Sun through the sky. The snake's body actually has fire signs along it, Xiuhcoatl, the fire serpent. It also has legs, and some have said, that looks like a dragon. But it's probably another one of those conflation creatures; it's the crocodile features on the snake.

Very near to the top of the stone is a date cartouche, and it's says 13 Reed. Many scholars believe that's denoting the year 1479, the year that it was carved, during Itzcoatl's reign. Others think that maybe it was Moctezuma II's work, and that it dated from his reign. Hard to tell when it's a 52-year cycle. Finally, a little known fact about the stone is that on the sides, not looking at the front, but the sides, it's really only eight inches thick there as it came out of the floor. There are images of Venus and flint knives going all the way around. Both Venus and flint knives are symbols of war. So, symbolically, they're saying that the Aztec universe is surrounded in war. For that reason, we think that probably was a sacrificial stone.

But we do have other sacrificial stones, and they're generally taller. They're usually about three foot in height; they're more practical for use so someone can bend over it. The Calendar Stone was actually carved into a slab, and what stuck out was only eight inches thick. So it might have also been one of these gladiatorial rings. The Spanish Chronicles told us about these shallower rings that were in the center of the city and that sacrificial victims would be made to fight to the death on top of these rings. The Calendar Stone typifies the Aztec dichotomy. A deep, elegantly combined statement of mythological history, time, astronomy, philosophy, and religion all carved into a single stone. And then, that stone was used to kill sacrificial victims.

The Calendar Stone was not the only important monument found during the 1790 cathedral repairs. Two other major carvings were found at the same time. The stone of Tizoc, and the statue of Coatlicue. The stone of Tizoc is somewhat like the calendar stone; it's a large disk. It's 10 feet in diameter and 3 feet thick. In weight, it's about 9.5 tons. It's sculpted all in the round. It's not inset like the calendar stone. And it has beautiful carvings, both on the top and the sides.

This one is clearly a sacrificial stone. I say that because of the bowl and channel carved into the top. In the center is a shallow bowl where they put the hearts. And then the channel leading out was for the blood drain off. The top image is a sun symbol. But it's not connected to the calendar or astronomy; it's just a symbol with jeweled designs, those same designs with the five dice symbols that mean turquoise.

Its name, Tizoc, comes from the side images. There are 15 different scenes of domination. They're Aztec warriors capturing various cities. Enemies are being grabbed up by the hair and dragged back to be captive sacrifices. They're wearing costumes of Huitzilopochtli and Tezcatlipoca. And it's said to be the King Tizoc himself in some of those images. His reign was from 1481 to '86.

The other important piece found in the 1790s was the statue of Coatlicue. It's three tons and eight foot tall. It's a monstrous image, and when they found it, it spooked the priests. It's a human with snake heads coming out where its head should be, and snakes on its skirt. The Aztec descendants knew exactly what it was in 1790. And they came up and they started leaving flowers and candles. The priests didn't like this, so they re-buried it.

Now, Humboldt heard about it, and he came to Mexico City and dug it up again in 1803. Then, once again, the priests asked, and they re-buried it. But it was unearthed again in 1823, and this time they made a cast of it. That cast was shown in an exhibition in London in Piccadilly Fair. They put it away inside the University and hid it away for years. But today, it's finally got its rightful place in the National Anthropology Museum.

I've stood beneath this thing just marveling at it. It's such a beautiful carving of such a terrible-looking thing. The skirt has serpents all over it, and its head is actually two heads of snakes going either direction, and the eyes of the snakes are the eyes of the statue looking forward. It has a necklace of human hearts and hands. And then on its belt line, there are skulls hanging off. It's a truly monstrous image. And we know who this is; it's the mother of Huitzilopochtli. She's lady serpent skirt, Coatlicue.

Her story is well-known. The story says that she was living at Coatepec with her children. She had a daughter, and she had 400 sons. And then one day while she was sweeping the temple, there was a cluster of humming bird feathers there, and as she tried to pick it up, it landed on her hand, and it impregnated her. Her daughter, Coyolxauhqui was enraged by this. So she rallies the boys to run up and murder the mother. And they chase her to the top of Coatepec mountain. There, they chop her head off, and the blood spews out like snakes; that's why the statue has these snakes where they head should be. But just at that moment, Huitzilopochtli is born in full war gear, and he kills all 400 boys, and then he chops up Coyolxauhqui into little pieces and throws her off the mountain.

So, we have this statue of Coatlicue, probably from the top of the Templo Mayor, like the other ones were. But then, there was another piece of the puzzle, an important find made in 1978. They were doing street repairs near the cathedral, and they found the base of the Templo Mayor. And attached to the base was another disk. This one showed the dismembered body of Coyolxauhqui. It was another one of these huge pieces. It was 10 foot in diameter. Now it's the centerpiece of the Templo Mayor Museum there in downtown Mexico City. Her name means face painted with bells. And on the stone, the face has bells on it, really confirming her identity.

So with that find with us too, we can securely say that the Templo Mayor is a symbolic representation of Coatepec mountain. We know that the Templo Mayor's right side was dedicated to Huitzilopochtli, and that they said it was a re-creation of Coatepec, his birthplace. These statues that we found together are a re-creation of that mythical moment. His mother is on top, beheaded. His half-sister is in pieces below. Both archaeology and the Chronicles in this case, agree it's a symbolic Coatepec. But what's more, this is another wonderful scene and a mixed message by the Aztecs. We have this horrible image of monsters and mutilation. But within it is a message about how much the god of war loved his mom.

There are so many Aztec artifacts that help us to understand who they were. But if I was given the choice of having only one with which to learn about their culture, I'd choose the Codex Mendoza, and let me tell you why. The term Aztec Codex has come to mean any ancient book regarding the Aztecs, both pre- and post-conquest books. There are certain chronicles that have actually been misnamed codices. For example, Sahagun's volumes are called the Florentine Codex. Or Duran's writing has come to be known as the Duran Codex.

Altogether, we have almost 500 Aztec documents. But I draw a distinction between those written by Europeans and those written, at least in part, by Aztec people. The Codex Mendoza was written at contact, and its authors were Aztec. Spaniards later came and looked at it and put European script over it. It was commissioned by Antonio de Mendoza, the first viceroy of New Spain, in 1535. He had the book made for Charles V. It was to be an assessment and explanation of the Aztec Empire. So Aztec scholars worked along with Spanish people to create the book. It's mostly an Aztec picture book, with Spanish annotations. It's written on normal European paper.

The Codex actually never made it to Charles V. Those ships were attacked by French privateers. The book was taken, and it went to France instead. It landed there about 1553. Someone there bought it for about 20 francs. In the by-and-by, it ended up in Oxford. And then Lord Kingsborough made the first copy of it in 1831.

There are 71 pages total and three sections. Section one was just 16 pages, and it was about Aztec history from the year 1325 up till 1521. It tells us about the founding of Tenochtitlan. It gives us a list of Aztec rulers, and along with that, the achievements of each. It also gives us a big list of the cities each one of them conquered.

Section two was 39 pages, and it was a list of all the conquered cities within the Triple Alliance territories. It was also about the tribute that was demanded from each one of those. And this was very important to the Spanish; it was a list of resources and wealth. For us today, it's an invaluable list of place names and trade goods.

Section three was 16 pages, and it was a description of Aztec life. That was probably of least interest to the Spanish and the King, but it's of great interest to me. There were so many wonderful details there, and all with drawings. There are lots of chronicles, but they're only words. This was better because there were actual drawings to look at what they were talking about. They talked about the lives of priests and warriors in great detail. It talked about the way they rose in ranks and the different clothes each rank wore. It also had detailed descriptions of battle methods. It told us about battles in which they would sneak in at night to take positions, and how they would specifically target leaders to be captives. It also talked about the establishment of tribute in each one of these places.

Each page has full-color drawings. I particularly like page 69, because it shows Moctezuma's palace, and it's just like Cortez described. It's two stories. And in the picture you see servants working below, and you see the King himself in a top window looking out. In that single picture book, the Aztec told us their history, the specifics of their entire wealth base, and all about the daily lives of their people. What a document. I wish we had something like that written for the Maya. So, in a strange way, the Spanish led the Aztecs to create a document that preserved their culture. And creating the Codex Mendoza as an Aztec piece of literature with Spanish intent, the two cultures together put together a piece of cultural patrimony that remains invaluable even today.

You know that the Aztec were fierce warriors, ruthless conquerors, and removers of hearts. But did you know they also loved poetry? Across the Triple Alliance, the ability to create a beautiful poem was respected as much as prowess in battle. The Aztecs memorized songs and poems. There were hundreds recorded at contact. And they were handed down from family to family. They were taught to everyone in school. There were songs for each one of the festivals.

Then there were poems. The Aztec called poems Flower Songs. They were spoken rhythmically and often accompanied with a drum or a flute. I envision them as kind of beatniks who are snapping along as someone's telling their poem. They're usually solo acts just like that, but there's an important distinction. We can see them in the codices. When they're doing a song or talking, it's just a [scroll] coming out of their mouth. But these speech scrolls when they have flowers on them, that means that they're speaking out a poem.

Rulers and nobles and statesmen were expected to be great speakers. Creating beautiful poems was a virtue, something they all had to do. Moctezuma created many original poems. And oftentimes he would stand up in his court and he would speak out a new poem he had created. They were all memorized, and the best ones were memorized and remembered for generations.

Nezahualcoyotl was the most famous of all Aztec poets. He was the King of Texcoco, and one of the founders of the Triple Alliance. That man was actually a legend across the board. He was an architect, an engineer, an artist, an orator, a seer of the future, and a reluctant warrior king. He's the guy who designed the incredible aqueducts and the levees. He was a true Renaissance man in the spirit of Thomas Jefferson or Egypt's Imhotep.

Nezahualcoyotl created the Aztecs greatest poems. I keep wanting to say he *wrote*, but they weren't written until contact. They had to be memorized. And every cultural person, everybody who had culture in their life, knew a few poems by heart. Nobles were expected to know hundreds. Poems were literally ingrained in Aztec thought.

The oldest poem we have from Nezahualcoyotl was from before the Triple Alliance. It was during a moment when the Tepanecs had driven him from his city in Texcoco. In exile, he was inspired to create a poem about his sorrow and the fleeting nature of human existence. It's called "Song of the Flight," and it goes like this.

In vain I was born. In vain I left the House of God and came to earth. I am so wretched. I wish I had never been born. Truly, that I had never come to earth. That's what I say. But what is there to do? Do I have to live among the people? What then, princes, tell me.

Do I have to stand on earth? What is my destiny? My heart suffers. I am unfortunate. You were hardly my friend here on earth, life giver. How to live among the people. Does he who sustains and lifts men have no discretion?

Go friends, live in peace. Pass your life in calm, while I have to live life stooped, with my head bent down when I am among the people. For this I cry, feeling desolate, abandoned among men on earth.

How do you decide your heart, life giver? Already your anger is vanishing. Your compassion is welling. I am at your side, God. Do you plan my death? Is it true we take pleasure, we who live on earth? Is it certain that we live to enjoy ourselves on earth?

But we are all so filled with grief. Are bitterness and anguish the destiny of the people on earth? But do not anguish, my heart. Recall nothing now. In truth, it hardly gains compassion here on earth.

Truly, you have come to increase bitterness at your side, next to you, oh life giver. I only look for, I remember my friends. Perhaps they will come one more time. Perhaps they will return to life. Or only once do we perish. Only once our time here on earth. If only our hearts did not suffer next to you, oh life giver.

Nezahualcoyotl created songs about the beauty of life and the inevitability of death. Here's another.

With flowers you paint, oh giver of life. With songs you give color. With songs you shade those who will live on earth. Later, you will destroy eagles and tigers. We live only in your painting here on earth.

With black ink, you will blot out all that was friendship, brotherhood, nobility. You give shading to those who live on earth. We are only in your book of paintings, here on earth.

There were certain songs that every Aztec warrior was to learn and keep close to their hearts. Songs like this one were sung before battle.

Heart, have no fright. There on the battlefield, I cannot wait to die by blade of sharp obsidian. Our hearts want nothing but a war death. You who are here in the struggle, I am anxious for a death from sharp obsidian. Our hearts want nothing but a war death.

For the Aztec, life was a series of paired dualities—men and women, darkness and light, life and death. I believe that through their arts and actions, we can see that they also saw beauty and horror as pair dualities, two sides of the same coin. I hope that this discussion of their arts has brought that to light for you.

Starting in the valley of Mexico, the Aztecs spread their doctrine of beauty and horror across Mesoamerica. In our next lecture, we'll turn to the Maya world in the Post-Classic, and see how that message eventually spread all the way across to the port City of Tulum.

Tulum—Aztecs at the Ancient Maya Port City
Lecture 40

Tulum was a small port city but of great strategic importance. By the time of Spanish contact, Tulum may well have been under the control of the powerful Aztec *pochteca* traders. In this lecture, we'll discuss a controversial theory: Tulum may have been the launching point for an Aztec invasion of the Maya to draw the Maya into their empire. This invasion, however, was cut short by the arrival of Hernan Cortes.

Tulum's Great Wall

- Tulum is surrounded by a massive wall; within that wall is a second wall called the inner enclosure, which holds most of the city's temples. Palaces are also found within that enclosure, which served as residences for the elites who controlled Tulum and possibly were places where the administration of trade was handled.

- The wall around the city, called the Great Wall, is 2,400 feet long, 20 feet thick in most places, and 10 to 15 feet tall. Clearly, it was excellent for defense, but some of its features call that defensive nature into question.

- First, it has five gates along its length—too many openings for proper defense. There are also large gaps, some more than 40 feet, in the area where the wall meets the cliff. An entire army could pass around the wall. What's more, archaeological surveys of the area found that most of Tulum's population actually lived outside the walls.

- Because of those odd features, archaeologists conclude that the wall was simply designed to restrict trade traffic in and out of the city, not used purely for defense.

In addition to restricting trade traffic, Tulum's Great Wall could have been a sign of the prestige and wealth of the city.

El Castillo

- At the center of the inner enclosure is El Castillo, Tulum's main temple. Three stories tall, the structure has stuccoes and murals on the interior walls. A wide staircase leads to the top, and at the bottom are rooms flanking the staircase. Those lower rooms date to some of the earliest phases of the city. The upper temple of El Castillo was built sometime after 1400. And on the top of the stairs is a small, upright stone—most likely, a sacrificial stone.

- There are two small windows on the back wall of the upper temple of El Castillo, almost like shafts going through the thick wall. These windows may have been navigation aids—they both look out precisely to a gap in the reef about a half a kilometer offshore.

- El Castillo was just one of many temples at Tulum that were significantly rebuilt after 1400. Earlier phases were clearly Maya constructions, but these new temples showed the influence of Central Mexico.

Council Houses at Tulum?

- Residential palaces are the most common form of structure at Tulum. There are only four to five houses of any significant size and a dozen smaller ones. In fact, there are only 68 structures in the entire city. With so few buildings, the population living within Tulum could have only been a couple hundred. Most of the people lived outside the city walls.

- The largest residential palace is the House of the Halach Winik—80 by 50 feet with patios at both the front and back. If Tulum did have a ruler, he probably lived in the Halach Winik.

- The common belief is that these palaces are elite residences, but some doubts are raised based on their architectural details. First, the houses do not have many rooms in them. The Halach Winik has only three large rooms. Typically, a Maya residence has more subdivisions within it, more rooms for more activities and sleeping spaces.

- Archaeologists have identified stone benches as the place where people laid pillows and made their beds. These buildings have no benches. They are also not very private places; they have a number of exterior doors and open patios.

- In fact, these houses are reminiscent of the council houses for clan representatives at Mayapan. Mayapan was also walled, and the League of Mayapan met inside. Perhaps Tulum had the same political system as Mayapan. Also like Mayapan, Tulum has a few temples scattered around these residences. One of them is the House of the Cenote, built directly over the entrance of a cenote. This cenote was Tulum's only source of freshwater within the walls.

Migrants from the Peten

- Tulum's history is in three phases: Early Post-Classic, from 1000 to 1200; Middle Post-Classic, from 1200 to 1400; and Late Post-Classic, from 1400 to 1521, or Spanish contact. Although Tulum itself originated later, the region had a much older occupation history.

- Area surveys found that Tulum was one of three cities in the immediate area. Close to Tulum were the sites of Tank-Ha and Xel-Ha. Excavations at Tank-Ha indicate that it is much older than Tulum. Tank-Ha was first settled in 300 B.C. It had continuous occupation all the way up until the conquest period—probably because of the reef, which provided abundant fishing and a place to control marine traffic.

- About 880, Tank-Ha's ceramics changed, which correlates to the Classic period collapse. That change was probably due to migrants from the Peten headed into the Yucatan. These migrants traveled east out of Belize, then up the coast. Belize's old name is Belikin, which means "road to the east." The migrants who went through Belikin were the Itza people.

- The Itza eventually established Chichen Itza and may have come from the Tulum area. The idea is that they landed at Tank-Ha, then moved into Chichen Itza. Murals at Chichen Itza seem to support that theory; they may depict a Peten military entrada from the east. Perhaps the Itza took over the coast while they were headed to Chichen Itza.

- If that interpretation is correct, it might explain Tulum's establishment. Because Xel-Ha and Tank-Ha already existed, Tulum was a new port created by Chichen Itza about the year 1000 to control and increase trade.

Changes in Ceramics and Architecture

- Tulum, Tank-Ha, and Xel-Ha acted as ports administering trade between the Peten and Yucatan for a 400-year period, from 800 to 1200. But then, in the 1200s, Chichen Itza fell, and Mayapan took over the peninsula.

- The major changes for Tulum came about 1400. Archaeologists call the last phase of pre-Columbian cultural activities, before the arrival of Spanish, the Late Post-Classic. This period began abruptly around 1400 and brought major changes not only to Tulum but also to the entire Yucatan Peninsula.

- The most significant changes were in ceramics and architecture. A ceramics change—to archaeologists—means a change in the attitudes of the people and, perhaps, a change in their trading partners. Sometimes such changes are even more accurate than carbon-14 samples. At Tulum, in a sudden ceramics change, craftspeople began producing a type called Tulum red.

- Buildings across Tulum were modified at the same time. Roof styles were changed to flat-topped roofs. Mini-shrines were placed inside the temples and palaces. A new architectural element was the outward sloping wall.

- The best example of the outward sloping wall is the Temple of the Diving God, which gets its name from the figure above its front doorway: a descending human figure with wings. This image was added to many of the doorways after 1400. Given that corn is in its headdress, this figure may have been the Corn God.

Connection to Coba

- Tulum's final days may well have been as an Aztec *pochteca* outpost. Tulum was transformed about 1400. Although El Castillo still looked very Maya, just south of El Castillo, in the inner enclosure, stands a building called the Temple of the Initial Series.

- Inside the Temple of the Initial Series is a Classic period stela. The Long Count date on the stela is 564—well before Tulum's inception. The style of carving, however, is similar to that of a nearby city in the interior, Coba. The theory is that the stela was carried about 30 kilometers from Coba, then enshrined in Tulum.

- Coba was abandoned during the Classic period but was resettled in the Post-Classic period, when diving gods were placed on the temple tops. The Coba stela was enshrined for the same reason that the people used the Chichen Itza snake columns: They were symbols of ancient Maya authority.

Temple of the Wind
- Just after 1400, Tulum had renewed prosperity and a strong Maya heritage. The city had connections to the interior; its people had wealth and a trade network. It was exactly the kind of place that *pochteca* traders wanted to take over. The Aztec may have found Tulum and literally painted over the town.

- The temples of Tulum were repainted inside and out. Maya murals can be detected underneath those last paintings, but the new ones are much more in the style of Central Mexico. The gods depicted are still identifiably Maya, but Central Mexican symbols of Venus are flying above them.

- The gods on the murals are similar to images from Aztec-controlled Oaxaca. This style has been termed the international Mixteca-Puebla style, a common sign of Aztec presence. Two Maya stela were decommissioned at that time. Stela 2 was reused in a shrine in front of the Temple of the Frescoes. Dated 1261, it is illustrated with Aztec-style imagery.

- Stela 3 was also reused. Its mini-shrine was in front of the most telling piece of Aztec evidence at the site, the newly built Temple of the Wind. Standing on the cliff side, the Temple of the Wind has a square temple base but a circular temple on top. There are none others like it in the area. It looks just like an Aztec Ehecatl temple. The Maya did not worship Ehecatl, the Wind God; in fact, he was the patron deity of the Aztec *pochteca*.

Launching Point for Invasion of the Maya

- The Aztec strategy for regional domination was this: They initially sent the *pochteca* to scout for trade networks. The *pochteca* established exchanges of goods. Then, the Aztec military arrived. Southwest Campeche was in this last stage when Cortes arrived.

- Tulum very well may have been an Aztec-controlled Maya port city, from which the Aztec planned an invasion of the Maya. The Aztec had to abort the invasion when Cortes conquered Tenochtitlan.

- In the next lecture, we'll discuss those moments of first contact with the Spanish—and the profound effects on Mesoamerica.

Suggested Reading

Lothrop, *Tulum*.

Miller, *On the Edge of the Seas*.

Questions to Consider

1. Do you find the evidence of Aztec intrusion at Tulum believable?

2. Why did the small city of Tulum need such a massive wall?

3. Give that virtually every other Maya coastal city is now a resort or an amusement park, how did Tulum survive into modern times?

Tulum—Aztecs at the Ancient Maya Port City
Lecture 40—Transcript

Tulum was a small, but strategically important place. From its very beginnings, the port city was a place where goods float in and out of the Yucatan. In its early days, those goods were flowing mostly from the Peten and point south. But by the contact period, Tulum may well have been under the control of the powerful Aztec *pochteca* traders.

The first European contact of Tulum comes in 1518 when a priest on a Spanish ship sailing Yucatan's east coast wrote this,

> We followed the shore day and night. And the next day toward sunset, we perceived a city or town so large that Seville would not have seemed more considerable nor better. One saw there a very large tower. On the shore was a great throng of Indians who bore two standards, which they raised and lowered to signal us to approach them. The commander did not wish it.

Now, that had to be the city of Tulum. From where they were sailing there was no other possible candidate in that area. The large tower was probably Tulum's Castillo. It wasn't actually a tower, it was their main temple. Later that year, Cortes ransomed a Spanish priest from the same area. And that priest said he was the captive of someone called the Lord of Zama. And Zama, meaning Don, was probably Tulum's ancient name.

Tulum wasn't mentioned again for another 300 years. Stephens and Catherwood visited there in in 1841. They spent three days at the site, and again, Catherwood made some wonderful drawings there. There were no roads into the area, so they had to approach by boat from Cozumel. The locals in the region said the general region's area's name was Tulum, and hence, Stephens gave the site the name Tulum.

That was the last stop along Stephen's journey in 1841. And he noted there that rituals were still taking place in the temples at Tulum. The area was completely unknown then. Stephens wrote in his book, "In fact, I conceive it to be not impossible that within this secluded region may exist, at this day unknown to white men, a living aboriginal city occupied by the relics of the ancient race who still worship in the temples of their fathers."

Aside from a few self-appointed explorers, the Carnegie Institution was the next to study Tulum in the year 1916. The director of the project was Samuel Lothrop. He did a survey, took some photos, and made a very accurate map. Then he returned in 1918, and again in 1922 to dig. And he excavated mostly toms, which was the goal of that day. Back in the '20s, treasure hunting was OK. But like Stephens, 80 years earlier, Lothrop found that the Maya controlled the wilderness beyond. He was allowed to hire local Maya as his workers, but he was not allowed to enter the interior of the Yucatan. There were tales of living cities still out there in the jungle. And in his memoirs, he often wrote that he was worried about an attack from the local Maya.

Lothrop's excavations were the biggest ever done at Tulum. Then, in 1937 through 1940, there was a Mexican survey project of the general area, and they found more sites along the coast. Those, like Tulum, had well preserved murals. In the 1950s the Carnegie Institution returned again. This time, William Sanders was the Director, and he did excavations that confirmed the Post-Classic chronology of Tulum, and he also established the region's first ceramic sequence.

Since then, there's been very little archaeology. In the 1970s there were some projects that conserved the murals. In the 1980s, tourism began and INAH shifted to consolidating buildings for tourism. Today, it's a beautifully restored site, and over one million tourists visit there every year.

Now that you know a little bit about the history of Tulum's discovery and excavation, let's talk about the city itself. There are many larger and more impressive Maya cities, but Tulum's coastal location makes it one of the most scenic ever built. Tulum is surrounded by a massive wall, and then there's a second wall inside the city that's called the inner enclosure, and it holds most of the city's temples. There are a few other temples scattered about the site, but most of them are structures that we name palaces. They were the residences for the elites who controlled Tulum. I personally think they were probably more than just houses. I think they were also places where the administration handled the trade that came into the port.

The wall around the city is the city's biggest feature. It's called the Great Wall. It's 2,400 feet in total length, and it has three sides. The east side is the coastline, and there, it's mostly covered by 40-foot-tall cliffs. The wall around is also very, very thick—20 feet thick in most places. And it's 10 to 15 feet tall. So clearly, it was good for defense, but its features call that defensive nature into question.

First, it has five gates along its length; there are two on the north end, two on the south end, and one really big one on the west. That's a few too many for proper defense. More though, there are also big gaps at the cliff where the wall hits the cliff, on either side north and south, there's over 40 feet of a gap; and entire army could pass through and around the wall. Then further, 1950s surveys found that most of Tulum's population was actually living outside the walls. So if the walls were for defense, why was most of the population living outside? Due to those odd features, Lothrop concluded that the wall was simply designed to restrict trade traffic in and out of the city, not purely for defense. It could have also been a sign of prestige and wealth, and I agree with his conclusion.

So returning to the walls inside the city, they cover an area called the inner enclosure. It's basically Tulum's downtown. And there are various temples within the inner enclosure, but no houses. At the center of it, backing up to the sea, stands the Castillo, Tulum's main temple. It's three stories tall and wonderfully well preserved. It still has its roof. And there are stuccoes on the interior walls and murals.

A wide staircase leads up to the top, and at the bottom place there are lower rooms flanking the staircase. Those lower rooms date to some of the earliest phases of the city. The upper temple was built sometime after 1400 A.D. And on the top there, on the top of the stairs, there's a small, upright stone right at the top of the stairs. Lothrop said it looked like an Aztec sacrificial stone, and I agree. And I'll tell you more about that in a little bit.

There were two small windows on the back wall of the upper temple of the Castillo. It's a very thick wall, so the windows are almost like shafts going through this thick wall. And a friend of mine came up with an interesting idea, that maybe these windows were navigation aids. They both look out exactly over a gap in the reef about a half a kilometer offshore. And he put two candles in each one of those windows, and then he tried to navigate a boat through the reef at night. And only when he could see both of the candles, was he lined up just right to pass through the reef at night. The Castillo was just one of many temples at Tulum that were significantly rebuilt after 1400. Earlier phases were clearly Maya constructions, but these new temples showed central Mexican influence. I'll talk more about that later in this lecture, when I get to why I think the Aztec controlled the city at European contact.

Next, let's talk about the most common form of structure at Tulum, its residential palaces. Since Stephens first recorded them, they've been discussed as residential, and they may well have been. I think, however, that they were more than just houses. It's all but gone today, but Tulum had a main street running north-south through the city. You can see it when you look at the map, there's a gap between all the buildings; it runs from one wall gate to another wall gate. And along its lengths are all these elite residences, and each one of them have steps that lead down to that now-gone street.

There really aren't many of those elite houses. There's only four to five of them of any significant size, and there's another dozen or so that are smaller. By my count, and I've walked around the entire site counting each one of the buildings, there are 68 structures total in the entire city, and most of them are low platforms that I have no idea what their use was. So, with that few amount of buildings, the inner population of Tulum could have only been a couple hundred people max. Most of the people were living outside the city walls.

The major houses are all clustered near the inner enclosure. We have the House of the Chultun, and it's named that because there's a *chultun*, or storage pit, in its patio. Then we have the House of the Columns, and it has a front colonnade of cylindrical columns; that's where it gets its name. Then the biggest one we have is the House of the Halach Winik. The House of Halach Winik is definitely big. It's 80 by 50 feet, and it has patios both on the front and backsides. People say that if Tulum did have a ruler, he probably lived there in the Halach Winik.

The common belief is that these are elite residences, but I myself have some doubts based on their architectural details. First, there aren't really many rooms in them. The Halach Winik only has three big rooms. The other palaces also have very few rooms. And typically, a Mayan residence is more subdivided; it would have more rooms for more activities and sleeping spaces. And speaking of sleeping spaces, there are absolutely no benches. We identify these stone benches as the place they laid pillows and made their beds, and these buildings have none of those benches. Also, they have lots of exterior doors and open patios. They're really not very private, if they're going to be a residence to an elite person.

To me, they remind me of Mayapan. They remind me of the council houses for clan representatives. Mayapan city was also walled, and the league of Mayapan met inside. They were families representing cities from around the region, and they were councils that got together to make group decisions for the entire region. The timing is just right, it's right around 1400. That's when Mayapan was living and when Tulum was building these buildings. So perhaps we're just seeing the same political system as Mayapan had in the city of Tulum.

Also, like Mayapan, there were a few temples that are scattered around between these residences. One of them is the House of the Cenote. It's in the northeast corner of the city; and it's built directly over the entrance of a cenote, and there's fresh water inside. That was very important for the city, because it's right up against the ocean where they have nothing but salt water. This cenote, protected by the House of the Cenote, was their only source of fresh water within the walls.

Another very different-looking building is the Temple of the Frescoes. It's two stories tall, and it's a tourist favorite. It's always crowded around by a bunch of tourists taking pictures. On the corners, there are faces of old men, and we identify them as the Pauahtuns. They are a group of four old men who held up the corners of the sky; back in the classic period they were called Bacabs, Post-Classic Pauahtuns. The building was covered with murals, both inside and out. Today, only the inside one is preserved. And they are part of my theory of the Aztec entrada, so I'll hold those until we start talking about the Aztecs.

As I've said, Tulum was rebuilt about 1400. Like other sites, we only see the end of the site's history on the surface. Most of what we see today wasn't there before 1400. But Tulum was earlier and always an important trade port. Understanding its early days can help us explain its later importance. Tulum's history had essentially three phases, an early Post-Classic from 1000 to 1200, a middle Post-Classic from 1200 to 1400, and a late Post-Classic from 1400 to 1521, Spanish contact. And while Tulum itself began late, the region had a much older occupation history.

Area surveys found that Tulum was one of three cities in the immediate area. Close by to Tulum were the sites of Tank-Ha and Xel-Ha. All three were coastal, and there was settlement between all of them, so there was a lot of people living there along the coast. Xel-Ha is now, unfortunately, a water amusement park, and it's gone. But Tank-Ha still exists, and it's been well studied. Excavations there show that it's actually much older than Tulum. In fact, Tank-Ha was first settled in 300 B.C. It had a continuous occupation all the way up until the conquest period.

It was probably because of the reef. There was a long strip of reef about a half a kilometer off the shore. And in between that and the shore were calm waters. And they were abundant fishing areas. It could also control marine traffic. So, this was a good place to live. There were only small gaps in that reef so they could actually protect what they had as well using that reef.

About 800 A.D., Tank-Ha's ceramics changed, and that correlates nicely to the classic period collapse. That change was probably due to migrants from the Peten headed into the Yucatan. They traveled east out of Belize and then up the coast. Belize's old name is actually Belikin, which means road to the east, indicting people from the Peten coming out. Nowadays, Belikin is the name of a beer in Belize. But these migrants who went through Belikin, those people were the Itza people.

Now the Itza eventually establish Chichen Itza. And Mayan contacts tell us that the Itza people came from the east, not directly from the south, so it makes sense they may have come from the Tulum area. The idea is that they landed at Tank-Ha, and then they moved into Chichen; that makes good sense. And murals at Chichen Itza seem to support that idea. They may show us a Peten military entrada from the east coast.

Murals at Chichen Itza's temple of warriors display a narrative, a sequence of events. First, we see traders in canoes; then we see warriors; then we see captives that are being led away by those warriors. There's a scene in which a walled coastal city is burning. And then excavations at Xel-Ha, before it became a water park, showed us that they once had a defensive wall, and it was burned, about that same time. So perhaps that is proof of an Itza takeover of that coast while they were going into Chichen Itza.

If that interpretation is correct, it might explain Tulum's establishment. Xel-Ha and Tank-Ha were already there. Tulum was a new port created by Chichen Itza to control trade and increase it right about 1,000 A.D. That would also explain why there are snake columns added to the top of Tulum's Castillo at 1,400. Chichen was gone at that time, but Tulum was probably looking to show symbols of their power foundation.

Tulum, Tank-Ha, and Xel-Ha all remained the same for a 400-year period, from 800 to 1200. They were trade ports that were administrating trade between the Peten and Yucatan. But then Chichen Itza fell in the 1200s. There was still little change there. Mayapan took over the peninsula, but it was further away. Tulum's ceramics did change a bit. And the area's population increased a bit. But there was nothing that was a major change. There was no new architecture or temples. The big changes really came about 1400, the late Post-Classic. At that time, there was a radical overhaul.

Archaeologists call the last phase of pre-Columbian cultural activities, before the arrival of Spanish, the late Post-Classic. It begins abruptly around 1400 and brings major changes to not just Tulum, but the entire Yucatan Peninsula. The biggest changes were in the ceramics and the architecture. The ceramics change, and that sort of thing makes archaeologists excited. That means that we're seeing a change in the attitudes of the people, perhaps a change in their trade partners. Changes in ceramics are a solid horizon marker that we can hang onto and learn from; sometimes they're even better than carbon-14 samples. At Tulum there was this sudden change. They started using a type that we call Tulum red; it was a type with a shiny red slip on the outside.

Buildings across Tulum were modified. Their roof styles were changed to flat tops. There were still corbeled arches on the inside, but they were hidden by those flat-topped roofs. They also started adding mini shrines; they were placed both inside the temples and the palaces. And then there was a very new architectural element, an outward-sloping wall technique.

Those outward-sloping walls are actually very ugly looking. Some people look at it and say, well, that's just sloppy architecture. The best example is the temple of the Diving God. Yes, it's ugly, but it's still standing. Some believe that this outward-sloping wall helped it be hurricane resistant. Whatever it was, that style spread across the Yucatan. It wasn't just a mistake at Tulum, it was a particular kind of architecture they were making then.

The Temple of the Diving God gets its name from the figure above its front doorway. It's a descending human figure with wings; it has feathers on its arms; and its legs are above its head, so it's descending. It was added to many of the doorways post-1400. Tulum's Castillo and palaces have them, too. They show up all across Yucatan. Personally, I think it's the Corn God, because in its headdress it has corn. But actually, we're still debating exactly who this god was. Whoever it was, it was signature architecture post-1400.

At the start of this lecture I told you that I think Tulum's last days were as an Aztec *pochteca* outpost. We finally come to the point in their history when that begins to happen. Let's talk about why I believe this controversial theory.

Tulum was transformed about 1400. Ceramics and diving gods were there, but they were still very Maya elements. The Castillo got its snake columns honoring Chichen Itza's heritage, again, very Maya. And just south of the Castillo, in the inner enclosure, stands a building called the Temple of the Initial Series, and inside of it, we found a classic period stela.

The stela is laying on its side; it's like it's enshrined inside this temple. When we read the long Count date on it, it says it's from 564 A.D.; that was well before Tulum's inception. This confused Lothrop about the dates of the site. Then, a woman named Joyce Marcus noted that the carving style was very much like a nearby interior city called Coba. It was the same size, and there was the same sort of jade-skirt style on the figure on the front. So she suggested it was actually carried about 30 kilometers from Coba and then enshrined in Tulum.

Coba was a classic-period city, and it was abandoned, like the rest of them, during the classic period. But then, someone resettled it in the Post-Classic, and they installed those diving gods on the temple tops. I personally think Tulum loom was the catalyst, and that they enshrined a Coba stela for the same reason that they used the Chichen snake columns. They were symbols of ancient Maya authority that they were using.

So, just after 1400, Tulum had renewed prosperity and a strong Maya heritage. They had connections to the interior, and they had wealth and a trade network. That was exactly the kind of place that *pochteca* traders wanted to find. I think they did, and they literally painted over the town. The temples of Tulum were repainted inside and out. We can see more Maya murals underneath those last paintings, but the new ones are much more Mexican in style. They have registers of gods walking in procession. Now, the gods are still identifiably Maya; they are the Corn God, the Moon Goddess, Itzamna, but Mexican symbols of Venus are flying above them.

The registers of the gods on those murals are like images from Aztec-controlled Oaxaca. On the walls of the site Zaachila we have the exact, same style. And in the Borgia Codices from the Puebla region, we have that same style. Mural expert Arthur Miller called it the international Mixteca-Puebla style. It was a common sign of Aztec presence, where we see that, the Aztec have been there.

There were also two Maya stela that were decommissioned about then. Stela 2 was reused in a shrine in front of the Temple of the Frescoes, and that was one that was full of this Aztec-style imagery. It's date was 1261 A.D., and its message was apparently no longer relevant at Tulum.

Stela 3 was also reused. It was broken up and used in a mini-shrine. It has no date, but it's the same style as stela 2. It's mini-shrine was in front of the most telling piece of Aztec evidence at the site, the newly built Temple of the Wind. Standing on the cliff side, it has a circular temple base, but a square temple on top. There are none other like it in the area. It looks just like an Aztec Ehecatl Temple. The Maya didn't have Ehecatl the Wind God. Ehecatl guided travelers and protected them. In fact, he was the patron deity of the Aztec *pochteca*. Events in wider Yucatan at that time may also be relevant clues. At 1450, Mayapan's league dissolves. The city burns to the ground. And we know that the Mexicans were there and part of it. There was a power vacuum. And trade networks were disrupted. At the same time, the Aztec are taking over Oaxaca. There were new murals at Oaxaca, just like Tulum's.

Recalling the Aztec strategy, they sent first the *pochteca*. They scout out for trade networks. They establish exchanges of goods. Then the Aztec military arrives. This last stage was happening in southwest Campeche when Cortes arrived. He landed at the Maya port of Xicalanco. There, he found a garrison of Aztec warriors led by Moctezuma's brother. That was where Cortes first got La Malinche, his translator. But what was a bilingual slave doing there? I think the Aztecs were preparing for an assault on the Maya, and they were called back to Tenochtitlan to fight against Cortes before they could.

So, I believe that Tulum was in the same position, that it was an Aztec-controlled Maya port city, and it was a place where they were about to launch their invasion from. They had to abort it when Cortes sieged Tenochtitlan. No Spaniards ever landed there to actually ask the people of Tulum what was going on, but Tulum's walls speak for themselves.

Would the Aztec have succeeded in pulling the Maya into their empire? We'll never know. Places like Tulum suggest that they were preparing to try just when the Spanish arrived. In my next lecture, we'll talk about those moments of first contact and the profound effects they had on Mesoamerica.

First Contact with Europe in Mesoamerica
Lecture 41

Europe had been using the Silk Road to trade with India and China for centuries. But when the Ottoman Turks conquered Constantinople in 1453, that route became dangerous. European nations needed new seafaring routes to Asia. This was the catalyst for the European discovery of the Americas. In this lecture, we'll describe the events that led up to the momentous encounter between the Old World and the New World.

A Flawed Map

- The Portuguese maintained trade routes to the Far East by sailing around Africa. Establishing resupply points was difficult, however, and the seas were very rough, especially around the Cape of Good Hope. What's more, it was a very long and costly journey.

- Christopher Columbus thought there was a better way. An Italian-born merchant, Columbus had traveled widely and was very well read. In 1485, Columbus was the first to propose a western route to the Indies, but the Portuguese turned down his request to finance an expedition.

- Columbus believed that the Indies were actually closer than they are in reality. He was influenced by the Italian astronomer Toscanelli, who had calculated the earth's circumference. Because Toscanelli used Arabic miles, not Roman miles, his calculation turned out to be somewhere around 30,000 kilometers, not the actual 40,000 kilometers.

- By using Toscanelli's map, Columbus estimated that it would be only 2,500 miles to Japan, but he was off by about 10,000 miles. Finally, however, Columbus convinced Spain to back his expedition. Ferdinand and Isabella were the rulers at the time, but most of his funding came from Italian merchants.

"Indios"

- In August 1492, Columbus sailed west in the *Nina*, *Pinta*, and *Santa Maria*. He was headed for Japan, but he hit the Bahamas. This was the first of four voyages he would take from Spain to the New World.

- In the Caribbean, after sailing around Cuba and several other islands, Columbus wrecked the *Santa Maria* on the island he called Hispaniola—modern-day Haiti and Dominican Republic. Because he went ashore on Christmas Day, he named the site La Navidad, which is "Christmas" in Spanish. There, in a peaceful encounter, he met the native Taino. From the Taino, the explorers acquired gold and other goods. The explorers called the natives "Indios," which is the origin of the term *Indians*. Columbus thought he had landed in India.

- Columbus returned to Spain to a hero's welcome and claimed to have found the East Indies. News of his discoveries spread throughout Europe. His second voyage was planned almost immediately.

Crimes against the Natives

- Six months after he returned to Spain, Columbus set sail on his second expedition. This time, he had 17 ships, 1,200 men, and tons of provisions. He was off not only to explore and acquire but to colonize.

- Arriving back in Hispaniola, Columbus found that La Navidad had been destroyed by the Taino; all the Spaniards left there had been killed. With La Navidad destroyed, Columbus made a new colony to the east. He called it La Isabella, after the queen. After a series of hurricanes and the onset of disease, Columbus moved the colony in 1496 south to Santo Domingo.

- In Columbus's third expedition, he landed in South America and explored the Orinoco River area. Returning to Hispaniola in 1499, he faced an angry population; there were charges of tyranny and genocide against the Taino people. Even Columbus's allies could not deny the acts of cruelty.

- Columbus and his brothers were convicted of those crimes in Hispaniola and sent back to Spain in chains in 1500. They spent a year in jail and were stripped of their titles and all their wealth. In another audience with the king, however, the accused denied the charges against them and begged for a final chance to find the passage to the Indian Ocean. Ferdinand agreed, and he backed them with more ships.

The Moment of Contact

- In 1502, Columbus embarked on his fourth and final expedition to the New World. It was on that journey that the first Mesoamerican and European contact actually took place. With a promise to find a route to India, Columbus left with four ships. He sailed into the Caribbean with a hurricane right behind him.

- Surviving the hurricane, Columbus sailed south to Honduras. There, his brother Bartolomeo saw a huge trading canoe with 25 men, women, and children aboard, carrying supplies of cotton clothing, cacao, copper bells, and pottery. The Maya traders were headed from the south up to the Yucatan.

- The explorers captured the canoe and commandeered its cargo. They released all the people but questioned the captain using a Taino interpreter. The old man told them stories about tremendous stores of gold farther south.

- Columbus's men searched the coastline for a way through to the Pacific Ocean, all the way down to Panama. After being stuck in Jamaica for a year, Columbus went back to Spain. He landed in 1504, but he was in v poor health. Two years later, in 1506, he died in Valladolid, Spain.

- Although Columbus never did find his route to the Indies, he had opened up communication to the New World—arguably, the most significant cultural contact moment in world history.

Balboa and the Discovery of the Pacific

- In 1500, a young man named Vasco Nunez de Balboa arrived on the shores of Hispaniola. Balboa would eventually create the first permanent mainland Spanish settlement. The son of a conquistador, Balboa had joined a treasure-hunting exploration to Panama and Colombia.

- For four years, Balboa went on various expeditions, and he learned the coast of Panama very well. After falling into debt, he stowed away on a ship to Colombia on an expedition led by the young Francisco Pizarro.

- Balboa suggested moving a settlement to Darien in Panama, which was more fertile and had fewer warlike natives. Pizarro agreed, and they decided to move the settlement. Balboa picked the landing point. A hard-fought battle took place, but ultimately, the Spaniards were victorious. What's more, the natives that had attacked possessed a vast amount of gold and wealth. Balboa became a hero to all the men.

- Eventually, Balboa became the governor of Santa Maria la Antigua del Darien in Panama. In 1513, he led his most famous expedition—to the Pacific Ocean. Pizarro was with him on that journey, as well—an adventure that led to the eventual conquest of the Inca Empire.

The First Spaniards in Mexico

- As Pedro de Valdivia sailed to Santo Domingo on a mission for Balboa, he and his crew were shipwrecked on the shores of the Yucatan Peninsula. Most scholars agree that these were the first Spaniards in Mexico.

- The men were immediately captured by the Maya. Valdivia and three others were sacrificed; the others became slaves. A priest named Jeronimo de Aguilar also became a slave and learned Chontal Maya and Maya customs. In 1518, he was ransomed by Cortes and became a translator.

- A soldier in the party named Gonzalo Guerrero "went native." He was given to the king of Chetumal; eventually, he married the king's daughter, and they had three children together. He is remembered in the Yucatan as the first mestizo. All over Yucatan are statues in his honor.

Although he claimed to remain a friend of Spain, Gonzalo Guerrero fought with the Maya against the Spanish for 25 years.

Guerrero and Aguilar

- In 1518, an expedition led by Juan de Grijalva appeared in the Yucatan with four ships—sent by Grijalva's uncle, Diego Velasquez, the governor of Cuba. By the time Grijalva returned to Cuba to report, his uncle had lost faith in him. Velasquez commissioned another expedition, led by Hernan Cortes. He gave Cortes numerous ships and 500 men. Cortes left for Cozumel late in 1518.

- Cortes landed on the island, immediately burned down the town, and erected a Christian cross in the ashes. He ransomed Aguilar and sent the former priest to retrieve Guerrero, as well. But Guerrero refused to return, saying that he now was a Maya.

- Guerrero actually helped the Maya fight the Spanish, teaching them the tricks of Spanish strategy and tactics. Guerrero became a phantom menace for the conquistadors and one of their most wanted. He lived for 25 years as a Maya war captain. He led

50 canoes to Honduras in 1536 to join a fight against Pedro de Alvarado, but the battle was lost. Guerrero's dead body was found among the Maya dead.

- Jeronimo de Aguilar joined Cortes's crew in an expedition that would eventually lead to the destruction of the Aztec civilization.

Dona Maria "La Malinche"

- Just before Cortes left Cozumel, he got word from the governor of Cuba that his permission had been revoked. But he ignored the message and went anyway. Along the way, he picked up more men and more horses. Rounding the Yucatan, Cortes landed in Tabasco.

- There, he conquered a large Maya port with many Aztec *pochteca* traders. The defeated people gave him 20 slave women, one of whom was Dona Maria "La Malinche." She spoke both Maya and Nahuatl; thus, she and Aguilar worked as a translation team. The locals told Cortes about the Aztec capital of Tenochtitlan.

- La Malinche was an infamous figure. On the one hand, she is the symbol of native betrayal. On the other hand, she is a symbol of mestizo heritage. She eventually became Cortes's wife and bore his favorite son, Diego. More than just a translator, she was key to Cortes's successful strategy against the Aztec.

A Clash of Cultures
- Cortes sailed west, landed at Veracruz, and conquered Chalchihuecan, or the "place of jade." Cortes renamed it Villa Rica de la Vera Cruz—Villa Rica because of all the gold, and Vera Cruz ("true cross") because he had landed on Good Friday.

- Veracruz became the second permanent mainland settlement in the Americas. Before that, it was actually an Aztec tribute community. Locals there told Cortes more about Tenochtitlan, the amazing city full of gold. Cortes sent messages to Moctezuma and requested a meeting, but all his messages were ignored.

- Cortes decided to march to Tenochtitlan. In August 1519, he began the march inland, with 700 men, 15 horses, and 15 cannons. At this point in history, the Spanish had been in the Americas for almost 30 years. They had explored, conquered, and learned the geography, history, and culture. Now, it was time for the showdown: Mesoamerica's most powerful nation, the Aztec, versus the mighty Spanish Crown.

Suggested Reading

Carrasco, *Quetzalcoatl and the Irony of the Empire.*

Diaz, *The Conquest of New Spain.*

Questions to Consider

1. Why did it take the Spanish almost 30 years to come into direct contact with the Aztec?

2. Should Columbus be viewed as a hero or a villain in world history?

3. If you were captured by the Maya, as Aguilar and Guerrero were, would you have gone native or resisted acculturation?

First Contact with Europe in Mesoamerica
Lecture 41—Transcript

Europe had been using the Silk Road to trade with India and China for centuries. But when the Ottoman Turks sacked and took over Constantinople in 1453, that route became dangerous. European nations needed to find new seafaring routes to Asia. That ended up being the catalyst for discovering the New World.

At first, going around Africa was the only known way, and establishing resupply points was difficult. The seas were very rough, especially around the Cape of Good Hope. But by 1488, the Portuguese had managed to make outposts. Their ships were making it around the Cape, but it was a very long and costly journey. Some people thought there was a better way. Among them: Christopher Columbus. He was an Italian-born merchant, and he had traveled widely, and he was very well read. He was the first one to propose a Western route in 1485. The Portuguese listened to him, but they turned him down. And he tried again to convince them in 1488, but again, they said, no, we're fine, we're going around Africa, and we don't believe your route would work.

So, he thought the Indies were actually closer than they are in reality. He was influenced by Italian astronomer Toscanelli. Toscanelli had calculated the Earth's circumference, but he had done it wrong. He was using Arabic miles, not Roman miles, so his calculation turned out to be somewhere around 30,000 kilometers, not the closer to 40,000 kilometers it actually is. So, with that, they also thought that Japan should be closer to Europe, and they thought it was farther south. Toscanelli had made a wrong map. But using that map, Columbus estimated that it was only going to be about 2,500 miles to Japan. Japan at that time was called the East Indies. But he was actually off by about 10,000 miles.

Finally, he convinced Spain to back him. Ferdinand and Isabella were the rulers at the time. And the truth was that Spain wasn't doing all that well; they weren't a very wealthy nation. A lot of the other European nations were doing much better than them. So they gave him permission in the name of

Spain, but they really couldn't fund it. So, most of his funding came from his Italian merchant friends.

In August of 1492, he sailed west. He had three ships, the *Niña*, the *Pinta*, and the *Santa Maria*. He was headed for Japan, but he hit the Bahamas. This was the first of four voyages he would take from Spain to the New World. And although American school children call him the discoverer of the Americas, the truth is he never actually touched or even saw the modern United States. And, by the way, Columbus was not the first European in the Americas. Viking Leif Ericson was there in 1000 A.D. He landed in Canada, and he established a small colony that he called Vinland; today, it's Newfoundland. And his colony didn't last. It was repelled by the locals. Columbus was actually up in Iceland in 1477. Perhaps he was there because he had heard the tales of Ericson. Maybe he was trying to find a route from there to upper China.

Columbus's first voyage was only into the Caribbean. He sailed around Cuba and a few other islands. Then, actually, he wrecked the *Santa Maria* into the island the he called Hispaniola. That's modern-day Haiti today, and the other half is the Dominican Republic. He wrecked there on Christmas day, so he named the site La Navidad, which is Christmas in Spanish. And he built a fort there and left 39 Spaniards to protect it.

They met the Taino Indians then. And at that point, it was a peaceful encounter. From the Taino, they acquired a lot of gold and other goods. They called those natives Indios. And that's where the term *Indian* comes from. Columbus thought maybe he had landed in India. In fact, he never, ever acknowledged that what he had found wasn't Asia.

Since he had wrecked his ship, the *Santa Maria*, he took the *Niña* back to Spain. He returns to Spain with a hero's welcome. He claims to have found the East Indies. And he shows off some of the Indios he had brought back with him. Because of his deeds, he got the title Admiral of the Seas. He was also proclaimed the governor of Hispaniola. And the news of his discoveries spreads around Europe. His second voyage was planned immediately.

Six months after he returned to Spain, Columbus set sail on his second expedition. This time, he had 17 ships, 1,200 men, and literally tons of provisions. He was off not just to explore and acquire, but to colonize. He arrived back to Hispaniola about one year after he had left that small Spanish settlement there. What he found was that La Navidad was destroyed by the Taino. All 39 Spaniards had been killed, and Columbus acted harshly. He punished the local natives. He enslaved them and forced them to pay tribute. The ones that continued to rebel, he cut their hands off.

La Navidad was actually, in modern day, Haiti. But with it gone, Columbus decided to make a new colony to the east. This time he called it La Isabella, after the queen. Today, it's in modern-day Dominican Republic. Settlers first stayed in that place, but there was bad luck there. Two huge hurricanes hit the area in 1494, and again, in 1495. They wrecked everything they had built. And hunger and disease set in. There was mutiny. And again, Columbus punished people harshly that didn't follow his orders. Finally, the colony was moved, in 1496, south to Santo Domingo.

Columbus went back to Spain again. And then in 1498, he returned with his third expedition. This time he had six ships, three to supply people, and three to go further explore. Columbus landed on South America this time. And he explored the Orinoco River Delta. Looking at it, he correctly identified that though he had been on islands, this had to be the mainland; the river was so large, it had to be coming from some mainland source.

Then he went back to Hispaniola in 1499. He arrived there to a very angry population. He and his brothers were despised on Hispaniola. They claimed that they were cruel and that they were bad leaders. There were charges of tyranny and genocide against the Taino people. Witnesses said that there were body parts cut off the natives to punish them, and, not just the natives, the colonists got the same treatment if they disobeyed. They said that Columbus and his brothers were enslaving all the natives and that they were working them to death. Even Columbus's allies really could not deny their cruelty.

Christopher and his brothers, Bartolomeo and Diego, were convicted of those crimes in Hispaniola. They were sent back to Spain in chains in the year 1500. And they spent a full year in jail. They were stripped of their titles and all their wealth. But then finally, they got another audience with the crown. They denied all the charges against them. They claimed that they were just simply political intrigue, that other people wanted what they had, and they lied about them. They begged for a final chance to find that passage through to the Indian Ocean. Ferdinand agreed. And this time, he backed them with more ships. Their wealth was reinstated. But, Columbus was never again to be the governor of Hispaniola.

In 1502, Columbus embarked on his fourth and final expedition to the New World. It was on that journey that the first true moment of Mesoamerican and European contact actually took place. With a promise to find a route to India, he leaves with four ships. He had built a new *Santa Maria*. He entered the Caribbean with a hurricane right behind him. And he got to Hispaniola, but they refused to let him enter the port. They still hated him. He warned them of the coming hurricanes, but they didn't listen to him. So those hurricanes hit on July 1, 1502. There were 29 ships at that time in their port, carrying gold that was going to go to Spain, and they were all lost in the storm. Columbus actually weathered it, sheltering in a bay around the other side of the island.

Surviving that, he sailed south to Honduras, and he was investigating the islands off the north coast of that current country. There, his brother Bartolomeo saw a trading canoe. It was huge; it was actually longer than his ship. And it was eight-foot wide. It was made out of a single tree trunk. There were 25 men and women, also children, and supplies on board this one ship. There were cotton clothes, cacao, copper bells, and pottery. The Maya traders were headed from the south up to the Yucatan.

So they captured that canoe and took its cargo. They let all the people go, except the captain, an old man. They had a Taino translator on board, and he could actually communicate with this old man. So the old man told them stories of lots of gold further south. So they said, great, come be our guide. So they went down the coast. And after a while, they let the old man off, probably somewhere around Nicaragua. Supposedly, they said they paid him well and he was happy.

They searched the coastline for a way through to the Pacific Ocean; they went all the way down to Panama. Natives there said rivers led through to another large ocean. They tried to establish a base camp there, but between native attacks and more hurricanes, it was undoable. So they abandoned the search. They tried to get back up into the Caribbean, but they actually wrecked on Jamaica on their way headed towards Hispaniola again.

Then Columbus was stuck in Jamaica for a whole year. Hispaniola's governor knew he was there, but he didn't like him, so he refused to rescue them. Finally, they were rescued, and Columbus went back to Spain. He landed in 1504, but he was in very, very poor health. Two years later in 1506, he died in Valladolid, Spain. So, Columbus never did find his route to the Indies. But, he had accidentally opened up communications to the New World. Arguably, that was the most important cultural contact moment in world history. Just imagine a world without the Americas.

Just while Columbus was being fired as governor and led away in chains in the year 1500, a young man was arriving to the shores of Hispaniola. His name was Vasco Nuñez de Balboa, and he would eventually create the first permanent mainland Spanish settlement.

Balboa was not particularly successful in Spain. He was the son of a conquistador, and he was a page in his youth. By 1500, Spanish ships had crossed the Atlantic hundreds of times. There was a ship leaving every week. And Balboa decided to board one. He joined a treasure-hunting mission, and that mission went down to Panama and Colombia. Rodrigo de Bastidas's expedition was the one he joined. It was licensed from the crown of Spain. They could find what they wanted, but they had to follow La Quinta, the rules of acquisition. That meant that there was $^1/_5$ for the crown and $^4/_5$ for the explorers.

He went on four years of various expeditions like that. And he learned the coast of Panama very, very well. He took all of his earnings to Hispaniola in 1505. There, he bought lands, and he started farming. He had crops, and he was doing pig farming. But he really wasn't very good at it. And eventually, he fell deeply into debt. To escape his creditors, he stowed away on a departing ship. He hid in a barrel, and that ship was on its way to

Colombia. The expedition was to secure terra firma there. They established a place called San Sebastian. But again, it was attacked by natives. A young Pizarro was there in charge of the group. And while they were waiting for reinforcements, the natives were constantly and fiercely attacking.

Balboa was discovered during the voyage, and the captain almost killed him. But his knowledge of the area was deemed valuable, so they spared him. He was a very charismatic person, and everyone on the crew liked him.

The crew was upset when they arrived to a nearly destroyed camp. Balboa suggested moving the settlement. He said the Darien in Panama might be a good spot. It was more fertile, and there were less warlike natives there. Pizarro agreed with him, and they decided all to move the settlement. Balboa picked the landing point. There was a hard-fought battle there, but ultimately, they were victorious. And, the natives that attacked them had a ton of gold and wealth. Balboa became a hero to all the men.

Santa Maria La Antigua del Darien was the first permanent colony on the mainland, and Balboa was elected to be in charge. Eventually, he became the governor. In 1513, he led his most famous expedition; he found the Pacific, the South Sea. A young Pizarro was with him on that journey as well. That opened the door to the eventual conquest of the Inca empire. But that's a different story.

We're focused on the first contact in Mesoamerica, not South America. Balboa accidentally made that moment happen, too, when he sent the ill-fated Captain Valdivia back to Hispaniola with the wealth he had captured for the crown. In 1511 Valdivia and his crew left Panama for Santo Domingo. As so often happened then, they were caught off guard by a hurricane and wrecked near Jamaica; 15 men made it into lifeboats and drifted for about two weeks. They landed on the shores of the Yucatan Peninsula.

There's scholarly debate, but most agree that these were the first Spaniards in Mexico. They were immediately captured by the Maya. Valdivia and three others were sacrificed that very first day. Others became slaves. All but two men eventually died. There was a priest named Geronimo de Aguilar, and there was a soldier named Gonzalo Guerrero.

Aguilar became a slave of the king, the K'inich of Zama, probably Tulum. He learned Chontal Maya and their customs. Eventually, he was ransomed by Cortes in 1518, and he became a translator for Cortes. But Guerrero goes native. His military knowledge was very valuable. He was given to the king of Chetumal in the southern part of that coast. Eventually, he married the king's daughter, and they had three children together. He's remembered there in the Yucatan as the father of the very first mestizo. His children are the mixed blood, like everyone today. In Yucatan, all over the peninsula, there are statues in his honor. He's a hero to the Maya.

Seven years passed until the next Spaniards arrived. In 1518, the Juan de Grijalva expedition showed up with four ships. They were sent by his uncle, Diego Velazquez; he was the governor of Cuba at the time. Grijalva first lands on the island of Cozumel. He takes a town on the south end of that island. Then he sails the coast, surveying for landing spots. He probably saw Tulum. Then he saw the gigantic Ascension Bay. He turned north, and he went around the Yucatan. Eventually, he lands in Tabasco for a brief time. The Grijalva River there is named after him.

He makes it all the way to Veracruz, and he notes greater wealth in that area. So then he returns to Cuba to report what he found. But by that time, his uncle had lost faith in him. He wasn't aggressive enough. So he commissioned another expedition. This one was led by a man named Hernan Cortes. He gave him many ships and 500 men. So Cortes leaves for Cozumel late in 1518. Cortes lands on the island, and he immediately burns the town on the north end. There, he erects a Christian cross in the ashes. The natives tell him about Aguilar, so he sends people and he ransoms this priest. The priest tells him about the shipwreck. He also tells him about Gonzalo Guerrero. Cortes sends Aguilar to go retrieve Guerrero as well.

But Guerrero says, no, that he's a Mayan now. And Guerrero's wife, who's a princess, is very angry with Aguilar. She says, who let this slave walk up and bother us? Gonzalo at the time was all tattooed and pierced. He said that he was still a friend of Spain, but that he's Mayan now. But he was lying about being a friend of Spain. Guerrero actually helped the Maya fight the Spanish. He taught them the tricks of Spanish warfare. So when Montejo attacks the west side of the Yucatan, Guerrero was there, leading warriors, and he knew all their tactics. He soundly defeated him at the site of Champoton. When Davila attacked the east coast of Yucatan, Guerrero was there, too, and he deceived them with letters. He sent notes to separate forces, tricking them to retreat, or that the other people were dead. He became a phantom menace for the conquistadors and one of their most wanted.

He lived for 25 years as a Maya war captain. He led 50 canoes to Honduras in 1536 to join a fight against Pedro de Alvarado, but he lost. His body was found dead among Maya bodies, all tattooed, and at that time, he had grey hair. As for the other Spanish castaway, the priest Geronimo de Aguilar, he joined Cortes's crew and recommended they follow Grijalva's route around the coast. That expedition would eventually lead to the destruction of the Aztec civilization.

Just before Cortes left Cozumel, he got word from the governor of Cuba that his permission had been revoked, but he ignored it, and he went anyway. That would cause him some trouble later. Along the way, he picked up more men and more horses, and he rounded the Yucatan. He landed in Tabasco, just where Grijalva had. There, he defeated the town of Xicalanco, a big Maya port. And there were Aztec *pochteca* traders there. The defeated people gave him 20 slave women, and one of them was Doña Maria "La Malinche." She spoke both Maya and Nahuatl. So between she and Aguilar, they could work as a team. The locals told Cortes about the Aztec capital of Tenochtitlan.

La Malinche is an infamous figure. On the one hand, she's the symbol of native betrayal. But she's also a symbol of mestizo heritage. She eventually became Cortes's wife. And she bore his favorite son, Diego. She was more than just a translator; she was actually very key to Cortes's successful strategy against the Aztecs.

Upon Tabascan advice, Cortes sails west. He lands at Veracruz and takes over another town. Grijalva had seen that same place a year before, and he had reported a lot of gold there. Bernal Diaz had been with Grijalva and was now with Cortes to confirm that that was the same place. It was called Chalchihuecan, a "place of jade." Cortes renamed it Villa Real de la Vera Cruz. He also called it Villa Rica because of all the gold there. The Veracruz part was because he had landed on Good Friday. "Veracruz" means "the true cross." It became the second mainland permanent settlement in the Americas.

Before that, it was actually an Aztec tribute community. Locals there told him more about Tenochtitlan, this amazing city full of gold. And Cortes sent messages to Moctezuma. He requested a meeting, but all those messages were ignored. So, he decided to march to Tenochtitlan. His advisers counseled not to do it, but Cortes ordered all of the boats burned. Then, his soldiers had no choice. So in August of 1519, they began their march inland. There were 700 men, 15 horses, and 15 cannons; 100 men were left behind to hold Veracruz.

At this point in history, the Spanish had been in the Americas for almost 30 years. They had explored, conquered, and learned the lay of the land. It was time for the big showdown. Mesoamerica's most powerful nation, the Aztecs, versus the mighty Spanish crown. In our next lecture, we'll discuss that fateful clash of cultures.

The Siege of Tenochtitlan
Lecture 42

Arguably, the defeat of the Aztec at Tenochtitlan at the hands of the Spanish conquistadors was one of the greatest military victories in all of world history: A few hundred Spaniards defeated hundreds of thousands of Aztec warriors. One of the best accounts of Cortes's siege of Tenochtitlan was *The True History of the Conquest of New Spain* by Bernal Diaz. Diaz was an eyewitness to the action and had a great deal of experience in the New World. What's more, he had read many other accounts of the battle and had respect for the native people. In this lecture, we'll tell the tale of how Cortes conquered Tenochtitlan—based on Diaz's document and on native accounts.

Enemies of the Aztec
- Cortes landed south of Vera Cruz in 1519 with 11 ships, 600 men, horses, and weapons. Almost immediately, an Aztec welcoming party showed up bearing gifts. The Aztec messengers said that Moctezuma welcomed the explorers but asked them not come to the capital. The Aztec would be happy to pay the Spanish whatever tribute they wanted.

- Moctezuma was back at his capital worried about a prophecy that conquerors from the east would destroy the Aztec civilization. The year 1519 was 1 Reed, the predicted time when Quetzalcoatl would return.

- Cortes finally settled at a site called Cempoala. There, he met Fat Cacique, a leader of the Totonac people, and learned a significant fact: The Totonac hated the Aztec tyranny and could be potential allies for the Spanish. Cortes promised to protect them and, thus, gained the support of the entire Totonac region.

- Cortes established Villa Rica de la Vera Cruz in July 1519. He became the leader of the settlement, which meant that he had direct authority over the new Spanish colony. He sent one of his ships back to Spain with his side of the story and some gifts for the Crown.

Battles with the Tlaxcalans

- Cortes decided to venture to Tenochtitlan. Aztec tax collectors arriving to meet Fat Cacique were immediately arrested. Cortes then secretly sent the Aztec collectors a message saying that the Spanish were friends of Moctezuma and would be visiting soon. Cortes took 400 men, horses, and weapons and headed for Tenochtitlan. The Totonac suggested that he go through Tlaxcala, whose people were the sworn enemies of the Aztec.

- A force of 3,000 Tlaxcalans, led by Xicotenga the Younger, prince of the Tlaxcalans, attacked the Spanish. Many Tlaxcalans were killed, and three of their captains were captured by Cortes. The next day, Cortes released the prisoners and sent them back with an offer of peace. The Tlaxcalans sent another 6,000 warriors to attack. Still, the Spanish held their ground.

- The Spanish soldiers deserve a great deal of credit; 400 fighters repelled thousands in multiple battles. Eventually, the Spanish won the Tlaxcalans' respect and loyalty.

"We Will Make History"

- Cortes and his men stayed among Tlaxcala for weeks and learned about Aztec dominance. They were housed in a large and beautiful city, with a thriving marketplace. In the marketplace, the Europeans were horrified by the sight of slaves in cages; thus, they broke open the cages and released the slaves.

- Another message was received from Moctezuma, inviting the Spanish to visit him at Tenochtitlan. The Spanish were advised to pass through the nearby city of Cholula. Cortes replied favorably, although the Tlaxcalans warned him not to go.

- At this point, the Cuban soldiers objected that 400 men could not conquer an entire nation. Never before had anyone done that, not even Alexander the Great or the mighty Roman Empire. And Cortes, in a splendid speech, replied that the men would make history. As it turned out, he was right.

Arrival in Tenochtitlan

- Cortes and his men marched on to Cholula, with 1,000 Tlaxcalans. Because Cortes was wary, he camped just outside Cholula and sent scouts and messengers to assess the situation. The scouts quickly learned that the men were marching into a trap; there were 20,000 Aztec warriors waiting in a ravine nearby.

- Cortes and his men then set a trap of their own. All the Cholula nobles were invited into a plaza, then surrounded by Tlaxcalan forces. The Spanish slaughtered every one of the Cholula nobles, and the Tlaxcalans sacked the city.

- On November 8, 1519, Cortes walked the causeway into the Aztec capital of Tenochtitlan. Moctezuma came out to meet him, accompanied by a huge entourage. Moctezuma was brought directly to Cortes on the causeway and stepped down to greet him personally.

- Moctezuma's greeting speech was legendary and has been confirmed in both native

Moctezuma was aware of the impressive victories of the Spanish and worried that these conquerors represented the fulfillment of a prophecy predicting the destruction of the Aztec.

and Spanish accounts. He told Cortes that Tenochtitlan was his city, his home. He welcomed the return of Cortes as a god. Moctezuma was sure that the prophecy was being fulfilled, and he publicly swore allegiance to Spain. The Spanish were led to extravagant quarters.

- The first week in Tenochtitlan was very cordial. The Europeans toured the city and its markets. Dances, music shows, and feasts were held in their honor. They witnessed human sacrifices—which appalled them. Moctezuma was a gracious host. Although the nobles did not trust Cortes and wanted him out of the city, Moctezuma still feared the prophecy. He gave the Spanish a great deal of gold and asked them to take the tribute and return to Spain.

Moctezuma Taken Hostage

- In communications with Vera Cruz, Cortes discovered that Moctezuma had sent an army to attack the city. He made the bold decision to take Moctezuma hostage. Six months passed with Moctezuma in captivity. It was a brilliant strategy by Cortes. Moctezuma still held court and participated in sacrifices every day. Cortes and Moctezuma talked for hours; Moctezuma knew all the soldiers by name, and they treated him with great respect.

- Moctezuma told all the caciques to surrender. Tributes started to pour in. Cortes verified that the gold was coming from three large gold mines, and Moctezuma surrendered an Aztec vault full of gold. Diaz helped weigh the gold: He reported that it was worth 700,000 pesos, or 42,000 pounds of gold.

- The situation seemed to be going well for the Spanish. The Aztec had surrendered without a fight, and the Europeans had become rich beyond their dreams. But then, in April 1520, 18 ships from Cuba arrived with orders to arrest Cortes and his men for mutiny and treason. Governor Velasquez sent Panfilo de Narvaez to arrest Cortes.

- When word reached Cortes at Tenochtitlan that Narvaez had landed and was headed inland with 900 men, Cortes immediately rode out to intercept him. He left Pedro de Alvarado in charge back in Tenochtitlan—the biggest mistake of his career.

Attack by the Aztec

- Cortes ambushed Narvaez using the Tlaxcalans. Then, crisis struck. Word came back from Tenochtitlan that Alvarado and his men had been attacked in their quarters by thousands of angry Aztec. While Cortes was gone, the Aztec invited Alvarado to a festival dedicated to Tezcatlipoca. There was feasting on human flesh, which infuriated Alvarado. He ordered all the exits blocked, then he killed everyone present. For the Aztec, this was the last straw. They needed to get the Tlatoani back.

- Cortes now returned with 1,200 men. The Aztec led him into the city but only to share the fate of Alvarado. Thousands of Aztec attacked the soldiers' compound. Moctezuma was forced up onto a roof and was hit in the head by a stone. Bernal Diaz reports that Moctezuma died soon after, and his body was sent out into the crowd.

- The Spanish knew that they had to escape. They built platforms from the doors in the compound and planned to lay them across the causeway gap at night. Then, they loaded up the Tlaxcalans with gold.

- The night escape was a disaster. It's called the Noche Triste, "sad night." The Aztec were ready with their own plans and attacked from canoes. The water was filled with the bodies of horses and men. Gold-laden Spaniards sunk to the bottom of the lake. Many of them were dragged to the temple and sacrificed.

- Cortes made it to land on June 30, 1520. Still, tens of thousands of Aztec warriors were on his trail. The Spanish reached Tlaxcala, where the Aztec attacked them again. The Europeans barely survived this battle. Now, Cortes was trapped in Tlaxcalan, with fewer than 400 of his 1,400 original men.

The Conquest of Tenochtitlan

- Any other man would have returned to Spain or Cuba at this point—but not Cortes. He remained in Mexico, rallied his Aztec-hating allies, and forged a new plan. He decided that if he could control Lake Texcoco, he could conquer Tenochtitlan.

- In Tlaxcala, Cortes and his men built boats in secret for months. Cortes finally convinced Velasquez to join the mission, and more men arrived. Just after Christmas, the Spanish celebrated mass at Tlaxcala, then dragged the boats to Texcoco and demanded that the city surrender. The city was then evacuated.

- In fact, all the towns in the area were empty—but Aztec warriors were hiding everywhere. Aztec attacks were futile, however. The Spanish continued to advance and launched their boats on Lake Texcoco. When Texcoco's supplies were exhausted, the Spaniards moved on to Iztapalapa—where there was another Aztec trap. The Aztec broke down the levees and flooded the town. The plan almost worked, but the Tlaxcalans figured it out at the last second and warned the Spanish.

- The breach in the levees ruined the freshwater barrier, and brackish water filled into the Tenochtitlan side. Now, the city had no more freshwater and no supplies. At that point, Cuauhtemoc was in charge of the Aztec. Cortes sent him repeated messages of peace, but the Aztec vowed to fight to the end. Tens of thousands defended the causeway; the siege went on for months.

- On the one-year anniversary of the Spanish landing, the Aztec attacked with more than 100,000 men. Still, the Aztec could not repel the Spanish. Eventually, the Spanish breached Tenochtitlan. Cuauhtemoc fled by canoe with his family, but he was captured and brought back to Cortes. Finally, Cuauhtemoc surrendered on August 13, 1521. The Aztec were defeated.

Suggested Reading

Carrasco, *The Aztecs: A Very Short Introduction.*

Diaz, *The Conquest of New Spain.*

Duran, *Book of the Gods and Rites and the Ancient Calendar.*

Gruzinski, *The Aztecs: Rise and Fall of an Empire.*

Smith, *The Aztecs.*

Stuart, *The Mighty Aztecs.*

Questions to Consider

1. What gave Cortes the confidence that a few hundred men could defeat an entire nation?

2. What was more important, Spanish military prowess or Cortes's negotiation skills?

3. How important was the role of religion in the meetings between these two great cultures?

The Siege of Tenochtitlan
Lecture 42—Transcript

Arguably, the defeat of the Aztecs at Tenochtitlan at the hands of the Spanish conquistadors was one of the greatest military victories in all of world history. A few hundred Spaniards defeated hundreds of thousands of Aztec warriors, well, a few hundred Spaniards, thousands of native allies, and 12 infectious diseases, that is.

In this lecture, I'll tell the tale. But first, again, what version to believe? There are Spanish versions and native versions. Some of them were written right at contact, others much later. And they also had different motivations. Cortes' letters were to convince the king. Duran's native informants wanted to justify the native reaction to the Spanish.

I think that the best possible sources are primary accounts, in other words, from someone who was actually there. Secondary accounts are stories told from others. Then, we even have another level that we would call tertiary accounts, and those are stories of people's stories. Of all the chronicles, I choose Bernal Diaz and his story, *The [True] History of the Conquest of New Spain.*

Diaz was there the whole way. This was actually his third expedition, and he was very experienced. He was in Panama with Balboa's settlement. He was with Grijalva on his expedition. And he was the last surviving member of the Cortes mission. He actually wrote his story at the age of 67 from Guatemala. And at that time, sadly, he was as poor as he had ever been in this life.

He wrote his account in response to what he called the lies of Gomara. The pros about his account is, one, he was really there, and two, he had read all the other accounts. Finally, three, he had respect for the native people. The cons of his account are, one, he was clearly a Cortes supporter. Two, he really downplays the native contributions in the battle. And three, he wrote it long after the fact, and maybe he did forget some of the details. So, I'll use mainly Diaz, but also a few native accounts that were supplied by Sahagun and Duran to create the story I'll tell you now.

Picking up where we left off in my last lecture, Cortes landed south of Veracruz in 1519. At the time, he had 11 ships, 600 men, some horses, crossbows and muskets, and a few canons as well. So, first he set up some huts in the dunes, but those areas had a lot of bugs, and there was a lot of wind that blew. Wasn't a good place for his first camp. But almost immediately, an Aztec welcoming party showed up and greeted them. They were tracked, and they knew they were coming, since they had landed in Tabasco. Moctezuma knew all about the Spanish.

An official named Tendile gave the Spanish gifts. He brought them gold, because he had learned from the informants in Tabasco that the Spanish were always asking about gold. He also gave them cotton clothes and feathers and jade. Then he gave them a name. He called them the "Teules," and *teule* means either "God" or "demon," a little of both; you know how the Aztec pantheon is. And he said that Moctezuma welcomes them. But please don't come to the capital, that the Aztecs are happy to pay them whatever tribute the powerful Spanish want, and they can take it and go away with it.

Moctezuma was back at his capital worried about a prophecy he had heard. Nezahualpilli, the current king of Texcoco, had warned him. He said that he had a vision that conquerors were going to come from the East, and that it was they who would destroy the Aztec civilization, and that perhaps it was connected to this legend of Quetzalcoatl's return. In 1519, One Reed was the year. It was a year of the new fire ceremony, and it also happened to be the year predicted when Quetzalcoatl was going to return. So, they had seen the Spanish victories, and they were impressive, so all the signs were very foreboding about these people.

A few weeks of messages passed back and forth. But eventually, the Aztec allies stopped bringing food to the Spanish. So Cortes was motivated at that point to survey the coast and look maybe for a better place to settle. He finds a place called Quiahuiztlan, and that becomes the actual city of Veracruz. He suggests that settlement, but there's protests, especially from the Cuban landowners that are with him. They remind him, listen, our mission is only for trading. We're not supposed to be settling here. And Cortes promises those people that after they settle and do this, that if they want to leave, they can leave.

So they move north up the coast, and they get to a site called Cempoala. And Cortes sends this city a message of peace, and that's accepted by somebody that Diaz calls the Fat Cacique, and they go to visit him. He's a leader of the Totonac people there. And there, they learn something exciting. The Fat Cacique and the Totonac hate the Aztec. The Aztecs have enemies. If they have enemies, these are potential allies. The Fat Cacique of Aztec tyranny; they demand massive tribute and capture men for sacrifice, and they rape their women. Cortes promises to protect them and gains the support of the whole Totonac region, including Quiahuiztlan, his future home base.

Villa Rica de Veracruz was established in July of 1519. It was a shrewd move, because it circumvented the authority of Governor Velazquez. All people present voted that Cortes, as the captain, would become the leader of this new settlement, and that meant he had direct authority over this new Spanish colony. So he sends one of his ships back to Spain with his side of the story and some gifts for the Crown.

He builds a fort, housing, and a church there. Then Cortes decides to go to Tenochtitlan. The Cubans demand to go back to Cuba. Cortes has them arrested and calls them all cowards. Then he sinks the ships on purpose. First of all, he brings off the provisions and the gear, of course. But now, everyone, including the Cubans, were committed until reinforcements came.

Cortes really was an excellent speaker. He won over Spaniards and natives alike. There were so many moments in the story where his speeches made the difference, and it makes sense because he was actually trained as a lawyer back in Spain. Like one of these stories, he convinced those Cubans to stay, or, along with Malinche's help, how he convinced the Totonacs to swear allegiance to him; they had really just met. That was a good job of talking.

Aztec tax collectors arrived to the Fat Cacique's place, and they were immediately arrested. The Totonacs were full of fear, but Cortes soothed them and said, don't worry. We've got this. But then, he secretly goes to those collectors with a message, saying that they're the friends of Moctezuma, and that they'll be coming for a visit soon. Then he lets those collectors go. And he tells the Totonacs that he's going to deal with the Aztecs personally, because he has the Spanish god on his side.

The Totonacs were the first of many to hear the standard Spanish line, that God wants you to stop what you're doing. Cortes gave them big speeches about not doing any more human sacrifices, and to stop eating each other, and please, no more sodomy. But the Fat Cacique says, look, this is really hard to stop. It's of vital importance to our gods and the people. Everybody here does it. We're not just going to stop this. So then a ship from Jamaica shows up. They're also trying to establish a first settlement there. Cortes captures some of them, and he poses in their clothes on the shore. He tries to lure the rest of them to land, but they figure it out and they sail off. So, at this point, Cortes knows the gig is up. His time is short. He's got to do what he's going to do before more come.

Leaving behind some to guard the fort, he takes 400 men, horses, crossbows, and muskets, and he heads for Tenochtitlan. Along with him, he has 2,000 porters and guards given to him by the Totonacs. The Totonacs suggest that he goes through Tlaxcala, who are the sworn enemies of the Aztec. As Cortes marched into Tlaxcala, the Tlaxcalans reacted much like one would expect a foreign enemy to be received, with an army of their own. In fact, they sent thousands. But somehow, Cortes and his men were able to stand their ground.

Two Totonac messengers were sent ahead with a message of peace. They were held and then released. The Tlaxcalans said that must just be Aztec lies, and they send a message back saying, we're going to sacrifice and eat you. So a force of 3,000 Tlaxcalans attack the Spanish. They're led by a man named Xicotenga the Younger, the prince of the Tlaxcalans. They fight all day, but the Spanish hold their ground. Many of them, the Tlaxcalans that is, are killed, and three of their captains are caught by Cortes. That night, the Spanish sleep by a river and tend their wounds.

The next day, Cortes releases those captain prisoners and sends them with another offer of peace. That struck the Tlaxcalans very odd. They thought to themselves, why didn't they just sacrifice those guys? And what odd gods these people warship. So they send another 6,000 warriors to attack. During that battle, one of the horses get their head cut off by one of these swords with the obsidian blades on the side. Other people are dismembered.

305

But still, the Spanish held their ground. This time about 60 of them were injured. But they took more prisoners and then released them with more messages of peace. It was September and in the mountains, so it was cold. They went into a small town and took it over where they would spend the night. They fortified the temple area. Temple areas in that area were called Cues by the locals. Tlaxcalan priests prayed and consulted their gods for what to do about these people. And the message came back from those priests that, aha, these Spaniards are powerless at night. So, they planned a night raid, again, led by Xicotenga, but it was a huge failure. The Spanish were always ready. They never slept. So the Tlaxcalan leaders finally decided, well, yes, these people must be Teules, because they're absolutely unbeatable. They're supernatural.

So, I really have to give the Spanish big credit at that moment; 400 people repelled thousands of people in multiple battles. Later, they had native allies, but this was the first battle, and it was just them. Doing this won the Tlaxcalan respect and eventual loyalty. They stayed among Tlaxcala for weeks, and they learned all about Aztec dominance. It was a big, beautiful city they were staying in, and they were given very nice lodging.

And they checked out the market, and there were all sorts of beautiful things in the market. But, there were also people in cages. And so they broke those cages open and let those people out, let the slaves escape. And they gave more big speeches about Christianity and told the Tlaxcalans, hey, no more sacrifice, no more eating people, no more sodomy. And the Tlaxcalans, again, did not understand this at all. They said, why do these people keep saying this? Don't say this out loud. You are insulting our gods.

Another message was received from Moctezuma, and that message said, don't stay with those terrible people, the Tlaxcalans. Come visit me at Tenochtitlan. Come through the nearby city of Cholula. So, Cortes replies favorably that, sure, we will. The Tlaxcalans warn him not to go, that the Aztecs are liars and they're evil.

At this point, the Cuban soldiers speak up again and object. They say, this is crazy. How can 400 men conquer a nation? Never before has anyone done this, not even Alexander or the Romans. And Cortes replies in a great speech, he says, that's right, no one until now. We're going to make history, and this is going to be the greatest campaign ever. And he turned to be right.

They march on to Cholula. And the Tlaxcalans offer 10,000 men, but Cortes only takes about 1,000. They gave the Spanish gifts of gold and cotton. And then every town that they went through kept giving them these gifts; they were heroes in the area. The common people, though, had a bit of fear in their eyes. Cortes was cautious, so he camped just outside of Cholula, and he sent scouts and messengers to assess the situation. They quickly learned that this was actually a trap. There were 20,000 Aztec warriors waiting in a ravine nearby, and they could that see the population was actually evacuating; that's why they were scared. There were trenches dug into city streets.

Cortes consulted his men, as he always did in making these decisions, and they decided that they were going to have to punish these people for doing it. So they lay a trap of their own. All the Cholulan nobles were invited into a plaza, then, they surrounded them. They closed them off with their Tlaxcalan forces, and the Spanish slaughter everyone in the plaza. They say nearly 3,000 nobles were slaughtered. And then the Tlaxcalans sacked the city.

Now the Spanish have an even better reputation. They've taken out Cholula. They must be gods. The message comes back from Moctezuma to Cortes, and he says, ah, those terrible Cholulans. I can't believe they treated you, my friend, like that. Oh, that's terrible. Please come and see me in my capital. So, at Cholula, actually, one of the soldiers scales Popocatepetl. It's an erupting volcano, and nobody's ever seen one among the Spanish. This guy was really crazy brave to climb it. And at the top is the first time any of them saw Tenochtitlan. From that top, he sees into the lake. And he reports back, and Cortes' army immediately departs. There are more gifts, and the caciques accompany them the entire way.

Then, on November 8, 1519, he starts walking along the causeway into the Aztec capital. Moctezuma comes out to meet them in a huge entourage of thousands of people. He's tall, thin, and wears a small beard on his chin. A team of servants carry him on a litter, and he's dressed in fine robes. He's brought directly to Cortes on the causeway and steps down to personally greet him.

His greeting speech is famous. It's been confirmed in both native and Spanish accounts. He tells Cortes that this is his city, his home. He welcomes the return of Cortes as a god. Moctezuma is sure that this is the prophecy, and he publicly swears allegiance to Spain right there. And they're led to their new fancy quarters.

The first week is very cordial. It's a beautiful palace, and they love their lodging. They get a tour of the city and all of its markets. Dance shows and music shows and feasts are held in their honor. They get a tour of all the Cues, the temples. And they see a whole lot of sacrifices, and every time they say, oh, please, no, stop that. And the Aztec reply is, well, you, please don't insult our gods. That's what we need to do.

But all through it, Moctezuma is a very gracious host. The nobles don't trust Cortes, and they want him out of the city. But Moctezuma still fears the prophecy. And then he gives the Spanish lots of the gold they're looking for. He asks them to go back and just take the tribute and go back to Spain.

Cortes communicates with Veracruz, and they discover, actually, that Moctezuma has sent an army to attack Veracruz. Things are getting out of hand, and something needs to be done. So they make the bold decision to take Moctezuma hostage. Just one week after they arrive, they walk into his palace and tell him, come peacefully or die right now. And he says, what? No, I can't do that. And they said, too bad. That's just what we're going to do. So, instead of causing a ruckus, he goes willingly to the Spanish quarters. The nobles go crazy. But, he's still the king; he still calls all the shots.

Six whole months pass in captivity. It's a brilliant strategy by Cortes. Moctezuma still holds court, and he still goes out and he participates in the sacrifices every day. And every day, the Spanish tell him, please cut that out. But they have become honest friends, Cortes and Moctezuma. They had hours of talks, and they played board games together every day. Moctezuma knew all of the soldiers by name, and they all treated him with great respect.

All the caciques were called in by Moctezuma and told to surrender. Moctezuma mandated their obedience, and tributes started to pour in. Cortes verifies that this gold is coming from three large gold mines, and Moctezuma gives up an Aztec vault full of gold. Diaz helped weigh it. In total, he said that it was 700,000 pesos. Doing the math, that's actually 42,000 pounds of gold. Things were going great for the Spanish. The Aztec had surrendered without a fight. They were rich beyond their dreams. Spain was going to be so happy. But then, in April of 1520, 18 ships from Cuba arrived with orders to arrest Cortes and his men for their mutiny and treason.

Governor Velazquez sent Captain Panfilo de Narvaez to arrest Cortes. When word reached Tenochtitlan that he had landed and that he was headed inland with 900 men, Cortes immediately rode out to intercept him. He left Pedro de Alvarado in charge back in Tenochtitlan, and that was the biggest mistake of his entire career.

Narvaez was not a problem. Cortes ambushed him with the Tlaxcalans. Narvaez had no idea what kind of power Cortes had at that point. He had been able to harness thousands of people in Mexico in a very short time. So, Narvaez was arrested and brought back to Veracruz. Then Cortes gave another one of his amazing speeches. He told all of these 900 men, who wants to be rich and famous? Come with me.

He explained how beloved all the Spanish were among the Aztecs and how he had a huge pile of gold waiting. Those 900 men that were sent to arrest him became his new army. But then a crisis struck. The word came back from Tenochtitlan that Alvarado was being attacked in their quarters by thousands of angry Aztecs. Pedro de Alvarado was a handsome man. The Aztecs called him Tonatiuh, the Son of the Sun, because he had this red hair, but he was also very cruel and ruthless.

While Cortes was gone, the Aztec invited him to a festival dedicated to Tezcatlipoca. There were dances and music and feasting. And then, the feasting was actually feasting on human flesh, and that made Alvarado crazy. And he ordered all of the exits of this party blocked, and then he killed everyone there, innocent, unarmed, hundreds of people.

Now, Bernal Diaz doesn't make a whole lot of this. He kind of glosses over it. But the native accounts do. They talk about it as a horror. Innocent women and children were killed. They say there were guts everywhere, and people were hiding under dead people, trying not to be killed. From their opinion, the Aztecs were just trying to show him how beautiful Aztec society could be. So this was the last straw. They need to attack, and they need to get the Tlatoani back.

Cortes now returned with his now 1,200 men. Many of them weren't soldiers. They were actually people that went there to settle. The Aztecs led him into the city, but only to share the fate of Alvarado. Thousands of Aztecs are attacking his compound. Cuitlahuac, the new Tlatoani, or leader of the Aztecs, is leading the charge. And they're all yelling, we will eat you. You can't leave. And the fight goes on for weeks. Moctezuma is very depressed. He says, just kill me. This is a disaster. But they force him up onto the roof and tell him to yell out that everybody needs to be peaceful. But darts and stones come from the angry mob, and one of the stones hits Moctezuma in the head. He's badly injured, and he's brought back inside.

Bernal Diaz says he died sometime soon after, and everyone wept. Even Diaz and all of the Spaniards loved him. There's a debate that says maybe the Spanish killed him. I tend not to believe that. Cortes was smart. Why would he kill his hostage? In any event, they send the body out to the crowd, and the crowd is now even more angry. They knew they had to escape. The causeways were blocked, and the drawbridges were burned. They had to make a plan to escape, maybe at night. So they build platforms from the doors within their compound, and they plan to lay them across the causeway gap so they can get away. And then they load up the Tlaxcalans with all of their gold. Narvaez's men load down too. Cortes tells everybody, take as much as you want, but know that we've got to run and you can't carry too much.

The night escape was a disaster. It's called the Noche Triste, the "sad night." The Aztecs were ready with their own plans. Those platforms did not the work. There were lots of canoes attacking. So the water fills with bodies of horses and men. Gold-laden Spanish sink to the bottom of the lake. Many of them are dragged to the Cue and sacrificed on top. Some Spaniards could hear and see the screaming of their companions on the causeway.

Cortes made it to land at Tacuba on June 30, 1520. Still, tens of thousands of Aztec warriors were on his trail and attacking. They move on, and finally they get to Tlaxcala. The Aztecs are waiting on the road, though, and they attack them again; they barely survive this battle. And when he gets there, he's got less than 400 of the 1,400 total people that were trapped within the city.

I think any other man would have returned to Spain or Cuba at this point, but not Cortes. He remained in Mexico, rallied up his Aztec-hating allies again, and made a new plan. He decided that if he could control Lake Texcoco, he could defeat Tenochtitlan. Rigging from the 18 ships was brought in, and they built 13 boats. Each boat was big enough to hold 25 men. They built them in secret in Tlaxcala for months. And more and more people around the valley were starting to get sick; the Spanish diseases were taking hold. Many of the Tlaxcalan nobles turned Christian, thinking if they accepted God they wouldn't be sick anymore.

Velazquez, during this time, sends four more ships, but he still doesn't know what's happening there. And Cortes convinces those to join him too, and he gets more men. Just after Christmas, they held a mass at Tlaxcala. And then they drag the boats to Texcoco, and they demand Texcoco's surrender. They do immediately, and the city's evacuated. In fact, all the towns in the area are empty. But the Aztec warriors are hiding everywhere, and they sneak attack. There are many more Aztecs in the lake with canoes. But the Aztec attacks are futile. The Spanish continue to advance.

They launch their boats to have lake dominion. They are faster and bigger than the canoes, which are no match against them. Texcoco's supplies eventually are exhausted, so they move on to a place called Iztapalapa, and there is another Aztec trap. They actually break the flood walls of the huge levees, and they flood the town. It almost works, but the Tlaxcalans figure it out at the last second, and they warn the Spanish.

It ruins the freshwater barrier, and now all of that brackish water fills into the Tenochtitlan side. It was really a disaster. They capture all three towns at the ends of the causeway, and then they break the aqueduct that's going from Chapultepec. Now the city has no more fresh water, and they're really not getting any more supplies. Canoes at night are trying to get there with supplies, but they're taken out by the Spanish boats. The Aztecs take a Spanish boat with their supply things, but it only works once.

Cuitlahuac died of smallpox months earlier. Cuauhtemoc was now in charge. Cortes sent repeated messages of peace, but they said, no way. The Aztecs vowed to fight to the end. Tens of thousands defended the causeway every day. It goes on for months and months. On the one-year anniversary of their landing, the Aztecs attack huge. With more than 100,000 Aztecs, they land on the Spanish on June 24.

Still, they can't repel the Spanish. Getting weak and sick, disease and famine starts kicking in. The Spanish finally fill the causeway gaps one by one, and eventually they breached Tenochtitlan. Cuauhtemoc retreats into the market at Tlatelolco, and they continue to resist for a few more weeks. They capture a few Spaniards, and they actually put them on stakes, their heads on stakes, to intimidate them. Finally, Alvarado breaks from Tacuba. They hold those temples at Tlatelolco. Sandoval corners them in a residence. Cuauhtemoc flees by canoe with his family, but then he's caught and brought back to Cortes. Finally, he surrenders on August 13, 1521. The Aztec were defeated.

They won, but where was all the gold? Cuauhtemoc was tortured, but he couldn't reveal much. He was really living as a puppet king at that time. Eventually, Cortes kills him in Tabasco in 1525. I always think about him when I pass the area called Cuauhtemoc in Tabasco. There's a nothing town there named after this once-famous king. Today at Tlatelolco, there's the Plaza of the Three Cultures, a solemn statue with the words, "Heroically defended by Cuauhtemoc, Tlatelolco fell to Hernan Cortes." It was neither a triumph nor a defeat. It was the painful birth of the Mestizo nation that is the Mexico of today.

As for the conquistadors, the gold they fought so hard for slipped through their fingers. None had their proper share. So they went looking for it in the Aztec tribute zones. Unfortunately for the Maya, soldiers like Pedro de Alvarado headed their way. Let's talk about that in my next lecture.

Conquest of the Maya and Landa's Legacy
Lecture 43

Once the Aztec were defeated, Cortes and his conquistadors turned their attention to the rest of Mesoamerica. Although the Europeans' war with the Aztecs was relatively quick and confined to the Valley of Mexico, the Maya region was spread across what today is five different countries, and the conquest of the Maya took decades of hard-fought military campaigns. In this lecture, we will study the Spanish conquest of the Maya area; compare and contrast the brutal cruelty of the conquistadors with the Dominicans, who advocated "voluntary conversion"; and consider the paradox of the Franciscan Diego de Landa, who tortured and killed the Maya in the name of God but who wrote the Maya's definitive ethnography and made it possible to decipher their hieroglyphics.

Invasion in Maya Territory

- After Tenochtitlan fell in August 1521, Cortes took charge of the Aztec tribute network and demanded allegiance of the tributary states to the Spanish Crown. Few opposed the Spanish after the Aztec were defeated. In 1523, emissaries headed all the way down to the Soconusco: Maya territory.

- The Maya met Cortes's scouts with representatives from the K'iche and the Kakchiquel people, the two largest language groups in the Guatemalan highlands. Both peoples swore obedience to the Spanish Crown. But the scouts returned to Cortes and insisted that the Spanish needed to invade the natives' territory and beat them into submission.

- Cortes decided to send Pedro de Alvarado on this mission. His 300 soldiers and 180 horsemen were accompanied by thousands of Tlaxcalans and Cholulans. They marched along the trade routes down toward the Soconusco, following the Pacific Coast from Oaxaca into Guatemala. At the Salama River, Alvarado turned inland. There, he was met by the K'iche army.

- The Maya of the Guatemalan highlands were vulnerable. Their many different groups were divided along language lines. Each group had its own territory and fortified capital. Alvarado used the conflicts between them to his advantage. After defeating the K'iche, Alvarado marched to the K'iche capital and burned it to the ground.

Pedro de Alvarado
- Following the demise of the K'iche, the Kakchiquel made an ill-fated decision. In April 1524, they invited Alvarado to their capital at Iximche and offered to ally with him against the other Maya groups. Alvarado accepted their help.

- The Kakchiquel troops led Alvarado to the other Maya groups. At Lake Atitlan, the Tz'utujil Maya were defeated. Next, the Mam were conquered. To the south and east were the Pipil, who were overcome by Pedro de Alvarado's brother Gonzalo. Gonzalo established the city that is now known as San Salvador.

- In July 1524, Alvarado claimed Iximche as the region's new capital. By August, the Kakchiquel rebelled against him and actually burned down their own capital of Iximche in 1526. Although there were many pockets of Maya holdouts, however, the region was Alvarado's.

- This was a particularly bad time for the Maya. Alvarado established *encomiendas*—places where Spaniards were given rights to the land and any people living on it. The Maya in those lands were enslaved and forced to work in the mines. Alvarado even imported black slaves to join the Maya working in his mines.

- In 1540, Alvarado hatched his final bold plan. He funded 13 ships and 550 men with his own money. His plan was to sail from western Mexico to China to complete the mission that Columbus never could. But bad luck befell him. In western Mexico, a horse fell on him and crushed him; he died in 1541.

For his work against slavery, Bartolome de las Casas is considered a pioneer of humanitarian philosophy, and he remains a beloved figure in Mexican history.

Bartolome de Las Casas

- Although the Spanish conquistadors were generally a cruel and ruthless lot, a shining example of a moral and upright man was Spanish historian and missionary Bartolome de Las Casas.

- Las Casas landed on Hispaniola in 1502. At that time, he was a slave owner. When the Dominicans arrived in 1510, they were appalled by the cruelty they saw—and they opened Bartolome's eyes.

- He began to lobby against slavery and asked for an end to the encomienda system. In 1522, Las Casas started a colony in Venezuela. There, he advocated treating natives with respect. Unfortunately, that mission was a disaster; the natives burned down his community and killed nearly everyone. Feeling deeply guilty, Las Casas became a friar in 1523.

- For a decade, he lobbied Spain to put an end to slavery and argued that the natives deserved respect and equal rights. In the mid-1530s, he journeyed to Guatemala, where he advocated "voluntary conversion." In 1542, Las Casas won his case against slavery—albeit briefly. The Holy Roman Emperor Charles V proclaimed a law for New Spain that abolished slavery, tribute, and the encomienda system. Las Casas was made bishop of Chiapas in 1545.

- However, the new law was repealed in the same year—the work of powerful landowners and nobles. Las Casas had to flee in 1546 and lived the rest of his life in Spain, where he continued to champion the dignity of the natives.

Francisco Cordoba

- Yucatan was the place of first contact as early as 1502, with the arrival of Columbus. Aguilar and Guerrero were there in 1511. Both of these were unintentional moments of contact, however. The third contact was also unintentional—the arrival of Francisco Cordoba in 1517.

- Cordoba sailed from Cuba with three ships and 100 men, looking for slaves to capture. He reached the northeast tip of the Yucatan, probably somewhere around modern-day Cancun. The Maya there gave him gifts and invited him ashore, where they ambushed him with arrows. The Spanish ransacked the area and ran.

- In need of fresh water, Cordoba sailed around the peninsula. But he and his men were surrounded at night by thousands of warriors. In the morning, there was a massacre, and more than half the Spanish were killed. After sailing into a storm, Cordoba and his men ended up in Florida. Finally, they returned to Cuba, where Governor Velasquez received a report of a mainland and possible stores of gold.

- Velasquez sent his nephew Juan Grijalva to Yucatan in 1518, where he established Cozumel as a base. But if the mission was to find gold, all fingers pointed to Vera Cruz. Thus, the next mission was led there. And the Maya were spared, at least for the time being.

Francisco de Montejo

- It was not until 1527 that Governor Velasquez would again fix his gaze on the Yucatan. In May of that year, he sent Francisco de Montejo to conquer Yucatan in the name of Spain. Montejo landed in Cozumel first and went ashore. There, he made a small settlement that he called Salamanca.

- The Spaniards tried to push inland, but they met with Maya resistance. The Spanish forces became seriously dwindled and had to recover for two months. They tried to push north again but were fought off by yet more Maya. Finally, they returned to Cozumel in 1528. Only 80 of Montejo's original 400 men survived.

- Stubborn and undaunted, Montejo took a supply vessel south. He took 40 men, leaving 40 more with Alonso Davila. They made it as far as the large Maya capital of Chetumal. The Maya had told Montejo that Gonzalo Guerrero lived in Chetumal. Guerrero and the Maya quickly fortified Chetumal.

- Montejo moved on to Tabasco, where he was appointed governor in 1529. Using Tabasco as a base, he approached Yucatan again, this time on the west coast. He established a garrison at Campeche, but it was continually attacked. His son Montejo the Younger made more progress inland but then lost everything he gained.

An Enormous Slave Colony

- The rebellion against the Spanish grew in Campeche. By 1534, Montejo's mission seemed pointless. Many of Montejo's men abandoned the garrison to join the conquistadors in Peru. Montejo was forced to retreat to Vera Cruz; Campeche reverted back to the Maya.

- By 1540, Montejo was in his 60s, and he assigned his powers to his son Montejo the Younger. His son returned to Campeche with another 400 men and finally took it in 1541. The Maya were becoming increasingly sick with infectious diseases brought by the Europeans, and they were demoralized. Finally, in 1542, Montejo the Younger conquered the city of Tiho and built Merida over its ashes. This was the new capital of Yucatan.

- With Merida as a power base, Montejo sent a new wave of conquistadors east, led by Gaspar Pacheco. In 1545, Pacheco organized a vicious attack on Chetumal—the Spanish took no prisoners. The Yucatan Maya had resisted for decades, but now they were tired, sick, and few in number. Pacheco enslaved them in encomiendas. By the 1550s, Yucatan was an enormous slave colony.

Diego de Landa

- Although the Dominicans and Bartolome de Las Casas were arguing for voluntary conversion in the Maya highlands, the Franciscans controlled Yucatan and took a different tack. The answer to the violent Maya resistance there was conversion by force.

- The greatest zealot among the Franciscans was Diego de Landa. Landa was born a nobleman in Spain. At the age of 25, in the year 1549, he landed in Yucatan. Adamantly opposed to human sacrifice, he would preach to the Maya and disrupt their rituals. He learned their language and studied their culture carefully.

- Convinced of a Maya underground resistance, Landa became increasingly violent and tortured and killed people for information. At Mani, he burned books, ritual objects, and even people. This was the final straw for Bishop Francisco de Toral of Yucatan, who had condoned Landa's methods. Now, even the conquistadors were calling him brutal and cruel. Landa was arrested and sent to Spain, where he was jailed for five years while awaiting trial.

- While in jail, Landa wrote a groundbreaking book, *Relacion de las cosas de Yucatan*—the single most significant Maya ethnography ever written. It recorded all aspects of Yucatec Maya life, from food to religion to calendar rituals. Most important, it was a comprehensive description of Maya hieroglyphic writing, which aided in its later decipherment.

- Landa used the book in his defense, arguing in favor of the forced conversion method. He won his case and he was sent back to Mexico. In 1573, he was appointed the new bishop of Yucatan.

Suggested Reading

Bricker, *The Indian Christ, the Indian King*.

Landa, *Yucatan before and after the Conquest*.

Maxwell and Hill, *Kaqchikel Chronicles*.

Roys, *The Indian Background of Colonial Yucatan*.

Questions to Consider

1. What was it about the Maya of Yucatan that allowed them to resist the conquistadors so much more effectively than others in Mesoamerica?

2. What would have happened to overall world history if Pedro Alvarado had been able to launch his expedition to China?

3. Did Landa's goals justify the means?

Conquest of the Maya and Landa's Legacy
Lecture 43—Transcript

Once the Aztec were defeated, Cortes and his conquistadors turned their eyes to the rest of Mesoamerica. While their fight with the Aztecs was relatively quick and confined to the valley of Mexico, the Maya area spread across what today is five different countries, and took decades of hard-fought military campaigns.

Tenochtitlan fell in August of 1521. Cortes took charge of their tribute network. And messengers were sent out to all different areas. They had requests for allegiance to the crown of Spain. Few opposed the Spanish after the Aztec were defeated. Emissaries headed all the way down to the Soconusco in 1523. That was the farthest-out tributary state, and it was Maya territory.

At first, Cortes sent Mexican scouts. And the Maya actually came out and met them in what's now Chiapas. There were representatives from the K'iche and the Kaqchikel people. Those were the two largest language groups in the Guatemalan highlands. Both of them swore obedience to the Spanish crown. But the Aztec scouts returned to Cortes and said, nope, we don't believe those people. You're probably going to have to go down there and beat them into submission.

So Cortes decided to send Pedro de Alvarado. He was the infamous character who triggered that massacre at the Aztec feast. He was the red-headed Tonatiuh, Son of the Sun, as the Aztecs called him. He had spent two years as the ruler of Texcoco. And he had collected many slaves, and he had put them all to work in gold mines. But now, he was ready to further expand his holdings. And he was noble-born, so he was very favored back in Spain.

His 300 soldiers and 180 horsemen were accompanied by thousands of Tlaxcalans and Cholulans. They followed the trade routes down towards the Soconusco, following the Pacific coast from Oaxaca, and they took this all the way down into Guatemala. At the Salama River Basin, he turned inland. And there, he was met by the K'iche army.

The Maya of the Guatemalan highlands were vulnerable. Their groups were divided along language lines. Each group had their own territory, and each group had their own fortified capital. There were the K'iche, the Kaqchikel, the Mam, the Tz'utujil, et cetera. There were many different groups. And Alvarado used the conflicts between them to his advantage.

Alvarado's first battle was decisive. On February 8, he was at Zapotitlan, and he beat the K'iche there. At the time, that place had another name; it was Xetulul. Many Guatemalan towns have now been given different names. As Alvarado and the Aztecs went down there, they gave them more Nahuatl names, so Nahuatl names came into Guatemala with that group. Any town that you see that ends in *-titlan* or *-tenango* is actually something that was renamed an Aztec name, and it had a former Maya name.

Alvarado followed the K'iche into the highlands. They planned to ambush him near Xelaju. Xelaju is now called Quetzaltenango; it's another one of those Nahuatl names. But their buses, even today, still say Xelaju. So, the K'iche were there, but they were shocked by these horses. They had never seen such horses, and they were a major factor in Alvarado's success. The K'iche ruler Tecun Uman died there at Xelaju. Alvarado himself probably killed him. Tecun Uman apparently struck Alvarado's horse. He was confused; he thought they were one being. So as he struck the horse in the head, Alvarado ran him through with his sword, right into his chest. And he had no idea how important that person was. For the K'iche, losing their leader like that, they were demoralized.

Maya chronicles tell us about the conquest and give us accounts of Tecun Uman and his generals. From the Maya point of view, these were magical, powerful warriors with supernatural powers. As they did their preparations for battle, they talk about them transforming into their animal spirits. Tecun Uman's *nahual*, or animal spirit, was the Quetzal bird. So nowadays, there's a legend that people still talk about in the highlands that says, that moment that Alvarado stabbed him in the chest is the moment that all Quetzals in the whole area of the highlands got a little red spot on their white chest. Forevermore, every male Quetzal had that red spot, and it happened the moment that Tecun Uman was killed by Alvarado.

Today, Tecun Uman is an official hero of Guatemala. There are many different statues in his honor. There's one right outside of Xelaju that makes him look a little like Arnold Schwarzenegger; very muscly. And Alvarado wrote to Cortes about that moment of his death. He, again, the letter made it seem like he did not know who that was. The letter simply said, today I took someone out who looked like a leader. It was the same day that Tecun Uman went down. So from there, he marched to Q'umarkaj, which is the K'iche capital, and he burned it to the ground. Today, we can still visit it, but we call it the ruins of Utatlan.

When the other Maya language groups saw the dominant force in the area, the K'iche, go down in less than two months, they were quite worried. The Kaqchikel made an ill-fated decision. In April of 1524, they invited Alvarado to their capital at Iximche and offered to ally with him against the other Maya groups. Alvarado accepted their help, and the Kaqchikel troops led him to the other Maya groups. First, they brought him to Lake Atitlan. And there, they took out the Tz'utujil Maya. They fought bravely there, but they lost. Their canoes were scattered around the lake. They hid for a while, but they couldn't beat Alvarado.

Next, the Kaqchikel brought them to the Mam and their capital at Zaculeu. Now, that one's also named another name. Today we know it as Huehuetenango, another Nahuatl name pasted over a Maya name. To the south and east were the Pipil people; they were the ones that fought the hardest. They went all the way down into El Salvador, and they teamed with other groups of indigenous, especially the Lenca. The Lenca are the culture right next to the Maya. They're not Maya, but they're their neighbors. And those people Alvarado could not suppress. In one of the battles against these folks, Alvarado actually took a very bad wound to his left leg. And for the rest of his life, he limped because of his encounters with the Lenca people.

Finally, his brother Gonzalo bested them in 1528, and he established the city that's now known as San Salvador in El Salvador. In July of 1524, Iximche was claimed as Alvarado's new regional capital. By August, the Kaqchikel realized what a horrible deal they had made with him. Alvarado was obviously cruel, and he was enslaving everyone he encountered. So the Kaqchikel rebelled against him, and they actually burned their own capital of

Iximche down in 1526. They held out the best they could against Alvarado, hiding in the mountains until the 1530s.

There were many, many pockets of Maya holdouts, but the region was Alvarado's. He was appointed governor by Spain in 1527. And he became, and he continued to be, the governor of Guatemala for the rest of his life. This was a particularly bad time for the Maya. He established *encomiendas* everywhere. These were places that Spaniards were given land-right grants, and not just the land, but any of the people that were living on it. So the Maya in those lands were enslaved and forced to work in the mines.

Alvarado went back to Spain for a little while, and he married there. But he brought his wife back to Latin America, and she died the first year upon arrival. But, marrying her increased his wealth and holdings even further. With that money, he actually imported black slaves to join the Maya working in his mines. The native populations by that time were beginning to dwindle from all of the diseases. There really weren't enough Maya to work his mines. Hence, he imported black slaves. But, all of this wealth and things actually ended up making Alvarado bored and restless. So when Pizarro began the Inca conquest down to the south in 1534, Alvarado tried to get in on it. He actually had no permission from Spain; he just went on his own. He tried to get to the city of Quito first, but on his way up into the mountains, he was met by Pizarro's men and threatened, because he had no authority. So he ended up wheeling and dealing, and he sold his army and the boats to Pizarro's forces. And he still made a tidy profit, but he had to go home.

In 1540, Alvarado hatched his final bold plan. He funded 13 ships and 550 men out of his own money. His plan was to sail from west Mexico to China. He was going to complete the mission that Columbus never could. But, bad luck befell him. In west Mexico, a horse fell on him and crushed him. And so he died there in west Mexico in 1541. I wonder whatever happened to all those ships and men.

Pedro de Alvarado was dead. But his legacy in Guatemala remained. The Maya there were considered less than human, savages who needed to be forcefully converted to Christianity. The Spanish crown supported that idea, and with it, the notion that the Maya could be forced to work as slaves while being "civilized."

One year before his death, Alvarado remarried. He married the sister of his first wife, a woman named Beatriz de la Cueva. She was a redhead just like Alvarado. It's hard to believe, but she was actually even more cruel than him. She became the new governor of Guatemala, and she was the only woman ever in colonial times to become a governor. And she ruled with an iron fist, and the Maya despised her.

But she met a bizarre end. Just weeks into her governorship, there was an earthquake, and a big volcano named Volcano Agua's crater broke above her capital city. The entire crater had a lake inside of it, and that lake flooded out, and it buried her palace and the entire town in a landslide. There are tours today where you can visit that. Maya guides tell us that the earth had had enough of her and just swallowed her up.

Now, we've been talking about conquest for a while. Generally, the Spanish conquistadors were a ruthless lot. They were cruel. But not everyone at the contact period was like that. I can point out at least one shining example, Bartolome de Las Casas. De Las Casas landed on Hispaniola in 1502. At that time, he was a slave owner, and his job was capturing Tainos to be slaves; it was his family business. Then the Dominicans arrived in 1510, and they were appalled by all of this cruelty, and it opened up Bartolome's eyes. He began to lobby against slavery.

He went to Spain to argue against slavery. And he asked for an end to the *encomienda* system. He said, they were going to give people rights and a new way of life. In 1522, he started a colony in Venezuela. And there, he advocated treating natives with respect, and no one was to become a slave. Unfortunately, that was a disaster. The natives burned down his community and killed most everyone. Feeling very guilty about that, he became a friar in 1523.

For a decade, he just studied and lobbied Spain. He was always arguing that the natives deserve respect and equal rights. In the mid-1530s, he went to Guatemala, and he was a big advocate of what they called "voluntary conversion." He had witnessed Alvarado's cruel world, and he used it as evidence to make a case back in Spain. In 1542, de Las Casas won his case, at least briefly. The Holy Roman Emperor Charles V proclaimed the new law for New Spain that abolished slavery, and tribute, and the *encomienda* system. Landowners absolutely hated it and de Las Casas. He was made the bishop of Chiapas in 1545, and he excommunicated a lot of nobles there at that time.

But, the new law was repealed in the same year. There were powerful friends back in Spain of those nobles who made it happen. De Las Casas had to flee in 1546, and he never did return. He lived the rest of his life in Spain. He continued to champion native dignity. And in the Valladolid debate of 1550, he pretty much won the argument of savages versus men of free will in regards to those natives.

Bartolome de Las Casas died in Madrid in 1566. He was considered a pioneer of humanitarian philosophy. He went from slave owner to champion. It's really an inspiring story. And he's a beloved figure in Mexican history. In 1848, San Cristobal in Chiapas was renamed "San Cristobal de Las Casas" in his honor.

While Alvarado's ruthless tactics were destroying the Maya in the highlands, his fellow conquistadors in Yucatan were not having nearly as much luck. In fact, Alvarado had already been proclaimed governor of Guatemala before the first permanent Spanish settlement could even be established in the Yucatan. As we've discussed, Yucatan was the place of first contact, as early as Columbus in 1502. Then, Aguilar and Guerrero were there in 1511. Both of those were unintentional moments of contact; they weren't seeking the mainland.

The third time was also unintentional; it was done by Francisco Cordoba in 1517. He sailed from Cuba with three ships and 100 men. He was just kind of out there in the Caribbean, mainly looking for more slaves to capture, because Cuba was low on slaves at that time. He sells west and hits the northeast tip of the Yucatan, probably somewhere around modern-day Cancun. And the Maya there gave him some gifts, and they invite him onshore. And then when he gets there, they ambush him with arrows. The Spanish ransack their area, and then they run. They had a couple of gold pieces, and they took two Maya prisoners on that first entrada onto the mainland.

He sailed around the peninsula, west and then south. But his water barrels were leaking, and they were running low; they needed freshwater to drink. So they find a big port in Campeche, a Maya port, and they go onshore to get water. Again, they're invited in. But in that community, they see blood-covered altars. And then warriors assemble, and they say, leave immediately or die. So they leave without a fight and with a little water.

They keep going south, but they get low on water again. Next, they saw the port town of Champoton. They go on shore for more water, but surrounding them suddenly at night were thousands of warriors. In the morning, there was a massacre, and more than half of them were killed. They escaped to their boats, but they had to leave at least one of their boats because it was damaged. They all flee with no water and badly wounded.

They sailed into a storm, and they ended up actually in Florida. They get water just before they die, and they finally get back to Cuba. Governor Velazquez gets the report of mainland and possible gold. Cordoba actually died of his wounds soon after, but the news of Yucatan's existence was there in Cuba now. Velazquez sent his nephew in 1518, Juan Grijalva, and Cozumel was established as a base. But his mission was to find gold, and all fingers pointed to Veracruz. So Cortes led the next mission there, and the Maya were spared, for at least the time.

It was not until 1527 that Governor Velazquez would again fix his gaze on Yucatan. In May of that year, he sent Francisco Montejo. With 400 men and 53 horses, Montejo's orders were to conquer Yucatan in the name of Spain. Montejo was with Grijalva in 1518, and he was also with Cortes. But Cortes sent him back to Spain with the message that they had made a colony. Now, he was finally in charge. He landed in Cozumel first and then went ashore. We believe he landed somewhere just north of Xelha in some swampy mangroves. And there, he made a small settlement that he called Salamanca. It wasn't a good choice, though. Because it was swamps, everyone started getting sick.

They tried to push inland, but they were met with Maya resistance. And then there was more sickness and more resistance. Their forces became seriously dwindled. They had to recover for two months at a Maya town called Mochi that welcomed them. They tried to push north again, but they were fought off by yet more Maya. Finally, they returned to Cozumel in 1528, and he only had 80 of his original 400 men that were still alive.

Stubborn and undaunted, he took a supply vessel south. With 40 men with him, he left 40 more with Alonso Davila, and he told him to follow him by land south. They make it as far as Chetumal, which is a big Maya capital, and they capture four Maya and a canoe. Those Maya tell him that Gonzalo Guerrero lives in Chetumal. So he sends a message to Guerrero, a promise of rewards.

The reply comes back that Guerrero is only a humble slave, that he can't do anything. Meanwhile, Guerrero is sending secret letters to each of them, Montejo and Davila. One says Davila is dead, and the other one says Montejo is dead. And they both say, you should retreat, because they're dead. It worked, and they both returned to Cozumel. They meet there and realize that they were tricked. In the meantime, Guerrero and the Maya quickly fortify Chetumal. And that way now seemed pointless to continue.

So, Montejo moved on to Tabasco, and he was actually appointed the governor there in 1529. Using it as a base, he approached Yucatan again, this time on the west coast. He established a garrison at Campeche, but that was continually attacked. His son Montejo the Younger makes more progress inland but then loses everything he gained. Alonso Davila went overland from Campeche back to Chetumal. He had 75 men, 15 horses, and established a base at Laguna Bacalar. The Guaymil Maya helped him fight Chetumal, and they were successful. But then, the Guaymil turned right around and turned on him. His men barely escaped by canoe into the Caribbean, and they end up in Trujillo, Honduras. Again, there's been absolutely no Spanish progress in the Yucatan.

The Montejos weren't doing any better. The rebellion grew in Campeche. And attempts to establish new bases all fail. By 1534, it seems pointless. Montejo's men, a lot of them at least, abandoned to go join the conquistadors in Peru. And he's forced to retreat to Veracruz. Campeche reverts back to the Maya.

By 1540, Montejo is in his 60s, and he assigns his powers to his son, Montejo the Younger. He returns to Campeche with another 400 men and finally takes it for good in 1541. The Maya at this point are becoming increasingly sick; all of those diseases are setting in, and they're becoming demoralized. So finally, in 1542, Montejo the Younger takes the giant city of Tijo and builds Merida over its ashes. Finally, they have the new capital of Yucatan.

With Merida as a power base, Montejo sends a new wave of conquistadors east. They're led by the brutal Gaspar Pacheco. In 1545, there's a vicious attack on Chetumal. They took no prisoners. They garroted all the men. They cut women's breasts off, and they killed innocent children. They were drowned, with gourds tied to their feet. Pacheco establishes the fort at Bacalar. The Yucatan Maya had resisted for decades. But now, they were tired, they were sick, and they were few in number. Pacheco enslaves them in *encomiendas* again. By the 1550s, Yucatan was really just one big slave colony.

While the Dominicans and Bartolome de Las Casas were arguing for voluntary conversion in the Maya highlands, the Franciscans controlled Yucatan and took a very different tact. The violent Maya resistance there resulted in the belief that conversion must be by force. The greatest zealot among the Franciscans was a young man named Diego de Landa. De Landa was born a nobleman in Spain. At the age of 25, he landed in Yucatan in the year 1549. He was stationed first in Izamal, a place that still had large Maya temples.

Quickly, he gained a reputation as fearless. For 10 years, he just walked the peninsula alone. He would preach, and he would bust into Maya communities and disrupt sacrificial rituals. He learned their language and their culture thoroughly. But his was a tough love; he wanted to know what they were doing, so he could stop it. He was convinced of a large Maya underground resistance. He said there were still thousands of people practicing the old religion, and I have no doubt he was right. But he became increasingly violent about it. He tortured and killed people for information. Ultimately, this led to his most infamous sack, an auto-da-fe at Mani in 1562.

At Mani, Landa burned books, ritual objects, and even people. It was in the yard in front of their church. I've stood in that same spot many times. The numbers vary, but for sure, dozens of books and thousands of cult images were burned there. There were tortured and killed Maya nobles at that same spot, too. As many as 127 people died there. I always wonder what were all the things we lost in that one spot when I stand there.

This was the final straw for the bishop. Bishop Francisco de Toral of Yucatan had been ignoring Landa's methods. But now, even conquistadors were calling him brutal and cruel. So he was arrested and sent to Spain in chains. And he was jailed for five years while he awaited trial. While in jail, he wrote an amazing book, *Relacion de las cosas en Yucatan*. It was the single, most important Maya ethnography that was ever written. It had all aspects of Yucatec Maya life, from food to rituals, it was very insightful. And it was a firsthand account of all of their calendar rituals. Most importantly, it told us all about Maya hieroglyphic writing, and those were the keys to its later decipherment.

Landa used the book in his defense, and he justified his tough acts in order to learn. He argued the forced conversion method. He won his case, and he was sent back to Mexico. In 1573, he was appointed the new bishop of Yucatan. He established the Yellow Monastery at Izamal. And from there, he continued his harsh conversion tactics. He built churches in every little village. He gained supreme power over Yucatan. Yucatan Governor Gijon opposed him, and he got excommunicated and replaced in 1577. Landa had a lot of power then. But Landa died in 1579. Behind him, he left a terrible legacy—religious justification for persecution, total control in order to save their souls. This translated to a justification for slavery. Yucatan would continue that way for the next 100 years.

But the Maya weren't done. Landa was right about that underground movement, and it continued, hidden away in the jungle. Eventually, it would reemerge in a series of rebellions called the Caste Wars. We'll talk about that. But first, in my next lecture, let's talk about the last independent Maya kingdom, the Itza.

Fall of the Last Maya Kingdom—The Itza
Lecture 44

Three centuries ago, the capital city of Nojpeten was the site of the demise of the last independent Maya kingdom: the Itza. At that time, at least 40,000 Itza lived around Lake Peten Itza, part of a loose confederation of independent cities and groups—the largest of which were the Itza, Yalain, and Kowoj—ruled by an Itza lord named Kan Ek. These indigenous groups were not unified, however, and in the end, this was their undoing. In this lecture, we'll describe the events that led to the fall of the last Maya kingdom.

First Contact with the Itza

- Pedro de Alvarado had taken Guatemala, and Francisco de Montejo had conquered Yucatan, but Peten was located in a gap between those two Spanish-controlled areas, and the Itza fiercely defended it. They created a no-man's-land that lasted for more than 150 years.

- Hernan Cortes made the first contact with the Itza. In 1525, Cortes passed through the area en route to punish an errant captain, Cristobal de Olid. This was also an opportunity to explore unknown parts of Mesoamerica.

© Georgios Kollidas/iStock/Thinkstock

To cross the lowland jungles of the Peten, Cortes had his men assemble a series of wooden platforms; these were placed ahead of the men and horses, enabling them to walk across swampy areas.

- Cortes embarked from the state of Tabasco, along with an entourage of about 3,000 Aztec warriors. Tabasco traders led him straight to Lake Peten Itza, and there, Cortes was invited by King Kan Ek to visit him on the island of Nojpeten.

- In a peaceful meeting. Cortes talked about God, and Kan Ek allowed him to erect a cross on the island. Kan Ek said that Captain Olid was in Honduras. Cortes moved on and eventually made it to Honduras, but by that time, Olid had already been killed in a rebellion. Cortes returned to Mexico by boat, and no one would contact the Itza for another 92 years.

The 12th *Bak'tun*

- In 1618, a group of 150 Itza emissaries emerged from the jungles south of the Spanish fort of Bacalar with a message from King Kan Ek to the governor of Yucatan. Franciscan friars were excited to accompany the emissaries to Merida, where they announced that they were ready to peacefully surrender to Spain. This was odd because at that time, the Itza were actually growing in power; refugees from other areas were joining them on a regular basis. Never once had they been successfully attacked by the Spanish.

- The Itza claimed that a great cycle was ending and that they were ready for the changes it would bring. The year was the beginning of the 12th *bak'tun* of the Long Count calendar. There was historical precedent for these dramatic voluntary changes. At the 11th *bak'tun*, in 1224, the Itza had voluntarily abandoned Chichen Itza. At the 10th *bak'tun* in 830, the Itza left Tikal.

- Franciscans returned with the Itza to Nojpeten. Juan de Orbita and Bartolome de Fuensalida celebrated mass for Kan Ek and preached the word of God. Orbita took a tour of the island's temples and discovered the statue of a horse. This was actually Cortes's horse, and the Itza had grown to love it. When it died, they deified it. This is an excellent example of the impact of the contact between the Europeans and Mesoamerica: The horse of Cortes became a new Itza deity.

- But Orbita was angered by this statue of the horse and destroyed it, infuriating the Itza priests. They demanded that he and his group be expelled. Orbita went back once more in 1619, and at that time, Kan Ek accepted a cross for his own house. The local leaders opposed Orbita, however, and demanded once again that the priests be expelled. Kan Ek did so. This was a significant moment because it demonstrated that Kan Ek did not have full authority.

Itza Massacre of the Spanish

- The Itza had presented themselves to the governor of Yucatan, and the governor wanted the glory of being the one who brought them under Spanish rule. If they would not be convinced through religion, it would be by the sword.

- Captain Francisco de Mirones was assigned to lead Yucatan's army against the Itza. He planned an armed conquest of the Itza with the permission of the Council of the Indies. The argument was that the Itza had already surrendered in 1618; thus, the military operation was to quell a rebellion, not make a conquest.

- Southwest of Bacalar were lands that were still not under Spanish control—lands where the Maya went for refuge. Jop'elch'en, a reduction town headed by the Franciscan Diego Delgado, was as far as the Spanish had gone into that area. Reductions were forced relocations of Maya people.

- Friar Delgado helped Captain Mirones establish a fort just south of Jop'elch'en in 1622. That was the launching point for the military expedition. While waiting for reinforcements, Friar Delgado went ahead to Nojpeten, where he was greeted by Kan Ek.

- It's not clear what happened thereafter, but something went exceedingly wrong. Every single Spaniard was killed. They were sacrificed, and Delgado's heart was removed. All their heads were mounted on stakes along the island's shore. Mirones sent scouts looking for them, and they, too, were sacrificed. One of the Maya guides escaped and returned to tell Mirones what had happened. Mirones sent word to Merida for more reinforcements.

- Reinforcements arrived—but too late. By the time they got there, the fort was burned and everyone had been massacred. Mirones's head was also on a stake, and his heart had been cut out. The Spaniards would not return to Itza territory for another 70 years.

An Itza Buffer Zone

- In the south, in Guatemala, the Spanish tried to enter the Peten but without much success. The Dominicans there sought voluntary conversion of the Mopan and the Ch'ol Maya.

- The buffer zone between Guatemala and the Itza lands was a destination for Maya refugees. In 1631, the reduction town of Manche was established by military force in that same area. Mopan peasants were forcibly moved into that reduction.

- Then, there was a sudden attack at night, in which thousands of Itza Maya descended on the Spanish. The Itza's strategy was to keep these buffer zones unoccupied by the Spanish. It worked—at least until the 1690s.

Camino Real

- The year 1692 was a significant turning point in the destiny of the kingdom of the Itza. The Council of the Indies gave permission to Guatemala and Yucatan to construct a road connecting those two regions. As a side benefit, the Spanish could finally address the threat of Maya rebels in the buffer zone in between.

- Yucatan's governor at the time was an ambitious and wealthy nobleman named Martin de Ursua y Arizmendi. Building this new road was a stepping stone in his career, as was conquering the Itza.

- The Camino Real was originally to run west of Itza territory, from Campeche all along the Usumacinta, but before it was begun, there had to be diplomatic contact with Kan Ek. However, an Itza-area civil war was brewing at the time. The Yalain and the Kowoj were fighting Kan Ek. When the road began in 1695, the work crews were repeatedly attacked and were forced to retreat back to Campeche.

- On the Guatemala side, President Barrios had a plan to secretly defeat the Itza and claim their territory before Yucatan could; thus, he launched an assault in 1695. That was hindered by the Mopan and the Ch'ol people, who were divided. But Ursua learned of Guatemala's plans and changed the direction of the road, pointing it straight at Lake Peten Itza.

A Divided Itza Nation
- In January 1696, Yucatan sent more priests to Nojpeten in a delegation headed by Friar Andreas de Avendaño. They presented gifts to Kan Ek as a new royal subject of Spain. Kan Ek acted his part and agreed to be baptized. Then, in an act that upset all his people, he allowed the priests to baptize 300 children.

- The leaders of the Kowoj arrived to Nojpeten and demanded that Kan Ek go to war against the Spanish. Because Kan Ek was still sympathetic to the Spanish, he let Avendaño flee at night—but Kan Ek's regional authority was finished. The Itza region at this point was now bitterly divided, which led to the demise of the Maya kingdom of the Itza.

- Avendaño was lost in the forest for a month. A company of soldiers sent to rescue him was slaughtered by the Itza. Avendaño managed to return, with reports of a divided Itza nation.

- Governor Ursua decided that if Kan Ek would not surrender, he would have to conquer the Itza. By December 1696, the Camino Real had reached the western edge of Lake Peten Itza, and preparations for an assault on Nojpeten began.

Demise of the Last Maya Kingdom

- Governor Ursua led the conquest himself. Although Kan Ek continued to offer peace, there were frequent night attacks, and fleets of canoes blockaded the lake. Another campaign was launched that same year from the Guatemala side. Juan Diaz de Valesco's troops made it to the lake, but Diaz was lured in and sacrificed, and his head was found later.

- Ursua's final plan was to build a galleon on the shore of Lake Peten Itza, which was launched at dawn on March 13, 1697. There was a blockade of Itza canoes, but the galleon rode through it. The Spanish maneuvered around Nojpeten, firing their cannons at the temples. The entire island was subdued in less than an hour. The soldiers stormed the temples and destroyed the idols. Ursua climbed to the island's peak and planted his flag.

- Kan Ek escaped by canoe, but he was eventually captured. The Yalain and the Kowoj continued to resist, but at that point, it was futile. Yalain's capital was burned in 1698; the Peten was ceded to Guatemala.

- For the Spanish, the Itza were a loose end, a bit of unfinished business. For the Maya, they were a last great hope. The Maya kingdom of the Itza that fell in 1697 was the very last in all of the Americas. The Maya of the Yucatan had lost the territories where they could escape the oppression of the encomiendas. Now, they had nowhere to run.

Suggested Reading

Bricker, *The Indian Christ, the Indian King.*

Jones, *The Conquest of the Last Maya Kingdom.*

1. The horse Tzimin Chak had an incredible effect on the Itza. What other incidents of momentary cultural contact had such an impact?

2. Would the Itza have held out indefinitely if had they not become embroiled in a civil war? Was their independent city-state model of governance their undoing?

3. Why did Yucatan give up the Peten after conquering it?

Fall of the Last Maya Kingdom—The Itza
Lecture 44—Transcript

Today the island of Flores is a colorful tourist destination in the middle of Lake Peten Itza, a place that travelers to Tikal spend the night. But three centuries ago, it was a capital city named Nojpeten, and the location of the last stand of the final independent Maya kingdom, the Itza.

Back then, the Itza lived all around the lake. There were at least 40,000 of them living there at their fall in the year 1697. It was a loose confederation of independent cities; the Itza, the Yalain, and the Kowoj where the largest of them. They were all ruled by an Itza lord named Kan Ek, and he lived on the island called Nojpeten. They weren't totally unified, and in the end, that was really their undoing.

They were the same people who had migrated to Chichen Itza, and then, hundreds of years later, they returned to the Peten in the 1200s. Alvarado had taken Guatemala, and Montejo had taken Yucatan, but Peten was this gap in between those two Spanish-controlled areas, and the Itza defended it viciously. They created a no-man's-land that lasted for over 150 years. The moment of first contact with the Itzas was actually with Hernan Cortes. In 1525, he passed through there en route to punish an errant captain. That captain was actually Cristobal de Olid; he was way down in Honduras, and he had gone rogue. That was the same captain, if you remember, that Cortes had sent to the Tarascans, and who had done that terrible deed of dragging their king behind a horse and killing him.

So, Cortes, at this point, had to put Olid down, and he decided to go overland. This was an opportunity to also explore unknown parts of Mesoamerica. So he launched from the state of Tabasco, along with an entourage of about 3,000 Aztec warriors. At Tabasco, he had actually executed Cuauhtemoc; he had Cuauhtemoc with him at the time, the King of the Aztecs, but through a series of events that made him untrustworthy, he ended up executing him there in Tabasco. Tabasco merchants led him east.

It was an amazing effort by Cortes. He had to cross the jungle, and what he did is he built wooden platforms, and he'd build them in front of his army and his horses, and then he had a crew disassembling them behind him and going up in front of the army again to lay down the platforms so they could walk across these swampy areas; that was the only way he could figure out to cross the lowland jungles of the Peten at the time with his horses. The traders led him straight to Lake Peten Itza, and there, Cortes was invited by King Kan Ek to visit him on the island of Nojpeten. His advisors said no, don't do that, but this was Cortes, he's supremely confident. Was he going to be scared now? So we went.

And it was a peaceful meeting. Cortes talked about God, and he was allowed to erect a cross there on the island. Kan Ek said that he had heard of the Spanish and that he had heard of this captain, and he pointed Cortes smartly towards Honduras, said oh, he's not around here, he's in Honduras, keep going that way. At the end of their meeting, Cortes gave the king the gift of a lame horse. And this is an interesting side note, that this king, Kan Ek, was the same name as the king that they found hundreds of years later. That's really not a normal pattern that every king in every generation would be called Kan Ek; it's not a normal pattern, and I'm not sure why that happened, but that's a little side note.

Cortes moved on, and it was a tough journey. There was illness and bad weather, and they moved very slowly through the jungle. Eventually, he made it to Honduras, but by that time, Olid had already been killed. His men actually got sick of him and killed him during a rebellion. So, Cortes returned to Mexico by boat, and no one would contact the Itza for another 92 years.

In the year 1618, a group of 150 Itza emissaries emerged from the jungles just south of the Spanish Fort of Bacalar. They said they had a message from there king, Kan Ek, for the governor of Yucatan. Franciscan friars were excited to accompany them to Merida, where they announced that they were ready to peacefully surrender to Spain. Why would they do that? They were actually growing in power down there in the jungle. Refugees from the other areas were joining them on a regular basis. Never once had they been successfully attacked by the Spanish.

But in the year 1618 they came out. Specifically, they claimed that a great cycle was ending and that they were ready for the changes it would bring. They said it was the year 3 Ahau in the *k'atun* cycle, but I've noticed a little bit more. It was also the same year as the opening of the 12th *bak'tun* of the Long Count calendar. It was that year exactly that the Itza predicted this change, and there was a historical precedent for this. On *bak'tun* 11, 1224 A.D., the Itza had voluntarily abandoned Chichen Itza. On *bak'tun* 10, 830 A.D., the Itza had left Tikal. It's a pattern of voluntary major change, and it fits into a theory I've mentioned a few times during this lecture series, that I believe that the Long Count was designed to let the Maya know when it was an appropriate time to change, namely, the turn of these *bak'tuns*.

But back to the Itza and the year 1618. Franciscans returned with them to Nojpeten. Juan de Orbita and Bartolome de Fuensalida held mass there on Nojpeten for Kan Ek, and they preached the word of God. Kan Ek politely watched that, but then he told them, no, it's really not time for us to convert to Christianity yet. Orbita took a tour of the island's temples, and in one of those temples, he found the statue of a horse. Now, I love this story. This was actually Cortes's horse. Cortes left it for them, and they grew to love it. They fed it flowers, and when it died, they deified it. They called it Tzimin Chac, and they made a statue in a temple in its honor. I think it's a great example of contact's impact. This was just one single meeting, a day, that resulted in the creation of a new Itza deity.

Locals around the lake still talk about Tzimin Chac. There's a legend that says the Spanish tried to take that statue off the island in a Spanish galleon, but that the statue became supernaturally heavy, and it sunk into the lake. Then they also say in the 1990s that four U.S. helicopters tried to pull it out of the lake, but again, it became supernaturally heavy. Everyone around the lake knows the general vicinity it's in, and Lake Peten does this interesting thing, where over a 40-year cycle, it goes lower and then higher, and the change is some 10 meters. So right now, it's on its way down, and people around the lake right now are saying, as soon as the lake lowers enough, we're going to see the horse; you'll see what we're talking about, that it's truly there. I wonder.

But Orbita was angered by this statue of the horse, so he smashed it with a rock, and that made the Itza priests furious. They demanded that he and his group be kicked out, and they were put on canoes that very night, and black-painted warriors accompanied them in other canoes and followed them out, making sure they'd leave. They eventually got back to Bacalar with reports of what happened. Orbita went back once more in 1619, and at that time, Kan Ek accepted a cross at his own house from Orbita. His wife, though, and the other local leaders opposed Orbita. They demanded once again that those priests be expelled, that Kan Ek had to do it, and he did, and this was an important moment because it proved that Kan Ek really didn't have full authority. He had to do what the other folks wanted him to do, as well. So he told those priests to leave and never come back.

But the cat was out of the bag. The Itza had presented themselves to the governor of Yucatan, and he wanted the glory of being the Spaniard who brought them under Spanish rule. If they were not going to be convinced through religion, it was going to have to be by the sword.

Captain Francisco de Mirones was assigned to lead Yucatan's army against the Itza. So he planned an armed conquest of the Itza, and he had the permission from the Council of the Indies. They had argued that the Itza had already surrendered in 1618, so, they got to couch it as a rebellion, not a conquest. Because at the time, the Council of the Indies said, look, we're really not going to be conquering anyone else; we're only going to control the people within our lands. So this was couched as a rebellion, and they just had to control an area of growing escaped wrongdoers, in their words.

Southwest of Bacalar were lands that were still not under Spanish control. It was an area that refugee Maya escaped to often. Hopelchen was as far as the Spanish had gotten into that area; that was one of these reduction towns on the frontier. Franciscan Diego Delgado was in charge there. Reductions were basically forced relocations of Maya people. Friar Delgado helped Captain Mirones establish a fort just south of Hopelchen. It was in the Ix Pimienta region, in a town called Sakalum. There, they put 20 Spanish soldiers and 80 Maya laborers. They captured runaways, but some of them escaped. Then they built a small fort and settlements in 1622. That was stage one, the launching point, and they sent word for reinforcements.

While waiting for those reinforcements, Friar Delgado went ahead. Mirones sent 13 soldiers and 8 Christianized Maya to lead him back to the lake. At the lake, they were greeted at the lake's shore, and they were invited cordially to Nojpeten. Canoes ferried them all the way to the island, and Kan Ek greeted Delgado's party. It's not really clear what went wrong, but it went very wrong. Every single Spaniard and the Maya were killed. They were sacrificed, and Delgado's heart was removed. All of their heads were mounted on stakes and mounted along the island's shore. Mirones sent scouts looking for them when they didn't return. They, too, were welcomed to Nojpeten, and they, too, were sacrificed. One of the Maya guides escaped, and he came back to tell Mirones what had happened. He gave them the reports of the heads on stakes. So Mirones sent word to Merida for more reinforcements; things were getting bad.

Reinforcements arrived, but too late. By the time they got there, Sacalum's fort was burned and everyone had been massacred, and there was Mirones's head himself on a stake. His body had been opened up, and his heart was gone. Surviving Maya in the area said it was the Itza, and that they were led by a war captain named Ajk'in P'ol. A bounty was put on Ajk'in P'ol's head, and there was a manhunt across lower Yucatan. Eventually he was caught, tortured, and hanged. His head was paraded around on a stake at that point. It was a public show to prevent rebellion of the Maya, but the Itza had clearly made their point; Yucatan wasn't going to return there for another 70 years.

In the south, in Guatemala, they were also trying to enter the Peten without much success. They pushed north into the Peten and Chiapas. The Dominicans there wanted voluntary conversion of the Mopan and the Ch'ol Maya people. There was a buffer zone between Guatemala and the Itza lands, and that was another free zone for Maya refugees; it was kind of a no-man's-land, and there were no Spanish settlements there. In 1631, the reduction town of Manche was established by military force in that same area. Mopan peasants were forcibly moved into that reduction. Then, there was another sudden attack at night; thousands of Itza Maya descended on it. The Spanish survived, but they were badly wounded, and in the morning, they found proof that it was, indeed, an Itza war camp nearby. This was an ambush, just like Sacalum had suffered.

That attack, and others, kept Guatemala from advancing any further. They said the Itza were inspiring Mopan rebellions. That was probably true; they were inspiring rebellion both in the north and the south. The Itza had a strategy. If they could just keep these buffer zones unoccupied, they could protect themselves. This was also an inspiration for all the other Maya that were slaves at the time, that there was a Maya free zone that they could escape to. It worked, at least until the 1690s.

In 1692, there was a big turning point in the destiny of the kingdom of the Itza. The Council of the Indies gave permission to Guatemala and Yucatan to work together on a road connecting those two regions. As a side result, the pesky Maya rebels in between could finally be reduced. Yucatan's governor at the time was an ambitious and wealthy nobleman. His name was Martin de Ursua y Arizmendi. Eventually, he was to become the governor of the Philippines for Spain. Building this new road was a stepping stone in his career, and so was conquering the Itza.

The Camino Real was originally to run west of Itza territory, from Campeche all along the Usumacinta, but before it was begun, there had to be diplomatic contact. Kan Ek's nephew, Aj Chan, went to Merida to discuss this. During that trip, he agrees to be baptized, and again, he offers the Itza surrender to the crown of Spain. But what governor Ursua doesn't know is that Kan Ek couldn't really offer that. An Itza area civil war was brewing at the time; the Yalains and the Kowoj were against Kan Ek, so, when that road began in 1695, the work crews were repeatedly attacked, and they had to retreat back to Campeche.

On the Guatemala side, President Barrios had a plan to secretly defeat the Itza and claim their territory before Yucatan could, so he launched an assault in 1695. That was hindered by the Mopan and the Ch'ol people, who were divided. They almost reached the lake, but then they turned back, because they were repelled by those Mopan and Ch'ol, but they planned to return as soon as they could.

But Ursua learned of Guatemala's plans, and he changed the direction of the road. This time, he pointed it straight at Lake Peten Itza. Captain Garcia de Paredes was in charge of making sure that road got there. They made a new base of operations at Chuntuki, and that was just 60 miles north of the lake. There was a work camp on the books, but really, that was a fort.

In January of 1696, Yucatan sent more priests. Friar Andreas de Avendaño was in charge of them. They followed the projected path of the new road down to the lake. The Chacon Itza welcomed them on the west shores, but it really wasn't a true welcome. These were actually Kowoj allies, and they allowed the priests through to Kan Ek. Eighty canoes came out to meet them. Many gifts followed, and they were given to Kan Ek, as the new royal subject of Spain. Kan Ek acted his part, and he got baptized. He ordered the Maya priests to serve Avendaño, and then he starts wearing a Spanish uniform around Nojpeten, a Spanish military uniform worn by their king. Then, in an act that upset everyone, he allowed the priests to baptize 300 children. The children were really too much for the community to bear, and outrage started.

The leaders of the Kowoj, a man named Aj Kowoj, specifically, arrived to Nojpeten, and he demanded that Kan Ek stop all this nonsense. He said, sacrifice these people, or we'll go to war against you. Kan Ek was still sympathetic to the Spanish, so he let Avendaño flee at night, but that ended his regional authority. The Itza region at this point was now bitterly divided, and that was their demise.

Avendaño was lost in the forest for a month. He's the one who probably stumbled across Tikal and recorded it. Word of his flight reached Garcia at Chuntuki, and he sent a company of soldiers down to the lake. At first they said everything was fine, and they invited them in canoes to come see, but when a few resist and don't want to get onto the canoes, they're all killed. Again, it was another Itza trap. They got back on shore, but there were 2,000 more Itza waiting, and a rain of arrows came out of the jungle. They were treated to the lake's edge, but there were more Itza in canoes; hundreds of canoes were hiding in the reeds, more arrows, and they had heavy losses. They barely retreated to Chuntuki with their lives. The Itza were on their heels the entire way.

So this new defeat gets back to Ursua. Avendaño returns with reports of the divided Itza nation, and this was an embarrassment. Ursua decided that it was clear; if Kan Ek would not or could not surrender, he'd have to conquer them. Governor Ursua invests his own money to ramp up operations, both road construction and amassing a military war machine. By December of 1696 the Camino Real reached the western edge of Lake Peten and preparations for an assault on Nojpeten itself began.

The Itza attacked the road all along the way. At the lake, the Spanish dug in at a place called Chich, that was an Itza town since the 1300s. We've actually done excavations there, and we can see that Chich was, indeed, once fortified. Governor Ursua himself showed up to the lake edge, and he was going to lead the conquest himself. Kan Ek continued to offer peace. His nephew, AjChan, now Don Martin, because he was baptized, visits the group of Spanish. He brings women and jewelry, lots of gifts, but other people around the lake undermined those attempts. There's trickery. As Kan Ek is trying to make good, other warriors are coming in. At one point they dress up like women, and then they get into the camp and attack once they shed their disguises. There were frequent night attacks, and there were fleets of canoes always blockading the lake.

From the Guatemala side there was another campaign launched that same year. It was supposed to be a three-pronged attack, but they never did meet up. Juan Diaz de Valesco's troops make it to the lake, but on the lake shore, they're once again tricked. The Itza on Nojpeten were wearing Franciscan robes and beckoning them over. Diaz was lured in and sacrificed, and his head was found later.

Ursua's plan was ambitious; he wanted to build a galleon on the shore of the lake. This was a massive undertaking. He was going to make one that was the size of an ocean vessel, and cannons were hauled down from Merida. Tools were brought down, as well, but it took months to build. They made it out of chicle wood, a very strong wood, and then they built a stone boat ramp. We've actually found that boat ramp archaeologically, so we know it's true. When finished, that galleon was 47-feet long. It had 12 oars on either side, and it had six mounted cannons. It had the capacity to hold 114 men. After a final fake offer of peace, on March 12, Ursua says, that's enough. The galleon was launched at dawn, March 13, 1697.

There was a blockade of Itza canoes, but they rode right through it. The arrows couldn't penetrate the galleon. They maneuvered around Nojpeten, firing their cannons at the temples. They destroyed bowmen on the rooftops, and then they landed the galleon on the south end. The entire island was subdued in less than an hour; 108 soldiers leaped out, all with muskets, and they shot everyone. They were indiscriminate; women and children were swimming to safety off the island. The soldiers stormed the temples and destroyed the idols. Ursua climbs to the island's peak and plants his flag. Nojpeten fell to the Spanish that morning.

Kan Ek escapes by canoe, but he's eventually captured. The Yalain gave him up, and his sons, as well. The Yalain and the Kowoj continue to resist, but at that point, it was futile. Yalain's capital was burned in 1698. Ursua doesn't care about the Peten; there are no resources of any real worth there. The credit for the conquest was his goal. He gives Kan Ek and his sons to Guatemala, and they live the rest of their lives as prisoners in the city of Antigua. Peten is also eventually Guatemala's. Ursua, having inflated his reputation through these deeds, goes on to be the governor of the Philippines.

For the Spanish, the Itza were a loose end; they were a bit of unfinished business. For the Maya, they were a last hope; a reason to believe that they could resist the Spanish was there in the jungle. When that last Maya kingdom fell in 1697, it was the very last one in all of the Americas. For the Maya of the Yucatan, especially, they lost the territories they could retreat to, and when they could escape the oppression of the *encomiendas*, now they had nowhere to run. Without the Itza to take them in, they were on their own. Their desperation created the subject of my next lecture, the Caste Wars.

The Caste Wars of Yucatan
Lecture 45

A Maya rebellion in the 1800s, known as the Caste Wars, still shapes the identities of the Yucatec Maya today. Although the Maya of southeast Yucatan resisted Spanish rule from the very beginning, by the 1600s, much of that area was under Spanish control. Many Maya were made to work in the haciendas, producing sisal and sugar cane. The Spanish developed a kind of caste system to control the Maya. In this lecture, we'll examine how that caste system led to a rebellion by the Maya, consider the phenomenon of the Talking Cross and the Cruzob movement, and discuss how the Mexican Revolution expanded the rights of indigenous people.

Yucatan's Caste System

- Yucatan's caste system had four main tiers. At the very top were the *peninsulares*, those people born in Spain. On the second level were the *criollos*, the Spanish people who were born in Yucatan. On the third level were the mestizos, or people of mixed blood—part Spanish and part Maya. At the lowest level were the Indios, who had no rights at all.

- In between was a group called the *hidalgos*. Hidalgos were Maya people who were trained to use guns and were in charge of controlling the Indios. They were also instrumental in finding renegade communities in the jungle.

- After the Itza kingdom fell in 1697, there were no places where the Maya could escape slavery. The entire area of the Yucatan was one slave labor pool. The Maya were paid but not equitably, and they were not permitted to leave or to stop working. By the mid-1700s, desperation set into the entire region. Some of the hidalgos had had enough and actually assisted the Maya slaves.

The Yucatan Break from Spain

- While the Mexican War of Independence was being fought, from 1810 to 1821, Yucatan stayed completely out of it. After Mexico won against the Spanish, Mexico put new laws in place outlawing slavery and giving land rights to all the indigenous people in Mexico.

- Yucatan also broke away from Spain in late 1821, but the Maya were not granted the same rights as the indigenous in Mexico. That was the final straw for the Maya.

- After the war, Texas rebelled and, with the backing of the United States, broke away from Mexico. Guatemala also rejected Mexico, deciding to join Central America instead.

- Yucatan decided to join Mexico in 1823—which meant it owed more taxes. The Yucatan elite simply passed the burden of those taxes along to the Maya. They gave some Maya land rights but only to impose taxes on them.

A Maya Army

- In 1839, a Spanish nobleman, Santiago Iman, started a movement in Tizimin to encourage the Spanish to break away from Mexico. Seeking an independent Yucatan, Iman asked the Maya people for their support. In return, he promised them land and exemption from taxes.

- Iman armed the Maya with guns and trained them to be soldiers. With his Maya army, he pushed all the way across Yucatan. First, he took over Campeche, then finally conquered Merida. In 1841, Iman had enough control of the entire peninsula to proclaim independence from Mexico.

- Mexican president Santa Anna had lost Texas and Guatemala. Chiapas was leaning toward Central America. Thus, in 1842, Santa Anna brought troops and subdued Chiapas, bringing it into Mexico. His next target was Yucatan, but he was repelled by Maya forces.

- A divide among the Yucatan elites grew. On one side, Miguel Barbachano in Merida was for rejoining Mexico. On the other side, Santiago Mendez in Campeche was against joining Mexico. He feared that the United States would attack them if they were part of Mexico—and he was right. The United States occupied Mexico City in 1847.

- In the chaos, the Maya retreated back to southeast Yucatan but kept their guns. In 1847, the Maya staged a rebellion that history calls the Caste Wars. Onerous taxes and brutal treatment could no longer be tolerated. The Maya began planning a break away from Yucatan to create their own state.

Maya Rebellion

- Three men led the Maya rebellion in 1847: Manuel Antonio Ay, mayor of Chichimila; Cecilio Chi, mayor of Tepich; and Jacinto Pat, a wealthy landowner in Tihosuco. Chi and Pat obtained weapons and gunpowder from British Honduras—today called Belize. The Maya forces gathered on Pat's land in Tihosuco.

- Santiago Mendez, the Yucatan governor at the time, intercepted letters between Ay and Chi and captured Ay and killed him. Mendez's soldiers burned Tepich to the ground. Chi and Pat responded by attacking Valladolid. The battle was a bloodbath; all non-Maya people in the town were killed.

- By 1848, all but Merida and Campeche were Maya territories. Cecilio Chi wanted to crush the Spanish and take all of Yucatan, but Jacinto Pat wanted to negotiate a peace treaty with Miguel Barbachano, the new governor of Yucatan.

- Miguel Barbachano was cornered by the Maya rebellion just as he took office. Finally, Barbachano decided Yucatan should rejoin Mexico; on August 17, 1848, he signed the agreements to make Yucatan a state of Mexico. Mexico responded by sending him the weapons and soldiers he needed to fight the Maya.

A Maya Retreat and the Talking Cross

- Suddenly, however, the Maya simply retreated to their homes. Some scholars theorize that this was a result of failed leadership, but most believe the reason was even simpler: It was planting season. The Maya were corn farmers.

- Whatever the reason, the Maya retreated, and the Spanish advanced. Chi was assassinated by his own men in December 1848. Pat was assassinated in September 1849. The Maya rebellion movement was then leaderless and fractured. By 1850, the Maya were concentrated in just the southeast portion of the Yucatan.

- Then, in the town of Chan Santa Cruz, legend has it that a cross began to speak to the Maya, inspiring them to keep fighting and advising them where and how to attack the Spanish. The advice of the cross turned out to be sound.

- At first, there were only a few witnesses to this miracle, but then many heard the cross speaking. A new movement of Maya leaders who had been trained by the Spanish army heard the advice of the Talking Cross. To this day, the Maya believe that the cross truly spoke. In fact, the shrine of the Talking Cross is still in existence in modern-day Felipe Carrillo Puerto.

The Cruzob Movement

- People who followed the Talking Cross were called the Cruzob. England actually recognized them as the official state of Chan Santa Cruz. A captured Spaniard at the time saw 200 white soldiers in Chan Santa Cruz. The English had sent troops there to maintain the city's defense.

- The Cruzob movement gained momentum. The problem, however, was that the Maya were not unified. Some groups of Maya wanted total independence; others wanted to negotiate. Some of them even fought against the Cruzob and expelled them from their own territories.

- The Icaiche Maya, living in the area where Belize, Mexico, and Guatemala intersect, attacked the English in Belize. Belize supported the Cruzob to stop the Icaiche. Mexico sent in troops on multiple occasions.

- For a short while, the Maya had what they wanted. In 1884, Mexico signed a treaty with the Cruzob, and boundaries were established for an official state of Chan Santa Cruz. Again, there was infighting among the Maya. A coup d'état a year later dissolved the treaty and, along with it, the state of Chan Santa Cruz.

- The Cruzob were dependent on Belize, or British Honduras, as their only source of gunpowder. And in 1893, the Mexican president, Porfirio Diaz, wooed the English away from the Maya and the Cruzob. Now, the Maya had no more supplies or gunpowder.

- Diaz sent in the Mexican army, led by General Ignacio Bravo, to take out Chan Santa Cruz. Bravo used cannons to smash the churches in the community. Throughout the entirety of the Caste Wars, 200,000 people—mostly Maya—died.

The Mexican Revolution

- Porfirio Diaz proclaimed that the territory of the Yucatan was Mexico's, but he was about to face a much bigger problem: the Mexican Revolution. Diaz had been promoting pro-business, anti-indigenous policies throughout his presidency. By the beginning of the 20th century, native people across Mexico had had enough, and rebellions broke out across the country.

- The Maya of southeast Yucatan were again part of these rebellions. 1915, Diaz proclaimed that he had officially subdued the Maya and they were now part of the state of Yucatan.

- In 1921, the Mexican Revolution was won. Diaz was out, and there was a new land reform program for the indigenous called the *ejido system*. Areas around towns were solely indigenous property that could be bought and sold only within that community. But the Maya of southeast Yucatan continued to defend their borders. They were left alone for decades.

Caste War Museum
- Even in the 1950s, the people who inspired the Caste Wars who called themselves the Cruzob were still in control in the Yucatan. The Mexican Revolution did improve the rights of indigenous people. Slave labor ended; taxation was fair and reasonable. And slowly, the southeast part of the Yucatan began to open up again.

- Tihosuco's church is still partly in ruins owing to the cannon fire from Bravo's men. The inhabitants leave it that way to remember the days of the Caste Wars. Tihosuco's Caste War Museum is an enormous source of community pride.

- Resistance against colonization in Mexico continues to this day. In the next lecture, we'll take a look at other areas of modern Mexico and discuss their fight to maintain cultural autonomy.

Suggested Reading

Bricker, *The Indian Christ, the Indian King.*

Jones, *The Conquest of the Last Maya Kingdom.*

Knab, *A War of Witches.*

Restall, *The Maya World.*

Roys, *The Indian Background of Colonial Yucatan.*

1. What is it about the Maya of southeast Yucatan that inspired them to keep fighting all those years?

2. Do you think the Talking Cross was a hoax to trick the people into fighting or something more?

3. Are we done with Maya rebellions, or do you think another one could take place?

The Caste Wars of Yucatan
Lecture 45—Transcript

In the tiny town of Tihosuco, Quintana Roo stands a museum dedicated to the colonial history of the region. It's called the Caste War Museum, and it tells the tale of a Maya rebellion in the 1800s, how it started, and how its results still shape the identities of Yucatec Maya today.

That museum is really a wonderful place. My students and I are always warmly welcomed there. I usually call ahead, and they'll make us a lunch in their courtyard. A few times they've even brought in a little Maya band and they've played for us during lunch. It's a fun time there. But the museum's content is deadly serious.

The Maya of Southeast Yucatan resisted Spanish rule from the very beginning. Gonzalo Guerrero was there helping them. They repelled Grijalva, and Davila, and Montejo. The Fort at Bacalar couldn't have even been established until 1543. The southeast section of Yucatan was a refuge for Maya fleeing Spanish persecution.

The Spanish reorganized the Maya into towns they called reductions. These were areas to Christianize them and also to put them to work. But the Maya were constantly escaping, and they fought back against these reductions. The Itza kingdom was just to the south. And in between there and the Yucatan was a buffer zone, a zone of free Maya people. But slowly, they were subdued. By the 1600s, much of that area was under Spanish control.

Many Maya were made to work in the haciendas, these big farms. On those farms they produced things like henequen, they called it sisal there, and sugar cane. The Yucatan was huge business, and there was incredible wealth there. These haciendas were owned by rich Spanish nobles, and some of them got so incredibly rich, they were minting their own coins there, just for their hacienda, with audacious pictures of their own heads on their coins. They were dependent on Maya slave labor. And the Spanish developed something that was akin to the caste system to control them.

Yucatan's caste system had four main tiers. At the very top were the *peninsulares*; those were people that were born in Spain. The second run was the *criollos*; they were Spanish people who were born in Yucatan. Then, the third one was mestizos, people of mixed blood; they were part Spanish and park Maya. The lowest level, the lowest of the low, were called the Indios; they were the lowest caste, and they had absolutely no rights. But in between them was a group called the *hidalgos*.

Hidalgos were Maya people who were trained to use guns. They were given the charge of controlling the Indios. They were the ones that made sure those Indio slaves kept working. And if they escaped, they were in charge of hunting them down. They were also instrumental in finding renegade communities out in the jungle. The hidalgos would lead these missions to go find Maya that had escaped. The conditions for Maya in those days were absolutely terrible.

But still, southeast Yucatan was a beacon of hope. It was a place that the Maya could escape slavery. But in 1697, a dark year came upon the Maya. That was the year that the Itzac kingdom fell, and slowly, there were no more places for the Maya to hide. The whole area became a slave-labor pool. They were paid, but not equitably at all. They were free, but not to leave or to stop working. By the mid-1700s, desperation set into the entire region. Some of the hidalgos had enough of it, and they turned around to actually help the Maya. In 1761, a man named Jacinto Canek at Cisteil started a rebellion. He led a big rebellion there against the Spanish. But the Spanish were able to quickly put it down. And Canek was tried, tortured, and then publicly executed. The town of Cisteil was burned, and its fields were salted.

Then, the Mexican War of Independence broke out; it went on from 1810 to 1821. Yucatan stayed completely out of it. They waited to see how Mexico would do against the Spanish. But in the end, Mexico won. And as a result of winning that war, they put new laws in place, namely, they outlawed slavery, and they gave land rights to all of the indigenous in Mexico.

Yucatan, at least in part, followed suit in the regard that they broke away from Spain. Spain was really in no position to control them at the time, so they also proclaimed their independence from Spain in late 1821. And that should have been a good thing for the Maya, but it wasn't. They didn't get the same rights as the indigenous in Mexico, and that became the final straw for them. Mexico had won their war against Spain, but the work of nation building had just begun.

Texas rebelled. And with the backing from the United States, they broke away from Mexico. Guatemala also rejected Mexico, deciding to join Central America instead. Yucatan weighed their options, and they decided to join Mexico in 1823. So they were part of a new country. But that meant they owed new taxes. The Yucatan elite just passed the burden of those taxes along to the Maya. They gave some of them land rights, but it was really only in order to allow them to pass the taxes along to them, as well. The Maya were mostly still forced labor. The Spanish had more taxes too, and some of them didn't like being part of Mexico.

Spaniard nobleman, Santiago Iman, wanted them to break away from Mexico. So in 1839, he started a movement in Tzimin. He wanted a new, independent Yucatan, and he asked the Maya people there for support. In return, he promised them land and exemption from the taxes. Iman armed the Maya with guns and trained them to be soldiers. And with his Maya army, he pushed all the way across Yucatan. First he took over Campeche and then finally he took over Merida. In 1841, he had enough control of the entire peninsula to once again proclaim independence from Mexico.

As an aside, Stephens and Catherwood were actually conducting their expeditions at the same time as Iman's coup. Their journeys, that they wrote in a book called *Incidents of Travel*, occurred between 1839 and 1841. They were sent by Martin Van Buren. They were ambassadors to the new Central America and these countries that were deciding what they were going to do in the wake of independence from Spain. They were traveling at the time through Chiapas and Yucatan, and they ended up in Tulum.

Mexico, essentially a brand new country, was still struggling. President Santa Anna had lost Texas and Guatemala. Chiapas was leaning toward Central America. So in 1842, Santa Anna brought troops and subdued Chiapas, bringing them into Mexico. His next target was Yucatan. But he couldn't do it; he was repelled by those same Maya forces at Campeche and Merida. So

Yucatan was independent again. But the elites just went back to their usual behavior; they started exploiting the Maya again, and they kept levying these huge taxes.

And a divide among the elites began. On one side, there was Miguel Barbachano in Merida, and he was for rejoining Mexico. On the other side, there was Santiago Mendez in Campeche, and he was against joining Mexico. He feared that the U.S. would attack them if they were part of Mexico. And he was actually right. The U.S. occupied Mexico City in the year 1847. In the chaos of the division and the Mexican American War, the Maya retreated back to the southeast part of Yucatan, but they kept their guns that Iman had supplied them. They were angry about Iman's broken promises, and discontentment grew.

In 1847, that same year, they staged a rebellion that history calls The Caste War. The leaders of Maya towns in southeastern Yucatan agreed that the taxes and the treatment could no longer be tolerated. They began planning a break away from Yucatan, forming their own, independent territory by force. When Spanish intercepted their letters, they reacted harshly.

The Maya movement began in that year, 1847, and there were three main leaders at the time. There was Manuel Antonio Ay, who was the cacique, the Maya word for mayor, of a town called Chichimila. There was also Cecilio Chi, he was the cacique of a town called Tepich. And finally, there was Jacinto Pat; he was a rich landowner in the town Tihosuco.

Chi and Pat contacted British Honduras for their support. By the way, British Honduras is now, today, called Belize. Back then it was British territory. They asked the Brits for weapons and gunpowder, and they explained about Iman's broken promises. The Brits agreed to supply the Maya with those arms, and the Maya forces gathered on Pat's land in Tihosuco.

Santiago Mendez was the Yucatan governor at the time. When I look for portraits of him, he's always shown with a monocle, and everybody knows that if you're shown with a monocle, you're obviously evil. This man had it out for the Maya, and when he intercepted those letters between Ay to Chi, he saw that they were discussing plans of a rebellion. So Mendez captures

Ay and kills him. He publicly puts him to death in the town of Valladolid. Mendez's soldiers continued to Tepich; they were looking for Cecilio Chi there, and they burned Tepich to the ground. Chi and Pat respond by attacking Valladolid. A loyal Maya army follows them, and it's a bloodbath. All non-Maya people in the town are killed. They went on to wipe out all of the whites in that upper part of Yucatan.

The Maya pushed Spain backwards. The Spanish were held to places. In 1848, all but Merida and Campeche were Maya territories, and the Spanish were very frightened. Cecilio Chi was young, and he was a fiery man. He wanted to crush the Spanish and take all of Yucatan, just repel them all. But Jacinto Pat was older and more thoughtful. He liked to read history books. He was a very educated man, and, he was a former friend of Barbachano, so he wanted to negotiate a peace treaty instead.

Pat's old friend, Miguel Barbachano, was named the new governor of Yucatan in March of 1848. And by the way, the Barbachano family is still very powerful in the Yucatan. Today, they're big landowners; they own lots of haciendas, and they own lots of hotels, mostly in Merida. They used to own all of Chichen Itza, but just recently, they sold it back to the governments of Yucatan. But back then, Miguel Barbachano was cornered by the Maya rebellion just as he took office.

He reached out for help. He contacted areas like Jamaica and Cuba and the U.S.A, and he even contacted Texas. But none of them would get involved. Jamaica and Cuba were new as well, and really too small to help. The U.S.A. had just finished signing the Treaty of Guadalupe Hidalgo and made peace with Mexico. Of course, that peace came along with them taking all of Texas, New Mexico, Arizona, and part of Utah as part of that exchange. California, as well, came along with the deal of Guadalupe Hidalgo. But the U.S didn't want to get involved; they had just gotten out of there. Texas was its own nation, too, at the time, but they were still recovering from Mexico's attack that had happened just a few years before.

Finally, Barbachano decided they should rejoin Mexico. So on August 17, 1848, Barbachano signed the agreements to make Yucatan a state of Mexico. Mexico responded by sending him the weapons and soldiers he needed. But the Maya were still too much to repel; they owned too much of the peninsula at that time, and even with the Mexican forces, they couldn't do anything about it.

But then suddenly, the Maya just retreated. Many of them returned to their homes. Some say it was because of leadership mistakes, but most scholars believe that it was simply that it was planting season, and the Maya were all corn farmers. So they returned to their crops so that they could plant. Whatever the reason, the Maya retreated and the Spanish advanced.

Blame flew around the Maya about this failure. Chi was assassinated by his own men in December of 1848. Pat was also assassinated in September of 1849. The movement was then leaderless and fractioned. By 1850, they were back to just that southeast portion of the Yucatan. But then, the Talking Cross started, and it started talking to the Maya.

In the town Chan Santa Cruz, modern-day Felipe Carrillo Puerto, now it's about an hour from Tulum, the people say a cross began to speak to the Maya, inspiring them to keep fighting and telling them where and how to attack the Spanish, and its advice was good. At first, there were only a few witnesses to this miracle, but then many came, and they all heard the cross speaking. There was a new movement of leaders who were Maya that had been trained by the Spanish army, by Iman. They knew military strategy, and they transmitted it through the Talking Cross.

Now, a lot of scholars believe that it was really just a ventriloquist trick, that it was these military leaders behind it speaking and people thought it was the cross. But Maya, to this day, believe that it truly spoke. In fact, the shrine of the cross is still there. I've brought students there many a time. It's on a sleepy backstreet of modern-day Felipe Carrillo Puerto. But there's always someone attending it. There's flowers, and the room has many different Maya festival objects within it along with the cross. There, there's actually five cross shrines. There's one in Tihosuco, there's another in a place called San Martin, there's one in Tulum, and I'm not sure where the fourth one is. I've gone looking around for them, and I've found one so far.

Actually, the last time that I visited the shrine in Felipe Carrillo Puerto was May of 2009. It was that trip that I heard there were these other shrines. So, the group I was with and I went looking for more of these shrines. We followed the directions of the old man that was tending the shrine in Felipe Carrillo Puerto to a little village, San Martin, just to the south. And we found the church he was looking for, but it was all closed up. In fact, as we looked around this little town, no one was on the street. As we looked closer, there were people just kind of peeking out of their doors. And then we realized why.

This was May of 2009, and just as we had landed in the Yucatan, we heard that H1N1 had broken out, this crazy swine flu. And everyone in Mexico was scared about it, and they were all hiding in their homes. So the church was closed up and people were peeking out their doors. The only thing in the churchyard were a bunch of pigs. And so, we decided that we would take some pictures with those pigs, and I sent them back to my wife on my phone. And she was upset. She said, don't send this to me by email. People will make me leave my work. Everybody is scared of this swine flu. But that was the moment, and I didn't actually get to see the shrine that time because swine flu had closed all the doors of the church.

People who followed the cross were called the Cruzob. England actually recognized them as the official state of Chan Santa Cruz. A captured Spaniard at the time saw 200 white soldiers there in Chan Santa Cruz. Apparently, the English had actually sent some troops. They were doing petty attacks and city defense for years. But in 1858, there was a massacre at Bacalar. All the Spaniards there were killed, and the fort was taken by the Maya. They held it, actually, until 1902.

The Cruzob movement gained momentum. But there was, again, one big problem; the Maya weren't unified. Some groups of Maya wanted total independence; others wanted to negotiate. Some of them even fought against the Cruzob themselves and kicked them out of their own Maya territories. The Icaiche Maya were some of them; they were in the three-corners area where now Belize, Mexico, and Guatemala connect. They were fiercely controlling their own territory and attacking the English in the Belizean town of Orange Walk. They attacked them twice. So Belize supported the Cruzob to stop the Icaiche.

Yucatan was now Mexico, and Mexico took these Cruzob seriously. They sent troops in multiple times to try to suppress them. The cross told them how to win wars against the Mexicans. They used jungle tricks that the Maya knew. For example, they poisoned all their wells with chechem, a kind of poison ivy from the jungle there, and then they pretended to retreat. And when the Mexicans came in and used their wells and drank from them, all their throats swelled from the inside and they died.

For a short while, they almost had what they wanted. In 1884, Mexico signed a treaty with the Cruzob and boundaries were established for an official state of Chan Santa Cruz. Crescencio Poot was appointed governor of Chan Santa Cruz. But again, there was infighting among the Maya; not all of them agreed. They didn't want to do this at all. Some of them didn't get the land they wanted in the deal, and they were disgruntled. So eventually, a coup d'etat a year later dissolved the treaty, and along with it, the state of Chan Santa Cruz.

The Cruzob were dependent on Belize, or at that time, it was British Honduras. That was their only source of gunpowder. And in 1893, Mexican president, Porfirio Diaz, wooed the English away from the Maya. He offered them great trade deals, but the deal was they had to shun the Cruzob. It worked, and they closed their borders. Now the Maya had no more supplies or gunpowder. That was a huge problem for their movement.

Then, Diaz sent the army in again. This time, it was led by General Ignacio Bravo. Pictures of him show he had this big, crazy mustache he liked to sport during battle. But he was a very tough leader. And he's the one who really takes out Chan Santa Cruz. There were heavy losses for the Maya when he came in. They scattered into all their villages. And Bravo hunted them down one by one. And he was using cannons, smashing their churches in each one of these communities. All said and done, through all of the Caste War times, they say about 200,000 people, mostly Maya, died in those wars.

In 1902, the Maya abandoned Fort Bacalar. Bravo was coming, and they had no gunpowder. When British Honduras turned their back, the Cruzob were boxed in. Diaz proclaimed that the territory was Mexico's, but he was about to have a much bigger problem; the Mexican Revolution was coming for him.

Porfirio Diaz had been promoting pro-business, anti-indigenous policies throughout his presidency. They were making the rich richer and the poor poorer. By the start of the 20th century, native people across Mexico had had enough, and rebellions broke out across the country. The Maya of Southeast Yucatan were, again, part of it. The cross had stopped speaking, but the Maya were still fighting. The Mexican army was already stationed there, so they were a focus of putting down the Maya rebellion.

In 1915, Diaz proclaimed that he had officially subdued the Maya and that they were now part of the state of Yucatan. In 1921, the Mexican Revolution was won. Diaz was out, and there was a new land reform program. The Ejido system began; it was land reform for the indigenous. This meant that areas around towns were only indigenous property, and they could only be bought and sold within that community. But the Maya of Southeast Yucatan could care less. They continued to defend their borders, and they were left alone for decades. Samuel Lothrop arrived to Tulum as an archaeologist in 1921. He came from the Cozumel side. Still, in 1921 there were no roads leading from the west. The local Maya allowed him into the ruins, but not beyond. He wrote about the old ways still hiding somewhere in the woods.

Now, a few months ago, Michael Coe wrote me about my Tulum app. He was praising this app that I had made that has lots of information on Tulum and a geonavigation system for tourists that visit the site. He's a class act like that. He's always taking a moment to encourage the current generation of Maya scholars. But in that letter, he also told me about his first visit to Tulum, that same area of Yucatan. He said it was in the 1950s, and that, again, he had to take a boat from Cozumel, because even at that time there were no roads.

During his visit there he camped out with people who called themselves the Cruzob, and he spent the night in the Castillo at Tulum with them. And within that temple, they had a shrine to the Talking Cross set up right inside the temple. So even in the 1950s, the people who inspired the Caste War, who called themselves the Cruzob, were still there and in control.

Slowly over the next decades, there was more contact from the outside. The revolution actually did improve the rights of indigenous people. Slave labor was actually ended. Taxation was fair and reasonable. And slowly, the southeast part of the Yucatan began to open up again. The Maya became more welcoming. Chetumal on the coast grew very large, and then in 1974, the whole area was called The State of Quintana Roo; it's the youngest of all the states in Mexico. It was named after Andres Quintana Roo, a statesman and an advocate of education.

There are beaches all along the coast, and those became vacation properties. Chetumal became the capital. Cancun was eventually built, and tourism increased even further. Today, Quintana Roo is a vacation destination. It has Cancun, and Playa Del Carmen, and Tulum is growing as well. There's dozens of resorts and millions of tourists. Tihosuco and Tepich are still out there in the jungle with Maya inhabitants.

Tihosuco's church is still half-destroyed from the cannon fire. They could fix it, but they don't. They leave it there to remember those days of the Caste War. Tihosuco's Caste War museum is a great source of community pride. In front, the plaque says, this is a museum not to the dead but to the living. It's a place where the living remember why they have their freedoms and they never forget to defend them. Once I asked the museum's director, Carlos Espinosa Chan, if the people of Tihosuco were worried that the Mexican army would return some day. And he looked at me and he smiled and he said, we're ready for them. And I believe him.

So, as this lecture illustrates, in many ways the resistance against colonization in Mexico continues to this day. In my next lecture, let's take a look at other parts of modern Mexico and discuss where the fight to maintain cultural autonomy continues in other spots.

Echoes of the Past in Mexico
Lecture 46

In the more than 500 years since the first Europeans landed on the coast of Yucatan, disease, conquest, and acculturation have threatened to completely wipe out Mesoamerican history, religion, culture, and practices. Despite tremendous pressures, the Mesoamerican way of life still thrives in the hearts and minds of the people living in Mesoamerica today. In this lecture, we'll study some of the indigenous people in Mexico, with a look at how they are maintaining the ancient traditions even today.

Indigenous Peoples in Mexico

- According to the National Institute of Statistics and Geography (INEGI), in 2010, the population of Mexico was 118 million, but only 16 million, or 14 percent, were indigenous.

- There are several complicated reasons for this seemingly low number. First of all, the indigenous are loath to participate in the census; being identified as an Indio can lead to discrimination. Second, indigenous people have a general distrust of the government.

- Third, the definition of *indigenous* is flawed. Basically, it refers to people who speak a native language or who self-identify as indigenous. The census used to have a category called mestizo for people of mixed blood, but now, the Mexican census has dropped that category. Another 60 percent of Mexicans used to call themselves mestizo. Together with the indigenous, the total is about 74 percent—a more realistic number.

Results of the Mexican Revolution

- Poverty among the indigenous in Mexico has shaped the country's modern history. After Spanish contact, three waves of 12 infectious diseases came over from Europe, which wiped out 90 to 95 percent of the indigenous population in the first 100 years. But slowly, the population grew back, both indigenous and mestizo.

- In 1810, a large population of indigenous people was controlled by a small group of Spanish landowners. That led to the Mexican War of Independence against Spain. Although this war was led by nobles, it was fought by the indigenous. In 1822, Mexico gained its independence. And with that, Mexico ended slavery and granted equal rights for native peoples.

- But the changes did not go far enough. Europeans still owned most of the land, and poverty continued for the indigenous people. In 1910, the Mexican Revolution began, with indigenous leaders. In the south was Emiliano Zapata. In the north was Pancho Villa. Although Villa was not an indigenous, his soldiers were Yaqui from the northern deserts.

- That revolution was about indigenous land rights, and the result was the ejido system. Under the ejido system, indigenous villages own their land collectively, and they cannot sell it outside the bounds of their own community. Much of the country's land was restructured in that way, and the system still functions today.

- Ancient heritage was more respected after the Mexican Revolution. The government started its own branch of archaeology, and efforts to recover and honor the past were made. A national identity as mestizo was born. The Law of Indigenous Linguistics Rights was signed in 2003, which recognized 62 different languages within the country of Mexico.

The Zapotec
- Oaxaca is the homeland of the Zapotec, a people who were already subjugated at Spanish contact. There were Aztec garrisons in the Valley of Oaxaca, and the Zapotec paid tribute to the foreigners. It was not a significant leap for the Zapotec to surrender to the Spanish without a fight.

- Sadly, surrender did not save them. Disease swept over Oaxaca quickly. In the Valley of Oaxaca, a 1521 Aztec census recorded 350,000 people. However, a 1650 census recorded only 300,000.

At that time, this sparse population was spread over a vast area. Black slaves were actually imported from the Caribbean because there were no natives left to enslave.

- But the population replenished over the centuries. Today's census in the Valley of Oaxaca is 777,000 Zapotec. In reality, the number is probably more than 1 million. The Zapotec cover all of central, south, and east Oaxaca now, and most are town-dwelling peasant farmers. Other Zapotec have migrated out of Oaxaca. In fact, there are tens of thousands of people of Zapotec heritage living in the United States.

Keeping the Ball Game Alive
- Zapotec make up the main indigenous culture in the Mexican state of Sinaloa. The original native population of Sinaloa is doing something significant to preserve ancient culture: keeping the Mesoamerican ball game alive.

- Locals play a game called *ulama*—the Aztec word for "ball game." *Ulama* seems to be quite similar to the ancient ball game. It has been played as long as anyone in Sinaloa can remember. What's more, it is played with a conscious recognition that it is performed in honor of the ancestors.

- There are three different versions of the game in Sinaloa: *ulama de cadera*, which is hip ball; *ulama de antebrazo*, or forearm ball; and *ulama de palo*, which is stickball. Hip ball is the most popular, played with a seven-pound solid rubber

Ulama **has been in Sinaloa since before Spanish contact, but now, after centuries, only about 150 people still play the game.**

ball, with the players wearing leather hip pads. Five or more players are on each side of the court.

- Forearm ball is gentler. It is played with one to three people on either side, and players hit a lighter, smaller ball back and forth with their forearms. Because women are not allowed to play hip ball, they often play forearm ball.

- Stickball is played by hitting a very small ball with paddles weighing about 15 pounds each. The images on the wall of the ball court at Chichen Itza also depict ball players holding bats. Chichen Itza was influenced by Tula, and Tula is not very far from Sinaloa.

- The ball games are scored in the same way. A point, called a *raya*, is scored when the ball goes out of the back of the opponent's court. Eight *rayas* will win the game. But if the game is tied at the end of a particular turn, both teams reset to zero—which can make the game last a very long time. The record length for a game in Sinaloa is two days.

The Huichol

- Just south of Sinaloa are the states of Jalisco and Nayarit. Up in the rugged mountains of those states lives a group of indigenous people who many consider to be Mexico's most traditional people: the Huichol. There are about 50,000 Huichol people today, living in the high Sierra Madres. They are very isolated there—or they were until the 1900s.

- Guadalajara's expansion lowered the water table in the entire area; thus, there are now fewer opportunities for hunting, and crops are not as easy to grow. Many of the Huichol have been forced out of their communities down into the plains, where they work on tobacco farms.

- The Huichol say that they migrated from a location near San Luis Potosi, and they make a pilgrimage back there every year. The Spanish reported these pilgrimages as early as the 1500s. But at that time, the Spanish said the Huichol were bellicose and had no gold; for these reasons, they were left alone.

Peyote Hunt
- Huichol religion revolves around the worship of four independent entities: deer, corn, rain, and peyote. Together, they create a symbolic cycle of human life. An annual pilgrimage, an arduous desert journey, is made between October and March that ties the entities together. The Huichol start in the Sierra Madres and travel 500 kilometers to a place called Wirikuta. The journey to and from Wirikuta takes a month.

- Arriving at Wirikuta, the Huichol hunt peyote. They look for what they call a peyote family, a cluster of five peyote buttons. The pilgrims make a tiny altar next to the buttons and give them thanks. Then, they gather up the peyote and eat it that evening.

- Around the fires in the evening, the elders tell the creation story. According to this story, the first men crossed the desert and arrived at a place called the Hill at Dawn, where the sun was born. When they arrived, the deer sacrificed themselves so that men could eat, and peyote is said to grow out of the dead bodies of the deer. When the men ate the peyote, they became gods.

- Research on rock art in the canyons of the Pecos River in Texas suggests that this peyote ritual has been going on for 4,000 years. In the 1990s, archaeologist Carolyn Boyd made some astonishing discoveries in the depictions at the White Shaman Cave.
  - One depiction at the cave shows five men walking. Nearby are deer with dots on their antlers. In other areas are men with spears standing near a hill.

○ Boyd literally connected the dots. She matched those images to the symbols of the Huichol pilgrimage: the walk, the hunt, the Hill at Dawn, and the peyote buttons, which are the small dots.

Curanderismo

- Most indigenous people—at home and in their own minds—are still strongly connected to their ancestors. The Nahua, living in Central Mexico, are an excellent case in point.

- The Nahua are Aztec descendants. Broadly, the group comprises anyone who speaks Nahuatl. The census reports about 2.4 million Nahua in Mexico today. They are dissimilar to such groups as the Huichol or Zapotec in that they do not wear traditional dress, and most live in urban settings.

- Although they may not look the part, the Nahua have strong native traditions. One of the best examples is the native healing practice called *curanderismo*. *Curanderos* heal people through prayers and visions and by using plant medicines. *Curanderos* speak to the plants, which have living spirits.

- The roots of *curanderismo* are clearly in shamanism. The source of a healer's power is the same source as another native practice that is much worse: witchcraft. Although people in modern-day Mexico City will not admit it, a *curandero* is a good witch. The same spirit power can also be used by bad witches, who ask the spirits to hurt or even kill people. The practice focuses on contact with the supernatural.

- Unfortunately, traditional life in Mexico is disappearing at an accelerated rate. Many indigenous practices have come to a permanent end. In some parts of Mesoamerica, ancient practices and cultural traditions are seen as impractical. But as we'll see in the next lecture, some modern Maya communities are in the middle of a cultural revival.

Suggested Reading

Morris Jr. and Foxx, *Living Maya*.

Spores and Balkansky, *The Mixtecs of Oaxaca*.

Stuart, *The Mighty Aztecs*.

Questions to Consider

1. Do you think the Mexican census is fairly counting its modern indigenous population?

2. Is tourism a good or a bad thing for indigenous ways of life?

3. Can today's remaining indigenous traditions survive modern technology?

Echoes of the Past in Mexico
Lecture 46—Transcript

It's been over 500 years since the first Europeans landed on the coast of Yucatan. Disease, conquest, and acculturation threatened to completely wipe out the Mesoamerican way of life. Despite that, it still thrives in the lives, hearts, and minds of the people living there today.

I was once interviewed in Palenque by a reporter. And that reporter asked me, where did the Maya go? And I replied, where did the Romans go? The article ended up calling me laconic for that. That's short to the point of being rude. Well, my point was actually this. The Romans are still here; we just call them Italians today. And the Maya are still here; we just tend to call them Mexicans or Guatemalans. And today, they don't live in just Mesoamerica; they're everywhere in the world. He's that guy at the convenience store, or she's that woman at the day care.

INEGI is the institution in Mexico that controls their census. In 2010, it said there was a population of 118 million people in Mexico. But it said there were only 16 million of those people that were indigenous; that's about 14 percent of the population. And I thought to myself, what? Have they been to Mexico? I think that's a crazy low number.

But it's that way for complicated reasons, and some of those reasons actually make sense. First off, the indigenous are allergic to census. Things are improving, but still, today, being identified as an Indio leads to discrimination. It used to lead to persecution. It immediately identifies someone as a lower status, and that equals less opportunity. Indigenous people have a general distrust of the government and a historical precedent for that. They tend to say, no thanks, I'll pass on discrimination. And they don't self-report that they're indigenous, and it skews the numbers.

I think we also have a flawed definition of the term *indigenous*. Basically, it's people who speak a native language today, or people who self-identify themselves as indigenous. They used to have a category called mestizo for people of mixed blood, but now the Mexican census has dropped that category. So, that is actually another 60 percent of Mexico that used to call themselves mestizo. Together with the indigenous, now we're getting to somewhere like 74 percent; that makes more sense to me.

There's an unfortunate correlation between being indigenous and being impoverished; 45 percent, or 53 million people in Mexico live dirt poor. Many of them have migrated into the cities in modern times, and that's really bad for them; 79 percent of people in all of Mexico are now living in an urban environment. Peasants who were living in a rural area could survive by just farming, but people in urban areas need work to survive, and it's few and far between there.

Poverty among indigenous in Mexico has shaped the country's modern history. At contact, disease wiped them out. There were 12 infectious diseases that came over from Europe, and there were three waves of those diseases that arrived. That wiped out 90 to 95 percent of the indigenous population in the first 100 years. But slowly, the population grew back, and they were both indigenous and mestizo people.

At 1810, a large population of indigenous people was controlled by a small group of Spanish landowners. That led to the Mexican War of Independence. It was led by nobles against Spain, but it was actually fought by the indigenous. In 1822, the country gained its independence. And with that, they ended slavery, and they gave many more equal rights for native peoples. Mexico actually gets its name honoring the Aztecs. The Aztecs were the Mexica, and the Mexican flag looks like the legendary place where they put their capital, the eagle on top of the cactus.

But the changes still weren't enough. Many Europeans still owned the land, and poverty continued for the indigenous people. So in 1910, the Mexican Revolution started. In 1872, Benito Juarez had died, and Porfirio Diaz took over as the president in 1876. He undid all the social reforms of Juarez. He ruled the country like a dictator. Indigenous land rights were revoked, and a lot of them were given to foreign companies in 1883. The response was revolution, and that revolution had indigenous leaders. In the south, there was Emiliano Zapata. In the north, there was Pancho Villa. Villa wasn't an indigenous, but all of his soldiers were Yaqui Indians from the northern deserts. That revolution was about indigenous land rights, and the result was the Ejido system. Under the Ejido system, indigenous villages own their land collectively, and they can't sell it outside the bounds of their own community. Much of the country's land was restructured in that way, and it still functions today.

Ancient heritage was more respected after that revolution. The government started their own branch of archaeology, INAH, and efforts to recover and honor the past were made. Artists, like Rivera and Orozco, honored them in their murals. And there was a national identity as mestizo that was born in that time. The Law of Indigenous Linguistics Rights was signed in 2003, and it recognized 62 different languages within the country of Mexico. Things like that are happening now, and there's more respect every year. But still, most indigenous people in Mexico live in dire poverty. Revolutions took the country in 1820, and 1920, and what year is it again? I wonder if history is going to repeat itself.

We've talked about the histories of various culture groups throughout this course. Now let's talk about some of them in the present tense and about what's become of them today. We'll start in Oaxaca. Oaxaca is the homeland of the Zapotec. And they were already a subjugated people at contact. There were Aztec garrisons in the Oaxaca Valley, and they were already paying tribute to foreigners. So, it wasn't a big leap for the Zapotecs to surrender to the Spanish without a fight.

Sadly, surrender didn't save them. Disease swept over Oaxaca quickly. In the Valley of Oaxaca, we had a very good census at contact. In 1521, Aztec records recorded that there were 350,000 people there. But a 1650 census recorded that there were only 30,000. That's a 92 percent die-off rate in Oaxaca in the first 100 years, and it probably happened a lot quicker than that. It must have been a strange time, so much land and so many abandoned towns. Indigenous all dead, and not many Spaniards either. It was a sparse population over a vast area. Black slaves were actually imported from the Caribbean, because there were no natives left to enslave.

But population regrew over the centuries. Today's census in Oaxaca's Valley says there are 777,000 Zapotec. And remember, the indigenous don't like census. That number is probably more like over 1 million. They cover all of central, south, and east Oaxaca now, and most are town-dwelling peasant farmers. In the Valley of Oaxaca, old ways combined with practical new ideas and crafts. The idea of each village specializing in a craft was very ancient; it went back to the days of Monte Alban. But what they specialize in and how they make it has changed over time.

Teotitlan del Valle is a good example. Those folks have been weavers for centuries. Now, they're famous for rugs, but it used to be clothes. Then a man named Isaac Vasquez and his family started making rugs. Isaac worked for a while in New York as a cabby in the 1980s, and his clients told him, hey, tourists really like rugs. So he went back to Teotitlan del Valle and he started making rugs. Now, there's about 150 different families there that are making rugs.

They use European looms. They're no longer using the backstrap loom. And artist Rufino Tamayo revived the local dyes, so now they're using traditional dyes in combination with these European looms. And they can make any design. They're amazing. They use these looms like a painter uses a canvas. Funny enough, their largest client are the Navajo up in the United States. They're making Navajo-style rugs for the Navajo to sell in their reservations. I like to call those Zapajo rugs.

And of course, the Zapotec are very proud to claim Mexican President Benito Juarez as one of their own. He was an orphan from a Zapotec village, and he was raised and educated by priests in Oaxaca. He was president five times in between 1858 and 1872. And under his leadership, education was expanded for everyone in the nation, also indigenous. He's one of only three indigenous presidents ever in Latin America's history. Alejandro Toledo in Peru and Evo Morales in Bolivia are the only other ones.

So there are still about 1 million Zapotec people today. Most live in Oaxaca State, and they're farmers or craftsmen. Others have migrated out of Oaxaca. In fact, there are tens of thousands of people of Zapotec heritage living in the United States. One of the places that the Zapotec have migrated to the most is the Mexican state of Sinaloa. They actually make up the main indigenous culture there today. But the original population of Sinaloa is also doing something important to preserve ancient culture, keeping the Mesoamerican ball game alive.

Locals play a game called *ulama*; that's the Aztec word for ball game. And it seems to be very much like the ancient ball game. It's not a new tradition; it's been there as long as anyone in Sinaloa can remember. No one can really say how old it is. And it's played with a conscious recognition that they're keeping it in honor of their ancestors.

There in Sinaloa they have three different versions. They have *ulama de cadera*, which is hip ball; they have *ulama de antebrazo*, which is forearm ball; and then they have *ulama de palo*, which is stickball. Hip ball is the most popular, and it's played just like old times. They're wearing leather hip pads, and it's a seven-pound, solid rubber ball. Five or more players are on each side of the court. Forearm ball is more gentle. It's played with one to three people on either side, and they hit it back and forth with their forearms. And it's a lighter, smaller ball. It's played mostly by women. Women aren't actually allowed to play hip ball, so they play forearm ball.

Stickball is played with heavy paddles. The paddles themselves are about 15 pounds, and they're hitting a ball that's very small, only about one pound. It seems like a really odd variant of the Mesoamerican ball game. But then I think of the images at Chichen Itza on the wall of their ball court. Those ball players are depicted holding bats too. Perhaps that's some sort of explanation of what's going on at Chichen Itza. Because remember, Chichen Itza was influenced by Tula, and Tula is not very far from Sinaloa. In terms of scoring the game, it's the same in all three versions. A point, called a rayo, is scored when the ball goes out of the back of your opponent's court. Eight rayos will win the game, but if it's tied at the end of a particular turn, both teams reset to zero, which can make the game last very, very long. The record length for a game in Sinaloa is two whole days.

Ulama has been in Sinaloa since before Spanish contact. But now, after centuries, it's in danger. There are really only about 150 people left playing the game in Sinaloa. They're mostly adults, but they're trying to teach kids. Gosh, I hope it survives. But in today's world of modern video games, I hope they can get the kids to participate.

Just south of Sinaloa, where the ball game is still played, lie the states of Jalisco and Nayarit. Up in the rugged mountains of those states live a group of indigenous that many consider to be Mexico's most traditional people, the Huichol. There are about 50,000 Huichol people today. They're living in the high Sierra Madres, and they are very isolated there, or they were until the 1900s. They weren't Christianized then, but things are changing. Guadalajara's expansion lowered the water table in the entire area, and it pulled the water out of their region. So now there's less hunting, and crops aren't as easy to grow there. So many of them have been forced out of their communities down into the plains where they're working as tobacco farmers for other folks.

The Huichol say they migrated from a location near San Luis Potosi, and they make a pilgrimage back there every year. Again, we're not sure how long that's been going on. The Spanish saw them doing it in the 1500s. But at that time, the Spanish said the Huichol were bellicose and they didn't have any gold, so they just left them alone. Carl Lumholtz met them again in the 1890s, and his records of who they are look very much like they are today.

Huichol worship revolves around a set of four interdependent things—deer, corn, rain, and peyote. Together, they create a cycle. It's a symbolic cycle of human life. An annual pilgrimage is made that ties them all together. That pilgrimage is a difficult journey across the desert. The pilgrimage occurs between October and March, and they start in the Sierra Madres, and they go all the way to a place called Wirikuta. It's near Real de Catorce; that's their final destination. The goal there, when they reach their destination, is to do what they call a peyote hunt. The pilgrims walk across the desert, and during that journey they can only drink water. They don't even get any salt, and sex is strictly prohibited. There are sacred spots that they stop along the way to rest. But in all, it's a 500-kilometer-long journey, a month there and back.

Arriving to Wirikuta, they hunt peyote; it's in the desert near San Luis Potosi. First, they have to find what they call a peyote family, a cluster of five of them. And the pilgrims will make a tiny little altar next to them and give them thanks. Then, they hunt peyote, like their hunting deer, with arrows, bows and arrows. And they gather up that peyote that they hunted, and they eat it that evening. At the fires, the elders tell the creation story. They say that the first men crossed the desert, and they were following deer at that time. They arrived to a place called the Hill at Dawn. The Sun was born there. When they arrive, the deer sacrifice themselves so that men can eat, and peyote grows out of their dead bodies. The men eat the peyote, and they become gods.

The Huichol pray for humanity and the universe at this final destination. The next morning, they climb Cerro de Amanecer, which is the Hill at Dawn. They eat more peyote up there, and they make offerings in two small caves. Then they walk home, and they believe they're actually leading the rain back to the mountains for their crops. Peyote really only surfaces when it starts to rain. So they arrive there when it's raining, and they bring it back home. About 1,000 Huichol make that journey every year.

So how old is this tradition? Again, no one really knows. But, some amazing rock art research suggests that maybe it's been going on for 4,000 years. The rock art I'm talking about is in the Lower Pecos region of Texas. It's in the canyons of the Pecos River. A woman named Carolyn Boyd made some amazing discoveries there in the 1990s. Boyd's first discoveries were made at a place called White Shaman Cave. It's one of hundreds of Pecos rock art sites, but it has a particularly complex scene. There's a lot going on in it.

In one area, we see five men walking. And then, nearby them, there are deer with dots on their antlers. Then in other places, there are men with spears standing near a hill. There are deer there that are speared. But also, there are just those little dots on their antlers being speared. Boyd literally connected the dots. She matched those images to the Huichol pilgrimage. It has the walk, the hunt, and those little dots are the peyote buttons. There's a connection between the deer and the dots; they're both being hunted in these images. Even the hills there, the Hill at Dawn is in these pictures.

There are other figures in the same scenes. They have elongated bodies, and they're stretching up into the sky. They're one of the most common images from Pecos rock art. I've actually found some of these images myself while doing surveys out there.

But in this context, this is talking about the final part of the Huichol myth. Men take peyote, and they become gods. To me, Boyd's theory is rock solid. There are others that take a more conservative view and disagree; they say that we really can't connect something 4,000 years ago to the Huichol today. But going with my more optimistic view, I think Boyd has discovered a 4,000-year-old tradition. And more importantly, the Huichol are the guardians of a 4,000-year-old tradition. Let's hope they can keep it in a changing world.

Not every indigenous person in Mexico looks like a native. Many, in fact, most, don't dress like it or act like it in public life. But at home and in their minds, they are still strongly connected to their ancestors. The Nahua, living in Central Mexico, are a great case in point. The Nahua are Aztec descendants. Broadly, they're anyone who's a Nahuatl speaker. The census says there's about 2.4 million of them living in Mexico today. They're unlike groups like the Huichol and the Zapotec in the regard that they really don't have much traditional dress, and most of them are living in urban settings. They have jobs, like store clerks and bus drivers and street sweepers.

So they don't look like it, and they don't talk about it, but they're still strongly native. One of the best examples is the native healing practice called *curanderismo*. This happens in every single community; it's in every little neighborhood of Mexico City. *Curanderos* heal people. Their diagnosis happens through prayers and visions. The healing also happens with prayers, rituals, and plants. These plants aren't things that they just prescribe, like a pharmacist does. These plants have living spirits that *curanderos* speak with, and they talk about them. There's a whole group of cold plants and warm plants, and they use those different spirits to help people get better.

Today, the things that *curanderos* do in a normal neighborhood are couched as simple consulting, but its roots are very much shamanism. The source of a healer's power is the same source as another native practice that has a much worse name. That name is witchcraft. A *curandero*, though people in modern-day Mexico City don't want to say it, everyone knows that a *curandero* is a good witch. They are basically asking spirits to help and heal people. But that very same power is used by people they call bad witches, and they can ask the spirits to hurt or even kill people. It's all about contact with the supernatural.

A book by anthropologist Timothy Knab, called *A War of Witches*, is one of my favorite examples. Timothy Knab was in Central Mexico in the mid-1970s, and he learned to speak fluent Nahuatl. Using that language proficiency, he was studying healing in the town of San Martin in the state of Puebla. There he had two informants, an old man named Inocente and an old woman named Rubia. They were both healers for about 50 years of their lives. And through them, he learned about the power of their dreams, and they talked about taking journeys to a place called Tlalocan. That's a place of the dead and the place where *curanderos* go when they dream.

Eventually, Knab learned that his informants were also practicing witchcraft for their clients, but they were hiding their abilities. Eventually, he heard about a story of witches in that town from the 1920s. Back in those days, it got very bad. Witches were fighting each other, and hundreds of people died as a result of witchcraft. In the end, they crucified a few of the witches right in the middle of the town square to end it. And today, the entire region knows that San Martin is full of witches.

Knab becomes an apprentice of theirs, and he learns to lucid dream and control his dreams. In these dreams, he talks about seeing caves and the tunnels of Tlalocan, and he learns that our souls have three different parts in their understanding. On Earth, our soul is a yollo. But the spirit that travels to Tlalocan is our tonal. Then, in Tlalocan, we have a third, co-essence kind of spirit; it's our animal spirit in Tlalocan, and that's called a nagual. Some people say that this exact sort of image, Tlalocan and people visiting there, are in the murals of Teotihuacan.

If your nagual is hurt or lost, you become sick on Earth. And witches can use that to attack people. They have the power to travel to the other world and affect that other world. This practice is done by regular people in regular clothes, but it's purely pre-Columbian. We're not talking about the 1570s; we're talking about the 1970s. This is a great example of the hidden cultural continuity that still exists in Mexico.

But if we went to San Martin today, there would probably be less healers. Traditions and traditional life in Mexico is dying at an accelerated rate these days. Even in my short lifetime, I've watched many indigenous practices come to a permanent end. Communication technology is especially bad. The internet and cellphones are breaking isolation everywhere. It's great for business and prosperity, but the side effect is the loss of culture. Cable TV is having a large effect too, especially in terms of native dress. After all, commercials are designed to influence people, and they're doing it.

People may think, you know, these traditions have survived for 500 years; they're here to stay. But that's really not true. Technology is a new challenge to them. There's a dire need for documentation, appreciation, and protection of these traditions. It'll take respect from the outside but also from within the communities. They have to have reasons to stay and continue these ways of life. In the end, the fate of these traditions are in the hands of the people who practice them. In some parts of Mesoamerica, they're becoming seen as impractical. But as you'll learn in my next lecture, some modern Maya communities are in the middle of a cultural revival.

Maya Survival and Revival
Lecture 47

aya traditions, religious ceremonies, and cultural practices are still very much alive today. Guatemala was and still is the heart of Maya civilization. A full 80 percent of Guatemalans are Maya—about 10 million people. They wear the traditional native clothing; they live in houses of thatch and stone; and they practice farming and trading in the markets—just as their ancestors did. In this lecture, we'll discuss the ways in which the Maya have taken the lead in reclaiming their own cultural heritage.

Maya Languages

- There are 21 different Maya languages in Guatemala and 8 more in Mexico. K'iche is the largest in Guatemala, with about 1 million speakers. Mam is next, with about 500,000 speakers. The Kakchiquel language ranks third, at 400,000 speakers.

- The tiniest language group is the Itza Maya, which has nearly disappeared. Only seven people on the planet speak Itza Maya. All of them are very old and live in one village, San Jose, on Lake Peten Itza. Sadly, because the young are not learning the language, Itza Maya will most likely disappear within the decade.

- The strongest Maya cultural traditions are in the highlands. There, the people still live in traditional houses; they cook on hearths in the middle of their homes; and they gather firewood from the forest and water from the rivers. Millions of them live separated from the formal economy. They have a general distrust of the government and big business.

In the highlands, Maya women still use backstrap looms, retaining the beautiful textile traditions of their ancestors.

Day Keeping

- The best evidence of Maya cultural survival is the tradition of day keeping. In each community are specialists called day keepers, Maya priests with powers of divination. They keep and honor the days of the Tzolk'in calendar. They haven't missed a day in 3,000 years.

- In the tradition of day keeping, each of the 260 days is a living being, with its own personality and soul. These spirits are part of a larger world called the Mam. People possess the qualities of the day on which they were born.

- People approach day keepers with questions about what days are auspicious or how to cure illnesses. Day keepers ask the spirits of the days for guidance. Day keepers use a bag of seeds and crystals to understand the will of the Mam. As they count the seeds, they wait to feel what they call "lightning blood."

- Lightning blood is a tingling in some part of the body. When the day keeper feels it, the count stops, and the body part provides the answer to the problem. Usually, those solutions involve offerings to particular shrines.

Maya Fire Ceremony

- There are said to be 260 shrines in Guatemala, each named for a specific day of the calendar they represent. Fire ceremonies are held at these shrines, run by day keepers. During the ceremony, the day keeper lights a fire and puts candles around it. Incense, chocolate, and other items are put in the fire. The ceremony involves naming and honoring all 260 days. A typical ceremony takes about four hours.

- This ritual is not seen as in conflict with Christianity. There are many day keepers who are also devout Christians. Their offerings and prayers are sometimes made in churches, representing a phenomenon called *syncretic religion*—the peaceful combination of two religions.

- Unfortunately, not all Christians are open to syncretic religion. Many Maya shrines have been desecrated. In Guatemala in former times, it was more than just the Maya shrines that were attacked. In fact, for decades, Maya people in Guatemala were the victims of an extermination program perpetrated by their own government.

Rigoberta Menchu

- The trouble started in the 1950s as a backlash to Guatemala's democratic elections following World War II. The leftist government was replaced by a military dictatorship, which sought to suppress the rebellion. Because the Maya population was part of that rebellion, the government's attack was against an ethnic group.

- Traditional Maya life was branded communist. The Maya were restricted in travel, and there were bans on the Maya language. The violence escalated in the 1970s. Maya people disappeared in the thousands. The military would raid villages and remove the men, ignoring their civil rights. The worst came in the 1980s, when Efrain Rios Montt authorized mass executions of Maya.

- But then Rigoberta Menchu wrote her famous book, titled *I, Rigoberta Menchu*, the story of her experiences as an indigenous woman in Guatemala and the horrors she witnessed. In 1992, she won the Nobel Peace Prize. The book eventually led to a peace accord in Guatemala in 1996. The government officially ceased hostilities against the Maya. The genocide against the Maya was one of the worst in history; more than 200,000 Maya were dead or missing by the time it ended.

Zapatista Movement

- Today, Maya culture is honored in Guatemala. A government department was created to address discrimination and racism. The government has permitted altars where the Maya can conduct fire ceremonies. A day keeper association flourishes, with more than 6,000 members.

- Although the Maya Guatemala are no longer persecuted, they have problems across the border in Chiapas, Mexico. A series of bad land deals left the Maya there at the mercy of the coffee industry. The situation sparked the Zapatista revolution, which began on January 1, 1994.

- The Maya coordinated a series of attacks in multiple highland towns. The rebels called themselves Zapatistas after Emiliano Zapata, the Mexican revolutionary leader. The Zapatistas wanted autonomy, not secession. They adopted January 1, 1994, as their start date, in part because that was the first day of the initiation of the North American Free Trade Agreement.

- The Zapatistas continue to be a strong Maya movement even today. The Zapatista movement sprung from a Maya community in the Chiapas highlands. There are dozens of Maya villages around San Cristobal de Las Casas. The largest community is Chamula, with a population of about 50,000 people. Tzotzil Maya is spoken in the streets there. No government police or military are allowed in; the community has its own police force.

Syncretic Religion

- Chamula's church is an excellent example of syncretic religion—it is both Maya and Catholic. However, no traditional masses have been celebrated there since 1968. Today, the floor is covered in pine needles, and there are no pews. Families sit on the floor praying and sacrificing chickens.

- The Maya allow baptisms in the church once every 20 days. There are statues of saints along the walls, but now they have mirrors on their chests—reminiscent of Maya shamanic images from the Classic period.

- According to the Maya, there is always a fixed amount of suffering in the world. Only by accepting suffering can one relieve someone else's suffering. Therefore, sacrifices consist of offerings in tears. As a result, an odd profession has arisen: professional criers.

The Lacandon

- The Lacandon Maya live deep in the forests of eastern Chiapas. Until recently, they were perhaps the most traditional group of Maya people. There were no paved roads into the Lacandon area until the 1980s. The Lacandon were very primitive at contact; they wore robes made out of tree bark. Both men and women wore their hair long and hunted with bows and arrows.

- What's more, the Lacandon followed a unique pantheon of gods. They prayed to a main god called Hacha'kyum. They had what they called *god houses* that held *god pots*. These pots were created from clay and tended for 52 days, after which, they were broken into pieces. The god pots were symbols of the cyclical nature of life.

- Very few Lacandon are left today—some estimate fewer than 1,000. They live in three villages: Naja, Lacanja, and Metzabok. The Lacandon are slowly becoming Christians, especially at Lacanja near Bonampak. In the 1990s, the Lacandon took over the ruins of Bonampak, claiming it as their ancestral property. The National Institute of Anthropology and History (INAH) still controls the site, but the Lacandon control the entrance.

Mayas for Ancient Mayan (MAM)

- An exciting development is the recent movement by modern Maya people to regain their written language. After almost 500 years, the modern Maya can once again read and write in the hieroglyphic script of their ancestors. The movement began in the late 1980s; it arose out of Linda Schele's seminars in Texas to teach Maya hieroglyphs.

- In 2005, an organization called the Friends of the Maya sponsored Maya travel to the Texas Maya meetings, as well as workshops in Maya communities. The Maya began to present their own research, and the first Maya teachers were fully trained.

- In 2012, Friends of the Maya became an international association called Mayas for Ancient Mayan (MAM). The association holds workshops taught purely by Maya to other Maya. The students not only read Maya texts but also write Maya hieroglyphs. New stelae are now being erected in Guatemala and Yucatan.

- The descendants of the Maya, the Zapotec, and the Aztec number in the millions today. And they have much to contribute to the study of their ancestors. What's more, they have an inherent right to be part of that conversation.

Suggested Reading

Collier, *Basta!*

Menchu, *I, Rigoberta Menchu.*

Restall, *The Maya World.*

Tedlock, *Time and The Highland Maya.*

1. Do you think there will come a day when modern Mesoamerican people will be once again in charge of relating their own histories?

2. Are the days of indigenous persecution behind us, or are we just living in a temporarily more peaceful time?

3. What are the greatest mysteries about Mesoamerica that remain to be solved?

Maya Survival and Revival
Lecture 47—Transcript

Despite over 500 years of acculturation, and at times overt persecution, Maya traditions, religious ceremonies, and technologies are still very much alive. In this lecture we'll discuss the challenges that modern Maya face and how they're overcoming them.

Guatemala was and still is the heart of Maya civilization; 80 percent of that country are still Maya people; that's about 10 million people. They're living in traditional homes. They're farming and trading in the markets like they used to. And they're wearing all of their traditional clothing.

There are 21 different Maya languages in Guatemala, and there are eight more in Mexico. K'iche is the largest one in Guatemala, with about a million speakers. Mam is next at half-a-million speakers. The Kakchiquel are third at 400,000 speakers. And those are low estimates. Like I said before, indigenous people are allergic to census.

The tiniest language group is the Itza' Maya, and they're almost gone. Right now, as far as I know, there are seven people left on the planet that speak Itza' Maya. And all of them are very old and living in one village, San Jose, on lake Peten Itza. I went there once with my students. And I found one of these Itza' speakers, an old man named Rosa. He explained to us that he's trying it to teach kids in the village, but they're not really getting it; they don't really speak it. That means that that language will probably disappear within this decade.

The strongest Maya cultural traditions are in the highlands. There, they're still living in houses of thatch and stone. They cook on hearths in the middle of their homes. They gather firewood and water from the rivers. There are millions of them living separate from the formal economy. They have a general distrust of the government and big business.

And they retain beautiful textile traditions. They're still using backstrap looms, which means sometimes it takes them months to complete a single work. Each community has its own style of dress. Up in the highlands, the clothes you wear is your identity. It's changing a bit these days, like many things. More men are wearing jeans. Women are wearing usually more traditional dresses. Their styles change slower. They wear *huipiles*, that are kind of like ponchos.

Allen Christenson tells a nice story of his time among the highland Maya. Back in the 1990s, he was a volunteer dentist there. And he was in a community that all had these nice black jackets. And on the black jackets were embroidered flowers on vines. And each family handed in all their jackets after a birth, and the seamstress put another flower bud on the vine. They were actually wearing their family lineage. An added element of beauty to it is that the Maya symbolize flowers as souls.

The best evidence of Maya cultural survival is the tradition of day keeping. There are specialists called ah k'in, date keepers. They are Maya priests and they have powers of divination. There are multiple ones in every single community. They keep and honor the days of the Tzolk'in calendar, and I guess they haven't missed a day in 3,000 years. In that tradition, each of the 260 days is a living being. Each has its own personality and soul. They're part of a larger world called the Mam. That's a mother/father spirit of the world. People have the qualities of the day they were born on. And as we've discussed, that same tradition existed across Mesoamerica, but in Guatemala it still does.

People come to day keepers with questions, things like whether or not to do something, to marry or to take a job. They also called come to them about illnesses, how to cure them. Day keepers ask the spirits of the days. And it's set up somewhat like a doctor's consultation. Day keepers use a bag of tsetse seeds and crystals to understand the will of the Mam. They take a handful out and put it on a table, and then they group them in sets of four and make those sets of four into a grid pattern. The questions are asked of the seeds, and the day keeper will start counting through the groups of seeds. The first one is named whatever today is. As they're counting through, they're waiting to feel what they call lightning blood.

Lightning blood is a tingling in some part of their body. When they feel it, the count stops. And the day that they stopped on, added to the body part they felt it in, provides the answer. For example, if they felt it in their left foot and they stopped on the day kimi, that probably has something to do with the ancestors. They count a couple of times through, and those counts provide the solution for the problem; it's divined in that way. Usually those solutions involve offerings to particular shrines.

There are said to be 260 shrines in Guatemala, one for each day of the calendar. They're named for that specific day they represent. There are ceremonies that occur at these shrines, mostly what we call fire ceremonies. The day keeper runs the ceremony, and the clients bring the things that it needs, and they participate. They light up a fire, and they put candles around it. They also put copal incense, and chocolate, and other things in the fire. The ceremony involves naming out all 260 days and honoring them. In all, a typical ceremony takes about four hours of time.

And this is not seen as in conflict with Christianity. There are many day keepers who are also devout Christians. The offerings and prayers they make are sometimes done in churches. Chichicastenango's church, for example, have ceremonies going on on it steps every single day. And the day keeper's office is right next to that church. That's something that we call syncretic religion, when two religions combine together without being in conflict. Unfortunately, not all Christians feel the same way. Many Maya shrines have been desecrated. It happens all the time; it's still happening today. Pascual Abaj, in Chichicastenango, had its altar destroyed just in the 1990s. So some of these shrines are actually hidden away to protect them.

In times past in Guatemala it was more than just the Maya shrines that were attacked. In fact, Maya people in Guatemala were the victims of an extermination program perpetrated by their own government for decades. The trouble started in the 1950s as a backlash to Guatemala's democratic elections following World War II. The leftist governments were replaced with military dictatorships. And their goal was to suppress what they call the leftist rebellion. And the whole Maya population was part of that. So it was really an attack against an ethnic group.

Traditional Maya life was branded communist, and they got restrictions on travel. There were bans on the Maya languages. The old man Rosa that I met in Lake Peten Itza, he was an Itza' speaker, and he told me when he went to school as a boy, he was beaten if he spoke Maya in public. So there were violent oppressions all the way across the country. And in response, rebels defended themselves. The violence escalated in the 1970s. Maya people disappeared in the thousands. The military would raid villages and remove the men. There were no civil rights or protection for them. In fact, rich landowners could just come into these communities and grab them as slaves and force them to work in the fincas along the coast.

The worst was in the 1980s. Efrain Rios Montt took power then, and he authorized terrible mass executions. Villages were burned, and everyone was murdered—women and children, everyone. The Ixil Triangle took the worst of it. Tens of thousands of defenseless Maya people were killed there. It continued into the 1990s. Community organizers and priests were also targeted. Especially people that could talk to the outside world were targeted because they wanted to keep it quiet internationally.

But then Rigoberta Menchu wrote her famous book with the help of a French author. And it was finally published in English in 1984. Her book was called *I, Rigoberta Menchu*. And it was a horror story of her life and all the murder she had witnessed. In 1992, that book won a Nobel Peace Prize. And it led eventually to a peace accord in Guatemala in 1996. The government officially stopped their hostilities against the Maya. Nowadays, history names that moment in time a genocide. In fact, it was one of the worst in world history; over 200,000 Maya were dead or missing by the time it ended.

But now, Maya culture is honored in Guatemala. There's actually a government department of discrimination and racism. The government has permitted altars in the ruins that the Maya can visit. The Maya are free to enter there and conduct their fire ceremonies. And today, Maya religion is flourishing. There's a day keeper association now with over 6,000 members.

In 2007 Rigoberta Menchu ran for president against Rios Montt, the man who was in charge of all those murders back in the '80s. He actually had to drop out because of death threats. She didn't win, but she ran again in 2011. That is definitely a sign of positive change in Guatemala.

Efrain Rios Montt is on trial, and he's charged with genocide. He's already been convicted a few times, but those were overturned. The government right now is saying to the Maya, just forget about it and let's move on. But the Maya say, no, there's going to be no justice until people like him are convicted of the crimes they perpetrated.

While things were calming down for the Maya in Guatemala, they were flaring up for the Maya across the border in Chiapas. A series of bad land deals left the Maya there at the mercy of the coffee industry. The situation worsened until it turned into the Zapatista Revolution. The revolution began January 1, 1994. It was a coordinated attack in multiple towns. They were only in the highland communities at that time. The caretaker of the ruins of Tonina was actually its first casualty; he was accidentally shot while walking in the town of Ocosingo.

I was actually there that summer, a young kid of 25 years old. I was both in Guatemala and Chiapas while these wars were going on. It was really a crazy introduction to the area. I saw men that were wearing black ski masks to hide their identity. Mostly these people were poor Maya farmers. They named themselves Zapatistas after Emiliano Zapata. He was a Mexican revolutionary leader. The Zapatistas wanted autonomy, not secession. They took January 1, 1994 as their start date in part because that was the first day of NAFTA; they said it would make the poor poorer, ad in the end, they were right. It did.

Their leader and spokesperson was a man named Subcommondante Marcos. He wasn't a Maya, and actually, we're still not sure of his identity. He was an eloquent speaker, but not a soldier. He used the Internet to tell the world the plight of the Zapatistas. In fact, I think it was one of the very first movements to ever do that. Leading the attack was left to other commanders that were actually soldiers; 3,000 rebels took the town of San Cristobal de las Casas. They burned the police stations, and they actually occupied the military base. The Mexican army responded quickly, and they repelled them in less than two weeks. They retreated into the jungle. But international pressures stopped the violence. The Zapatistas continued to protest. The Zapatista movement today continues. But now it's primarily a political organization. A core group of them are still hiding in the jungle. Marcos is now part of what he calls Delegate Zero. They do peaceful marches, and they've done them as far as Mexico City. I saw one of these huge marches in Palenque on December 21, 2012, the end of the 13th *bak'tun*. So even to this day, it's a strongly Maya movement.

The Zapatista movement sprung from a very strong Maya community in Chiapas. Across the mountains and into the jungles, very traditional Maya life ways continue in Chiapas. Nowhere are they better represented than in the Chiapas highlands. There are dozens of Maya villages around San Cristobal de las Casas. They're proud, traditional, and autonomous. The largest of them is Chamula, and it has a population of about 50,000 people. Tzotzil Maya is spoken in the streets there, and there are no government police or military allowed in. They have their own police force.

Its church is another great example of syncretic religion; it's both Maya and Catholic. But there have been no traditional masses there since 1968. Today when you walk in, the floor is covered in pine needles, and there's no pews. There are families sitting on the floor praying. And they have candles and moonshine, and they're sacrificing chickens. No pictures are allowed inside the church, but tourists are free to come in. The Maya there feel like it's their obligation. They want to show foreigners the proper way to live.

They do allow baptisms in the church, but once every 20 days they'll let Catholic priests in to do it. The saints are still statues along the walls. But now they have mirrors on their chest. That reminds me very much of Maya shamanic images from the classic period. Carnival at Chamula is another great example of syncretism. On the last day of Carnival they have what they call the fire walk. Maya with banners run across coals in front of the church. It's very interesting to see, but it's like no Catholic ceremony I've ever seen.

Nearby, the village of Zinacantan is also very syncretic. There, I learned an interesting Maya concept, the concept of a fixed amount of suffering. They have almost a scientific explanation of it. They say there's always the same amount of suffering in the world. And only accepting suffering can relieve someone else's suffering. Therefore, offerings in tears are the sacrifices to relieve it. As a result, there's an odd profession there; there are people who are professional criers. Some people really just can't cry very well, so they hire a person to come and cry for them. I've been in the church and seen it. I've seen people over-the-top wailing, and it's been explained to me that they are these professionals. But both the money they spend on that person and the tears they shed are offerings to help the sick. Really, I think it's very pragmatic of them.

A lot of what I know about the Maya in Chiapas comes from my friend Chip Morris. He's a Maya textile expert, and he's been there for 40 years. Back when he was 21 years old he won the MacArthur Genius Award. He did so for connecting ancient and modern textile traditions among the Maya. They gave him $1 million. He felt a little guilty about it, though, and he ended up giving most of that money to the Maya. He used it just to buy himself a house and gave the rest to the communities. He continues to study and live there.

Chip speaks fluent Tzotzil, and all the communities love him. He's always helping women to do things like create weaving co-ops. And he learns the meanings of the patterns of their textiles, even today. And he studies changes over time in their textiles. He sees hints of Maya religion and history within the ways they weave. Culture is preserved through weaving up there.

Chip once told me a funny story about changing traditions and textiles. He said there was an Ivy League project that went up there to study traditional textiles. And they documented for 10 years that the styles were absolutely static. But it turns out that the Maya were just being polite. They talked to these guests, and they said they wanted to see us in our traditional dress. So, they didn't change anything. But the second they left there was a fashion explosion, all sorts of new patterns. I think it's a great example of how ethnographies affect the people they study, whether they think they do or not.

Lately, Chip has been helping another group of Maya who live deep in the forests of Eastern Chiapas. Those people are called the Lacandon. And at least until recently, they were perhaps the most traditional group of modern Maya people. The Lacandon were very primitive at contact. They had robes that they made out of tree bark, and they all wore their hair very long, both men and women. And they were constantly smoking these cigars. They were hunters who used a bow and arrow. They had just small garden plots, and they were following a unique pantheon of gods.

Trudi Blom dedicated her life to them; she was the wife of explorer Frans Blom. And she created, from her own home, a place called Na Bolom as a Lacandon center. But with the good of that came bad. More and more Lacandon came out for help, and they learned ways of other cultures. People also came into their territory. First it was just anthropologists, but nowadays it's tourists.

There were no paved roads into their area until the 1980s. And they were back there praying to their main god Hacha'kyum. They had what they called "god houses" and ceremonies around them. Their god houses held their god pots. God pots were created from clay and then cared for, but only for a 52-day cycle. They were made and they were fed, but then at the end they were broken. They were symbols of a cyclical life conception that they held. Things really changed for the Lacandon when Chan Kin Viejo died in the 1990s. He was their spiritual leader, and they say he was well over 100 when he died. And it's clear that he had hundreds of children, most of them living in the town of Naja. When he died, nobody made a god house anymore. There are less and less people that follow their traditional ways every year.

There are very few Lacandon people left today; some say less than 1,000. They live in three villages—Naja, Lacanja, and Metzabok. The government deeded lots of land to them, but the Ch'ol Maya that live nearby are not very happy about it. There's encroachment and outside world contact. The Lacandon are slowly becoming Christians, especially at Lacanja near Bonampak; there are now churches there.

In the 1990s, they took over the ruins of Bonampak. They said it was their ancestral property. INAH still controls the site, but the Lacandon control the entrance. That, again, is good and bad for them. It's a point of pride and self-determination. But again, it's increasing contact with the modern world, and it's helping their traditions fade all the faster.

Once I brought a group of students into the Lacandon Forest to a waterfall. There was a Lacandon guard standing there, but he was wearing jeans, and he was embarrassed. He said, oh I'm sorry, I didn't know you were going to show up. I would have been wearing my robes. So I told them a story. I told them about the Greeks and their togas, and I made a comparison. I said, you know, the Greeks don't wear their togas anymore either. But it's not what you're wearing, it's who you are. If you, as a Lacandon, continue your culture, then it continues no matter what you're wearing.

Now I want to talk about a subject that I'm very excited about, a recent movement by modern Maya people to regain their written language. After almost 500 years, some modern Maya can once again read and write in the hieroglyphic script of their ancestors. It began in the late 1980s, and it sprung out of Linda Schele's Texas Maya meetings; those were seminars to teach Maya hieroglyphs to whoever wanted to learn them. And from the beginning, she also invited Maya people to come learn with us. Donations paid their way up to the United States. A few returned year after year.

Then in the 1990s, she started giving summer classes in Mesoamerica. It was she and a man named Nikolai Grube that went down there. They started in Guatemala, but they were also in places in Mexico. There were a whole classes of Maya people, and they taught it in Spanish. It was different than in Texas, because it was about reclaiming their own personal history.

Schele told the story of one particular summer when she was doing a workshop in Hormiguero, Mexico. She was going through a text, and a man in the class began to cry. She asked him, what's going on. And he said that she had just mentioned a king's title in that text, and that that was his family name, and that his family had lived there for generations, but it wasn't until just then that he realized they were descended from the kings who made that city. I think that was a really powerful moment of cultural reclamation. Always gives me goosebumps when I tell that story.

Schele passed in 1998, but Nikolai Grube continued the work. Kathryn Josserand and Nick Hopkins also helped. Then a woman named Sue Glenn started the Friends of the Maya in 2005. It sponsored Maya travel up to the Texas Maya meetings. It also sponsored workshops in Maya communities.

The Maya started presenting their own research. And then, the first Maya teachers were fully trained.

In 2012, Friends of the Maya became an association called MAM, Maya for ancient Mayan. Now, there are workshops taught purely by Maya to other Maya. It's an international association. And they're not just reading them, but they're writing Maya hieroglyphs. New stele are being erected right now. At the time of this filming, I know of six new stele; they're both in Guatemala and in Yucatan. I think it's amazing. When in world history has a culture lost their written language for 500 years and then regained it? The Maya are going through a true cultural revival.

I think that's a great note upon which to end this lecture about the modern Maya. I hope I've engendered in you a respect for not just the Maya, but all Mesoamerican cultures and a desire to learn more about them. In conclusion, let me leave you with this thought. The Egyptians are gone. Egypt still exists, but that culture is now Islamic. That's not true in Mesoamerica. The descendants of the Maya, the Zapotecs, and the Aztecs, are still here in the millions, and they have much to contribute to the study of their ancestors. And what's more, they have an inherent right to be part of that conversation.

The Maya have taken the lead in reclaiming their own cultural history, and I hope the other culture groups of Mesoamerica follow that lead. I dream of a day when the tables are turned and Westerners like me learn about the ancient Aztec and the Maya directly from their modern descendants.

Frontiers of Mesoamerican Archaeology
Lecture 48

A lthough some people think that all the major cities of ancient Mesoamerica have already been found, that is far from true. Less than 1 percent of Mesoamerica has been professionally surveyed and studied, especially in the jungle areas. In fact, the central part of Yucatan is mostly unknown. However, every tiny village in the middle of nowhere knows the ancient cities in that area, and the villagers are willing to lead archaeologists to see them. To conclude this course, we'll explore the frontiers of Mesoamerican archaeology and discuss what is left to discover— and where to find it.

Unknown within the Known
- Ivan Sprajc, a Slovenian archaeologist, has done 20 years of survey work in southern Campeche. In a systematic search of the jungles since the 1990s, he and his team have found more than 90 cities.

- Some are midsized cities, but others are truly massive. Sprajc has found pyramids taller than 30 meters, as well as hundreds of stelae. Many of the stelae have hieroglyphs dating back to the Classic period. What Sprajc has found has profoundly changed our knowledge of the extent of the Classic period.

- Just south of Sprajc's survey area is the northwestern Peten jungle— one of the largest areas yet to be explored. Archaeologist Richard Hansen has been working at El Mirador for 20 years now and has looked to the west of that area. However, he has much work to do at El Mirador. One of the most significant frontiers of Mesoamerican archaeology is the search for the unknown within the known.

Tikal and Palenque

- Dozens of ancient cities across Mesoamerica have been known for decades, some of them for more than 100 years. Many of those cities have been the subject of intensive excavation and study. Still, because they encompass wide areas, even the best known have been only fractionally revealed.

- Tikal is an excellent case in point. It's one of the best-known Maya cities, but archaeologists have just scratched the surface. Within Tikal's core, the ceremonial center, archaeologists have mapped hundreds of temples, but only about 50 have been excavated.

- In fact, Tikal's most famous temple, Temple IV, still has its entire base covered with trees. Excavations of that base finally started in 2008, but archaeologists are not nearly finished. Visitors to Tikal see buried structures everywhere.

- At Palenque, even after 100 years of archaeology, a 3-year survey found more than 1,000 new buildings—including the largest temple at Palenque, which was actually larger than its palace. To date, at Palenque, only 40 structures have been excavated. The map shows about 1,500 structures—only 2.5 percent of the city has been excavated in 100 years.

Nohpat, Xultun, and Sak Tz'i

- Other major cities have not seen any archaeological research at all. The city of Nohpat, a crucial Terminal classic site in Yucatan, has a temple that is so huge, it can be seen from the site of Uxmal far away.

- Xultun is a megacity in the Peten, possibly even larger than Tikal. Xultun has been known since 1915, and archaeologists have recorded many stelae there, but excavations did not begin until 2008.

- In 2010, researchers found a small house that they identified as an astronomer's house, and on the walls were all sorts of calculations. This significant find taught us much about the kinds of data that Mesoamerican astronomers collected. This is just the beginning of work at Xultun.

- There are some cities named in the hieroglyphs that have yet to be found, such as Sak Tz'i, the enemy city we see in the murals of Bonampak. That same site is also mentioned at Piedras Negras and Yaxchilan, and archaeologists have no idea where it is.

- Sak Tz'i was clearly a major city, and scholars have a partial list of its kings from other sites. What's more, there is a looted Sak Tz'i stela in Europe, meaning that someone knew the location of Sak Tz'i.

Ancient Mesoamerica underneath Modern Cities

- When the Spanish arrived in Mesoamerica, there were already hundreds of cities located strategically near resources and with functioning infrastructure. It would not have made sense to build entirely new cities when perfectly good ones already existed. As a result, much of ancient Mesoamerica lies underneath modern cities.

- Mexico's largest city sits on top of the Aztec capital, Tenochtitlan. Subway construction projects located parts of the old city underneath Mexico City. In 1978, street projects located the base of the Templo Mayor, its main temple.

- Traces of the old city are being looted and destroyed. Hundreds of thousands of artifacts have already been stolen from Tenochtitlan. Recently, however, the National Institute of Anthropology and History (INAH) started a new initiative called the Urban Archaeology Program. All around the city, archaeologists are conducting controlled excavations. Their goal is to better understand the life of the Aztec common people. Such research is called *household archaeology*, and it is an admirable trend.

- Guatemala City is built on top of the ancient city of Kaminaljuyu—the highlands' greatest ancient city. A shopping mall sits right over one of its major temple groups. A large city park in Guatemala City contains massive temples that are vitally important because they are built in the Teotihuacan style. They hold clues to Teotihuacan's entrada into the highlands.

Hiding in Plain Sight

- Ancient cities are not just underneath modern cities; they are also found buried under remote villages and towns. Underneath the town of Frontera Corozal are multiple stone monuments sitting atop an ancestral site.

- In a humble village called Chajul in the highlands of Guatemala, an ancient mural was found behind the plaster wall of an abandoned house. That mural depicts a Maya lord sitting in a Spanish-style chair, with other Maya dancing around him in European clothes. It has been interpreted as an illustration of a victory dance after the Maya won a battle against the Spanish.

- The fact that the mural dates from the 1600s was enlightening. Archaeologists thought that the Maya had been conquered by that time. Apparently, however, the Maya who lived in Chajul were still resisting the Spanish in the 1600s. Other houses in Chajul are revealing yet more murals—a fine example of evidence and artifacts hiding in plain sight.

Cenote Diving

- There is another place where undiscovered evidence lies just underneath our feet: in caves and cenotes. Yucatan has thousands of cenotes. Chichen Itza's cenote held astonishing finds.

- Archaeologist James Brady pioneered cenote diving; he explored many cenotes in the 1980s and 1990s, revealing that offerings were made in cenotes everywhere, not just at Chichen Itza. Today, a university in Merida has a diving program, with the first underwater archaeology professor, Guillermo de Anda.

Today, cenote diving is opening new doors to our understanding of Maya life and religion.

- Anda has found architecture inside caves, with roads and temples leading under the water. His believes that these structures are evidence that at some point, the water table was much lower, and ladders were built inside the caves to seek water. If he is correct, these are new insights into the challenges Mesoamericans faced during drought periods.

Cave Archaeology

- In Mesoamerica, caves are significant symbolic places. They are entrances to the land of the dead. Consider the Olmec cave paintings in Chalcatzingo, or the cave underneath Teotihuacan's Pyramid of the Sun, or the Aztec origin stories of the Place of 7 Caves in Chicomoztoc.

- Important caves, such as Naj Tunich in the Peten, have taught archaeologists much. Naj Tunich has hieroglyphs on the walls and dozens of texts—all in perfect condition. Excavations have revealed stone tombs with elite burials and offerings.

401

- Loltun Cave in Yucatan has charcoal handprints that date to 10,000 years ago. These are the tiny hands of Maya people. There are also bison and mammoth bones in the cave—evidence that extends Maya history back for 7,000 years.

- Caves are an excellent frontier for discovery. What's more, the constancy of climate in a cave makes for excellent preservation of artifacts. The Grolier Codex was found in a cave in Chiapas in 1974.

Goals for the Next Generation of Archaeologists

- For an archaeologist studying Mesoamerica, one of the major goals is additional mapping. An ideal mapping project would be to find another Preclassic megacity in the Peten. Northwest Guatemala remains virtually untouched, with hardly any modern settlement.

- A second ideal project would be to find the evidence of South American settlements in western Mexico. Metallurgy finds in western Mexico prove that there was contact with South America. Metal works first show up in western Mexico about 300; then, there was a hiatus until about 1100, when the Mixtec placed gold into Tomb 7 at Monte Alban.
  - In deciding where to look for these settlements, archaeologists should consider this: When Cortes wanted to assess the gold resources of Mexico, he sent Spaniards along with guides to find the mines. They came back with reports that gold and silver were being taken out of certain riverbeds.

  - Archaeologists know where those riverbeds are, and that is where we will find South American settlements, as well.

- A third goal—and the most ambitious—is to find an Olmec Pompeii. Olmec monuments were made of basalt quarried from around volcanoes. El Chichon is an active volcano near the Olmec area in northwest Chiapas.

- El Chichon erupted massively multiple times in human history. It exploded around 800, and some scholars believe this was connected to the Classic period Maya collapse.

- El Chichon also erupted three times during Olmec times. There is a good possibility that it buried cities in one of these eruptions.

A Quickening Pace of Discovery

- In Mesoamerica, there is much left to find and to understand. Even in the best-studied ruins, archaeological knowledge is based on only a fractional sample. The existence of the Aztec capital was unknown until the 1960s. The Maya code of hieroglyphics was not broken until the 1970s. And, unfortunately, looting continues to outpace archaeology.

- On the other hand, the pace of discovery is quickening every year. The need for further investigations is clear and present—and downright exciting.

Suggested Reading

Blom and La Farge, *Tribes and Temples*.

Questions to Consider

1. What are the current ideas about Mesoamerican life ways that you think are the most likely to be completely wrong?

2. If you could run an archaeological project anywhere in Mesoamerica, where would you do it?

Frontiers of Mesoamerican Archaeology
Lecture 48—Transcript

I've had a lot of fun presenting this course. And as long as it's been, it's really just a fraction of what there is to be learned about Mesoamerica. But to conclude, let's talk about the frontiers of Mesoamerican archaeology. What's still left to discover? And where do we need to look to find it?

Most people think that all the major cities of ancient Mesoamerica have been found, but that's actually far from true. My estimate is that less than one percent of the actual land area of Mesoamerica has been professionally surveyed and studied, especially in the jungles.

When I started my career, my mentors and fellow students believed exactly that; they thought that the early explorers had found them all. And indeed, they did find a lot. Many of the known cities that were found long ago are still out there, and researchers have yet to return to them.

During Blom's surveys of Chiapas in the 1920s, he found dozens of major Maya cities, places like Lacanja; that's a major city. It has temples and ball courts, lots of carved stelae. It's about three hours walk into the jungle from a Lacandon village. I've brought my students out there once in a while to see. An entire lifetime could be spent just returning to the cities Blom found on horseback.

I myself found a major Maya city in 1995. I found it in a place called Programme for Belize, about 300 square miles of a reserve in the country of Belize. And that area is virtually unexplored to this day. The city I found I called Ma'ax Na, and I could tell from its long range buildings that it was a Terminal Classic city. It had two pyramids that were 25 meters tall, ball courts, palaces, stelae, and even a reservoir. I found hundreds of buildings, but there are many more out there.

And Programme for Belize is tiny compared to the other unexplored parts of the Maya jungle. The entire central part of Yucatan is mostly unknown. Every little village out there knows of these ancient cities, and people in those villages are willing to lead an archaeologist out to see them. But there are so many other cities that we already know about, those have yet to become a priority, or sometimes they're just not a possibility.

A great case in point are the modern explorations of Ivan Sprajc. He's a Slovenian archaeologist who works with INAH, and he's done 20 years of survey in southern Campeche. He's done a systematic search of that part of the jungle since the 1990s, and he and his team have found over 90 cities during that time. Some of them are mid-sized cities, but others are truly massive. He's found 30-plus-meter tall pyramids and hundreds of stelae. Many of them have kings' portraits on them, and they have hieroglyphs dating back to the Classic period. What he's found there actually changes our known extent of where the Classic cities were. Sprajc's surveys are a model and an inspiration to me.

Just south of Sprajc's survey area in Guatemala sits one of the largest unexplored areas. It's the northwest part of the Peten jungle. It's deep, low jungle. On the eastern edge of that same jungle sits El Mirador, Nakbe, and Tintal; those are the largest known Preclassic cities. But what's just to the west of those? Still, no one knows.

Richard Hansen has been working at El Mirador for 20 years now, and he's looked out there; he knows there's more out there, but he has his hands full at El Mirador. And that leads to another aspect of what more there is to be discovered. I like to call it the unknown within the known. We have dozens of ancient cities across Mesoamerica that have been known for decades, some of them for over 100 years. Many of those have been the subject of intensive excavation and study. Still, they're the size of cities, and even the best known have, in reality, only been fractionally revealed.

Tikal is a great case in point. It's one of the best known Maya cities, but actually, we've only barely studied the entire city. Textbooks say that it's 16 square kilometers in area, and they give it a population estimate of some 70,000 people. But in reality, that number is based on a survey sample. It was grid lines that were walked by surveyors, and they mapped off of those grid lines, but not completely into the blocks that the grid represents. So, what we ended up getting was an estimated total from a much smaller sample of the entire city.

And even within Tikal's core, the ceremonial center, we've mapped in hundreds of temples, but really, only about 50 have been excavated. Many of them are cleared just of trees so they're not getting any more damage from those trees, but they're not excavated. In fact, its most famous temple, Temple IV, still has its entire base covered with trees. Excavations of that base finally started in 2008, but they're still not nearly done with it. Visitors who visit Tikal see buried structures everywhere.

My own work at Palenque was a revelation too. There were 100 years of archaeology there when I arrived. I did a three-year survey, and I found over 1,000 new buildings. In fact, I found the largest temple at Palenque. It was about a kilometer west of its palace, and it was actually larger than its palace. To date at Palenque, they've actually only excavated about 40 structures. My map has about 1,500 structures; that's 2.5 percent of the city excavated in 100 years.

Another great example is Yaxchilan. It's a very famous city, but in reality, it's virtually unknown. There's absolutely no settlement survey there. Colleagues of mine have poked around in the woods, and they've said that the entire river bow is full of houses. Only the ceremonial center has been mapped so far, and even that is only partially excavated.

I actually wanted to do that settlement survey at Yaxchilan, and I almost had the chance. The World Monument Fund had the money to do it, and they recommended me to the Mexican government, but INAH said, no, that project can't go on. As it turned out, in those years, the country of Mexico and Guatemala were teaming together to make a dam on the Usumacinta River. It hasn't happened yet, but they were planning it at that time, and so they didn't want any projects going on for political reasons. If they had built that dam, it would have flooded all of Yaxchilan up to only the very top temples, and the entire area would become the largest lake in all of Central America. It would have flooded huge amounts of areas, a lot of them with unknown ruins.

It's a difficult thing. What do we do? Do we preserve history? Or do we create infrastructure and electricity for millions of people in Mexico and Central America that need it? These are issues sometimes that we come up with. Do we preserve history, or do we help modern people? It's complicated. But I'm an archaeologist, and I'm glad the dam hasn't happened yet. And I hope it never does, because there's still a lot to learn out there.

But at least Yaxchilan had some study. Other major cities don't even have that. Another good example is the city of Nohpat in Yucatan. It has a temple that's so huge you can see it from the site of Uxmal far away. One time I actually walked out there to Nohpat with some colleagues, and we saw and climbed its massive temples. I saw open, looted tomb chambers, and there was a stela there from the Classic period, which is important; that's a Terminal Classic area. It's a very important site, and yet, there's been absolutely no research there.

Another site that's been in the news is Xultun. It's a megacity in the Peten; some say it's even larger than Tikal. It's been known since 1915, and we've recorded many stelae out there, but excavations didn't actually start until 2008. Then in 2010, they found a little house that they identified as an astronomer's house, and on the walls were all sorts of calculations. They taught us brand-new things about the kind of data that astronomers were collecting. And that's just the beginning of work at Xultun.

And then, there are some cities named in the hieroglyphs that have yet to be found, like Sak Tz'i, or White Dog; that's a great example. That's the enemy city we see in the murals of Bonampak. That same site is also mentioned at Piedras Negras and Yaxchilan, and we have no idea where it is. Sak Tz'i was clearly a major city, and we have a partial list of its kings from those other sites mentioning them. And, there's a Sak Tz'i stela in Europe. It was looted. So, obviously someone knows where the site is, just not archaeologists.

Personally, I think it's the site of Plan de Ayutla, which is near a little town called Nuevo Palestina. They've been doing excavations there, but in my opinion, not in the right places to solve the question of whether it's Sak Tz'i. They've done the ball court. They've done the top of the temples. But where they should be digging is at the base of the big temples. As the rocks fall off the temples, they cover the bottom plaza right next to the temples, and that's where they usually put the stelae. So I hope one day they actually dig at the base there, and we might finally answer the question of whether or not we even know where Sak Tz'i is.

Or maybe Sak Tz'i are the three huge pyramids on the horizon that I see every time I bring students to the top of the Golondrinas Waterfalls. There's so much out there in the remote jungles. But not all of the unknown are out there in the forest; some of them are literally under our noses.

When the Spanish arrived, there were already hundreds of cities located strategically near resources and with functioning infrastructure. Why would they choose to build new cities when perfectly good ones were already there? As a result, much of ancient Mesoamerica lies underneath its modern cities.

Mexico's largest city sits on top of the Aztec capital, Tenochtitlan. We thought it was totally gone until the 1960s. And then, subway construction projects located parts of the old city underneath it. Then in 1978, street projects located the base of the Temple Mayor, their main temple. So, we discovered that the old city is still there, but everywhere in the city it's being looted and destroyed.

Hundreds of thousands of artifacts have already been looted from Tenochtitlan. They're on the shelves of many houses in Mexico City. But recently, INAH started a new initiative; they call it the Urban Archaeology Program, and all around the city, they're doing controlled excavations. Their goal is to better understand common Aztec life. One of them is occurring in the basement of a tattoo parlor.

I think it's great that they're looking for common Aztec people. That's what we call *household archaeology*, and we don't have near enough of it. We've really just begun to focus on that aspect of these communities. But in this case, I think that their urban project has other potential as well. Through it, we could actually reconstruct the siege of Tenochtitlan. We could look for the evidence of the battles at Tacuba, or the last stand at Tlatelolco. Or how about all that gold that fell off the causeways with the Spanish during the Noche Triste? There's great potential for recovering history right under Mexico City.

Guatemala City is another example. It's built on top of the ancient city of Kaminaljuyu. That was the highlands' greatest ancient city, and the evidence of that city is everywhere in Guatemala City. There's a mall on top of one of their major temple groups. And there's a museum in that mall, and it's right next to a shoe store. But there's a lot more to be done there.

There's a major city park in Zone 1, which is actually the worst and most dangerous part of town, but it contains massive temples. And those are vitally important because they're Teotihuacan-style temples. They hold clues to Teotihuacan's entrada into the highlands. There was a brief project there in the 1960s, but that was the only research that's ever really been done there. It's high time to return to that park and study those Teotihuacan temples.

And it's not just underneath big cities. Ancient cities are also under villages and towns everywhere. Another good example is the town of Frontera Corozal. That's a little sleepy town where you hire a boat to go upriver to Yaxchilan. And lately, they've been improving their town; they've been doing street improvement projects and sewer systems. While they were doing those, they found multiple stone monuments under the village, and the modern people had no idea they were there. They're sitting on top of an ancestral site. Now they've made a local museum for all of the different things that they're finding as they improve their town.

One more neat example is the discovery made in 2012. There's a humble village called Chajul in the highlands of Guatemala. There we find the victims of the genocide years. They've moved back into that village that was abandoned during the wars, and they're re-inhabiting the old abandoned houses. One particular squatter family was restoring the home they chose, and they removed the old plaster of the walls, and it revealed a very old mural. That mural depicts a Maya lord sitting in a Spanish-style chair, and then there are other Maya dancing around him in European clothes. It's been interpreted as a victory dance, after they won a battle against the Spanish. And it's from the 1600s, which is very enlightening. We thought that the Maya were all conquered by then. But apparently, the Maya who lived in Chajul were still resisting the Spanish in the 1600s. Other houses in Chajul are revealing yet more murals. It's a great example of what's hiding right in front of us.

Like the modern cities and villages hiding important frontiers of Mesoamerican archaeology, there's another place where undiscovered evidence lies just underneath our feet. This time, I'm talking about caves and cenotes. In Yucatan, there are thousands of cenotes. Landa wrote about the offerings that were thrown into them, and also the sacrifices that were thrown into them. Chichen Itza's cenote held incredible finds. But cenote archaeology is in its infancy. Today, diving cenotes is opening new doors to our understanding of Maya life and religion.

James Brady pioneered cenote diving. He dove many cenotes in the '80s and '90s, and he showed that those offerings were everywhere, not just Chichen Itza. Now, UNAM Yucatan, which is a university in the city of Merida, has a diving program. They have the first underwater archaeology professor, and he's teaching the students to dive cenotes. The professor's name is Guillermo de Anda. He was a dive shop owner for years, but he turned professor. In his projects, he's been finding architecture inside caves with roads and temples that are leading down to under the water. His theory is that they're evidence of a drought period; that at some point, the water table was much lower, and that those structures were built inside the caves seeking that water, that they were temples to pray for rain. If he's right, these are new insights into the migrations and the challenges that they faced during drought periods.

Caves are symbolic, important places. They're entrances to the Land of the Dead, and not just for the Maya, for all of Mesoamerica. Chalcatzingo is an Olmec cave with paintings in it. Or how about the cave underneath Teotihuacan's Pyramid of the Sun? It might be the reason that they put the city there. Or the Aztec origin stories that say that they started in a cave, the Seven Caves of Chicomoztoc.

Famous caves have taught us much, like Naj Tunich in the Peten; it was found in 1979. There are hieroglyphs all over the wall, dozens of texts, and they're in perfect condition. They discuss rituals that were going on in the cave. And we've found stone-built tombs with elite burials in Naj Tunich. There are offerings to the dead and many burials down there. It's enlightening, and it tells us about the importance of caves.

And consider Loltun Cave in Yucatan; it has charcoal hand prints that date to 10,000 years ago. They're tiny, little hands; they're Maya people. There's also bison and mammoth bones down there. And that evidence extends Maya history back for 7,000 years. In a cave you have a constant climate, and that leads to great preservation. Caves have super potential.

And caves are everywhere. In Chiapas, I heard a story about a new cave every week, for example, the site of Chinikiha. My friends and I went on a weekend exploration trip to that site. We asked the local village for permission, and they agreed to guide us to the site. And in the site, they showed us this section of seven different caves. And the old man who was guiding us pointed to one of them and he said, that goes on for kilometers and kilometers, and at the bottom of it is a big underground lake. I used to go there as a boy, but now it's too hard for me to get to.

My most recent encounter with a cave was on a farm in Chiapas. I was guiding a group of professors, and the locals heard I was coming through, so they asked me to look at this new cave they found, and a boy led me across the farm to go see it. We all went inside, and it was huge and deep and very slippery, so it was dangerous. I didn't let the professors hang out very long. But I could see it had already been looted. There was broken pottery all over the place. And I told the boy, no one's coming to protect this. This is your patrimony, and you guys will either protect it or ruin it. It's your choice.

Again, there's so much on the surface. Caves really haven't become priorities yet, but their preservation potential is great. We can find things in there that we can't find anywhere else. To me, it's a great frontier for discovery. I think of the fourth codex that we found, the Grolier Codex. It was actually found in a cave in Chiapas in 1974.

One of the most frequent questions I get asked as an archaeologist is, if money, permits, and time were non-issues, what projects would you do? That's a fun question, and I have tons of ideas and dreams, but I'll give you just my top three here. My first goal would be more mapping. I'd love to continue my maps at Ma'ax Na or Palenque; both have hundreds of more buildings to be found, and they have caves to explore as well. But my dream mapping project would be something different, finding another Preclassic megacity in the Peten.

As I said, Northwest Guatemala remains virtually untouched. There's barely even any modern settlement out there. For decades, it was guerrilla territory. It was a place where rebels were hiding and fighting against the government. It was dangerous to go out there. But now they're all gone these days. Projects could actually enter safely. Well, that is except for drug runners and giant crocodiles and jaguars.

Years ago, I met Richard Hansen at the Palenque Roundtable; I think it was 1997. And I asked if I could use his El Mirador base camp to go further out there to the west. And he agreed with me; there are big cities out there. But he cautioned me. He said, if you're going to do that, you better have the cojones to deal with five-meter crocodiles. He had seen them, and they had spooked him.

If I did it today, there'd be three main phases to the project. First, I'd do an aerial survey. I'd fly real low back and forth and look for temple tops, and I'd GPS mark the location. Number two, I'd look at topo maps and plan a land route, something that didn't go through too many swamps. Then number three, we'd hike in, and we'd map the city. It could be done. And if not me, someone's going to do it one of these days. Those cities are out there.

My second dream project ties into my love of ancient South America. I would love to find the evidence of South American settlements in West Mexico. The metallurgy out there proves that they made contact, and teaching such a complex skill took more than just a casual meeting.

Metalwork first shows up in West Mexico about 300 A.D. It's mostly copper and some silver and gold, all from West Mexico, Michoacan, Jalisco, and Nayarit. Then there's a hiatus until about 1100 A.D. when the Mixtec put all that gold into Tomb 7 at Monte Alban. The time periods match northern coastal Peru's history very neatly.

Some say it was people from Colombia or Ecuador, but the many Tumi knives recovered make me think it was Peru. Regardless of who it was, the question is, where to find the settlement evidence to prove their permanent presence in Mexico? And I think I know where to look. Cortes wanted to assess the gold resources of Mexico, so he sent Spaniards along with guides to go find the mines. They came back with the report that gold and silver were being taken out of the riverbeds in locations that he named, and we know where they are. So, we should return to those river basins and look for the mining sites. That's where we're going to find the South American settlements as well.

My third and most ambitious dream would be finding an Olmec Pompeii. Olmec monuments are basalt, and they were quarried from around volcanoes. We know there are quarries at the Tuxtla Mountains, and those are extinct volcanoes. But there's another active volcano near the Olmec as well, El Chichon in Northwest Chiapas.

El Chichon erupted massively multiple times in human history, most recently in 1982, and thousands of people died during that eruption. Entire villages were covered in meters of ash. River valleys were filled in. It also exploded around 800 A.D., and some people think it was connected to the Classic Maya collapse.

It also erupted three times during Olmec times. In fact, between 1700 and 1982, there were at least nine eruptions, and some of them were larger than the one during the 1982 eruption. There's a good chance for buried cities out there, but the area is vast. Where and how would we look? Again, I have some ideas.

First, I'd use satellite maps and look for areas that look like extinct river basins; that's where all the Olmec put their cities, in these river basins. Then I'd use ground-penetrating radar, which is getting better every year.

A city like that would probably be deep, maybe 30 meters deep. But it'd be basalt against ash, and the signal would come back right. Then we'd use backhoes to get down to the settlement. Imagine if we found an intact Olmec city. I dream of finding something like that one day.

For as much as I've imparted over this lecture series, I hope I've also demonstrated how much there is still left to find and understand. In my well-informed opinion, we've barely scratched the surface of ancient Mesoamerica. Even in the best-studied of ruins, our knowledge is based on a fractional sample. The continued existence of the Aztec capital was unknown until the 1960s. The Maya code of hieroglyphics wasn't broken until the 1970s. Looting continues to outpace archaeology. We lose things every day. We're losing things right now.

Unlike Egypt, where settlement clustered along the Nile under easily-removed sand, Mesoamerica is spread over a huge area, and it's buried under thick jungles, or on top of remote mountains, or deep inside caves. It's not easy work. And I can say, that from years of experience, it's difficult.

On the other hand, the pace of discovery is quickening every year. I can't believe the paradigm shifts I've witnessed in just my lifetime. I wonder, how much of what I've imparted here will be totally overturned by the next generation of archaeologists? The need for further investigations is clear, present, and to me, downright exciting.

Bibliography

Adams, Richard. *Prehistoric Mesoamerica*. Rev. ed. University of Oklahoma Press, 1996. A rare textbook that covers the entire region of Mesoamerica; written by one of the most well-respected of archaeologists doing work in the 1970s and 1980s.

Adams, Richard E. W., and R. C. Jones. "Spatial Patterns and Regional Growth among Classic Maya Cities." *American Antiquity* 46 (1981): 301–332. Adam's theory that Classic Maya cities were spaced at least 20 kilometers away from one another.

Aldana y Villalobos, Geraldo, and Edwin L. Barnhart, eds. *Archaeoastronomy and the Maya*. Oxbow Books, 2014. A collection of papers on the astronomical alignments of temples, astronomy in codices, and the lunar series.

Andrews, E. Wyllys V. "Dzibilchaltun." In *Supplement to the Handbook of Middle American Indians*. Vol. 1, *Archaeology*. Edited by V. R. Bricker and J. A. Sabloff, pp. 313–341. University of Texas Press, 1981. Andrews conducted seasons of excavations at Dzibilchaltun in the 1960s and 1970s. This report is an excellent summary of his findings.

Andrews, George. *Maya Cities: Placemaking and Urbanization*. University of Oklahoma Press, 1975. One of the first publications to explain Maya cities as urban places rather than isolated ceremonial centers.

Ashmore, Wendy. "The Classic Maya Settlement at Quirigua." *Expedition* 23, no. 1 (1980): 20–27. One of the first papers to discuss Quirigua's importance as a Classic Maya city.

———, ed. *Lowland Maya Settlement Patterns*. University of New Mexico Press, 1981. A collection of papers focused on surveys of the residential areas surrounding the ceremonial centers of the Peten rainforest.

Aveni, Anthony F. *Sky Watchers of Ancient Mexico*. Rev. ed. University of Texas Press, 2000. A great source for information on

Mesoamerican archaeoastronomy written by one of the fathers of the field of archaeoastronomy.

————, ed. *Foundations of New World Cultural Astronomy: A Reader with Commentary*. University of Colorado Press, 2008. A large volume of many important papers written over the years about New World archaeoastronomy. A great collection picked by Aveni.

Barnhart, Edwin. "The First Twenty Three Pages of the Dresden Codex, the Divination Pages." 2005. Online at www.mayaexploration.org/research_pubs.php. A report translating the texts of each almanac of the first 23 pages and the mathematics behind the tables.

————. *The Palenque Mapping Project: Settlement and Urbanism in an Ancient Maya City*. Dissertation presented to the University of Texas at Austin Anthropology Department, 2001. Online at www.mayaexploration.org/research_pmp.php. The report and conclusions from a three-year survey and mapping project that located more than 1,100 new structures at the Classic Maya city of Palenque.

————. "Residential Burials and Ancestor Worship: A Reexamination of Classic Maya Settlement Patterns." Paper presented at the Third Palenque Round Table, Palenque, Chiapas, Mexico, 1999. Online at www.mayaexploration.org/research_pubs.php. A paper about how the practice of burying the dead under houses and venerating the graves gives a false impression of how many homes were actually living spaces in the Classic period.

Blom, Franz, and O. La Farge. *Tribes and Temples*. MARI Publications 1 and 2. 1926–1927. The report of Blom and La Farge's extensive survey of the ruins of Chiapas and Tabasco. A record of dozens of major cities, many of which are still yet to be further studied.

Braswell, Geoffrey E., ed. *The Maya and Teotihuacan: Reinterpreting Early Classic Interaction*. University of Texas Press, 2003. A collection of papers discussing the evidence of how and why Teotihuacan reached down into the Maya world.

Bricker, Victoria. *The Indian Christ, the Indian King: The Historical Substrate of Maya Myth and Ritual.* University of Texas Press, 1981. Focused on post-contact Yucatan Maya, the Caste Wars, and the Books of Chilam Balam. Great insights into how Maya cultural traditions persisted into the post-contact period.

Butterwick, Kristi. *Heritage of Power: Ancient Sculpture from West Mexico, the Andrall E. Pearson Family Collection.* Yale University Press, 2004. A catalog and discussion of the west Mexico artifacts in the Metropolitan Museum of Art in New York City. Includes a discussion of west Mexico's ancient history and the history of archaeological research.

Byers, Douglas S., ed. *The Prehistory of the Tehuacan Valley: Environment and Subsistence.* University of Texas Press, 1967. A collection of papers about early evidence of domestication of crops in the Tehuacan Valley. Includes MacNeish's early rock shelter studies.

Byland, Brice, and John Pohl. *In the Realm of 8 Deer: The Archaeology of the Mixtec Codices.* University of Oklahoma Press, 1994. A book detailing the archaeological quest to find and document the cities and towns mentioned in the Mixtec codices written in the 11th and 12th centuries A.D.

Carrasco, David. *The Aztecs: A Very Short Introduction.* Oxford University Press, 2012. A short but very inclusive summary of Aztec civilization by a leading Aztec authority.

———. *Quetzalcoatl and the Irony of the Empire: Myths and Prophecies in the Aztec Tradition.* University of Chicago Press, 1992. A discussion of Quetzalcoatl's importance to the Aztecs, both as a role model of civilized behavior and a feared prophecy of his return to reclaim his throne.

Christenson, Allen J. *Popol Vuh: The Sacred Book of the Maya.* O Books, 2003. A masterful translation by a scholar fluent in Quiche Maya. This edition catches many double meanings that other translations do not.

Clark, John E., and Mary E. Pye, eds. *Olmec Art and Archaeology in Mesoamerica.* National Gallery of Art, 2006 (distributed by Yale University

Press). A collection of papers about Olmec settlement patterns, artifacts, cultural evolution, and art.

Coe, Michael D. *Breaking the Maya Code*. 3rd ed. Thames and Hudson, 2012. The story of how the Maya script was finally deciphered and the people who did it.

————. *The Maya*. 8th ed. Thames and Hudson, 2011. A well-written textbook on Maya civilization.

Coe, Michael D., and Rex Koontz. *Mexico: From the Olmecs to the Aztecs*. 7th ed. Thames and Hudson, 2013. The best textbook for an overview of all Mesoamerican cultures except the Maya. The Maya are covered in Coe's book *The Maya*.

Coe, Michael D., and Mark Van Stone. *Reading the Maya Glyphs*. 2nd ed. Thames and Hudson, 2011. The most up-to-date text on how to read Maya hieroglyphics.

Coe, Sophie D. *America's First Cuisines*. University of Texas Press, 1994. A well-researched book about the foods eaten by the Maya, the Aztec, and the Inca. Includes recipes and how they were prepared.

Coggins, Clemency. *Cenote of Sacrifice: Maya Treasures from the Sacred Well of Sacrifice at Chichen Itza*. University of Texas Press, 1984. A description and discussion of many of the artifacts that were dredged from the main cenote at Chichen Itza.

Collier, George A. *Basta! Land and the Zapatista Rebellion in Chiapas*. Rev. ed. First Food Books, 1999. A detailed history of the events that led up to the Zapatista revolution, who actually led it, and how it ended up affecting the Maya communities of the Chiapas highlands.

Diaz, Bernal. *The Conquest of New Spain*. Translated by J. M. Cohen. Penguin Books, 1963. The firsthand account of Cortes's expedition to Mexico and defeat of the Aztecs. Told by a soldier who was with Cortes the entire time.

Diehl, Richard A. *The Olmecs: America's First Civilization.* Thames and Hudson, 2004. A textbook-style overview of Olmec civilization. A great single source for Olmec history.

————. *Tula: The Toltec Capital of Ancient Mexico.* Thames and Hudson, 1983. An in-depth study of Tula based on the field projects conducted over a decade on the site. The most complete source of information on the city.

Duran, Fray Diego. *Book of the Gods and Rites and the Ancient Calendar.* Translated and edited by Fernando Horcasitas and Doris Heyden. University of Oklahoma Press, 1971. A chronicle written by a Spaniard who grew up in Mexico just after the conquest. An unparalleled source for understanding Aztec ritual life.

Edmonson, Munro S., trans. *The Ancient Future of the Itza: The Book of Chilam Balam of Tizimin.* University of Texas Press, 1982. A translation of one of the Books of Chilam Balam. A great primary source document for the history of Yucatan as recorded by the Maya themselves.

Fash, William. *Scribes, Warriors and Kings: The City of Copan and the Ancient Maya,* Thames and Hudson, 1991. A complete description of Copan's recent history up until the late 1980s.

Foster, George M. *Tzintzuntzan: Mexican Peasants in a Changing World.* Little Brown, 1967. An ethnography about modern Tzintzuntzan and its inhabitants. The study harkens back to the pre-Columbian times to explain the culture traditions still alive today.

Freidel, David, Linda Schele, and Joy Parker. *Maya Cosmos: Three Thousand Years on the Shaman's Path.* William Morrow and Company, 1993. A groundbreaking study of the connections between modern Maya star lore and ancient Maya astronomy.

Gruzinski, Serge. *The Aztecs: Rise and Fall of an Empire.* Harry N. Abrams, 1992. A small book with accurate information and great full-color photos from the colonial period.

Harris, John, and Stephen Stearns. *Understanding Maya Inscriptions*. University of Pennsylvania Museum, 1992. A simple primer for learning to translate Maya hieroglyphs.

Haviland, William. "A New Population Estimate for Tikal, Guatemala." *American Antiquity* 34 (1969): 424–433. One of the first reports to present Tikal's extremely large population estimate.

———. "Tikal, Guatemala and Mesoamerican Urbanism." *World Archaeology* 2 (1970): 186–198. An early paper arguing for the urban nature of the city of Tikal.

Jones, Grant D. *The Conquest of the Last Maya Kingdom*. Stanford University Press, 1998. The history of how the Itza of Lake Peten were finally defeated by the Spanish in the 1600s. Very well researched and compiled from numerous colonial-period documents.

Kan, Michael, Clement Mieghan, and H. B. Nicholson. *Sculpture of Ancient West Mexico: Nayarit, Jalisco, Colima, a Catalogue of the Proctor Stafford Collection at the Los Angeles County Museum of Art*. Los Angeles County Museum of Art, 1989. Photo catalog of the collection accompanied by papers about various archaeological sites and the tradition of shaft tomb burials.

Knab, Timothy J. *A War of Witches: A Journey into the Underworld of the Contemporary Aztecs*. HarperSanFrancisco, 1995. The author's experience being trained as a modern-day witch in a Nahuat community near Puebla. Great description of modern beliefs about ancient religion.

Koontz, Rex. *Lightning Gods and Feathered Serpents: The Public Sculpture of El Tajin*. University of Texas Press, 2009. An in-depth discussion of the stone carvings of El Tajin and interpretations of what they depict, from a scholar who has studied the site for more than 20 years.

Kowalski, Jeff K., and Cynthia Kristan-Graham, eds. *Twin Tollans: Chichen Itza, Tula, and the Epiclassic to Early Postclassic Mesoamerican World*. Dumbarton Oaks, 2011. A collection of papers that challenge old ideas regarding the relationship between Tula and Chichen Itza.

Kricher, John. *A Neotropical Companion: An Introduction to the Animals, Plants and Ecosystems of the New World Tropics*. 2nd ed. University of Princeton Press, 1997. A biologically oriented field guide to the New World tropics. A very complete source of information.

Landa, Friar Diego de. *Yucatan before and after the Conquest*. Translated by William Gates. Dover Publications, 1978. An abridged version of Landa's *Relation of Things of Yucatan* with extra notes by Gates. Landa's chronicle is the single best source of information about the Maya at the time of conquest.

Leon-Portilla, Miguel. *Fifteen Poets of the Aztec World*. University of Oklahoma Press, 1992. A well-documented collection of Aztec poetry; organized by time period and region.

Lothrop, Samuel K. *Tulum: An Archaeological Study of the East Coast of Yucatan*. The Carnegie Institute of Washington, 1924. The report of the first professional archaeological project conducted at Tulum. Many photos of things that are now gone.

Malmstrom, Vincent H. *Cycles of the Sun, Mysteries of the Moon: The Calendar in Mesoamerican Civilization*. University of Texas Press, 1997. Theories about where and how the Maya calendar was created and how it's linked to astronomy, especially the solar zenith passage.

Marcus, Joyce, and Kent Flannery. *Zapotec Civilization: How Urban Society Evolved in Mexico's Oaxaca Valley*. Thames and Hudson, 1996. An exhaustive study of chronology and population estimates in the Oaxaca Valley based on the authors' extensive surveys of the region.

Martin, Simon, and Nikolai Grube. *Chronicle of the Maya Kings and Queens: Deciphering the Dynasties of the Ancient Maya*. 2nd ed. Thames and Hudson, 2008. One of the most recent books on ancient Maya politics and the first to discuss it as written history instead of anthropology.

Maudslay, Alfred. *Biologia Centrali-Americana: Archaeology*. 5 vols. R. H. Porter and Dulau and Co., 1889–1902. A five-volume set of all of the photos taken of the Maya ruins at the turn of the 20th century.

Maxwell, Judith, and Robert Hill. *Kaqchikel Chronicles*. University of Texas Press. 2006. A collection and translation of various Maya written documents from the highlands of Guatemala that discuss their pre-Columbian history and fateful meeting with the Spanish conquistadors.

Menchu, Rigoberta. *I, Rigoberta Menchu: An Indian Woman in Guatemala*. Edited by Elisabeth Burgos-Dabray and translated by Ann Wright. Verso, 1984. The prize-winning story of a woman growing up during the worst years of the Maya genocide in Guatemala.

Michels, Joseph W. *The Kaminaljuyu Chiefdom*. Pennsylvania State University Press, 1979. A comprehensive study of Kaminaljuyu and its area of influence from 500 B.C. to A.D. 1500.

Milbrath, Susan. *Star Gods of the Maya: Astronomy in Art, Folklore and Calendars*. University of Texas Press, 1999. A detailed review of both modern and ancient Maya astronomy ordered by observation phenomena.

Miller, Arthur G. *On the Edge of the Seas: Mural Painting at Tancah-Tulum, Quintana Roo, Mexico*. Dumbarton Oaks, 1982. Wonderful reproductions and explanations of Tulum's murals. Also a good argument for an Aztec presence in the city's late history.

Miller, Mary. *The Art of Mesoamerica: From Olmec to Aztec*. 3rd ed. Thames and Hudson, 2001. In-depth discussions of Mesoamerican art and iconography, organized chronologically through time and space.

Miller, Mary, and Karl Taube. *The Gods and Symbols of Ancient Mexico and the Maya: An Illustrated Dictionary of Mesoamerican Religion*. Thames and Hudson, 1993. Descriptions of Mesoamerican gods and religious terms arranged alphabetically. One of the few publications to cover Mesoamerican religion as a whole.

Millon, Rene. *The Study of Urbanism at Teotihuacan, Mexico*. Vol. 1. University of Texas Press, 1974. Millon's conclusions about the city's urban nature after completing his landmark survey of the valley.

Bibliography

————. "Teotihuacan." *Scientific American* 216, no. 6 (1967): 38–48. The results of Millon's survey of Teotihuacan, presenting its massive population size.

Morris, Walter F., Jr., and Jeffrey Jay Foxx. *Living Maya.* Harry N. Abrams, 1987. Studies connecting modern Maya textile traditions with ancient weaving techniques and iconographic symbolism.

Nuttall, Zelia, ed. *The Codex Nuttall: A Picture Manuscript from Ancient Mexico.* Dover Publications, 1975. A full-color publication of the 86-page Mixtec Codex Nuttall with an introduction by Arthur Miller.

Paddock, John, ed. *Ancient Oaxaca: Discoveries in Mexican Archaeology and History.* Stanford University Press, 1970. A collection of early papers and theories about Oaxaca's development; includes a great deal of information about Monte Alban and the Valley of Oaxaca.

Pool, Christopher A. *Olmec Archaeology and Early Mesoamerica.* University of Cambridge Press, 2007. An archaeologist's perspective on the Olmecs—focused on environmental adaptation and material culture. Good information on the Olmec trade network.

Powell, Christopher. *The Shapes of Sacred Space: A Proposed System of Geometry Used to Layout and Design Maya Art and Architecture and Some Implications Concerning Maya Cosmology.* Dissertation presented to the University of Texas at Austin Latin American Studies Department. 2008. Online at www.mayaexploration.org/research_pubs.php. A groundbreaking study showing the existence of a set of repeated proportions used by the Maya and other Mesoamerican cultures for designing and laying out art and architecture.

Powell, Melissa, ed. *Secrets of Casas Grandes.* Museum of New Mexico Press, 2006. A collection of papers about pottery and art forms from Casas Grandes (Paquime) and interpretations of its iconography.

Restall, Matthew. *The Maya World: Yucatec Culture and Society, 1550–1850*. Stanford University Press, 1997. A reconstruction of Maya life in the colonial period put together from a variety of written sources, including letters, census records, taxation laws, and maps.

Robertson, Merle Greene. *The Sculpture of Palenque*. 4 vols. Princeton University Press, 1983–1991. An exhaustive study of everything known about Palenque as of the 1980s. Specifically focused on art and iconography.

Roys, Ralph. *The Indian Background of Colonial Yucatan*. University of Oklahoma Press, 1972. A description of Maya society during the colonial period based on Spanish accounts and the Chilam Balam of Chumayel, a Maya history book written in our alphabet by the Maya themselves in the 1600s.

Scarborough, Vernon, and David Wilcox, eds. *The Mesoamerican Ballgame*. University of Arizona Press, 1993. A good collection of papers about ball courts across Mesoamerica and the mythological stories that surround the ball game.

Schaafsma, Curtis F., and Carroll L. Riley, eds., *The Casas Grandes World*. University of Utah Press, 1999. A volume of papers about the Casas Grandes (Paquime) settlement and the sites of the surrounding region.

Schele, Linda, and David Friedel. *A Forest of Kings: The Untold Story of the Ancient Maya*. William Morrow, 1990. A portrayal of ancient Maya life presented in the form of vignettes about days in the lives of Maya kings.

Schele, Linda, and Peter Mathews. *The Code of Kings*. William Morrow, 1998. The functions of Maya buildings discussed by building types and supported by translations and artifact assemblages.

Schele, Linda, and Mary Miller. *Blood of Kings: Dynasty and Ritual in Maya Art*. George Braziller, 1992. A landmark publication that explained bloodletting and many other Maya religious rituals that had to do with divine kingship.

Schlesinger, Victoria. *Animals and Plants of the Ancient Maya*. University of Texas Press, 2001. An overview of flora and fauna in the Maya area arranged by region. Includes a long opening about Maya cultural history.

Sharer, Robert. *The Ancient Maya*. 6th ed. Stanford University Press, 2006. An exhaustive textbook of almost 1,000 pages that covers all aspects and time periods of ancient Maya civilization.

Shook, Edwin. *The Great Wall of Mayapan*. Carnegie Institution of Washington, Department of Archaeology, Current Reports, No. 2, Washington, DC, 1952. Field report of the project that first recorded the wall surrounding Mayapan. Includes many other excavations.

Smith, Michael E. *The Aztecs*. 3rd ed. Wiley-Blackwell, 2012. A book that discusses not just the Aztec capital but many of the other, lesser known Aztec sites. A good source for studying various aspects of Aztec everyday life.

Spores, Ronald, and Andrew K. Balkansky. *The Mixtecs of Oaxaca: Ancient Times to Present*. University of Oklahoma Press, 2013. A good summary of Mixtec codex studies and archaeology. Part 2 is a study of colonial documents to explain what happened to the Mixtecs from conquest up until the modern day.

Stephens, John Lloyd. *Incidents of Travel in Central America, Chiapas and Yucatan*. 2 vols. Harper (1841), reprinted by Dover, 1962. The chronicles of some of the first travelers to visit the Maya ruins, John Lloyd Stephens and his artist, Frederick Catherwood.

Stuart, David, and George Stuart. *Palenque: Eternal City of the Maya*. Thames and Hudson, 2008. An in-depth look at Palenque's dynasty and mythological texts that reinterprets many of the old ideas regarding its patron deities and relationship with other Classic Maya cities.

Stuart, Gene S. *The Mighty Aztecs*. National Geographic Society, 1981. A book about Aztec history that connects the Aztecs' modern descendants to traditions and places. Great photos and drawings.

Tedlock, Barbara. *Time and the Highland Maya*. Rev. ed. University of New Mexico Press, 1992. An ethnography about the day keeper shamans of highland Guatemala. Written by an American scholar who was herself initiated as a shaman.

Tedlock, Dennis. *Popol Vu: A Translation*. 2nd ed. Simon and Schuster, 1996. The story of the Maya creation myth, which is key to understanding Maya religion.

Thompson, J. Eric S. *Maya Hieroglyphic Writing*. University of Oklahoma Press 1971. One of the original books on Maya hieroglyphs. Includes Thompson's T Numbers system, still used by scholars today.

Townsend, Richard F., ed. *Ancient West Mexico: Art and Archaeology of the Unknown Past*, Thames and Hudson, 1998. A great collection of papers from the top authorities on west Mexico's ancient culture. Many ceramics photos.

Webster, David. *The Fall of the Ancient Maya*. Thames and Hudson, 2002. A book dedicated to the various theories about why the Classic Maya abandoned their cities.

Willey, Gordon, and Richard Leventhal. "Prehistoric Settlement at Copan." In *Maya Archaeology and Ethnohistory*, edited by N. Hammond, pp. 75–102. University of Texas Press, 1979. Important baseline study of Copan's settlement of the surrounding valley.

Notes

Notes

Notes

Notes

Notes

Notes